A History of Catholic Antisemitism

A History of Catholic Antisemitism
The Dark Side of the Church

Robert Michael

palgrave
macmillan

First published in 2008 by
PALGRAVE MACMILLAN™
175 Fifth Avenue, New York, N.Y. 10010 and
Houndmills, Basingstoke, Hampshire, England RG21 6XS.
Companies and representatives throughout the world.

PALGRAVE MACMILLAN is the global academic imprint of the Palgrave Macmillan division of St. Martin's Press, LLC and of Palgrave Macmillan Ltd. Macmillan® is a registered trademark in the United States, United Kingdom and other countries. Palgrave is a registered trademark in the European Union and other countries.

ISBN-13: 978-0-230-60388-2
ISBN-10: 0-230-60388-2

Library of Congress Cataloging-in-Publication Data

Michael, Robert, 1936–
    A history of Catholic antisemitism : the dark side of the church / Robert Michael.
       p. cm.
    Includes bibliographical references and index.
    ISBN 0-230-60388-2
    1. Judaism—Relations—Catholic Church. 2. Catholic Church—Relations—Judaism. 3. Christianity and antisemitism—History. 4. Antisemitism—History. 5. Catholic Church—History. 6. Holocaust, Jewish (1939–1945) I. Title.
BM535.M5 2007
261.2'609—dc22   2007035490

A catalogue record of the book is available from the British Library.

Design by Scribe Inc.

First edition: April 2008

10 9 8 7 6 5 4 3 2 1

Printed in the United States of America.

I dedicate this book to the patience and inspiration of my wife Susan, and my children, Stephanie, Andrew, and Carolyn.

To my parents, Gilbert E. Friedberg and Jeanne Greene Friedberg.

To my brother, Stephen H. Friedberg. When Steve and I were children, our second mother was Ruth Mary Hubbard Miller, a Roman Catholic. This loving person, who was married to a Protestant, expressed no prejudice toward us or our Jewish family. Not until researching the earliest origins of the Holocaust did I discover the Church Fathers and from there the whole sorry history of Catholic antisemitism. This book is also dedicated to Ruth Mary Hubbard Miller.

Finally, I want to dedicate my work to my late friend, the Reverend Father Edward Flannery, a human exemplar of the kind of Catholic that followed the tradition of authentic love for Jews his whole life long.

Contents

Preface

The search for truth is imperative if Catholics and Jews are to be reconciled. This search requires us to remember the bitterest facts. Without memory, past evils will replicate themselves in new forms. Without memory, we cannot complete a healing process that requires us to understand the dark side of things we cherish. Without memory, there can be no solid foundation for a compassionate and productive relationship between Catholics and Jews, in which human similarities override human differences. As the Ba'al Shem Tov has indicated, without memory there can be no redemption.

The Catholic Church and the Jews

More significant than a problem of blood, of life or physical death for the Jews, anti-semitism is a spiritual issue, an issue of spiritual life and death for Christians.

—Jacques Maritain

Catholic Antisemitism

It is almost impossible to find examples of antisemitism that are exclusively racial, economic, or political, and free of religious configuration. The infamous, secular, and "racial" Nuremberg Laws of 1935, for example, employed the religious affiliation of Jews in order to identify them for discrimination. What else could they do? There is no such thing as race and so there was no authentic scientific way to detect the racial nature of a Jew.[1] So the Nazis had to resort to using birth and baptismal records to establish who was a Jew, who was not. They checked seven records: four grandparents, two parents, and the person him or herself.

Many lay Catholics and widely respected Catholic writers still hesitate to come to grips with the two millennia of Catholic antisemitism that not only prepared Catholics to perceive Jews in a negative way but also primed them to accept the anti-Jewish aspects of secular ideas—and to take action on them. "Catholic," as distinguished from "Orthodox" and "Protestant," refers to those Christians in communion with the Holy See of Rome, to the whole ecclesiastical structure of the Church, and to the popes at the top of an extensive episcopal hierarchy.[2] "Catholic antisemitism" refers to the anti-Jewish elements in the theology of the Church Fathers, both Latin and Greek, the pronouncements and actions of the papacy and Catholic orders, the teachings and actions of clerics, the content of canon law, the laws and behaviors of secular Catholic princes, as well as the works and behaviors of secular Catholic faithfuls, including writers and artists. This definition does not deny that some Catholics have thought positively of, and acted benificently toward, Jews—especially since *Nostra Aetate* in 1965 offered official sanction to such humane and philosemitic behaviors. Nor does it deny that official Church doctrine, based on St. Augustine, regarded the Jews as suffering witnesses, not to be murdered—though Catholics violated this restriction time and again. But until 1965, the Catholic Church's "dark side" in regard to the Jews, Jewishness, and Judaism was predominant.

According to some authors, the Church's early hostility to Jews grew out of a Gentile antisemitism that converted pagans brought into the Church.[3] These writers do not take into account the positive pagan attitudes, pagan indifference toward Jews, or the qualitative differences between pagan and early Catholic antisemitism. Of the approximately 25 percent of pagan writers who disliked the Jews, almost all of them felt Jews were an annoying people who ate differently, wasted time on the Sabbath, believed in a ridiculous invisible God, and so forth.[4] But the earliest and strongest Catholic charge against the Jews was "Christ-killer" and the charge exploded beyond Jesus of Nazareth's generation of Jews when Catholics cited holy writ: "Let his blood be on our heads and the heads of our children" (Matt. 27:25).

Other authors argue that Christianity taught contempt of Jews only during the medieval period and that modern antisemitism is essentially secular. Such writers find no definite connecting link or continuity between Christian antisemitism and Nazism.[5]

Still other scholars dismiss the continuing power of Catholic antisemitism; instead, they believe that modern antisemitism originated in the "secular" Enlightenment period.[6] Robert Wistrich argued that if modern Catholics were antisemitic, then Jews would never have been granted any civil rights or other freedoms in modern Christian society. Wistrich assumed that Christian antisemitism was unambiguous and could not be hidden, disguised, or modified, and he ignored the fact that many Catholics based their behavior on St. Augustine's Witness-People dictum that all Jews were responsible for killing Christ but should be treated like Cain, that is, not murdered but made to suffer as living witnesses to their "crime." Wistrich also observed that Hitler's "either-or" policy of destruction of the Jews did not reflect the essential beliefs of Catholic orthodoxy but followed instead the path of Catholic heresy.[7] But Catholic anti-Jewishness has been the predominant position on the Jews, as this book will show, not the product of heterodoxy. Michael Marrus believes that the causes of the Holocaust have no roots earlier than the nineteenth century. In discussing Uriel Tal's analysis of nineteenth-century antisemitism, for example, Marrus misses Tal's point that even when racist antisemitism is theoretically anti-Catholic, it involves crucial elements of Catholic beliefs and of Catholic culture. Marrus mentions Peter

Pulzer's analysis of Austrian antisemitism at the turn of the century but omits Pulzer's recent appreciation of the continuing importance of religious factors in modern antisemitism. Pulzer's point is similar to that of Tal's: "I am more strongly convinced than I was when I wrote the book that a tradition of religiously-inspired Jew hatred . . . was a necessary condition for the success of antisemitic propaganda, even when expressed in non-religious terms and absorbed by those no longer religiously observant."[8] Marrus writes as though the Nazis were the first to demonize the Jews and ignores the crucial importance of Christian antisemitism in their mentality. St. Augustine, for example, called all Jews "Cains," St. Jerome saw all Jews as "Judases," St. John Chrysostom regarded all Jews as useless animals fit for slaughter. Catholic ideas such as these are not the kind that exist in a detached Platonic realm, but idées-forces—that is, ideas with emotional punch affecting the real world.[9] "Ideas, endlessly repeated, furnished justification for the vilest acts."[10]

James Parkes, John Gager, Robert Willis, and Alan Davies have all made provocative statements concerning the enduring negative effects of Catholic-Christian theology. Robert Willis concluded, "There are obviously, political, social, and economic factors that must be taken into account in assessing the causes of the Holocaust. What is at stake is a proper understanding of the contribution of theological antisemitism to the creation of a social and moral climate that allowed the 'final solution' to become a reality. . . . It is necessary . . . to appreciate the cumulative impact of a centuries-long tradition of hostility towards Judaism and Jews within the church as a crucial condition enabling [Hitler's] mobilization [of public opinion] to take place."[11]

Just as the Catholic attitude toward the Jews was bipolar, so Catholic antisemitism was not without exception. Indeed, had the Church attempted to eradicate all the Jews as it did the heretics, Jews would have disappeared by the fourth or fifth century, when Catholicism came to dominate the Roman Empire, or certainly by the High Middle Ages, when at times the Church's influence was almost totalitarian. Let us briefly examine the contradictory attitudes and actions of St. Bernard of Clairvaux (d.1153)[12]—certainly the greatest spiritual figure, and perhaps the greatest historical figure, of the twelfth century. He was the Church's most respected and influential cleric, the leading figure of the Latin Church, its greatest writer and preacher, a reformer of the powerful and prestigious Benedictine order, confidant of Pope Innocent II, and teacher of Pope Eugenius III. Like the popes, Bernard believed that religion should control every aspect of society. He was one of the founders of the Cistercian monastic order, encouraged the cult of Mary, and contributed to popular piety. We shall see in chapters 4, 5, and 6 that Bernard wrote against the Jews as deicides, slaves, and racially evil. But the case at hand is his relationship to the French Cistercian monk Rodolphe and the Second Crusade. Rodolphe was believed to perform miracles and attracted enormous crowds; he preached that the Jewish enemies of God must be punished.[13] His preaching was followed by massacres in Strasbourg, Cologne, Mainz, Worms, Speyer, Würzburg, and in other French and German cities[14] to the Crusader cry of HEP, HEP (*H*ierosolyma *e*st *p*erdita, Jerusalem Is Lost).[15] His demagogy was finally terminated by St. Bernard, who spoke out against the murder of Jews in England, France, and Germany. Bernard warned the English people that "the Jews are not to be persecuted, killed, or even put to flight."[16] An adherent of St. Augustine's precept about the Jews as the Witness People, Bernard traveled to Germany in late 1146 both to preach Crusade and to hush Rodolphe: "It is good that you go off to fight the Ishmaelites [Turks]. But whoever touches a Jew to take his life is like one who had touched the apple of the eye of Jesus; for [Jews] are his flesh and bone. My disciple Rodolphe has spoken in error—for it is said in Psalms [59:11], 'Slay them not, lest my people forget.'"[17] The psalm continues, "My God will let me look in triumph on my enemies. Do not kill them, or my people may forget; make them totter by your power, and bring them down, O Lord . . . consume them in wrath, consume them until they are no more" (Psalm 59:11–13)—which are words themselves quoted earlier by St. Augustine.

Yet Bernard's motives were not clearly mercy, charity, or human decency. He told the Archbishop of Mainz that Rodolphe's murderous preaching against the Jews was the *least* of his three offenses, namely, "unauthorized preaching, contempt for episcopal authority, and incitation to murder."[18] Again following St. Augustine, Bernard held that "the Jews ought not to die in consequence of the immensity of their crimes, but rather to suffer the Diaspora."[19] Bernard recalled to his English audience that Jews must "remind us always of what our Lord suffered." Bernard also noted that at the Second Coming of Christ, Jews who were already dead would remain in hell.[20] Likewise, he called the Jews hard-hearted and regarded the synagogue as a "cruel mother" who had crowned Jesus with thorns.[21] He used the servile condition of the Jews ("no slavery is as demeaning as that of the Jews"[22]), along with their lack of kingdom, priesthood, prophets, and Temple, to demonstrate that the Jews were being punished for history's greatest sin, the crucifixion of Christ. For Bernard, the Jews were venomous vipers whose bestial stupidity and blindness caused them to "lay impious hands upon the Lord of Glory."[23] Bernard also wrote that a Christian who neglected Christ's sufferings was "a sharer in the unparalleled sin of the Jews."[24] He commended the Abbot Warren of the Alps for attacking the indiscipline of churlish monks as "destroying those synagogues of Satan"—a phrase from Revelation. Following St. John Chrysostom, Bernard condemned the Jews as ever ungrateful to God and as always resisting the Holy Spirit, calling them the minions of Satan. He preached that "[t]he Jews, ever mindful of the hatred wherewith they hate his Father, take this opportunity to vent it on the Son . . . these wicked men" and that "Judaea hates the Light."[25]

The intimate connection between Judaism and Catholicism has motivated authentic Catholics—those who follow *theologia crucis* within Catholic thought—to treat Jews decently, and some in every generation have genuinely respected Jews. The Roman Catholic Church's historical prohibitions against Catholic-Jewish fraternization presumed the existence of social relationships between Catholics and Jews. Catholic theologians continually complained about the faithful who grew too close to Jews or treated them as human beings rather than as theological types. In every era, some Catholics steadfastly taught their children to respect other human beings, Jews included. "For most rescuers [of Jews during the Holocaust,] helping Jews was an expression of ethical principles that extended to all of humanity."[26]

Even though the Church has often sought to preserve Jews—at least a remnant thereof—and Judaism as historic forebears of Christianity,[27] most Catholic writers, thinkers, theologians, politicians, and prelates have expressed a profound hostility toward Jews, and their attitudes have incontestably influenced average Catholics. In the earliest centuries of the Christian era, a relatively bland preexisting pagan antagonism toward Jews was replaced by historical and theological beliefs that the Jewish people were abhorrent and that any injustice done to them, short of murder, was justified. Jews became the archetypal evil-doers in Catholic societies. This anti-Jewish attitude was a permanent element in the fundamental identity of Western Christian civilization and, for the purposes of this book, in the national identities of countries with large Catholic populations like Poland, Austria, and France. Catholics who took this antagonistic position toward Jews adhered to triumphalism, or *theologia gloriae*.[28]

The Churches' predominant, normative theological position in regard to the Jews has been called *theologia gloriae*, which according to James Parkes, is an "inbred religious paranoia [that] has been a perversion of everything Jesus meant."[29] This antisemitic theology of glory, this dark side of the Church, generally holds that: (1) the Christian Church, the new Israel—"ordained and sanctioned by God himself"—has triumphantly succeeded the cursed and rejected old Israel morally, historically, and metaphysically; (2) Jews denied the true Messiah, the Christ, and murdered him, for which all Jews are forever collectively guilty; (3) the Jews were paradigmatic evil-doers even

before their atrocious act of deicide; (4) Jews are not to be totally exterminated since they adhered to the Law and gave Christianity the history that it
needed to legitimize itself.

Moral perception and behavior are shaped by the society into which we
have been socialized and even more by the community we acknowledge as
our own. What the Church thought about Christ and itself as an institution
determined what most Catholics believed about Judaism and Jews. Anti-
Jewish theological defamations, communicated and empowered by the
Church, justified most Catholics in their antisemitic ideas. Moreover, this
anti-Jewish repugnance has not been restricted to the realm of ideas; like any
ideology, it has boiled over into contemptuous feelings and behaviors.
Tragically, to love Christ for many if not most Catholics came to mean hatred
of his alleged murderers. How could Catholics have ever learned to love the
Jewish people, asked Pierre Pierrard, when favorable religious ideas about
Jews "were lost in the blood of Calvary. 'The History of the Church' made
[Jews] appear only as an antithesis of the glorious epic of the Roman
Church?"[30]

Until 1965 and beyond, the most significant ideology about Jews within
the Church, that is, the theology of glory, has encouraged Catholics to view
Judaism as little more than the work of Satan and the Antichrist, and to
regard Jews with sacred horror. This anti-Jewish theology has been so perva-
sive that even decent Christians have sometimes uttered the most "factually
untrue and grossly libelous" statements about Jews.[31] Moreover, these negative perceptions have existed independent of what Jews themselves have actually done, or, indeed, of a Jewish presence at all. In their ideological assault on
the Jews, the Fathers of the Church, for example, never cited the misdeeds of
their contemporary Jewish neighbors. It was *mythical* Jewish actions—their
alleged deicide and later medieval defamations—that stood as the basis of
resentful Catholic misperceptions.[32] God was always pictured as "in there
punching" on the side of Catholics and Catholicism against Jews and
Judaism.[33]

These religious antagonisms, elaborated by the theological and popular
writings and preachings of the Church's great theologians and popes,
exploited by Catholic authorities, and enhanced by the liturgy, art, and literature of the Church, created in most of the faithful an automatic hostility
toward Jewishness. This diabolizing of the Jews has continued into the modern period with only minor deviations.[34]

Just as Catholic theology denied Jews salvation in the next life, so it disqual-
ified Jews from legitimate citizenship in Christendom. In a sense, Jews were
ostracized from full human status. Some protective Roman legal traditions,
some Catholic feelings of charity, and the Jews' ambivalent role as suffering

examples of the consequences of offending God provided Jews with a precarious place within Catholic society. But until their emancipation in the eighteenth and nineteenth centuries—and to this day, for some—Jews had only a very tenuous legal and moral right to exist, let alone act as citizens. The Jews had to plead with Catholic authorities—kings and princes, bishops and dictators, popes and presidents—to protect them. Sometimes this worked. Other times the authorities turned their backs on the Jews or collaborated with those Catholics who were intent on cursing, expropriating, expelling, or murdering them.

Despite the close theological relationship between Judaism and Catholicism, despite Jesus's commandment about love of neighbor, despite the modern Roman Catholic Church's insistence on "justice and charity" in the treatment of Jews, despite the Church's emphasis on *caritas* (love within families that extended outward toward neighborhood, city, and nation) and *agape* (the self-sacrificial love taught by Jesus on the cross that extended to love of enemies), most Catholics found it impossible to love Jews. When Catholicism was a new religion and had to fight for its own individual identity, churchmen and theologians found it necessary to distance themselves from Jews. Furthermore, humane behavior toward Jews required Catholics to follow the difficult moral precepts of Jesus as expressed in the Gospels. Although the Church professed the same moral precepts, it usually followed anti-Jewish policies. Some Catholic writers called on the faithful to love Jews but only as a first step toward converting them, that is, this kind of love was meant to precede the elimination of Jews as Jews.

This book will analyze and summarize the history of Catholic antisemitism and the set of beliefs that created a climate of opinion that led to untold suffering and millions of Jewish deaths before the Holocaust,[35] and not only made the Holocaust possible, but likely. What does it take for a nation's workers, middle class, aristocracy, artists, and intellectuals to, in just a few years, collaborate in the slaughter of hundreds of thousands of its Jewish neighbors and fellow citizens, and millions of Jewish coreligionists outside the national borders? As historian Walter Zwi Bacharach wrote, "no human being gets up one fine morning and sets out to kill Jews, just because he is ordered to do so."[36] This comment was mirrored decades later by James O'Gara, editor of the Catholic *Commonweal*: "Could the Nazi horror have sprung full-blown out of nowhere, without centuries of [Christian] antisemitism to nourish it and give it strength."[37] It takes centuries of preparation, tradition, and religion to enable people to see others as inhuman monsters and act on this perception. The distinguished psychologist Gordon Allport points out that Christianity stands as the focus of prejudice because "it is the pivot of the cultural tradition."[38] Catholic theological and Catholic racist antisemitism[39] prepared, conditioned, and encouraged Catholic anti-semites and others[40] to collaborate actively or passively with individual and institutional antisemitic behaviors—avoidance, antilocution, discrimination, expropriation, physical assault and torture, murder, and mass murder.[41] This Catholic antisemitism paved the long via dolorosa that led to Auschwitz and beyond.

Catholic antisemitism has been exported to the Middle East where Christian Arabs were the conduit for entry, so that traditional antisemitism has been grafted on to preexisting Muslim Jew-hatred and portends a grave danger for Jews in the future. *The Protocols of the Elders of Zion* (translated into Arabic by a Lebanese Christian in the early 1920s), Hitler's *Mein Kampf*, and Ford's *International Jew* are readily available all over the Muslim world. Mel Gibson's antisemitic film, *The Passion of the Christ*, gained instant popu-larity in the Middle East.[42] Neither Arab immigrants to Europe nor reac-tions to the Palestinian-Israeli conflict explains "the resurgence of European antisemitism after the Holocaust." On the contrary, explains Manfred Gerstenstein, the facts suggest that continuing antisemitism "is integral to European [Christian] culture." Leftists, Rightists, and those in between express hatred of Jews. At the beginning of the twenty-first century, most European nations are exhibiting significant levels of antisemitism. The dou-ble-thinking European Union attacks Israel and at the same time seems to oppose traditional antisemitism.[43] (In 2005, the European Union Monitoring Center on Racism and Xenophobia established a "Working Definition of Antisemitism."[44])

Unanswerable questions remain. Can the Church truly eliminate the anti-Jewish elements in its teachings? Can the Church admit to the mythic nature of the Gospel stories, which may contain some fact but more fully convey the authors' anti-Jewish perspectives and the Church's anti-Jewish interpreta-tions—especially in the Crucifixion story, which fixes on the Jews eternal responsibility and collective guilt for the murder of God?[45] A final question is whether the Catholic Church can give up its anti-Jewish position and remain as an intact institution.

CHAPTER 1

Pagans and Early Catholics

The Jews will never regain their former situation, since they committed a despicable crime by conspiring against the savior of humankind.

Origen, Contra Celsum

Pagan versus Catholic Antisemitism

It has been maintained that early Christianity unconsciously adopted pagan hostility toward Jews and that when Christianity conquered Roman civilization in the fourth century, the Christianized Empire reflected and elaborated the preexisting secular antagonism. But widespread pagan antisemitism is a myth. Whereas Greek and Roman writers did provide some material taken by Catholics to use against the Jews, nowhere among the pre-Christians do we find the elemental hatred of the Jewish spirit that we discover among early Catholic writers and Christianized Roman officials. The word "Jew" may have occasionally been employed derisively in the Roman Empire before Catholicism came to dominate it, but it was only after Catholic influence was felt in the Empire that "Jew" was considered almost universally foul and degrading.

Most pre-Christian pagan authors were neutral or friendly to Jews and accepted Judaism as it was. Out of 161 Greek and Roman authors who discussed the Jews, only 28 disparaged them.[1] Even in an extreme case, when the Jews of Judea revolted against the Romans in the first and second centuries CE, the Romans treated them no more savagely than any other seditious people of the empire. The Greeks and Romans found many reasons to respect the Jews: their antiquity, their well-documented history, and their great sacred literature. Up to the fourth century CE, many non-Jews, both pagan and Catholic, also admired the Jews' family and community life, their monotheism, their rejection of images, their elevated moral code, and their emphasis on the inherent value of human life. Considerable numbers of God-fearing Gentiles, although not properly converted to Judaism, worshipped at the gates of the synagogues. Roman and Catholic law and custom early on recognized the Jews as a *gens* (a people) and Judaism, according to Church Father Tertullian, as "a most distinguished and undoubtedly legal religion."[2]

A few Greek and Roman authors urged people shun the Jews, just as they were to avoid Christians. Some pagans identified certain practices as particularly Jewish and ridiculed the circumcision procedure, Sabbath observance, the eating of kosher foods, and the worship of one God.[3] Pagan authors Democritus and Apion charged the Jews with sacrilege and ritual murder. But most of their readers doubted the truth of these charges, as evidenced by the few, if any, pagan pogroms against the Jews.

The contrast between the almost incidental pagan aversion to Jews and the fundamental Catholic bitterness is striking. Even among this minority of non-Christian Greek and Roman writers who were inimical to the Jews, we do not find attempts to restrict Jewish civil liberties or segregate Jews from the rest of society. What there was of pagan hostility had no theological basis and no Church to sanction anti-Jewish policies. The pagan Gentiles saw the Jews neither as theological constructs nor as murderers of God. They did not demand that Judaism had to be defeated in this world and that the Jews had to suffer in this world and the next. The pagan Posidonius argued that Jews were atheists because they refused to believe in the pagan gods; in Catholic theology, Jews were not atheists—they were murderers of God. Philostratus reproached the Jews for keeping themselves apart; the Catholics Origen, St. Jerome,[4] and Emperor Theodosius perceived the Jews as hating their neighbors and the law. Apion and Celsus saw the Jews as ineffectual; St. Augustine saw them as models of evil. Apion and Tacitus called the Jews fugitive slaves from Egypt, but both Origen ("the Jews will never regain their former situation, since they committed a despicable crime by conspiring against the savior of humankind") and St. Jerome believed that God punished the Jews with perpetual slavery for the murder of the Christian Messiah.[5] Appolonius charged Jews with occasional cruelty, but the Catholic Commodius believed that Jews were possessed by a frenzied cruelty unique to them, which they called the *furor judaicus*. Plutarch accused the Jews of being physically dirty, but Catholic theologians like the fourth-century Ephraem of Syria saw the Jews as morally and religiously filthy—the Jews' odor corrupted by their "stench and unbelief." Tacitus accused the Jews of an annoying stubbornness and of regarding others with "hate and enmity." But many Catholic theologians, such as St. Ambrose and St. Augustine, radicalized Jewish stubbornness into a continuous, malicious refusal to believe in the goodness, beauty, and grace of Christ. Apion considered Jews politically seditious, but Chrysostom perceived them as rebels against God and against all that was holy and as worthy of slaughter.[6]

Are the Christian Scriptures Antisemitic?

Pagan hostility to Jews was founded on secular Jewish nonconformity, but Catholic antisemitism was defined first in the Christian Scriptures, the foundation of the Catholic faith. The Scriptural attitude toward Jews is, as John Gager writes, "the heart of the matter."[7] Scholars continue to disagree as to whether, on the whole, the Christian Testament is essentially pro-Christian[8] or "defamatory and meant to be defamatory."[9] But all can agree that crucial Gospel passages deemed the Jews as alien to the Christian cause and looked upon Judaism as Christianity's enemy.[10]

These devastatingly anti-Jewish passages of the Christian Testament gave birth to antisemitism.[11] At the least, portions of the Christian Scriptures have provided an array of theological ideas supporting, justifying, legitimizing, and sanctifying anti-Jewish hostility. Generally ignoring the Jewishness of Jesus and any positive relationships with Jews, both early and later Christian theologians, popes, politicians, and other antisemites[12] treated the anti-Jewish Christian Testament verses as storehouses of material to defame the Jewish people.[13] The antisemitic words of the Scriptures, the negative images conjured up, and the hostile emotions aroused all conditioned how Catholics treated Jews.[14] In 1991, Jack Sanders wrote, "It is the Christians, not Jews, who need to see that the problem of antisemitism is ingredient to the [Christian] Testament itself. . . . Those Christian groups where the Bible is read as literal truth . . . find again the divine sanction for the rejection and destruction of Jews that resides in parts of the [Christian] Testament."[15] The Gospels and letters of St. Paul have supplied historical figures as diverse as the Church Fathers, Thomas Jefferson, Richard Wagner, and Adolf Hitler with an arsenal of anti-Jewish material.[16] Even today, many average Christians interpret the Christian Testament as supporting an uncritical antisemitism.[17]

The Scriptural passages damning the Jews as rapacious hypocrites, children of hell and the devil, God-haters in turn rejected by God, and murderers of Jesus the Christ, God incarnate, were the focus of nearly all Catholic writers of the apostolic and patristic periods, which occurred in the first seven or eight centuries CE.[18] Catholics designated themselves as God's new Chosen People through their faith in Jesus; they displaced the Jews now cut asunder from God's grace and abandoned to play out their devilish role in history. These perceptions have dominated the West's attitudes toward the Jews for nearly two thousand years. As William Wilson has written, even to the present day, "many readers of the Christian Testament find no difficulty in accepting this bitter calumny against the Jewish people of Jesus's day. This is evidence of how effectively the Gospels have laid the blame for Jesus's death at the feet of his own people."[19] Even when we factor in the competition between Latin Christianity and a thriving Jewish community that denied the validity of the new religion, the anti-Jewish polemic of several passages in the Christian Testament remains the keystone of Catholic antisemitism.

St. Paul's Letters[20]

Saul of Tarsus (St. Paul) wrote his epistles before the Gospels were composed, and his letters reveal his perspective on the Jews. A Jew called to be an apostle of Jesus, Paul sometimes seemed to argue for peace and harmony between the two religions. He stated that God, who would not renege on his promises, had "certainly not" rejected the Jews, "God's people" (Rom. 11:1–5), for they possessed "the sonship, the glory, the covenants, the giving of the Torah, the worship, and the promises. The fathers are theirs, and of them is the Christ, as a human person"[21] According to Romans 11:16, Paul regarded Jews and Christians as parts of one olive tree, each a people uniquely chosen by God. In these passages St. Paul repudiated neither the Jews nor the Torah. John Gager, Clark Williamson, Norman Beck, and several others have argued that Paul saw the "old Law" of the Torah valid for the Jews and the "new Law" of Jesus authentic for Christians.[22] Professor Frederick Schweitzer has pointed out that "with all his shortcomings, St. Paul provides the central texts for *Nostra Aetate*, because nothing else in the Christian Scriptures or in Patristics or in Church council canons or papal decrees, early, medieval, or modern can serve the purpose of a new theology of acceptance."[23]

But Paul discounted many of the essential principles of Judaism, and introjected a high level of emotional polemic into the controversy between Jews and Catholics. Citing critical passages from Isaiah and Psalms (God made the Jews persistently sluggish, blind, and deaf, their Judaism "a snare and a trap, a stumbling block and a retribution for them"[24]), Paul claimed that "As regards the gospel [the Jews] are enemies of God for your sake; but as regards election they are beloved, for the sake of their ancestors; for the gifts and the calling of God are irrevocable."[25] Did Paul mean that the Jews were a holy people compared to pagans but an unholy people compared to Christians? Or were the Jews just stuck in their own lethargy, their hearts hardened so that Gentiles could become Christians and be saved? Whatever he meant, Paul's description of the Jews as "enemies" was the message that was communicated most clearly to Christians.

Paul's persistent and severe criticism of the religion in which he was raised helped lead to Christian rejection of Jews. His sometimes emotional attack on the Torah encouraged Christian opposition to the Jewish way of life, which was supposedly deemed unacceptable to God. In Romans, Paul acknowledged the glory, the covenants, the Torah, the promises, the patriarchs, and the messiah as Jewish. But he rejected his former coreligionists as the true descendants of Abraham: "[I]t is not the children of the flesh who are the children of God, but the children of the promise are counted as descendants."[26] Living according to the Torah means living to "gratify the desires of the flesh"; whereas to "live by the spirit" means not to be not subject to Torah.[27] Most of the time, Paul saw room for only one Chosen People. The future clearly belonged to the Gentiles who would become Christians.

Other material attributed to Paul expressed an intense emotional antagonism to aspects of Judaism and Judaizing Christians (those sympathetic to Judaism and practicing some Jewish rites and rituals). He wrote that "the written code [the Torah] kills"; it is "the dispensation of death"; circumcision, the physical sign of the Torah, was a "mutilation" and the whole Torah "a curse."[28] In Philippians, he referred to his former Jewish way of life as "garbage" (the King James translates it as "dung") and called adherents of the law (Torah) "dogs" and "evil-workers."[29] In Galatians, frustrated with his Jewish opponents, he chillingly wishes that "those who unsettle you would castrate themselves."[30] The two letters to the Thessalonians attributed to Paul but perhaps not written by him[31] pictured the Jews as the great theological enemies of God and of all humankind.[32] They attack the whole Jewish people as murderers of Christ and associate them with the Antichrist, the false Jewish messiah whom God allowed Satan to send to the Jews because they refused to believe in the true, Christianized Messiah, Jesus Christ.[33]

Whether Paul was responsible for all this anti-Jewish writing is far less important than the use Christian theologians from the late empire to the twentieth century made of this material as an ideological paradigm and an emotional attack on Jews, Judaism, and Judaizing Christians. Revelation, for instance, twice calls the Jews a "synagogue of Satan" (2:9, 3:9). St. Cyril of Alexandria adopted Paul's interpretations of Moses and the Torah as death, Christ as life. Cyril wrote that Paul "considered [the Torah] rubbish," and then gained Christ.[34] The Church Father most antagonistic to the Jews, St. John Chrysostom, employed Paul's ideas for his anti-Jewish purposes throughout his most antisemitic work, the *Homilies Against the Jews*.

Acts and the Gospels

The Acts of the Apostles is at the same time a historical account of early Christianity's development and an antisemitic morality play. Although it describes Jesus's disciples as observant Jews, Acts is full of specific anti-Jewish statements attributed to these disciples. According to Norman Beck, Acts comprises the most savage anti-Jewish polemic of the Christian holy books.[35]

Mixing theology and politics, Acts portrays the Jews, in sharp contrast to the Christians, as hostile to Roman authority, and in league with Herod and idolaters.[36] The notion of Jewish materialism and idolatry—the story of the worship of the golden calf and of Moloch—is repeated in St. Stephen's speech to the Sanhedrin after which the Jews stoned him to death, one of the few instances of Jewish attacks on Jewish-Christians.[37]

Acts insists that Jews who remain Jews are enemies of Christ. Although Jews who repented of their sin of deicide could become Christians, Jews who remained Jews were no longer considered God's people.[38] The author of Acts uses the term "the Jews" to indicate those who reviled and plotted against Paul and his colleagues, secured Paul's arrest, and wanted Paul dead.[39] According to Acts, all Jews, whether within or outside of Palestine, not the Romans, crucified Jesus. Jewish visitors from Rome were held responsible for having nailed Jesus to the cross, simply because they were Jews.[40]

Many anti-Jewish passages also occur in the Gospels, written between fifty and two hundred years after the death of Jesus and reflecting Christianity's continuing animosity toward the Jews. Although these books are essentially expressions of Christian faith, they leave the dangerous impression that they are objective history. Some passages refer only to a few Jews as evil, or make positive statements about Jews.[41] More often, Jews are dramatically portrayed as antagonists or disloyal followers of Jesus, or as persons or a people who misunderstood him. The Jews are said to have denied that Jesus was the Christ. He, in turn, is reported to have repudiated them, calling them "hypocrites" and "evil-speakers" (Matt. 23: 33, 37, where the Pharisees represent the Jews) who deserved to die. The Gospels assaulted the Jewish people, their leaders, and their institutions and indicted them for rejecting and crucifying Jesus.[42] When the Gospels portrayed the Jews as selecting Barabbas rather than Jesus (there never was a historical example of this practice of calling for the reprieve of a convicted rebel in Roman law or Jewish law on Passover), they are made to appear to be so depraved that they would sooner ask for the pardon of a thief than a savior and to choose Judaism over Christianity, that is, eternal damnation over redemption.[43]

The Gospel of St. Mark, earliest of the four, attempts to "dejudaize" Christianity. Mark, a Greek, reflects the bitterness of the Gentile Church toward the Jews,[44] depicting Jesus as alienated from his family,[45] describing how the Jewish leaders plot "against him, how to destroy him," and stating that the "chief priests and scribes were seeking how to arrest him by stealth, and kill him."[46] St. Mark portrays Jesus's own Jewish disciples as complaining about his anointment, then betraying and abandoning him.[47] Mark also involves the Jewish leaders and people in Jesus's murder. By neglecting the historical facts of Jesus's Jewishness and the involvement of the Romans in his crucifixion, Mark and other writers of the Christian Testament transformed the crucifixion into an exclusively Jewish event, describing Pilate[48]—despite his record of antagonism to, and murder and crucifixion of Jews—as an innocent person who is completely under the control of the malicious Jews.[49] When Pilate wanted to release Jesus, asking "Why, what evil has he done?" the chief priests "stirred up the crowd," which called repeatedly "Crucify him."[50] (Neither crucifixion nor burial were permitted on the Sabbath, from sundown Friday to sundown Saturday.)

The most likely historical scenario was that with the possible collusion of a handful of Sadducees, the oppressive Roman occupation forces in Palestine tortured and crucified Jesus because they perceived him as a threat to their security.[51] Pilate was described as "by nature [an] unyielding, self-willed, and hard" man, guilty of "endless and insufferable cruelties" against the Jews.[52] Though Roman historian Tacitus described Jesus's crucifixion itself as being ordered *by* Pilate, the Church saw to it that this became simply *under* Pilate, implying that the responsibility was Jewish, not Roman. As Clark Williamson points out, this distorted version of, Jesus being crucified "under Pontius Pilate" is still repeated as part of the Apostles' Creed.[53]

Mark identifies a Roman soldier as the first person to truly recognize Jesus's divinity, although his earliest disciples and followers were Jews.[54] Mark consigned those Jews who chose to remain Jews to damnation: "He who believes and is baptized will be saved; but he who does not believe will be condemned."[55]

The Gospel according to St. Matthew stresses that Jesus fulfilled Jewish prophecy and that the Jews' rejection of Jesus led to Jesus's rejection of the Jews.[56] It is full of polemic against Jewish religious traditions[57] and leadership.[58] Most importantly, Matthew implicates the whole Jewish people in crimes against God and humanity both before and during the present generation. The most significant single crime, that is, deicide, was but one manifestation of the inherent and preexisting Jewish evil, from Cain's crime onward.[59] In some of the most sustained invective of the Christian Scriptures, Matthew portrayed all Pharisees, and by implication all Jews, as "hypocrites," "children of hell," "blind fools," unclean sons of the murderers of the prophets, "serpents and vipers," all of them sentenced to hell.[60] Upon these Jewish "snakes [and] brood of vipers," these sons of bitches,[61] would "come all the righteous blood shed on earth."[62] The diatribe against the Jewish capital of Jerusalem as a "city that kills the prophets and stones those who are sent to it" and the frightening prediction about the destruction of the Jewish Temple confirm that in Matthew's view, God has abandoned the Jewish people.[63]

Anti-Jewish Catholics most frequently cite the following passage in which the Jewish people cry, "Let him be crucified! . . . His blood be on us and on our children."[64] This passage, according to one Jewish scholar, has "been responsible for oceans of human blood and a ceaseless stream of misery and desolation."[65] Matthew also refers to the triumphal Christian belief that, because of the Jews' rejection and murder of the Christ, they will lose not only their spiritual election as the Chosen People but also their worldly valuables, nationhood, government, capital city, house of worship, priesthood, and system of worship: Israel, king, Jerusalem, Temple, and Judaism.[66]

Matthew's report of the clash between Jesus and the Jews tells us far more about the later competition between the Pharisees (who then represented the main line of Judaism) and the early Roman Church than it tells us about the historical Jews of Jesus's time.[67] Because early Christianity bristled with hostility at the Jewish-Pharisee establishment, Matthew created a fictitious type of Jew, a terrifying and malicious Pharisee whom the Church later identified with all Jews who did not accept Jesus as the Christ.

Like Matthew's, St. Luke's Gospel concluded that of the whole evil and adulterous generation of Jews that had rejected Jesus as the Christ, only a remnant would be saved,[68] for Jews neither accepted the Gospel nor were they faithful to their own covenant with God.[69] Luke emphasized that the Jews were the villains in Jesus's life story and the evil subjects of Jesus's parables.[70] Writing for a Gentile audience,[71] Luke revealed that the Jews have been replaced by a new Chosen People: the Gentile followers of Jesus; that the Jews would reject Jesus, his new Church, and his divine revelations; and that the entire Jewish people merited any ruination that befell them.[72] Appropo of this, Luke described Jesus's rejection by the synagogue congregation of Nazareth, Jesus's hometown, and the congregation's attempt to kill him on the Sabbath.[73] "The chief priests and the rulers and the people . . . all cried out together, 'Away with this Man.' . . . They shouted out, 'Crucify him, crucify him!'" Luke combined Mark's attack on the Jewish leaders and Matthew's emphasis on the guilt of the Jewish people.[74]

Anti-Jewish statements reached their antagonistic peak in John 5–12.[75] Recent research indicates that John and Matthew reflect a bitter antagonism between Jews and Jewish-Christians.[76] Like the other Gospels, John regards the Jews as having lost their place, that is, their chosen status, to the sincere believers in Jesus Christ. John has Jesus accuse Jews who had been his followers but changed their minds and returned to their original faith, Judaism, of seeking to kill him.[77] John quotes Jesus as condemning these faithful Jews as Godless people whose father is the devil and who do the devil's work. They "are not of God."[78]

In the Synoptic Gospels (Matthew, Mark, and Luke), "the Jews" are mentioned only sixteen times; in John, they are cited seventy-one times (surpassed only by Acts, with nearly eighty mentions). Although Jesus's Jewishness is established early in the Gospel—he is twice called "rabbi"—and he quotes from the Jewish Scriptures throughout, the Jews have now become sons of Satan, whose goal is to murder Christ, "the light of the world."[79] In John's Gospel, the Pharisees, scribes, and priests of the Synoptic Gospels have now become "the Jews," all of whom seem to be enemies of Christ, indeed, veritable Antichrists.[80] Two later professions of faith, written specifically for Jewish converts to Christianity, contain a mention of the Antichrist as well: "Above all I renounce Antichrist whom all the Jews await."[81] The early second-century Apostolic Father, St. Polycarp of Smyrna, wrote to the church at Phillipi that "[t]o deny that Jesus Christ has come in the flesh is to be Antichrist[,] to be of the devil."[82]

Early Catholic Creeds and Liturgy

To fight off pagan opponents and heretics, the Church claimed to revere Jewish Scriptures and traditions, which it replicated in such Catholic practices as the priesthood, church discipline, fasting, and the keeping of the Sabbath (Lord's Day).[83] But once Christianity was ensconced as the official religion of the Roman Empire, in the fourth century, the Church openly claimed the inheritance of God's promises, which were initially promised to the Jews, and carried out a full-blown theological and political attack on the Jews. The existence of Judaizing Catholics and the flourishing of Jewish civilization helped convince the Church to create anti-Jewish creeds and liturgy as essential to the faith.[84]

The rites that converted pagans into Catholics were replete with anti-Jewish invective. The early Apostles' Creed emphasized that the true Messiah was Jesus Christ, whom the Jews had rejected and murdered. As St. Cyril of Jerusalem explained, the Creed was directed not at pagans, who did not believe in the coming of any Messiah, but at the Jews.[85] A sermon St. Augustine preached to converts being trained in Catholic doctrine (catechumens) is typical of sermons based on the Creed. St. Augustine believed it important to set the catechumens straight about the Jews from the beginning. He began by focusing on the importance of the catechism itself: "Receive, my Children, the Rule of Faith. . . . Write it in your heart, and say it to yourselves daily; even before you go to sleep, before you go out, arm yourself in your Creed."[86] He then described Christ's Passion in a dramatically anti-Jewish fashion: "The end of the Lord has come. It was the Jews who held him; the Jews who insulted him; the Jews who bound him; the Jews who crowned him with thorns; who soiled him with their spit; who whipped him; who ridiculed him; who hung him on the cross; who stabbed his body with their spears."[87] Jules Isaac has commented, "What a text! What an exegesis! It is a vivid model for the Christian literature, art, and teaching to come."[88] Isaac might have added, "What a pretext! What an excuse for future defamation and violence against Jews!"

The Church has used the liturgy of Easter and the seven days of Holy Week for nearly two millennia as an opportunity to defame Judaism,[89] which in turn has made Catholic attacks on their Jewish neighbors more likely.[90] The *Didascalia Apostolorum* identified the days of Holy Week with alleged evils of the Jews: Jesus's trial on "Wednesday, when they began to lose their souls," the crucifixion on "Friday, . . . when they crucified [Jesus Christ] as part of their Passover festival," and Saturday, the Sabbath day that God imposed on the Jews not as a day of joy and rest but as "mourning for their damnation."[91]

By the eighth or ninth century, about the time that St. John Chrysostom's viciously antisemitic sermons, treasured and preserved by Antiochian Catholics, became part of the curriculum in seminaries, the Church suppressed the slightest positive liturgical references to the Jews, such as bending one's knee and saying "Amen" after the Good Friday prayer for the Jews.[92] The Good Friday service is conciliatory and mild toward heretics, schismatics, and pagans, but *not* toward the Jews. Heretics and schismatics are in "error," and the pagans worship "idols." The faithful are instructed to genuflect and say, "Amen," at the conclusion of each of these prayers, but *not* after the prayer for the Jews.

Although some scholars deny that these parts of the service were intended to be anti-Jewish,[93] the *Oremus* singles out the "perfidious" Jews for special treatment, focusing on their "blindness."[94] Initially, the term *perfidus* may have simply meant unfaithful.[95] But because of its association with the Jews as having no faith in Jesus as the Christ, *perfidus* (and by the Middle Ages, *infidus* and *infidelis*) attracted the pejorative connotations of stubborn, blind, hostile, intentionally disbelieving, maliciously unfaithful, malevolent, and treacherous.[96] By the fourth century, St. Ambrose would write of the "*perfidia* of the stiff-necked Jewish people whose ears listen but do not hear, whose eyes look but do not see."[97]

Catholic congregations also refused to genuflect at the prayer for the Jews. The ninth-century Amalarius of Metz (d. 850), acting archbishop of Trier and superintendent of the archbishopric of Lyon, provides us with an explanation for the wording and instructions for the *Oremus*. He wrote: "When we pray for the perfidious Jews, we do not genuflect. For they had genuflected in mockery [of Christ in His Passion]. Let us demonstrate our revulsion at this act by not genuflecting when we pray for the Jews. . . . In like manner, let us abstain from the kiss of peace . . . so as not to duplicate the evil Judas kiss, which led to Christ's suffering. . . . We should abstain from doing things that associate us with the Jews. As St. Augustine has said, Easter should be commemorated on a Sunday so that it will be distinguished from the Jewish holiday.[98]

St. Jerome established the anti-Jewish basis for the next portion of the Good Friday Liturgy, called the *Improperia*, or the Reproaches, in a homily.[99] The Reproaches were first mentioned in the sixth century by St. Gregory, bishop of Tours, introduced into Western liturgy from the East (perhaps Jerusalem) in the eighth century, and fully developed by the eleventh century. They consist of a series of contrasting parallels between the good deeds God had done for the Jews and the Jews' malicious behavior in return. Purportedly spoken by Jesus while suspended from the cross,[100] this portion of the Easter Week liturgy was delivered in emotional and devastatingly anti-Jewish language. Each part of Jesus's speech is introduced by the question "My people, what have I done to you?" It imagines Jesus Christ directly addressing the Jewish people: Despite God's (Christ's) blessings, the Jews have "prepared a cross [for] your savior . . . pierced the body of your savior . . . delivered me flogged . . . opened my body with a lance. . . . led me to the tribunal of Pilate . . . fell on me with slaps and whips . . . gave me gall and vinegar to drink . . . hit my head with a stick . . . granted me a crown of thorns . . . hanged me at the gallows of the cross."[101]

Repeated reports of Catholic violence against Jews on, or just after, Good Friday provide ample evidence of the anti-Jewish feelings the service provokes. The French historian Pierre Pierrard can "still feel the emotions" he felt as a Catholic schoolboy at the Good Friday prayer for the Jews and its accompanying instruction *not* to genuflect. "I try to imagine what a 'moral ghetto' is, then I refer to the discomfort that grasped me at that moment."[102]

Not simply a matter of the sequence and timing of ritual events, the liturgical calendar was intended to reaffirm Catholic identity and the growing schism between Jews and Catholics[103] by clearly separating the holy days of the two faiths. As the second-century *Didache*[104] indicated, Catholic holidays supplant those of the Jews in order that Catholics "have nothing in common with the hypocritical Jews."[105] Eusebius of Alexandria indicated that Sundays should remind Catholics of "the resurrection of the Lord, the victory over the Jews."[106]

The theologians of the Church converted the joyous Jewish Passover holiday celebrating freedom and liberation into a tragic Good Friday commemorating the Jewish crime of deicide. Melito of Sardis argued that each time his Jewish neighbors celebrated Passover instead of Easter, they were denying the salvific power of Christ on the cross, in effect re-crucifying Christ.[107] Easter week reinforced the alienation of the Catholic faithful from the Jews and helped break whatever social affiliations Jews and Catholics had already established. The Council of Nicaea (325 CE) determined that the date of Easter be calculated so that it would not be synchronized with Passover. Catholics who celebrated Passover with Jews were subject to severe punishment, even excommunication.[108] The Jewish Passover, with its sacrifice of a lamb, was considered only a prototype of the true Passover—that is, the sacrifice of Jesus Christ, who was celebrated as "the Lamb of God" in prayer and ritual.[109] Aphraates, a fourth-century Syriac theologian, described the Jewish tribes as fornicators and adulterers compared to the tribe of Christians, which was the authentic church, and claimed that Moses, the prophets, and God were never "well disposed towards the Jews." He argued that the Jews should not be allowed to celebrate Passover any longer, since God had abolished it by dispersing the Jews and destroying the Temple at Jerusalem.[110]

Based on Matthew 7:6, early Christians excluded Jews during the Mass. The very presence of the Jewish "dogs," as they were called,[111] would profane the true sacrifice inherent in the service. The Church held that only the Catholic Mass could serve as a true spiritual communion with God. The Mass replaced the Jewish religious service, which, early Catholics argued, allowed communion only between the Jews and the physical altar. Homilies and readings from the Jewish Scriptures misused the Jewish prophets' criticisms to prove that all Jews were forever evil. Sermons based on the Christian Scriptures attacked the sinful Jews, their religion, and their unsatisfied Messianic hopes. The Church's goal was to ensure that the Jews and Judaism were portrayed so negatively that they could have no influence on Catholics.

The hymns of the sacred service were also intended to prove the validity of the Catholic interpretation of Scripture and Christianity's triumph over Judaism. Some hymns were sung in the form of a dialogue in which Church and Synagogue debated, which was perhaps the forerunner of medieval anti-Jewish drama. St. Jerome argued that the Jews did not understand the true meaning of the psalms they sang. Hostile and unkind, he called the Jewish hymns, the "grunting of pigs and the braying of jackasses."[112] Catholic liturgy adopted Jewish psalms "to announce Christ, retell his suffering, describe the salvation he brings, exalt their faith and solemnize their victory [over the Jews]." By employing these most touchingly beautiful songs, Catholic theologians sought to show that only Catholics were the authentic Chosen People, the true Israel, and that the evil Jews were now the false Israel. *Theologia gloriae* was consecrated as a regular part of the religious service.

In the fourth and fifth centuries, paganism declined and the service could concentrate even more on the Jews. Catholic services marking specifically Catholic occasions—Christmas, Ascension, and saints' days—were filled with anti-Jewish theology. Beginning in the sixth century, new rites celebrated the Blessed Virgin as mother of God and proclaimed Jewish evil. Into the twentieth century, the celebration of the cross throughout the Catholic Latin liturgy also emphasized the role of the Jews in the crucifixion.[113]

At this time, the Latin Church changed its baptismal rites to reflect the belief that the Jews were more satanic and less receptive to Catholic truth than any other converts. Not only was the conversion process more protracted for Jews, but the Church also required only the Jewish converts to curse themselves, the Jewish people, and their history. The Jewish convert was required to renounce the "errors of our fathers" and undertake not to "associate with the accursed Jews who remain unbaptized. . . . I will never return to the vomit of Jewish superstition, the vomit of my former error, or [associate] with the wicked Jews. . . . If I wander from the straight path . . . I shall be handed over to the eternal fire, in the company of the Devil . . . sharing . . . with Judas the punishment of burning."[114]

To alienate Catholics from Jews, the Church enforced the Christian Scriptures, creeds, and holidays, as well as the divine service itself, as part of a theological assault on Judaism and the Jewish people. The Church disguised the Jewish roots of the Catholic service and conditioned the faithful to believe that Christianity had no roots in Judaism and that Jews were wholly unconnected to Catholics. Only the Church and its Catholic tenets deserved allegiance on this earth. Eternal life was a Christian reward, eternal damnation the fate of the Jews.

CHAPTER 2

Value Inversion and Vilification

> Don't you realize, if the Jewish rites are holy and venerable, our way of life must be false.
> *St. John Chrysostom,* Adversus Judaeos

Most ancient peoples, both Jews and Gentiles, regarded crucifixion as demeaning. But the followers of Christ converted the "scandal of the Cross" into an act of metaphysical and escatological importance. An apparently meaningless execution in the political life of the Roman Empire and Judean politics became, for Christians, the most meaningful act in history, because Jesus's death would lead to his resurrection and potentially to eternal life for all the faithful.[1]

The Jews claimed to have discovered a spiritual God who they believed created all humanity, and with whom they had entered into a covenant. In it, they agreed to fulfill moral and ritual obligations in return for which God would make them the Chosen People, with the males marked by the holy ritual of circumcision. Their covenant with God carried with it the obligation for Jews to act as a kingdom of priests and a holy nation (Exodus 19:6), whose purpose was to set an example by their lives to help human beings toward righteousness. Thus Jews saw themselves as living witnesses to God's moral purpose for mankind, even if, as God's servants, they had to suffer and die for it. All this was recorded in the Jewish Scriptures, which the Jews considered sacred, besides being the historical record of their covenant with God and their history as a people. But Catholic theologians resorted to value-inversion to destroy Judaism's credibility. They turned Judaism on its head. They reinterpreted, modified, and adopted the traits and ideas most identified as Jewish (the covenant, monotheism, synagogue, kosher rules, circumcision, chosenness, the Promised Land, Jerusalem, and Temple) to fit the requirements of the Catholic self-image. The theology of glory, Martin Luther wrote, "calls evil good and good evil . . . everything has been completely turned up-side-down."[2]

In the patristic mind, the Jews were God-murderers—that is, people who first rejected and then slew God, incarnated in the form of Jesus Christ. Replaced by the "newly and truly chosen" Christians, Jews became hated by "God the Father." According to St. Augustine, the Jews were no longer witnesses to their positive relationship to God's existence and goodness. Instead, like Cain, Jews were to suffer throughout history so that all human beings would realize the penalty for deicide and other religious crimes. This dogma became the predominant position of the Church. The Jews' circumcision no longer marked their covenant with God, instead, it became the mark of the devil or of Cain the murderer. Fathers of the Church held that the Jews were taught circumcision by God to soften their hardness of heart, or to identify them so that the Romans would exclude them from Jerusalem. The fourth-century theologian Ephraem of Syria called the Jews circumcised dogs; for St. John Chrysostom, they were marked by circumcision like beasts.[3]

Judaism and Jews served four negative functions and one positive function for churchmen of the patristic period and of the Middle Ages. First, the Church utilized the Judaism of the past to supply Christianity with an unimpeachable history and with the prestige the new Church otherwise would not have possessed. Catholic history was allegedly older than Jewish history, having begun not with Abraham or Moses, but at the beginning of time. The early Church claimed all the Jewish Scriptures as their own birthright, with the "Old" Testament patriarchs treated like the first Catholics. The Church co-opted all the Jewish saints and true believers in God all the way back to Adam as Catholics: Abraham was "father of the faithful"; Abel was progenitor of the Church.[4] Cain was progenitor of the Jews.

A second goal of Catholic theologians was to render the persistent Jews hateful so that the faithful would not be attracted to Judaism.[5] The Church Fathers falsified the whole of Jewish moral history. They announced that the Jews were, are, and will always be evil. No evil was too great for the Jews not to have reveled in; no crime too appalling for the Jews not to have rejoiced in. Whatever good the ancient Jews apparently did was in reality Catholic; only their evil deeds were Jewish. Besides the most atrocious sin of deicide, the Jews were collectively guilty of all the sins of their fathers, "sins" they repeated over and over again each year. By the time of the Middle Ages, this charge included that of ritual murder of an innocent Catholic child during Holy Week. The Jews were no longer pictured as the Chosen People, heroes of holiness and moral living; they were instead the very models of radical evil, "the earthly representatives of the power of Darkness."[6] For these crimes, Jews had to suffer continual punishment on earth and eternal damnation, unless they sought salvation through the one true faith, Christianity. And even some

Church Fathers and medieval clerics doubted this possibility. The patristic writers thus employed not only the words of the Christian Scriptures against the Jews but also the texts of the Jewish prophets themselves. According to St. Irenaeus, had the Jews realized to what use their law and prophets would be put by Catholics, "they would never have hesitated themselves to burn their own Scriptures."[7]

Third, in order for Christianity to establish its own self-identity, legitimacy, and sanctity, it had to overthrow the theological dominance of Judaism. Jews therefore served as "an indispensable reference group, enabling Christians to know themselves as Christians and to incarnate good by contrast with [Jewish] evil."[8] When Jews persisted as authentic Jews proudly asserting their Judaism, by the time of the Middle Ages Catholic authorities with the instigation or support of churchmen ghettoized, expelled, forcibly converted, or sometimes killed them; for their loyalty to their own beliefs was seen as an insult and a danger to the Christian image. As St. John Chrysostom so bluntly put it, "Don't you realize, if the Jewish rites are holy and venerable, our way of life must be false."[9] The Catholic dilemma was that without Judaism, Christianity had no independent meaning. Judaism therefore had to be preserved, but in a condition where it could do no "harm" to Christianity, as a corpse in suspended animation.

Fourth, by focusing on the Jewish scapegoat and villain as the cause of all the specific historical ills of Europe, the Church could explain away the evidence that contravened its claim that the Kingdom of God had truly arrived with Christ, and it could account for the continued existence of evil in the world. The Jewish people served as a "magic betrayer" to help Catholics explain the ills that history visited upon them.[10]

There are indications that in every generation there were Christians friendly toward Jews. Every time we read of medieval prohibitions against Catholic-Jewish fraternization, we must assume that worthwhile relationships existed. Medieval Catholic theologians continually complained about Catholics who grew close to Jews or treated them as human beings rather than as theological types. This pro-Jewish, indeed, pro-human stance, *theologia crucis*, required the faithful to follow the moral teachings of the Jewish Scriptures as interpreted by Jesus of Nazareth in the Christian Scriptures, even in regard to the Jews. This perspective underscores the solidarity of suffering among all human beings. Moreover, Wolfgang Seiferth has identified a spirit of *Concordia* that saw an inner harmony between the two testaments. To be fully understood and appreciated, Christianity needed the ethical, monotheistic, and prophetic aspects of Judaism. This motif can also be discerned in some of the art and literature of the Middle Ages.[11]

Vilification

When the Church Fathers confronted the pagans outside of the Catholic community, they insisted that Christianity fulfilled the prophecies of the Jewish Holy Books, especially concerning the Messiah. It was, therefore, incumbent upon them to establish the validity of Judaism, this "very distinguished religion."[12] Origen's anti-pagan critique, *Contra Celsum* (Against Celsus), praised the Torah as inspired by the holy spirit of God and as the moral and legal principles upon which Christian thinking was based. Yet this praise of the Jewish foundations of Christianity was of *past* Jewish achievement and made for external, pagan consumption.[13]

But the existence of an independently thriving Jewish community, which persisted in denying the validity of Christianity by its refusal to convert, gave pagan anti-Catholics ammunition for their attack on Christianity and justified pagan rejection of Catholic missionizing. As a result, Catholic theological writers increasingly came to write of contemporary Jews as paragons of evil and satanic adversaries. It seemed to be a *theological* necessity that *all* Jews, whether Biblical or contemporary, be implicated in mythic religious crimes. "The phrase[s] 'a Jew,' or 'some Jews,' is almost unknown in patristic literature."[14] The Church Fathers argued that God had damned the Jewish people because of their continuous history of crime, which climaxed in the gravest crime and sin of all, deicide. Here is how three different early theologians summarized the Church's predominant theological position on the Jews, Judaism, and Jewish history.

- St. Gregory, the fourth-century Bishop of Nyssa: "Murderers of the Lord, killers of the prophets, enemies and slanderers of God; violators of the law, adversaries of grace, aliens to the faith of their fathers, advocates of the devil, progeny of poison snakes, . . . whose minds are held in darkness, filled with the anger of the Pharisees, a sanhedrin of satans. Criminals, degenerates, . . . enemies of all that is decent and beautiful. They are guilty of shouting: Away with him, away with him. Crucify him. He who was God in the flesh!"[15]
- St. Hilary of Poitiers: Judaism was "ever . . . mighty in wickedness; . . . when it cursed Moses; when it hated God; when it vowed its sons to demons; when it killed the prophets, and finally when it betrayed to the Praetor and crucified our God Himself and Lord. . . . And so glorying through all its existence in iniquity."
- Pseudo-Cyprian: "Moses [the Jews] cursed because he proclaimed Christ, . . . David they hated because he sang of Christ, . . . Isaiah they sawed asunder shouting [Christ's] glories, . . . John they slew revealing Christ, . . . Judas they loved betraying [Christ]."[16]

In *internal* communications among Catholics, their authentic anti-Jewish attitudes were expressed.[17] In the East as well as in the West, Catholic theology said to the Jews that their God, holy books, Messiah, and a portion of their law belonged to the New Israel, the Catholic Church; whereas the Jews themselves were disinherited and survived only as a warning of the consequences of obdurate wickedness.[18] The effect was devastating for the future status of Jews in Christendom. Patristic theologians regarded the habits and institutions of the Jews as hateful indications of the sinfulness and criminality of a Judaism that was so deaf and so blind to Catholic truth and goodness that it dared not to have died with the Coming of Christ, the supposed Jewish Messiah. The effect of these patristic ideas was devastating for the future status of Jews in Christendom, where Jews would be considered stateless beings long before the Nazi Nuremberg Laws of 1935, and where they would be murdered in their hundreds of thousands, if not millions, long before the Holocaust.

According to triumphalism, *theologia gloriae*, and the *adversus judaeos* tradition, Jews were Devilish Cains, and anti-Christs. Eusebius of Alexandria coupled the devil and the Jews. He began *every* paragraph in the first half of his sermon on the Resurrection thus: "Woe to you wretches, . . . you were called sons and became dogs. Woe to you, stiff-necked and uncircumcized, from being the Elect of God you became wolves, and sharpened your teeth upon the Lamb of God. You are estranged from His Glory; woe to you, ungrateful wretches, who have loved Hell and its eternal fires. . . . Hell . . . shall imprison you with your father the devil."[19]

For Tertullian, the outstanding North African theologian of the second and third century, antisemitism was as crucial to his religious beliefs as it was essential to his rhetoric. Anti-Jewish diatribes, for instance, are contained in twenty-seven of his thirty-two extant works. Like the other Fathers of the Church, Tertullian "needed Jews and Judaism as a kind of antitype to define nearly everything he was and stood for. . . . He uses [anti-Judaism] rhetorically to win arguments against his opponents and he uses it theologically . . . to construct a Christianity, a Christian social identity, which is centrally, crucially, un-Jewish, anti-Jewish."[20] Theological antisemitism thus seemed to define for him what it meant to be a Christian. And to be a Christian was to denigrate Jews, Judaism, and Jewishness.

Like the other Fathers of the Church, Tertullian's writings were replete with attacks on the Jewish people for a whole panoply of "crimes"—for him there were twenty-three categories of Jewish sin—from deicide and prophet-bashing to "bad habits" like clinging to the past. He held that the Jews were "the very anti-type of true virtue."[21] His major charge was that "though Israel may wash all its members every day, it is never clean. Its hands . . . are always stained, covered forever with the blood of the prophets and of our Lord himself."[22]

Like several other Fathers of the Church, Tertullian identified Jews with heresy, implying that it was the Jews who most inspired heretics. "From the Jew the heretic has accepted guidance in this discussion [that Jesus was not the Christ]. Let the heretic now give up borrowing poison from the Jew . . . the asp, as they say, from the adder." Deviations from Orthodox Christianity were seen not merely as Catholic splinter groups but as heresies that were essentially Jewish in spirit. The iconoclasts, who opposed the worship of religious images, were referred to as having "Jewish minds" by Peter of Antioch. When the Byzantine theologians' debated Latin theologians on the issue of the Latin use of *azymes*, unleavened bread for the Eucharist, the Eastern Church condemned their opponents as "sharing in fellowship with the Jews."[23] Tertullian gloated and exulted when he imagined how Christ would punish the Jews for having "thrown God, i.e., Christ, out." Israel was not merely *extra ecclesiam* (outside the Church); it was "*extra Deum*" (outside of God).[24]

What was new in St. Jerome was the identification of all Jews with Judas and with the immoral use of money, two themes that would bedevil Christian-Jewish relations for two millennia. Judas's sin and punishment was and would continue to be that of all Jews.[25] In his bitter, anti-historical, and anti-Jewish theology, Jerome sermonized that "Judas is cursed, that in Judas the Jews may be accursed. [Just as] you see the Jew praying; . . . nevertheless, their prayer turns into sin. . . . Whom do you suppose are the sons of Judas? The Jews. . . . Iscariot means *money and price*. . . . Synagogue was divorced by the Savior and became the wife of Judas, the betrayer."[26] In another emotional passage that may have served as the basis of the later anti-Jewish Good Friday liturgy called the Reproaches, discussed in Chapter 1, Jerome contrasted the gifts God had given the Jews with the "evil" with which the Jews repaid them. This homilitic assault went on for four thousand words like these:

> My enemies are the Jews;
> they have conspired in hatred against Me,
> crucified Me,
> heaped evils of all kinds upon Me,
> blasphemed Me.

Curiously, Jerome ended his sermon by asking his parishioners to forgive the Jews. Reminiscent of Paul, he argued that this should be done since God "has not altogether uprooted them. . . . We have been grafted upon their root; we are the branches, they the root. We must not curse our roots; rather we ought to pray for them."[27] Yet one must wonder about the effect of this sermon on a Catholic audience when after thousands of words of bitter attack, St. Jerome changed course to remind the faithful to pray for the Jews as an act of moral conviction. The words that ring down through history are not Jerome's plea for forgiveness, but his complaint that "the ceremonies of the Jews are harmful and deadly to Christians, and . . . whoever keeps them, whether Jew or Gentile, is doomed to the abyss of the Devil."[28]

Perhaps the most influential Father of the Church was the fourth to fifth century bishop of Hippo, St. Augustine. Like Paul, although he felt ambivalently about the Jews, in the end he came down hard on them. He did mention the need to "love" the Jews, although it was in the context of trying to convince them to leave their Judaism and convert to Christianity.[29] Like Jerome, he sometimes identified all Jews with Judas. He and St. Cyprian developed the idea that "there is no salvation outside the Church," a notion that dominated the triumphant Church until at least 1965. Like his teacher, the virulently anti-Jewish St. Ambrose, bishop of Milan, St. Augustine made the Jews a special subset of those damned to hell.

His theological construct in regard to the Jews, repeated at least twenty times in his work, was the "Witness People."[30] This proposition—that Jews are to survive as suffering Cains in collective punishment for their deicide until their conversion to Christ—has served to legitimize, even to sanctify, the enslavement of Jews to Catholics at least through the Middle Ages. At the same time, by establishing a limit to such suffering—that is, the Jews were not to be killed—this principle served to protect Jewish people from mass murder for the next eight hundred years despite the fact that many Christian theologians continued to question the Jews' right to exist at all.[31] St. Augustine believed that the stigmatic "mark of Cain" was, for the Jews, *Judaism* itself. He wrote,

> Not by bodily death, shall the ungodly race of carnal Jews perish. . . . To the end of the seven days of time, the continued preservation of the Jews will be a proof to believing Christians of the subjection merited by those who, in the pride of their kingdom, put the Lord to death. . . . Only when a Jew comes over to Christ, is he no longer Cain. . . . The Jews have been scattered throughout all nations as witnesses to their own sin and to our truth. . . . If a pagan doubts Christ, we can prove his Messiahship because he was predicted in the writings of the Jews themselves a long time ago. And so by means of one enemy [the Jews] we confound another enemy [the pagans]. 'Scatter them abroad, take away their strength. And bring them down O Lord.' (Ver. 12).[32]

The most bitter of early Christians in regard to the Jews was St. John Chrysostom. It is a positive sign of changing times that in the most recent edition of his works, his Catholic editor, Paul Harkins, wrote that Chrysostom's anti-Jewish theological position "is no longer tenable. Even if he was motivated by an overzealous pastoral spirit, many of his remarks are patently antisemitic. For these objectively unchristian acts he cannot be excused, even if he is the product of his times."[33]

We find in Chrysostom as in most of the Church Fathers, and later in Christian theologians, a kind of presents in his assault on the Jews. All Jewish sins whenever they were committed were associated with the Jews of the contemporary generation. The sins of the Jews were communal and endless, committed by the Jewish people both before the advent of Christ, during his lifetime, and into the present day. Chrysostom saw in his Jewish neighbors the alleged crimes of all preexisting Jews. If, for example, a Scriptural passage referred to Jews as having worshipped idols, Chrysostom applied this prophetic self-criticism to the Jews of his own day.[34] In his exegesis on Psalm 106:37, he wrote that the Jews "slaughtered their progeny with their own hands to serve the accursed demons, who *are* the enemies of our life."[35] And, like the other Church Fathers, he applied the Christian Testament passages concerning the Jewish involvement in the crucifixion to the Jews of his own day. He quoted a Jew of Antioch as saying to him proudly, 350 years after the event, "*I* crucified him."[36]

Although Chrysostom was critical of many groups, for him as for so many other of the Fathers, the Jews were the ultimate evil. In expounding on his program of hostility, Chrysostom sought to alienate any Catholic feelings of affinity with, or of common humanity toward, the Jews. The goal of "the Church's greatest preacher" was to situate the Jews in "the realm of the demonic."[37] His "intention [was] to expel the Jews once and for all from humanity,"[38] as evidenced by his words below.

- "Here [in the synagogue, he wrote,] the slayers of Christ gather together, here the cross is driven out, here God is blasphemed, here the Father is ignored, here the Son is outraged, here the grace of the Spirit is rejected. Does not greater harm come from this place [than from pagan temples] since the Jews themselves are demons?"[39]
- "[Jews] fought against the commands of God and danced with the Devil."[40]
- "It was not by their own power that the Caesars did what they did to you [Jews]; it was done by the wrath of God, and his absolute rejection of you."[41]
- In a stunning passage, Chrysostom went so far as to assert that because Jews rejected Christ, they therefore deserved to be killed.[42] Like other obstinate animals, the Jews "are *fit for killing*. And this is

what happened to the Jews: while they were making themselves unfit for work, they grew *fit for slaughter.*"[43]

- Chrysostom made the same argument about murdering Jews elsewhere. Quoting St. Luke 19:27, he claimed that Jesus was referring to the Jews when he said, "As for these enemies of mine who did not want me to reign over them, bring them here and *slay them* before me."[44]

Chrysostom contributed a profound sense of rage to the anti-Jewish polemic that resulted in violence against the Jews and their communities. Even though his diatribes against the Jews of Antioch seemed to have had no immediate effect, there were riots twenty-eight years later against the synagogues there. Can there be any doubt that his verbal and written assaults on the Jews helped form the attitudes of many Catholics toward their Jewish neighbors? Moreover, Eastern Emperor Arcadius, who confirmed the Jews in certain privileges in 396 and 397 CE, with the arrival of Chrysostom as Bishop of Constantinople issued anti-Jewish edicts; in 404, when Chrysostom was expelled from Constantinople, Arcadius reestablished a policy favorable to the Jews.[45]

From the eighth until the twentieth century, the great preacher's homilies against the Jews, considered among the greatest examples of rhetoric ever uttered, were used in Catholic schools and seminaries where priests were taught to preach and hate Jews.[46]

CHAPTER 3

Roman Law

[The Jew in Christianized Roman law was considered] a monster, a theological abstraction of superhuman cunning and malice, and more than superhuman blindness.[1]

James Parkes, The Conflict of the Church and the Synagogue

Constantine and the Nicaean Council

The fourth century realized the triumph of Catholic power and influence within the Roman Empire.[2] At the same time, the imperial government and its laws turned permanently anti-Jewish under the influence of the early Catholic theologians—all of whom were apparently Gentile and had lost all sympathy with the Jewish people.[3] The Catholic Church's predominant theological perspective was that Jews were evil beings with whom Catholics should have no social or religious relationships lest they become polluted.[4] The council of Elvira (300 CE) prohibited Jews from blessing Catholic fields and forbade Catholics from sharing meals with Jews, or from sex or marriage with Jews.[5] The council at Antioch (341 CE) disallowed the sharing of the Passover Seder with Jews. Laodicea (360 CE) required the Gospels to be read and Catholics to work on the Jewish Sabbath and prohibited Catholics from sharing feasts with Jews. Should Catholics persist in observing the Jewish Sabbath, they were to be considered "Jews . . . anathema to Christ."[6]

Constantine made Christianity the preferred religion of the Roman Empire, and at the end of the century Christianity became the official religion. Under the centrifugal pressure of invasion from outside the empire, Constantine may have decided to use the already well-established hierarchically arranged Catholic Church. Like the absolutist king Louis XIV fourteen centuries later, Emperor Constantine sought une loi, une foi, un roi—one law, one religion, one political authority.[7] In 312, under a Catholic symbol for Christ—called the *labarum*, consisting of the first two letters (X and P) of the Greek for Christ, *Christos*—Constantine defeated his rival for the imperial throne. In 313, he and Eastern Emperor Licinius agreed, in the Edict of Milan, to recognize Christianity as a lawful religion. In 321 he declared Sunday a public holiday. As W. H. C. Frend put it, "everything [Constantine did] was subordinated to the unity and perhaps even the universality of the Church." Considering himself "the equal of the Apostles" and universal protector of Christians, Constantine wrote to the Persian king in 326, proclaiming that the Christians in the Persian Empire under his protectorship.[8] He publicly recommended Christianity to his whole empire, Christianized the army, delivered Christian sermons in court, favored Christian individuals and communities, rewarded converts to the faith with rank and wealth, tightened the divorce laws, and prohibited gladiatorial combat.[9]

In 324, Constantine's victory at Chrysopolis had made him emperor of a unified empire whose capital was a rebuilt Byzantium, which he renamed Constantinople. The next year Constantine convened the landmark Church Council of Nicaea to resolve the Arian controversy (Arianism was the principal heresy of the time; it emphasized the dominance of God the Father and assigned a lesser role to Jesus) and establish religious peace and Christian uniformity in his newly united empire.[10] The council defined the nature of Jesus, developed a uniform Catholic creed, declared Arianism a heresy, and attacked Judaism. Constantine's convocation mentioned that Judaizing was detrimental to the Church,[11] and the council clearly distinguished the celebration of the Christian Easter from the Jewish Passover. The council's disengagement of the dates assigned to Easter from those of Passover was widely supported in the western Church at the time. Pseudo-Cyprian had already scornfully addressed the issue: "It should never be possible for Christians to stray from the way of truth and to trail like ignorant people after the blind and stupid Jews as to the correct day for Easter."[12] The council's decisions were sanctioned and published to the empire on June 19, 325 in Constantine's letter, signaling that the break with Judaism would be official and emotional.

> [The Jews are] a people who, having imbrued their hands in a most heinous outrage [Jesus' crucifixion], have thus polluted their souls and are deservedly blind. . . . Therefore we have nothing in common with that most hostile of people the Jews. We have received from the Savior another way . . . our holy religion. . . . On what subject will that detestable association be competent to form a correct judgment, who after that murder of their Lord . . . are led . . . by . . . their innate fury?[13]

Four years before Nicaea, Constantine had been willing to grant the Jews some concessions by guaranteeing Judaism's established practices.[14] But after

Nicaea, Constantine referred to Judaism in the same tone as the council; his law of October 329 described Judaism as a "deadly [and] sacrilegious sect." The same law called the Jewish synagogue—the center of Jewish worship since the destruction of the Temple—a *conciliabulum*—literally, "a place of assembly," but in Latin slang, "a brothel."[15] In his homilies, St. John Chrysostom twice alluded to the synagogue as a brothel.

Church Jewish Policy and Roman Law

Thanks to St. Augustine's doctrine of the Witness People, Church policy determined that the Jews were to be degraded, not murdered. Imperial Jewish policy, influenced by the emperor's Christian faith and the bishops, mirrored the Church's Jewish policy. The "Jewish problem" in the Christianized Roman Empire "was a religious problem."[16] Following the same path, Emperor Justinian invited ecclesiastical authorities to oversee laws affecting the Jews' status and rights. The Church's canons concerning the Jews assumed the force of law.[17]

Imperial laws were based on the principle that Jews were generally to be protected against violence but deserved less protection under the law than Catholics. Not slaves or foreigners, the Jews were legally considered *cives romani*, or Roman citizens. This was established in 212 CE when Caracalla granted the Jews citizenship.[18] The fundamental description of Jews living in the Christianized empire was that of a detested group protected from eradication.[19] This legal status mirrored the predominant patristic theology on the Jews.

Hostile laws affected pagans and heretics, but the enormous number of anti-Jewish laws and their theological rhetoric indicated that the "perfidious Jews" were the Empire's main victims of discrimination. The Jews could never occupy a status of equality with the faithful, who recognized in Jesus Christ the true Son of God. The *Codex Theodosianus* (Theodosian Code) followed another of the Church's principles, which is that Jews should never be put in a position of authority over any of the faithful. "No Jew . . . may receive any honors and dignities of office. For it is abominable that an enemy of God and of the Roman laws shall be empowered to execute these laws . . . and have the power to judge and pronounce sentence against Christians, many of whom are priests of that sacred religion, thereby insulting our faith."[20] By the fifth century, Jews could not serve as attorneys, could not bring criminal suits against Christians, and could not testify in criminal cases. If a Jew violated a Christian's rights, he was punished more severely than the Christian who oppressed a Jew. Roman law stated that "If Jews shall circumcise purchased slaves of anther nation, they shall be banished or suffer capital punishment."

Gentile Roman citizens who allow themselves or their slaves to be circumcised "according to Jewish custom" will be forever banished and expropriated; circumcising doctors will be killed.[21]

Based on this principle, the Church influenced the imperial government to exclude Jews from military rank and its accompanying privileges. Throughout the Roman Empire, with the possible exception of Italy, many Jews had served in the Roman Army. So many Jewish soldiers served the Romans that, by the end of the fourth century, the Church had become alarmed. In 418 the Church succeeded in having a law passed that excluded Jews from the army, although they still could serve in the defense of their towns. For a Jew to serve in the military, the law required that he have himself baptized as a Catholic.[22]

Whereas conversion to Christianity was encouraged, several laws of the Christianized Roman Empire severely punished converts to Judaism. Although neither the Church nor the Empire ever outlawed Judaism itself, Constantine's law of October 18, 329, made it a criminal offense to become a Jew: exile or death were the penalties set for Jews who tried to prevent their coreligionists from apostatizing to Christianity or who encouraged Romans to convert to Judaism.[23] "The Jews must be informed that if they . . . dare attack anyone escaping from their deadly sect and choosing to join the cult of God [Christianity] . . . they shall be delivered immediately to the flames and burnt with all their associates."[24] Two laws of 383–84 punished Catholic conversion to Judaism by exile, expropriation, or death. "Those Christians who have insulted the dignity of their own religion and name and have contaminated themselves with the Jewish disease will be punished for these shameful acts."[25] Another law noted that "To convert a Christian to Judaism meant contaminating him with Jewish sacraments."[26] A third law stated: "The blind and senseless Jews [are] heretics [and] abominable. . . . Whoever coerces or persuades any Roman, slave or free, to leave the cult of the Christian religion and join instead that abominable sect and rite [Judaism] shall be sentenced to death and expropriation."[27]

The Catholic Anti-Jewish Rhetoric of *Codex Theodosianus*

Emperor Theodosius II's collection of Roman law, the *Codex Theodosianus* of 438, contained a compilation of all the then-current legislation regarding the Jews. This legislation demonstrates that the Jewish communities' rights, privileges, and security had declined and that Christianity was the primary cause. The Jews were

"sacrilegious assemblies" (353),
"polluted with the Jewish disease" (383),

"contaminated with Jewish sacraments" (384),
"insulters of the Christian faith"
and a "plague that spreads widely" (408),
"the abominable and vile" (409),
"enemies of Roman law,"
"monstrous heretics,"
"the worst of men,"
and "blindly senseless" (438).

Judaism was referred to as

"a deadly and sacriligious sect"
and "a brothel" (329),
"the Jewish perversity, alien and hostile to the Roman Empire" (409),
"the mark of Jewish filth" (415),
"corrupt with the filth of its particular sect" (417),
"the insanity of the Jewish blasphemy" (425),
"an abominable sect and rite" (438),
"frightful and hideous" (438).[28]

Several laws repeat that "Whatever differs from the faith of the Christians, is contrary to Christian [Roman] law." One of the last laws of the *Codex*, a decree of Emperors Honorius and Theodosius II of April 1, 409, elaborated the Catholic position: "[It is prohibited to] cease being a Christian and adopt the abominable and disgusting name of the Jews [that is,] to adopt the Jewish perversity, which is alien to the Roman Empire which has now become Christianized. . . . For it is an issue of life and death when someone rejects the Christian faith and replaces it with with the disgusting Jewish form of perverse belief."[29]

During the Early Middle Ages the good relations that sometimes existed between Jews and Catholics troubled Churchmen, and several Church Councils at Elvira, Nicaea, Laodicaea, Vannes, Agde, Epaon, Orléans, Maçon, Clichy, Rheims, Metz, and Coyaca ordered the isolation of Jews from Catholics.[30] Embodied in conciliar proclamations, papal letters, and liturgical formulae, the Latin Church considered Judaism to be its most formidable ideological opponent.[31] The Church justified almost any harm done to Jews because of their "continuing crimes" of deicide, blasphemy, and heresy. As we approach the High Middle Ages, Jewish lives were now completely in the hands of their worst enemies.

CHAPTER 4

Medieval Deterioration

Damn you, you shameful Jews, you must be forever damned! I must blind you, you evil Jews, and all your children and send you all at once into the deep abyss of hell.
                                                              Christiana, the Alsfeld Passion Play

S alo Baron denied that medieval Jews lived in a state of "extreme wretchedness, . . . subject to incessant persecution and violence. . . . Prisoner in the Ghetto, denied access to the resources and activities of Western society, distorted intellectually, morally, spiritually by centuries of isolation and torture."[1] It is true that positive developments in Jewish life and thought did occur and good relationships between Catholics and Jews did exist during the High Middle Ages; besides, a few Jews prospered, some had residence and movement rights, and Jews were the only non-Catholic community to be tolerated at all. It is also true that in the Early Middle Ages, when European society was not fully Christianized, Jews lived comparatively well under Arian, not Trinitarian, Christians.

But the fact is that by the eleventh century, almost all Europeans were self-conscious Catholics, their lives rooted in Catholic liturgy and creed, conditioned by religious art and literature, canon law, and the ecclesiastical structure of the Church,[2] and during this period, the Church's anti-Jewish propaganda became more virulent and far more effective.[3] Most Jews suffered continual degradation, and hundreds of thousands of Jews were murdered by Catholics.

This period saw intensified Christian self-doubt, the development of new Christian heresies and Church Orders, Church reform movements, increased political conflict between Church and state, new demands for credit, urban development, missionizing, and Christendom's most intense crusading activity,[4] as well as the greatest outpouring of Catholic polemic against Jews.[5] In his *Exposito in Lucam*, St. Thomas Aquinas quoted St. Ambrose's bitter attack on the Jews word for word, referring to them as poisoned serpents and devils "possessed by the unclean spirit of demons . . . caught in the snare of the devil . . . polluted . . . with the inner filth of its soul."[6]

Christians saw denials of the Christological meanings of Scripture in Jewish prayer. The daily prayer called the *Aleinu le-Shabb'ah* criticized those who "prostrate themselves before vanity and emptiness and pray to a God that saveth not."[7] Christians observed that Jews spat when the words "vanity" and "emptiness" were recited. Even though the prayer derived from Isaiah 45:20 and therefore preceded Christianity, Catholic theologians as early as St. Jerome interpreted these words and actions as an indication that the Jews intended to curse Jesus and blaspheme Christianity.[8] The Inquisition ultimately pressured the Jews to excise the controversial phrases.[9] The Inquisition also examined and condemned Rashi's commentaries, Maimonides' *Mishneh Torah*, David Kimhi's (d.1235) vociferous denial of Jesus's Messiahship,[10] the Talmud, and other Jewish polemical writing.

Jews and Christians had to deal with one another socially on a daily basis. Many Jews depended on their Christian neighbors for the necessities of life, such as food and shelter. Christians depended on Jews for vital services as well: Jews lent money, sold food, and acted as middlemen.[11] Despite prohibitions, some Christians and Jews ate, drank, bathed, or had sex together, as indicated by several papal and princely laws that forbade such shared activities.

Artistic Representations

Through many of the preachings, writings, and artistic works of the articulate and creative faithful, the Church encouraged Latin Christians to regard the deicidal Jews as first among sinners, as cohorts of the devil, and as minions of the Antichrist. This antisemitic material kept contemporary Jews' complicity in the events surrounding the Passion of Christ ever in the forefront of the Christian mind. Medieval art and literature, most of it concerned with religious themes, indelibly imprinted the theology of triumph on the Christian psyche.

It is a medieval commonplace that art, second only to the Church itself, communicated God's voice to Catholic society. This idea appears as early as the sixth century, in the words of Pope Gregory the Great, and was restated in the twelfth century by Bernard of Clairvaux. Works of art acted as "literature of the illiterate."[12] Pope St. Gregory stated that "paintings are placed in the churches to enable the illiterate to read on the walls what they cannot read in the books."[13] Positive and neutral portrayals of Jews did exist in the Middle Ages but were most likely commissioned by the Jews themselves. Denigrating images of Jews appear in illustrated Bibles, prayer books, and psalters; in statues and bas-reliefs, both inside and outside of churches and alongside public ways; on portals and wall; in tapestries, stained-glass windows, and furniture; on stoves, plates, bric-a-brac, and even urinals.[14] A twelfth-century illustration in the *Hortus Deliciarium* (Garden of Delights) shows Jews roasting in the first cauldron in hell.[15] In a thirteenth-century Augsburg Psalter, St. Michael and a devil collaborate in damning a Jew, who is portrayed as the first to enter the jaws of hell.

The Gospels gave the medieval Catholic artist many opportunities to demonstrate his antipathy.[16] The artist disregarded the Jewishness of Jesus, his apostles, and his followers, as well as the Jewishness of his ideas and beliefs, while the Romans were exculpated from any involvement in his death. Only the Jews were seen as responsible. Later, great artists used this subject matter. Hieronymous Bosch (d. 1516) painted *The Crucifixion*, which shows Jesus en route to Golgotha, his face at peace; he is spiritually transported beyond the frenzied Jewish mob that surrounded him. In sharp contrast to the sublime Jesus, the Jewish crowd is portrayed as a collection of dehumanized monstrosities.

Besides the linking of the Jew, the Devil, ritual-murder, and blood-libel, the scatological *Judensau* (Jewish sow) motif pictured the Jews as sucking a sow's teats and eating its feces, which were identified with the Talmud. (The patriotic and secular German Economics Minister during World War I, Walter Rathenau, was assassinated simply because he was a Jew. His antisemitic murderers called for his death as "a goddamned *Judensau*." Nazis and Neo-Nazis also associated the Jews with the *Judensau*.[17]) The most famous representation of the *Judensau* was a fifteenth-century mural painted at eye level on a wall of the Brückenturm, Frankfurt's busiest public way, where it could be seen by all who entered the city. This mural portrayed the Jews, the Devil, a *Judensau*, and Simon of Trent (the alleged victim of Jewish ritual murder) and was accompanied by this obscene caption: "Drink the milk, eat the feces; this is your best sweet." Drawn first in the fifteenth century and restored several times by the city council, the mural's religious intention was made obvious because the painting was positioned next to one of the Crucifixion and because some reprints were printed on the reverse side of a mural depicting the crucifixion.[18]

The defeated Jewish *Synagoga* (female figure representing the synagogue and Jews) was positioned in the pictorial art of the time on the left side, associating the Jews with hell, strife, and danger. The triumphant Catholic *Ecclesia* (female figure representing the Church and Catholics) was positioned on the right-hand side, thereby associating Catholics with heaven, election, and safety. By the end of the Middle Ages, the artistic trappings of Ecclesia would be transferred to Mary, *mater et sponsa Christi* (mother and bride of Christ) as the universal symbol of Christian belief.[19] The faithful saw these figures much more often than they caught a glimpse of their own rulers.[20] Although she was sometimes portrayed as an attractive woman, almost a twin sister of Ecclesia, Synagoga was placed on Jesus's left (Matthew 25:41 reports Jesus as saying "to those at his left hand. 'You that are accursed, depart from me into the eternal fire prepared for the devil and his angels'"), and she was depicted as a defeated adversary. Her beauty did not denote equality with Ecclesia; accepting that all creatures, good and evil, ugly and beautiful, were created by God, medieval artists sometimes portrayed evil people as attractive.[21]

As hatred of Jews increased, so did "the gracelessness of Synagoga's image."[22] In the altar of Stavelot, Belgium, in the evangelistary of Bruchsal, Germany, and in the cathedral window at Chalons-sur-Marne, France, Catholic artists associated Synagoga more and more with the Jewish "Christ killers" and sometimes provided her with all the instruments of Christ's murder: the spear, sponge, vinegar, and crown of thorns.[23] She was usually blinded or blindfolded, often by the Devil.[24] Frequently, her head was bowed, her spear (perhaps an allusion to the spear that stabbed Christ on the cross or symbolic of the Jewish Scriptures breaking with Christianity) was broken into three parts (representing the power of the Holy Trinity), the tablets of the law were falling from her hand, and her crown lay at her feet. At Notre Dame de Paris, the Devil in the form of a serpent with fangs ready to strike coils its body around Synagoga's head and eyes, blinding her to the "truth" of Christianity. A window in Chartres Cathedral, which depicts the Passion shows a demon shooting an arrow into Synagoga's eye.[25] Other depictions of Synagoga defame her with symbols of stubbornness, deviltry, and evil.[26] Depictions of attacks against Synagoga reflect increasing violence against European Jews.

Literature

Latin and vernacular literature reflected and endorsed theological defamations of Jews. Throughout the twelfth and thirteenth centuries, the Jews of England and France were accused of ritual murder.[27] The most famous of these "martyrs to Jewish evil" was Hugh of Lincoln. In 1255, eight-year-old Hugh apparently accidentally drowned in the cesspool of a Jew's house in Lincoln. Jews discovered his body and, fearing for their lives, removed and hid it—but to no avail. The canon of Lincoln Cathedral and royal official John of Lexington, accused the Jews of ritual murder. (An English monk, Thomas of Monmouth, in the case of William of Norwich—the earliest alleged victim of ritual murder—invented the myth of Jewish ritual murder at least in part to increase the tourist trade.[28]) King Henry III ruled that all the Jews of England were guilty and seized this opportunity to extort money from them. Hugh's story came to be enormously popular, with twenty-seven versions of the story elaborated in gruesome detail by the imagination of balladeers, broadcast across England. Elements of *theologia gloriae* were evident in the reports of the monastic historian Matthew Paris (d.1259) and the monastic annalist of Burton,[29] who claimed that "Little St. Hugh" was allegedly crucified after being horribly tortured. Matthew noted that the Jews had collaborated in their crime in "almost all the cities of England" and that they tortured and "crucified [Hugh] in contempt and reproach of Jesus Christ."[30]

Chaucer was familiar with the traditional religious sources of theological antisemitism on which ritual-murder defamations were based. He read the Church Fathers and often quoted from the Christian Scriptures, the Apocrypha, and the lives of the saints.[31] Chaucer gave the accusation renewed respectability when he included it in his *Canterbury Tales* (1390) as "The Prioress' Tale," published about a century after the Jews had been brutally forced out of England. Although Chaucer's version is set in an Asian city, all the details are clearly European—"a Christian town, in which, long since, a Ghetto used to be where there were Jews supported by the Crown for the foul lucre of their usury, hateful to Christ and all his company."

Chaucer's prioress describes the "litel child" as an innocent, deeply devoted to Mary, Christ's mother. The prioress then mentions the association of Jews with the devil, claiming that Satan urged the Jews not to permit this goodness to exist any longer but instead to murder the child. "First of our foes, the serpent Satan shook those Jewish hearts that are his waspish nest." She alleged that the Jews hired one among them to kill the child and maliciously throw his body into their cesspool. The nun then exclaimed: "O cursed folk of Herod . . . blood cries out upon your cursed deed." And after her story was done, the prioress referred specifically to Hugh of Lincoln, as "likewise murdered so by cursed Jews, as is notorious (for it was but a little time ago)."[32]

Even though Chaucer may have been satirizing the prioress for her naiveté and ignorance, many literary scholars agree that he was not satirizing the prioress's "religious prejudice" against Jews.[33] While we can never know Chaucer's own attitude toward Jews, his prioress' tale has stimulated and confirmed antisemitism among his readers by perpetuating the degrading and deadly myth that Jews are ritual murderers of Catholic children.

Other lesser known, secular writers also depicted the Jews as evil. The twelfth-century Norman poet Philip de Thaun, for example, compared Jews with owls that fly at night and "sing at the approach of evil." Following tradition, he observed that when the Jews "crucified God," Christians replaced them as God's children.[34] But some authors, devout but at odds with the Church hierarchy, like Boccaccio, were arguably free of Jew-hatred.[35] Catholic theologian Peter Abelard, much like twenty-first century Evangelicals, seemed sympathetic to Jews in this life (he wrote that the Jews had not sinned grievously in crucifying Christ) but condemned them in the next life because those who refused to believe in Christ or receive the sacraments would end up in hell.[36]

Drama

Medieval drama stemmed from Catholic liturgy and the Mass, with its transubstantiation of consecrated wine and bread into Christ's blood and body. Jews remained quintessential outsiders.[37] Medieval theater was extraordinarily popular, and the plays covered many topics: morality, miracle, mystery, Passion, resurrection, redemption, Antichrist, and Corpus Christi, as well as the *planctus Mariae*, or laments of Mary.[38] People left their homes and businesses for days to watch the dramas, which were intended to teach the medieval audience about Christ and the Catholic faith. Yet medieval religious drama demonstrates "a mood of unrelenting hostility . . . directed in large part toward the disbeliever, the Jew." [39] Even when no Jews lived in the local area or within the whole nation, the Jew was denigrated. The theme of winning the reprobate Jews over to Christianity was one of the roots of European theater.[40]

If literary scholar Stephen Spector is correct, the Jews were assigned attributes that the playwright and audience could not accept in themselves.[41] Staged in churches or market places, religious dramas including Jews in the dramatis personae stereotyped them in terms of traditional Catholic defamations as disloyal, mean, treacherous, angry, duplicitous, greedy, contemptuous, and criminal.[42] In many of these dramas Jews appeared as enemies of Christ and Christianity who knew the truth of Christianity but maliciously denied it.[43] As in medieval sermons, liturgy, and graphic art, the Jews were often portrayed as cohorts of the devil, exploiting the power of money, plotting and acting against Christ and all Catholics. The drama of the Christian-Jewish conflict, already over a thousand years old, came to life on stage as a war between the forces of Catholic good and Jewish evil.

Corpus Christi plays celebrated the power of the consecrated host by dramatizing miracles involving the Eucharist. These dramas portrayed the Jews in distinctive Jewish costume as protagonists who viciously attacked the host, driving nails through it, making it bleed.[44] The Jews thus played an important role in Catholic teaching about Christ's real presence in the consecrated host.[45]

Reflecting traditional religious conflict, the medieval English mystery plays of Townley, York, and Chester, denigrated the Jews, who refused to depart from their Torah and accept the divinity or messiahship of Jesus. Jews are portrayed as demons who, blind to the truth of Christianity, stubbornly insist on their own religion. The Jews are shown seizing, torturing, and murdering Christ, doing most of what the Scriptures assigned to the Romans. Again, like demons, Jews defend the Torah and maliciously celebrate Jesus's crucifixion by dancing joyously around the cross. The Jews were shown as incapable of faith, as "demonic forces of destruction." The audience was urged to expel disbelief, symbolized by the Jew, from itself.[46]

Following antagonistic Catholic tradition, in some of these plays, Jews were condemned by their own prophets. In the twelfth-century *Jeu d'Adam* (Game of Adam), the prophet Isaiah, depicted as a Catholic who foresees the birth of Jesus Christ, told a historical Jew that,

Isaiah: You have the felon's disease, from which you will never be cured!

Jew: Am I really sick then?

Isaiah: Yes, sick with error![47]

Whereas the Romans were exculpated from any involvement in Jesus's death, Jews were repeatedly shown torturing and abusing Jesus. In the Frankfurt Passion Play of 1493, based on a version written one hundred years earlier, the Jews dragged Jesus before Pilate, "accusando, trudendo, spuendo, ridendo," accusing him, jostling him, spitting on him, ridiculing him. When Pilate pleaded with them, "Ecce homo! Ir Iudden, seht: ist er eynem menschen glich?" ("You Jews, look at this man. Is he not human?"), the merciless Jews answered, "Crucifige, crucifige eum!" Jesus was again beaten, pinched, spit on, stretched to fit the predrilled holes, and nailed to the cross with purposefully dull nails. In these plays, Jews were nothing less than blind, deceitful, perfidious, damned murderers.[48]

In the Alsfeld Passion Play (1501), like several other plays, the Jews employed money to corrupt those around them. The Jewish authorities tried to pay Judas his money with counterfeit pieces, reinforcing the stereotype of Jews as greedy cheats. Thomas of Froidmont explained that "Judas sold Christ out of cupidity."[49] More important, the Alsfeld play identified the Jews as minions of Lucifer. Jews were on his satanic council of war against

Christianity. The driving force behind this play was the principle that the Jews were the primary evil-doers in Catholic society. Anything done by Catholics to cause Jews to suffer was therefore psychologically, morally, and theologically justified. The play emphasized that Jews profaned their own religion and mocked Jesus. The Jews perverted their Passover holiday by drinking from the arse of a calf, "*Judei bibunt ex culo vituli.*" In a scene that continues for more than seven hundred lines, a patient Jesus and pleading Mary are contrasted with the monstrous Jews, who serenade Jesus and dance around him as he dies on the cross. The play ends with a vow to take revenge on the Jews by a character called *Christiana* (Ecclesia): "Damn you, you shameful Jews . . . you must be forever damned!" *Christiana* then promised the Jews great suffering in the future and blindfolded *Judea*, breaking her banner that carried a black idol on it. "Thus I must end this matter and blind you evil Jews so that you and all your children are blind . . . and send you all at once into the deep abyss of hell."[50]

Other plays embodied the same anti-Jewish themes. In one, a doctor of the Church declared that the Jews could not be redeemed; they were to be cursed in this world and damned to hell thereafter.[51] A medieval English play, *The Mystery of the Redemption*, associated the Jews, Judas (often portrayed as having red hair, associating him with the devil[52]), and Satan with money and the torture and murder of Jesus.[53] Judas is made to betray Jesus saying, "I shall earn some Jewish gold." The Jews call for Jesus's death. The High Priest Annas orders the Jews, "Take Him, beat him The crowd beats Jesus, spits in His face, and pulls Him about. All this occurs before the Jews take Jesus to Pilate. Pilate tells Jesus that, although he wants to spare Jesus, the Jews want Jesus's blood on a cross. Thereupon, the Jews, not the Romans, are portrayed as soldiers erecting the cross and nailing Jesus to it, mocking, scorning, and offering him gall and vinegar.[54] As a result of the impact of such dramas on the faithful, some city ordinances restricted the Jews—under guard—to their separate seating section during the performances, presumably to protect the Jews from Catholic attack. In Frankfurt am Main in Germany, the presentation of an Antichrist drama in 1469 required city officials to protect the Jewish quarter because the play seemed to confirm the association of Jews and the Antichrist in conspiracy against Christendom. Comparable situations arose in Freiburg, Rome, and in Toulouse.[55]

Serfs of Church and State

The idea of the Jews as slaves (in medieval Latin *servus* meant both slave and serf, although other terms, such as *coloni* and *ascriptii*, were also used for serf[56]) began with Paul, who compared the Jews with slaves and Christians with free men.[57] St. Augustine put it bluntly: "The Jew is the slave of the Christian."[58] Origen, St. Jerome, Chrysostom, and others argued that God was punishing the Jews with perpetual slavery for their murder of Jesus.[59] The Seventeenth Church Council of Toledo in 694 justified the legal status of Jews in Catholic Spain as serfs of the Spanish prince. In the mid-eleventh century, while praising a bishop for protecting Jews, Pope Alexander II observed that Jews "served Christians everywhere."[60] As we shall see, several medieval theologians and popes stated that the Jews were not free people, not citizens, but permanent slaves to Catholics.

Beginning in the eleventh century, the medieval Church began to exploit both canon law and secular law to destroy whatever legal and social privileges the Jews still possessed. By the twelfth century, the status of the Jews in Catholic Europe dropped below that of all Catholics. According to canon 24 of the Third Lateran Council of 1179, "Jews should be slaves to Christians and at the same time treated kindly due of humanitarian considerations."[61] Canon 26 held that "the testimony of Christians against Jews is to be preferred in all causes where they use their own witnesses against Christians. And we decree that those are to be anathematized whosoever prefer Jews to Christians in this regard, for they ought to be under Christians."[62] St. Bernard of Clairvaux observed that "there is no more dishonorable or serious serfdom than that of the Jews. They carry it with them wherever they go, and everywhere they find their masters."[63]

The most influential of medieval theologians, the thirteenth-century Dominican St. Thomas Aquinas, wrote that "the Jews are themselves the subjects of the church and she can dispose of their possessions as do secular princes. . . . The Jews are the slaves [or serfs] of kings and princes."[64] His perspective greatly influenced the mendicant orders, the Inquisition, and the entire Church ever since. Although he felt that the Jews could keep property sufficient to their survival, he wrote to the Duchess of Brabant that "Jews, in consequence of their sins, are or were destined to perpetual slavery," and as a result the princes can treat Jewish property as their own.[65] It might have been this letter that the Vichy regime employed to justify its anti-Jewish laws.[66] Opposed to Jewish usury (lending money at interest), he felt that "the Jews should be forced to work [the land] and should not be allowed to live only by means of usury as they do in Italy, where they spend the whole day doing nothing."[67]

Pope Innocent III regarded Jews as the perpetual slaves, serfs, and outcast "Cains" of Christendom. In 1205 he wrote to the archbishops of Sens and Paris that "the Jews, by their own guilt, are consigned to perpetual servitude because they crucified the Lord. . . . As slaves rejected by God, in whose death they wickedly conspired, they shall by the effect of this very action, recognize themselves as the slaves of those whom Christ's death set free."[68] In 1234, Pope Gregory IX wrote that "the perfidious Jews . . . are by their own guilt condemned to perpetual slavery."[69] This conception of Jews was established in canon law through the *Decretals* (letters containing papal decisions) of Pope Gregory IX in the same year and was used by Holy Roman Emperor Frederick II two years later. As late as 1581, Pope Gregory XIII concluded that the Jews were to be "eternal slaves" since their guilt for murdering Jesus grew deeper with each generation.

The Church sanctioned the Catholic princes' treatment of Jews as property that could be sold, traded, or lent; the only traditional restrictions— which were often violated—were those against mass murder and forced conversion. Although the Jews had a status distinct from slaves, serfs, or any other Catholic,[70] Catholic princes found them economically and practically useful, and reduced the Jews to servile status. Legal documents resound with the language of Jewish servitude: *servi camere, servi regis, servi nostrae, servi camerae regis,* and *servi camerae imperialis* (serfs of the court, serfs of the king, our serfs, serfs of the royal court, and serfs of the imperial court). From the early twelfth century, Catholic princes began to refer to Jews as *Judeus meus* (my Jew) and *Judeus suus* (his Jew).[71] The twelfth-century town charters in Aragón and Castile confirmed that "[t]he Jews are the slaves [serfs] of the crown and belong exclusively to the royal treasury."[72] In 1190, the English king Richard I gave a charter to a leading English Jew, Isaac, son of Joce. But it repeated twice that the Jews should be treated "as our property." King John, his brother and successor, felt that the English Jews were under the monarchy's protection as royal property and should live in peace. "We say this not only for our Jews, . . . for if we gave our peace to a dog it should be inviolably observed."[73] In 1236, the German emperor Frederick II coined the term "household serf" to indicate the Jews' personal, involuntary, and hereditary dependence on the emperor alone.[74] The Holy Roman Emperor Louis IV of Bavaria (1287–1347) put it this way in 1343: "You, the Jews, your bodies— as well as your property—belong to us and to the empire, and we can do to you, treat you, and handle you the way we want and consider proper."[75]

Although the condition of *Catholic* serfs varied enormously,[76] they held an inherent right to exist. They were Catholic souls who were members of the Catholic community and had an established status in the medieval social hierarchy. Catholic serfs could be freed at their Lord's will, but Jews could be liberated only by conversion to Catholicism.[77] Jews were often degraded, usually landless, politically powerless, frequently dishonored, and denied any inherent right to exist in Catholic Europe; they lived there on the sufferance of popes and Catholic princes. On occasion, the Jews were granted privileges, but these privileges depended entirely on the power and the whim of the grantor.[78]

Once the Jews' utility to the princes diminished—often because of ecclesiastical pressure—the Jews' lives and property were often forfeit. Because the Church had a theological and psychological need for Jewish status to be lower than that of any Catholic, Catholic authorities often dealt with Jews in ways they would not treat the lowliest Catholic peasant. In the 1180s, the French king Philip Augustus seized the Jews' property and then expelled them from his domain, without troubling to find legal justification. As Langmuir noted, "the king never could have treated his serfs this way and never did so."[79] No pope would warn *Catholic* peasants that their very right to exist depended on his feelings of kindness; yet in his mandate to the archbishops of Sens and Paris in July 1205, Pope Innocent III noted that only because of "kind[ness] we have tolerated these Jews."[80] The theological doctrine of the "Witness People," enunciated by most medieval theologians, among them, Peter the Chanter, Cassiodorus, Peter Damien, Peter Lombard, and Pseudo-Bede,[81] gave medieval Jews at best a precarious protection. These two principles, Catholic "kindness" and the Witness People doctrine, were the unsteady ideological bases for Jewish existence in Christendom.[82]

Forced Separation

Another cause and consequence of the deteriorating Jewish condition all over Catholic Europe in the High Middle Ages was the isolation of the Jewish community, which would later develop into a ghetto. Since pre-Christian times, the Diaspora Jews had voluntarily segregated themselves from non-Jews. Although Jews were free to live outside their section and non-Jews could live among the Jews, many Jews chose to live together for social, religious, and protective reasons.[83]

The first walled ghetto for Jews might have been located in Speyer, where on September 13, 1084, Rudiger, bishop of Speyer, gave the Jews a charter in which they were to live in an area encircled by a wall "in order that they not be easily disrupted by the insolence of the mob." Rudiger himself called this "the height of kindness." Six years later, the Jewish charter was confirmed and extended by Emperor Henry IV (d.1106).[84] By the end of the twelfth century, a walled ghetto marked most of Catholic Europe's towns.[85]

Although isolated residential areas might have helped the Jews maintain their identity, the increasingly stigmatized nature of these sections, their unhealthful location, overcrowding, and the legal compulsion forcing the Jews to live there made them dreadful places. Most visitors to the ghettos not only noticed the Jews' abysmal physical condition, but also attributed their situation to their absurd and evil religion. A seventeenth-century French traveler described the Jewish ghetto in the papal city of Avignon as "a place filled with infection. . . . It is not possible to see anything as disgusting as this whole place, as repulsive as their apartments, nothing is wretched and as stupid as the people: All these afflictions have justly befallen them for their crimes."[86] In 1783, an exceptionally frank traveler described the still-medieval *carrière* (ghetto) of papal Carpentras:[87]

> The dirtiest and most inextricable [streets in Carpentras] are those in which the Jews are penned up, like some evil and dangerous beast, which has to be locked up at night. . . . It is a disgusting thing to see this unhappy tribe banished from ordinary schools, from agriculture, from employment generally, while they are crushed beneath their taxes, branded by special clothing, and [forced] like vermin, to breed in cesspools.[88]

The papal ghetto for the Jews of Rome in *1836* was described as "untold misery. Tiny fetid rooms [that] lack any air, and light . . . in three miserable rooms seven families."[89]

Although it may have afforded Jews some protection, the ghetto not only kept Jews and Catholics apart but also maintained Jews in their subordinate and degraded status. The Church was especially sensitive to Catholic attitudes toward Jews and recognized that some Catholics, even an occasional Inquisitor, held a limited degree of respect for Judaism.[90] In fact, in 1286 Pope Honorius IV had to warn the archbishops of Canterbury, York, and Evreux that Catholics were worshiping with Jews in the synagogue on the Sabbath and other holidays, daring to show respect for the Jewish holy books, and ignoring the fact that Judaism was a "pernicious and dangerous disease."[91] The ghetto, therefore, was important in separating the faithful: the Church feared that, if exposed to the Jewish way of life, Catholics might be tempted to leave the Church and convert to Judaism. The English historian Travers Herford has observed that "[t]o the Christian the ghetto was a cage where certain dangerous and repulsive animals were confined. To the Jew it was the prison in which he was shut up from the free world outside, where as a man he ought to take his part."[92]

Other Stigmatic Notions

The Church created stigmatic emblems for Jews to keep them apart from Catholics. Canon 68 of the Fourth Lateran Council in 1215 decreed that the Jews had to be set off from Catholics "by the quality of their clothes." Thus secular authorities, pressured by the Church and churchmen, imposed on the

Jews the pariah's hat and badge of shame,[93] as another version of the mark of Cain. The *Judenhut* (Jew hat) was also employed publicly to ridicule Catholic usurers, women convicted of sexual relations with Jews, and Jews who had been sentenced to death.

The Jew badge took various colors—red (for hell) and yellow (for gold) were perhaps the most often used. The badge was usually round (called, in French, the *rouelle*), probably signaling the association of Jews with money, with Judas Iscariot's betrayal of Jesus for thirty silver coins, with usury, and with the desecration of the host. Yellow, orange, red, and white badges appeared in England as tablets of the law; in France, a wheel; in Sicily, the Greek letter tau; in Rome, a circular patch.[94] In 1227 the Synod of Narbonne ruled: "That Jews may be distinguished from others, we decree and emphatically command that in the center of the breast [of their garments] they shall wear an oval badge. . . . We forbid them moreover to work publicly on Sundays and on festivals. And lest they scandalize Christians or be scandalized by Christians, we wish and ordain that during Holy Week they shall not leave their houses at all except in case of urgent necessity, and the prelates shall during that week especially have them guarded from vexation by the Christians."[95] The Jew badge was sometimes tablet-shaped, evocative of the tablets of the law. Other times, as in Portugal in the early fourteenth century, the six-pointed star of David was introduced. Such signs marked out perjurers, witches, whores, and heretics as well. (The witches' ceremonies were called sabbaths.)[96] Jews who were unwilling to wear this mark of Cain faced the penalties of the loss of their clothes and everything they carried, imprisonment, corporal punishment, expulsion, or death.[97] Not until 1798 was the *rouelle* abolished in the papal states, when the French invaded.

The Catholic myth of the Wandering Jew began to circulate throughout Europe as early as the thirteenth century, although it was not widespread until the early seventeenth century. The Wandering Jew myth originated with a man named Ahasverus who had supposedly refused to help Christ on the way to his crucifixion and who was therefore cursed to wander the world until the end of time as an exemplar of his sin. By the Middle Ages, the myth of the suffering wanderer guilty of fratricide (like Cain) had developed into the story of the rootless, Wandering Jew. Ahasverus' continued suffering served as a witness to Jesus's sufferings and death, and as a warning to unbelievers.[98] As with so many other Catholic myths about Jews, the Wandering Jew fantasy affirmed a positive identity for Catholics at the same time as it confirmed the pariahship of the Jews.[99]

Canon and Secular Law

The Church's anti-Jewish theology served as the basis for its *magisterium*, that is, the teachings and structure of the Roman Catholic Church from the ordinary authoritative proclamations of bishop and pope, through the infallible proclamations of the bishops "in unison," bishops and pope, and pope speaking ex cathedra, which in turn was embodied in ecclesiastical legislation, such as papal decree and canon law. Inevitably the Church's law influenced the laws of the land, the secular law codes.

Alfonso X el Sabio (the Wise), King of Castile and León (1252–84) was sometimes hostile to "his" Jews and at other times he was the most tolerant of all medieval Spanish kings.[100] The papacy took note when, for his own practical purposes, Alfonso occasionally allowed Jews in his court to perform economic, administrative, and intellectual functions that gave them authority over Catholics.[101] This violated theological precepts and contravened the Theodosian Code, which closed state service "to those living in the Jewish superstition."[102] On March 23, 1279, Pope Nicholas III ordered Peter Guerra, bishop of Rieti, to investigate a series of complaints against the king, which stated, for example, that he assigned money claimed by the Church to Jews and appointed Jews to public office.[103] The pope's action, combined with the Infante (Prince) Sancho's expropriation of a large sum due to the king from his Jewish tax-farmers, influenced the king to murder or force conversion on several important Jews. Furthermore, in January 1281, following the example of the French king Philip Augustus a century before, Alfonso ordered all Jews in his kingdom arrested (with some tortured) and not releasing them until they paid more than four million gold *maravedis*, a confiscatory sum.[104]

This marked the beginning of the end of the Spanish Jews' glorious history. Henceforth, mistreatment of the Jews would be justified, as Alfonso's law put it, because "they crucified Our Lord Jesus Christ."[105] Further laws within the *Siete Partidas* stated that Jews were permitted to reside in the kingdom so "that they might live forever in captivity and serve as a reminder to mankind that they are descended from those who crucified Our Lord Jesus Christ." Although the synagogues were protected by the laws as a "place where the name of God is praised," the ritual-murder myth was mentioned, and Jews who converted Catholics to Judaism were to suffer the death penalty along with the convert, who was to be treated "just as though he had become a heretic." Jews could not appear in public on Good Friday nor hold public office, because as Christ-killers they had lost their chosen status as "people of God."[106] Almost a century later in 1377, the Spanish Cortes at Burgos revoked the collective fine that had been the traditional penalty for murdering a Jew. As Yitzhak Baer observed, "now the lives of the Jews were at any man's mercy."[107]

The very influential south-German *Schwabenspiegel* (1275) included specific references to canon law and was authored by a Franciscan friar who believed that nothing in secular law should conflict with canon law and the Catholic faith. He helped transpose ecclesiastical legislation into Jewish secular life. Following papal decrees, the *Schwabenspiegel* prevented Catholics and Jews from sharing meals; it prohibited Jews from holding public office and Jewish doctors from treating Catholics; and it forbade Jews from leaving the *Judengasse*, or ghetto, or to open their doors or windows on Good Friday. Other secular law codes influenced by anti-Jewish theology and replicating papal and conciliar restrictions prohibited Catholics from eating matzot; from buying the meat of animals slaughtered by Jews; from bathing with Jews; from accepting medical treatment from Jews; from using, under penalty of excommunication, Jewish servants or nurses; from giving gifts or bequests to Jews, although receiving gifts and bequests from Jews was permitted; from private religious discussions with Jews; from sexual intercourse with Jews; from playing with Jews in the streets. Jews could not appear in public during Holy Week, nor could they appear on the streets when the host passed by. As early as the end of the third century, the Council of Elvira, the first in Spain to legislate on Jews, declared that "if any person, whether clerical or one of the faithful, shall take food with the Jews, he is to abstain from our communion." The canons of the Church Council at Basle, 1431–43, decreed the same kinds of restrictions, adding compulsory sermons. These canons were not rescinded until 1846.[108]

The *Schwabenspiegel* assumed that Jews were essentially perfidious, that is, treacherous and prone to perjury, and required Jews to take a humiliating oath[109] while standing on the bloody skin of a pig, an animal that they considered an abomination and unclean, and which the Catholics related to the devil. "So that the blood and the curse ever remain upon thee which thy kindred wrought upon themselves when they tortured Jesus Christ and spake thus: His blood be upon us and upon our children: it is true."[110]The version of the oath employed in Frankfurt as late as 1847 read similarly that "the Jew shall stand on a sow's skin" with his hand on the Torah. "May a bleeding and a flowing come forth from you and never cease, as your people wished upon themselves when they condemned God, Jesus Christ, among themselves, and tortured Him and said: 'His blood be upon us and our children.'"[111]

Moneylending

In the Graeco-Roman world and in Catholic Europe up to the eleventh century, the Jews were rarely considered usurers (*usurarii*) although the Church had associated them with materialism and carnality since the first century. Some Jews may have been wealthy, but until the eleventh century Jews engaged in business were identified as *mercatores* (merchants). In the Early Middle Ages the same economic regulations often applied to Jews and Catholics without distinction,[112] because Jews were able to make a living by engaging in many of the same occupations as Catholics. In the High Middle Ages, in some places at some times, Jews were able to engage in a variety of occupations. In Angevin England, for example, Jews served as physicians, goldsmiths, soldiers, vintners, fishmongers, cheesemongers, grain and wool merchants, refurbishers of second-hand goods, pawnbrokers, and moneylenders.[113]

But for much of the High Middle Ages in most of Europe, the Jews were marked out by special commercial legislation[114] and severely restricted in their possibilities for making a living. And so they resorted to usury. The Jews were left little choice, for they lived in scattered communities and suffered frequent expropriations, periodic expulsions, and were taxed in their coming and going, in their buying and selling, in their praying and marrying, and in their birthing and dying. They were usually barred from owning land, from hiring non-Jewish workers, and from joining Catholic craft and merchant guilds.[115]

The Jews had the perfect qualifications for moneylending. Their international connections lent their business affairs efficiency, and their pariah status meant that the Church and princes could easily control them. Especially in Germany, but also in many other parts of Europe, usury and trade became the major means for them to make a decent living or to live at all. In Aragón, for example, a royal *privilegium* of March 15, 1298 stated that "given the poverty of the Jews of Lerida no process concerning usury will be instigated against them in the coming five years."[116] Gathered together in their own section of town, later ghetto, partly for their own religious, cultural, and security reasons, whole Jewish communities were probably supported by the moneylending of a few leading families, particularly in the eleventh through the thirteenth centuries. "[A] handful of very powerful patriarchs . . . encouraged for its own purposes by the royal government" dominated medieval Jewish communities.[117] Making the most of necessity, leading Jewish families, through their intelligence, knowledge, and industry, as well as creativity and daring, became desperate economic pioneers. They had fewer inhibitions about the process than Catholics, they were more willing to take risks, and they were accessible to people from each of the three medieval estates.

Medieval Europe's economic expansion inevitably required access to capital and credit.[118] Jewish money was as indispensable for the simple everyday necessities of medieval economic life as it was for the most characteristic medieval achievements—that is, cathedrals, pilgrimages, and wars, especially the Crusades.[119] In Angevin England, nine Cistercian monasteries, two cathedrals, and the Abbey of St. Albans were built thanks to the moneylending activities of several Jews, particularly Aaron of Lincoln (d. 1186).[120]

The Church determined who was a usurer and who was not. The so-called supreme court of medieval Germany at Magdeburg, the *Schöffen*, explicitly acknowledged the competence of ecclesiastical courts to determine the definition of usury. As early as the fourth century, Jerome identified all Jews with Judas and associated both with the immoral use of money. John Chrysostom, distorting Deuteronomy 23:19, claimed that "the [Jewish] creditor heaps up for himself a multitude of sins along with the surplus of his wealth. Hence from the very beginning [God] laid down this law on the Jews with their materialistic mentality, namely, 'You shall not lend money with interest to your brother or your neighbor.'"[121] Chrysostom's deception consisted of adding "to your neighbor" to his citation, implying that the neighbor could be a Catholic, to whom Jews should *not* lend at interest. But the passage, in fact, specifically permits lending at interest to "a foreigner," in this context, to a Catholic. Jewish authorities permitted such loans. Rashi of Troyes, perhaps the greatest medieval rabbinic authority, taught that Jews should not lend to Gentiles at interest unless no other means of earning a livelihood was possible. Two generations later, Rabbi Eliezer ben Nathan also ruled that without any other resources, Jews could lend at interest to non-Jews.[122]

Some Catholics were grateful for Jewish moneylending[123] but most seemed to resent their dependence on the hated Jews for this financial necessity.[124] The medieval Church was never comfortable with any kind of usury, Jewish or Catholic.[125] The canons of the Councils of Elvira, Nicaea, and Clichy in the fourth and seventh centuries opposed any sort of usury.[126] In the fifth century, Pope St. Leo I had stated that "usurius profit from money means the death of the soul" (*Fenus pecuniae, Funus est animae*).[127] The Second and Third Lateran Councils of 1139 and 1179 condemned Catholic usury and denied a consecrated burial to Catholics who lent at interest.

But by condemning Catholic usury the Church indirectly encouraged the Jews. Emperor Frederick II stated that Jewish usury was legitimate, because "the divine law does not prohibit it. They are not under the law established by the most blessed Fathers."[128] Indeed, the Church justified Jewish usury in canon law so long as the interest charged was "not immoderate," a phrase that was left undefined.[129] The papacy "tolerated" Jewish usury because Catholic Europe increasingly required a system of credit and because with Jews lending money, Catholics could keep their hands "clean."[130] By the twelfth century, "Jew" and "usurer" became nearly synonymous all across Catholic Europe.[131]

From the eleventh through the thirteenth centuries, just as the Jewish involvement in moneylending was at its peak, the seeds of its destruction were already sprouting. Churchmen came to realize that money was power, and they found it intolerable that the Jews could have such power over

Catholics. Elements of all three secular orders of medieval society—the upper and lower clergy, the aristocracy, and the commons—were in debt to Jews. The children of the devil could not hold sway over the children of God so long as the Church had the power to prevent it. Leading thinkers also condemned usury in general, although they were probably thinking about Jewish usury in particular. Pope Urban III (d.1187) and Peter Lombard (d.1160) wrote against it, and their views were later absorbed into canon law.

Although many of the same arguments were used against Jews as had been used against Catholic usury, the Jews' Jewishness made their moneylending most obnoxious.[132] Already in the late twelfth century, Rigord, a monk of Saint-Denis, was outraged that the Jews were growing wealthy by taking money from Catholics through lending at interest. His specific charges were that with this wealth Jews could own as much property as Catholics and that they could hire servants who "judaized with the Jews." These charges were all the more telling since they followed Rigord's accusation that "the Jews who dwelt in Paris were wont every year on Easter day . . . to go down secretly into underground vaults and kill a Christian as a sort of sacrifice in contempt of the Christian religion. For a long time they had continued in this wickedness, inspired by the devil."[133] Berthold of Regensburg, Walter von der Vogelweide, Ulrich of Liechtenstein, Foulque de Neuilly, Robert de Courçon, and others singled out the Jew as the arch-usurer.[134] The oldest English caricature of any sort, drawn in 1233, showed several moneylending Jews of Norwich about to be dragged away to hell by devils.[135] Richard de Morins, prior of Dunstable Abbey, in the early thirteenth century envisioned two Jews foretelling the coming of the Antichrist. Richard then resolved to end his house's dependence on Jewish moneylenders.[136]

Catholics were horrified that churches and monasteries offered sacramental objects to Jews as security for loans.[137] One of the earliest to complain that Jews received ecclesiastical articles was Peter the Venerable, who ended his letter of 1146 by advocating that such Jews have their property expropriated and "suffer a fate worse than death." In his letter of 1205 to Philip-Augustus, King of France, Pope Innocent III wrote that "the sons of the crucifiers, against whom to this day the blood resounds in the Father's ears . . . appropriate ecclesiastical goods."[138] In 1205, Innocent III noted that the insolent Jews through their "vicious usury" had gotten possession of even ecclesiastical goods. In 1208, he ordered Philip-Augustus "to induce the Jews subject to you, and to compel them by your royal power, completely to remit all usury to such debtors as are departing for the service of their God." Despite the objections of the French barons, who profited from Jewish usury, the king, greatly under the influence of the Church and its theology, responded with legislation limiting Jewish moneylending.[139]

The Church's decrees against Jewish usury were often couched in the most emotion-laden theological terms, calling the Jews eternal slaves who nailed Jesus to the cross, blasphemers who profane the name of God and who murder Catholics. Even Catholic usurers were condemned as Jews. Ecclesiastical chroniclers William of Chartres, Matthew of Paris, and an anonymous fourteenth-century ecclesiastical chronicler called Catholics more greedy than the Jews.[140] In 1146, Bernard of Clairvaux wrote an encyclical meant to halt violence against Jews in England but complained about "Christian usurers jewing worse than Jews."[141] In using *judaizare* to mean "to jew," Bernard might have been the first to give a new meaning to judaize, which up to this point meant to convert to Judaism.[142]

The popes might have officially tolerated Jewish usury but they continually took or supported measures against it. Pope Eugenius III (1145–53), who had at times been heavily influenced by Bernard of Clairvaux, issued a bull (*Quantum praedecessores*)[143] that formally relieved participants in the Second Crusade from paying interest on loans. In 1198, reflecting the increased Jewish role in moneylending, Innocent III called for a new Crusade and decreed that Crusaders would get back their interest on loans from Jewish usurers. And until the Jews conformed, they would be "excommunicated," or isolated from the faithful.[144] In 1219, Honorius III ordered that "Jews should be compelled . . . to return the usury to Crusaders." In 1228, Gregory IX decreed that crusaders did not have to repay debts to Jews because Jews "extort exorbitant usury from Christians."[145] About 1230, Raymond Peñaforte and other Catholic theologians demanded that all Jewish moneylenders refund their usuries.[146] In 1236, Crusaders, aided by clergymen, coerced the Duke of Nantes to cancel Crusader debts to Jews, forgive them for murdering Jews, and expel those Jews who stayed after the massacre.[147] In 1493, the poet Sebastian Brant wrote in his *Ship of Fools* that Catholic usurers were "Christian Jews" acting like "the Jewish cut-throat."[148] As late as 1592, a bull of Pope Clement VIII stated that Catholics owing money to Jews were not obliged to pay it back once a period of ten years had elapsed.[149]

The Church, increasingly offended by the relationships—especially monetary—between the faithful and the Jews, began to restrict Jewish usury and encourage Catholics to replace Jews as Europe's moneylenders. At the end of the twelfth and the beginning of the thirteenth century, scholastic theologians began to develop justifications for Catholic lending. In fact, according to Jacques Le Goff, the whole idea of purgatory (*purgatorium*) might have been created and elaborated in order to give Catholic usurers a hope that in the hereafter they would have a place to do penance for their sin of usury, thereby escaping hell and ending up in heaven.[150] Even after Catholic usurers outnumbered Jewish moneylenders, the Jews were forced to bear the burden of Catholic guilt about morally unacceptable usury.[151] In the late thirteenth century, Pope Boniface VIII (d.1303) reversed papal condemnations of usury, condoning Catholic usurers in the papal states but ordering Jewish usurers expelled. Soon, popes, ordinary clergy, canon lawyers, theologians, and friars stood universally opposed to Jewish moneylending at interest.[152] Catholic monarchs such as Philip Augustus, Louis IX, Philip III and Philip IV of France, Henry III of England, Alfonso X of Castille, and Albert III of Brandenburg supported the Church's policies.[153] In the fifteenth century, several Observant Franciscans, who emphasized asceticism, roused the populace against Jewish moneylenders. One of these Observants, Bernardino of Siena, added a virulent metaphor to the Church's prior condemnation of Jewish usurers. He accused them of sucking the blood from Catholics and of slitting the throats of the poor and feeding on their substance. Other antisemitic Franciscans were Giovanni di Capistrano, Jacob della Marca, Michele Carcano, Bernardino da Feltre, and Bernardino de Busti.[154]Only the faithful could use the full force of law to collect on their loans; the papacy helped Catholics collect on debts owed to them all over Europe, even using its power of excommunication to this end.

By the end of the Middle Ages, the Church and most princes had essentially abandoned the Jews as no longer economically useful, and they were for the most part driven into the interstices of medieval economic life. A few Jews continued to have the good fortune to be allowed to indulge in moneylending and overseas trade, but most were reduced to pawnbroking, peddling, and selling second-hand jewelry, furniture, and other such articles.[155] The long-term results, until Jewish emancipation, were poverty and stench that were considered "natural and endemic to the Jews."[156]

Even after the Jews lost control of moneylending, they continued to be stigmatized as the greedy betrayers of God. One monastic writer made it clear that "these things that have been said concerning Judas the traitor extend to the entire Jewish people."[157] To the Judas image was added that of Shakespeare's cruel and usurious Shylock. Up to the present day, many Christians have persisted in identifying Jews with the unwanted social change involved in the new money economy.[158]

Secular Princes

Most secular princes supported Jewish usury, for they had great control over the economics of Jewish moneylending. They could arbitrarily tax the Jews or confiscate their property. As a result, much princely wealth depended on the presence of the Jews whom they owned, traded, pawned, or even gave as valuable gifts. But as the Church became more dominant, the feudal powers often submitted to its anti-Jewish demands. The Church exerted pressure in France during the reign of Philip-Augustus (1180–1223),[159] whose policies included repeated extortions of money and seizures of Jewish property, including synagogues, which he donated to the Church as Catholic places of worship; Philip also had some Jews killed.[160] Appropriately, the main portal of Notre Dame de Paris, built during Philip's reign, portrayed *Synagoga* whose eyes were covered by a devilish serpent.

Louis IX (St. Louis, d.1270) was particularly susceptible to the suasion of the Church in Jewish matters. (English kings Henry III and Edward I were likewise pious Catholics and very responsive to the Church's anti-Jewish policy, basing their decrees on canon law, remitting to Parliament the charge of ritual murder, and compelling Jews to listen to Dominican sermons.[161]) Publicly committed to Catholic virtue, Louis was considered by medieval Christendom as the ideal Catholic monarch, concerned with peace, justice, and religious purity. His entourage was filled with Dominicans and Franciscans.[162] Despite adulation, even from modern authors, for his "austere and prayerful private life [and] his determination that every man should have his due,"[163] Louis collaborated with the Inquisition, the popes (seven held office during his reign), and the friars in anti-Jewish policies. Louis mercilessly punished blasphemers and heretics of all sorts, especially the Jews. His campaign against the sanctums of Judaism and the lives and the livelihoods of Jews not only resulted in the destruction of Jewish culture in France during the period but also set a model for the anti-Jewish decrees of the Cortes of Gerona in Spain in 1241.[164] Jewish moneylending was attacked and the Talmud, like the Kabbalah, was tried, condemned as blasphemous, and burned; French Crusaders massacred Jews with impunity in 1236 and 1251. Louis also confiscated Jewish property, including homes, fields, schools, synagogues, and even cemeteries. When he returned from a Crusade in 1254, he cancelled all debts owed to Jews, taking 20 percent for himself, and expelled the Jews—who were readmitted more than once in medieval France.

Despite—perhaps because of—his often cruel and violent attitudes toward Jews, Louis IX, this most "pious" of Catholic kings, was canonized only twenty-seven years after his death, an extraordinarily brief period for a layman. (Louis' royal status and the avid support of his royal grandson, Philip IV [the Fair] helped his cause.) Well aware of the Church's teachings on the Jews—whom one of Louis' biographers, William of Chartres, called "abominable" and "damned"—St. Louis stated that "the Jews . . . infect my land with their poison. . . . Let them give up their usury or all must leave my land, so that they no longer defile it with their filth."[165] At another time,[166] Louis confided to his seneschal and hagiographer, Jean de Joinville, that Catholics must not dispute religion in public with Jews, "that only a very learned scholar and perfect theologian should dispute with Jews, but a layman, as soon as he hears the Christian faith maligned, should defend it not only with words but also by striking the slandering evil-doers with a good sword thrust into the belly as far as the sword will go."[167]

In consultation with bishops and clergy, as well as with his barons, another French monarch, Charles II (d. 1309), King of Naples, Count of Anjou and Maine, also railed against the perfidious Jews as serpents and vipers. His 1289 edict of expulsion stated: "Jews, enemies of the life-giving Cross and of all of Christianity, perfidiously subvert Christians . . . from the way of truth." "Exhibiting zeal for the life-giving Cross" and relinquishing "extensive temporal benefit from the aforesaid Jews," Charles lost the funds he was accustomed to extorting from these Jews.[168]

St. Louis' grandson, Philip IV (d. 1314), issued his most anti-Jewish decree during a period of cordial relations with the Church and when the religious climate in France was extremely hostile to Jews.[169] Pope Clement V had granted him a pardon for having confiscated Jewish possessions just before Philip expelled the Jews from France in 1306.[170] During this period of rapprochement, Philip wrote more like the pope than a king. He instructed his officials to work closely with the Inquisition, and he warned that the Jews

> solicit Christians on behalf of heresy and ensnare many with their wiles and with their promises and bribes, to the extent that they receive from many and presume to handle wretchedly the most holy body of Christ and to blaspheme the other sacraments of our faith, by seducing many simple men and by circumcising those seduced. They receive and conceal fugitive heretics. To the scandal of our faith, they complete new synagogues, singing in a loud voice as though they were officiating in a Church service. They multiply copies of the condemned Talmud, containing innumerable blasphemies about the most glorious Virgin Mary.[171]

Despite expulsions, Jews remained in France, in legal terms as "people without consent," that is, they were considered by the authorities as New Christians, vagabonds, wanderers. Their continued residence was pragmatically accepted because they remained economically useful as used-clothes dealers, junkmen, and pawnbrokers.[172]

Public Debates

The Church also campaigned against medieval Jews by attacking their spiritual life centered in the Talmud. As early as 553, recognizing the rabbinic nature of the Talmud, Emperor Justinian had condemned the Mishnah as hostile to Christianity.[173] Sometimes, a Catholic prince, collaborating with the Church, would force a Jewish scholar to debate either a Catholic or an apostate Jew on the value and validity of the Talmud. The results were foreordained. In the thirteenth century, Nicholas Donin, a Jewish convert to Catholicism (he criticized the Franciscan Order in 1287 and was condemned to death by Pope Nicholas III in the same year) convinced Pope Gregory IX that the Jews ignored the law that God gave to Moses in writing and obeyed another law, much longer than the Scriptures and handed down orally. In 1239, Gregory sent outraged letters to the bishop of Paris to be transmitted to the bishops and kings of France, England, Portugal, Aragón, Navarre, Castile, and Leon that said the so-called Talmud "contained matter so abusive and so unspeakable that it arouses shame in those who mention it and horror in those who hear it." Gregory's ominous conclusions were that this Talmud is the "chief cause" of the Jewish "perfidy" and if these charges against the Jews prove true, then "no punishment would be sufficiently great or sufficiently worthy of their crime."[174] He ordered that on the first Jewish Sabbath of Lent, while the Jews were praying in their synagogues, all Jewish books were to be confiscated by the secular authorities and given over to the Dominican and Franciscan friars.[175]

A Talmudic scholar himself, Nicholas Donin had split from main-line Judaism and had been excommunicated by the rabbis in 1225.[176] Donin may also have accused the Jews of ritual murder and blood-libel.[177] The pious Louis IX had copies of the Talmud seized in March 1240 and ordered a disputation that took place in June in Paris, which was probably conducted with the cooperation of the Inquisition. This institution was allowed to deal with Jews who blasphemed Christianity, hindered the practice of Catholicism (for example, by Judaizing), or heretically challenged the authority of the Scriptures.[178]

During the Paris disputation itself, Donin held all contemporary Jews responsible for pronouncements taken out of context, of uneven authority, and written centuries earlier.[179] He argued that various Talmudic dicta hostile to Gentiles applied without qualification to Catholics and that the Talmud is the source of the Jewish refusal to convert, that Jewish loyalty to it insults the Bible and prophets, and that it contains passages that literally permitted Jews to cheat, plunder, and kill Christians, who were guilty of fornication, adultery, and sodomy.[180] Rabbi Yehiel, head of the Talmudic Academy of Paris, represented the Jews at the Disputation.[181] He did not deny Jewish hostility to idolaters but claimed, correctly, that the Talmud[182] did not refer to Christians and that the Jesus it condemned was not Jesus of Nazareth.[183] Finally, Yehiel pointed out that "[w]e sell cattle to Gentiles, we enter into companionship with them, we stay with them alone, we entrust our infants to them to be suckled in their own homes, and we do teach Torah to the Gentiles." His discussion was climaxed with the statement that whereas the Jewish apostate will be damned, Christians who keep the Seven Laws of Noah will be saved.[184]

Despite Rabbi Yehiel's denials, Donin's arguments reinforced the anti-Talmud movement among Catholic theologians and politicians. Canonists had already justified the Church's interference in Jewish affairs and claimed that Jews were subject to canon law.[185] Louis IX ruled that the Talmud was "full of errors, and that the veil covers the heart of these people to such a degree, that these books turn the Jews . . . to fables and lies."[186] In 1242, perhaps ten thousand copies of the Talmud were burned at the stake before the eyes of grieving Parisian Jews kept at bay by royal soldiers. Jewish communities all over Europe mourned this and later destructions of these holy books.[187] The Talmud played such an essential role in Jewish religion, culture, and spiritual and material life that since the Talmud had been declared blasphemous, no medieval Jew could easily avoid the charge of defamation of Christianity.[188]

Because of the resistance of thirteenth-century Spanish monarchs to fully cooperate with the Church, the results of the Jewish-Christian Disputation called by King James I at Barcelona in the summer of 1263 were less clear than those in France and elsewhere. Instigators of the disputation were the leading Aragónese Dominicans, Raymond de Peñaforte and Raymond Martini. The Barcelona disputation of 1263 was not a genuine debate,[189] for Christianity's certitude and truth was never in question. The purpose of this meeting was, according to the Latin report, "to destroy the Jews' errors and to shake the confidence of many Jews." The Catholics set out to demonstrate to the Jews that Christ was the Messiah who has already come; Christ was both divine and human; he suffered and was killed for mankind's salvation; the Jewish law and religious practices should have ceased with Christ's advent.[190]

The settings were a convent and the king's palace. Formidable Dominicans like Raymond Martini and Raymond Peñaforte (at the time of the debate the king's confessor, before that Pope Gregory IX's chaplain, papal canonist, Domincan General, missionary, and later canonized), as well as the knowledgeable Jewish apostate Pablo (or Paulo) Christiani were present on one side. In his *Dagger of Faith against the Moors and the Jews*—an anti-Jewish diatribe that influenced antisemitic literature up to and through the Third Reich—Martini called the Jews even worse enemies of Christianity than the Moslems. He paired the Jews with the devil as "enemies of the human race" who, following the Talmud, deliberately attacked Christians by killing them and their children. A precursor of Luther in his scatological attack on the Talmud, Martini believed that most of it was "a very great dung heap," full of "absurdities" and false beliefs about the Messiah that the Jews have believed from the time of Jesus.[191]

On the other side, the Jewish representative Rabbi Moses ben Nachman (also called Ramban and Nachmanides) (d. 1270) more than held his own, even under the threat of mob action.[192] In April 1265, Nachman was charged with having reviled Christ and the Catholic Faith in this work, *Vikuah Ramban*, and the king banished him for two years and had his book burned. The Dominicans wanted a more severe sentence.[193] In 1266, Pope Clement IV urged King James I to punish Rabbi Nachman for having published his version of the disputation, as well as reminding King James not to allow Jews to hold public office.[194] In July 1267, Clement IV wrote a second letter condemning the "Jews' damned treachery" and their lack of faith and gratitude; they were a "blind and grievously sinful people," whose sin was too great for forgiveness. In the face of Jesus's mission offering them salvation, these same Jews had tortured and killed him, bringing his blood down on their children. Even though Christian pity permits these wicked Jews to live in Christendom, they repay Catholic "kindness with insult, friendliness with contempt [like] a mouse in the pocket, a serpent about the waist, or a fire in one's bosom."[195] As late as 1553, under Pope Julius III, Cardinal Giovanni Caraffa, head of the Inquisition and the future Pope Paul IV, ordered copies of the Talmud burned in the papal states and all across Italy.[196]

Fair Treatment

Positive social and intellectual contacts had existed from the start between Christians and Jews.[197] Besides Boccaccio, other exceptional Christians wrote realistically or acted positively in regard to the Jews—for example, Gilbert Crispin, King Louis the Pious, and King Wenceslas II. German poet Heinrich der Teichner insisted that all human beings are God's children, including the Jews, and should be protected by the law; and the Flemish poet Jan van Boendale (de Clerk) argued "that they are human beings like us and have also come from Adam."[198] A fifteenth-century hymn noted that "it is our [Christian] great sin and grievous misdeeds that nailed Jesus the true Son of God to the cross. For this reason we must not revile you, Poor Judah, and the host of Jews. The guilt is indeed ours."[199] Many other Catholics also tried to help Jews in their times of trouble. Hugues Aubriot—the prévôt of Paris who built the fortifications surrounding the city and was suspected of leaving his wife for a Jewish woman—had punished anti-Jewish rioters and allowed the Jews of Paris to recover their children who had been forcibly baptized in the riots of 1380. But the bishop compelled him to restore the children to the Church[200] and threw him into a dungeon and forced him to "make amends and ask forgiveness for having practiced the Judaic perfidy."[201] A few other Christians attempted to treat Jews with respect.[202] In 1522, for example, Trieste authorities declared that "all Jews were God's creatures, and so no one should stone their houses or harass them."[203]

Jewish Reactions

Although Jewish authorities wanted neighborly relations with Christians, they opposed a sociability that Christianized Jews,[204] just as Christian authorities feared a judaization of Christians. In general, Jews repaid kindness with kindness, hatred with hatred. When Christians acted well toward Jews, they held these Christians to be "civilized people." When Christians acted cruelly, the Jews regarded them as vicious, bloodthirsty idolaters.[205] Jewish writers used expository treatises, poems, letters, parodies, biblical commentaries, poetry, liturgy, histories, legal works, and philosophical essays in their controversies with Christians.[206] Profiat Duran's *Sefer Kelimat Ha-Goyim* (c. 1400), for example, attacked the accuracy of St. Jerome's translation of Scriptures from Hebrew to Latin and analyzed the inconsistencies between the Christian Scriptures and Christian doctrines of the Virgin Birth, the Trinity, abrogation of the Law, transubstantiation, and papal authority.[207]

Anti-Christian Jewish polemic occurred as a delayed reaction to the Christological exploitation of the Jewish Scriptures. Jewish polemical writings tried to show that Christianity was a false religion and that Judaism was the true one. The Jews attempted to rebut all the crucial points of Christian belief, among them original sin, the Virgin Birth, the resurrection, and the Trinity.[208] Only a few polemics were written before the twelfth century[209] when, in response to the increased Catholic assault, many Jewish books were published wholly dedicated to defending the Jewish position.[210] One of the earliest Jewish polemical books was the *Toledot Jeshu*, containing both positive and negative material initially in the Jewish oral tradition concerning Jesus, and written down between the second and fifth centuries.[211] The title, *Toledot Jeshu*, or *Genealogy of Jesus*, might have been a parody of the opening of the Gospel of St. Matthew, "The book of the genealogy of Jesus Christ, the son of David, the son of Abraham."[212] Some Jewish writers have pointed out that the *Toledot Jeshu* did not claim that Jesus was unhistorical, only that he produced his deeds by means of magic, not divinity.[213] Other Jewish polemicists argued that the Jesus referred to in the *Toledot* was not Jesus of Nazareth but another, Talmudic, Jesus—student of Joshua ben Perahya, who lived a century before Jesus of Nazareth.[214] By ridiculing the most sacred Christian beliefs and supplying an alternative biography of Jesus, the book helped preserve Jewish identity and encourage Jewish resistance to Christian missionizing.

By the fifteenth century, as a result of Catholic expulsions and mass murders of Jews, all of Europe except for a north–south swathe in Eastern Europe and parts of Italy were Jew-free.[215] During the Middle Ages—which for the Jews lasted until their emancipation starting with the French Revolution—Jews could do little to confront Christianity, secure their legal status, or reinforce the fragility of their existence but bribe or beg Catholic authorities to act on their behalf.[216] Although Jews intermittently hovered near the centers of political power,[217] scapegoating, defamation, expropriation, and mass murder of Jews and the exile of all the Jewish communities in Western and much of Central Europe demonstrated the vulnerability of Jews to violent behavior on the part of Catholics in the Crusades,[218] and to the false antisemitic defamations that stirred medieval Catholics to further violence, such as ritual murder and blood-libel, profanation of the Host,[219] conspiring to murder Catholics by poisoning the wells,[220] the attacks sponsored by the mendicant orders,[221] and the Spanish Inquisition.[222]

The Middle Ages established that the most terrible things could be done to Jews, including mass murder, and these actions would be justified by Church doctrine. Economic and political factors undoubtedly contributed to Catholic violence against Jews. But Catholic theological antisemitism, continually repeated by theologians, clergy, and artists, was the fundamental cause and justification of the degradation and killing of Jews. As Richard Rubenstein has noted, "Once the fantasy of murdering Jews has become a fact, it invites repetition."[223] The Church sometimes collaborated in these events but usually stood by in silence, allowing the violence to happen. The most powerful institution within the Church and therefore the one most responsible for its silence was the papacy. Its Jewish policy of degradation and half-hearted protection was clearly and convincingly based on the Church's anti-Jewish theology.

In the end, all the Jews could do was mourn their fate:

> Dead that day was the crown of Israel,
> Dead were the students of the Torah,
> Dead were the outstanding scholars.
> Dead was the glory of the Torah
> Dead were the fearers of sin,
> Dead were the virtuous men;
> Dead were the radiance of wisdom and purity of abstinence;
> Dead was the glory of the priesthood and of the men of perfect faith;

Dead were the repairers of the breach,
Dead were the nullifiers of evil decrees,
Dead were the placaters of the wrath of their Creator;
Dead were many who give charity in secret.
Dead was truth;
Dead were the explicators of the Word and the Law;
Dead were the people of eminence and the sage—
All of them dead on this day on which so many sorrows befell us, and we could turn neither to the right nor to the left from the fury of the oppressor.[224]

CHAPTER 5

Crusades and Defamations

Either the Jews must convert to our belief, or they will be totally exterminated—
they and their children down to the last baby at the breast.

The Chronicler of Mainz, quoting Crusaders

Crusades

During the Crusades, traditional Catholic hostility toward Jews became radicalized, with the Jews coming more and more to represent an alien enemy residing in the heart of Christendom.[1] A despised minority of Christendom's "greatest sinners," scattered and unarmed, barely protected by the era's most powerful authorities, the Jews easily fell prey to Catholic Crusaders. The Jewish communities hardest hit by Crusader attacks—Worms, Mainz, and Cologne—were the greatest western European centers of Jewish intellectual and cultural vitality.[2] Some Crusaders put it bluntly, "either the Jews must convert to our belief, or they will be totally exterminated—they and their children down to the last baby at the breast."[3] But if the Crusaders had wanted simply to convert Jews, surely Jewish children would have been saved and raised as Catholics. This was seldom done.[4] The Jews' reputation as stubborn, stiffnecked reprobates led many Crusaders to believe that the Jews could easily ward off the oceans of baptismal water required for a real conversion. With authentic conversion a lost cause, all the Jewish enemies of Christ might as well be killed. Crusader assaults were territorially widespread,[5] religiously motivated,[6] savage, murderous, and characterized by communal Jewish martyrdom and an ambivalent attitude on the part of secular and religious authorities.[7]

Neither Pope Urban II nor any pope acted to stop anti-Jewish pogroms during the First Crusade.[8] By their silence, these First Crusade popes seemed to signal that they saw the end of Jewishness—by murder and conversion—as a good thing. Many Crusaders asked why not attack the Jews, Christ's greatest enemies living among Catholics, *before* setting out to fight the Turks in the Holy Land,[9] especially after Urban II granted the Crusaders absolution from penance even before they sinned.[10] The soldiers of Christ could now take up the cross and find immediate salvation no matter what they did to the Jews of Europe and the Near East.[11] The Jews were geographically closer and politically and militarily weaker than the Moslems. Besides, the Jews were guilty of a much more grievous injury to Christ than the Moslems, namely, his crucifixion.[12]

Admittedly, greed, envy, and need were also motives for Crusade attacks on the Jews.[13] But had the Crusaders' behavior been based on economic factors alone, instead of slaughtering thousands of Jews they would have only taken their goods or extorted money from them.[14] Crusaders burned synagogues (often with Jews in them)[15] and destroyed Jewish cemeteries.[16] Religious hostility was also obvious when, at Jerusalem in 1099, soldiers of the First Crusade slaughtered Jewish men, women, and children as other Crusaders had done in Europe. Before departing on Crusade, Crusade commander Godfrey of Bouillon swore to avenge "the blood of the Crucified with the blood of Israel and that he would not leave 'a remnant or residue.'"[17] Burning some of the Jews alive in Jerusalem's great synagogue, the Crusaders marched around it singing, "Christ, we adore Thee." They then proceeded to the Church of the Holy Sepulchre, singing in joy and exaltation of their victory as the confirmation of Christianity.[18]

Although on occasion upper clergy, sometimes responding to Jewish bribes, tried to protect the Jews,[19] neither they nor the Jews could match the combined forces of the townspeople and Crusaders.[20] These attacks on Jews would recur during the Second and Third Crusades. The first half of the thirteenth century was the "golden age of crusading," with Crusades occurring nearly every decade. In this century, the papacy often reacted to any threat to the Church by directing a Crusade against it.[21] Jews were often caught in the crossfire. In 1203, Crusaders burned down Constantinople's Jewish quarter.[22] Two hundred French Jews were murdered during the Albigensian Crusade of the early thirteenth century.[23] During the Sixth Crusade and after, several thousand Jews were murdered before the Crusaders left Europe.[24] Where and when Crusades were preached, Jews were killed: 1236 in France, England, and Spain; 1309 in Germany, the Low Countries, and Brabant.[25]

In the fourteenth century Catholics assaulted Jews during crisis situations, although Jews sometimes found temporary safety and comfort among their Catholic neighbors. In 1315, famine-riots in France became the Shepherds' Crusade in 1320. The "Crusading" shepherds attacked communities of Jews in the English territories of southwest France. The shepherds found many sympathizers among Catholic townspeople.[26] Although there may have been economic motives for such collaboration, the primary cause was religious.[27] One hundred and twenty Jewish communites in France and Spain were destroyed.[28] In 1321, false rumors were put forth that Jewish lepers were poisoning wells in order to kill all Christians. The Jews of France and Spain were believed to be part of the conspiracy and perhaps an additional five thousand were consequently burned in the south of France.[29]

Ritual Murder and Blood-libel

Catholic fantasies about Jews as devilish Antichrists capable of any atrocity existed from the time of the early Church and was propagated in Antichrist plays.[30] By the High Middle Ages, Jews were considered "the incarnation of disbelief in [Christendom's] midst."[31] It was widely believed during the Middle Ages that any Catholic blood was, in essence, Christ's blood[32] possessing sacred magic properties and sought out by the Jews. Jews were accused of ritually slaughtering a Catholic child, usually at Passover or Purim.[33] (This Christian myth might represent a reversal of the Christian habit of kidnapping and forcibly baptizing Jewish children.[34]) The triumph of Christianity and the vindication of Jesus's sacrifice were confirmed by the "exposure" of the Jews' alleged ritual murder and by their punishment.[35] (The Nazis also used the ritual-murder and blood-libel myths in their propaganda campaign against the Jews.[36]) By 1155, a Benedictine monk[37] made the first ritual-murder accusation about William of Norwich,[38] the scene of widespread massacres of Jews later in the century.[39] In 1255, the pious English king, Henry III, was the first official to order the execution of Jews for ritual murder.[40] The first ritual murder defamation on the continent occurred in Pontoise in 1163 but was soon followed by a more notorious case at Blois, France, in 1171.[41] Although political intrigue was involved, priests incited Count Theobald of Blois to burn thirty-two Jews, seventeen of them women, on unsubstantiated charges that they murdered a Catholic child, whose body could *not* be found.[42]

Despite the Jewish prohibitions against shedding innocent blood,[43] the consumption of any blood being seen as an abomination,[44] the blood-libel most often charged that the Jews used the blood of a ritually murdered Catholic child as an ingredient in matzot, the unleavened Passover breads. The Jews allegedly crucified a child, who bled Christ's blood. It was sometimes alleged that the Jews used the blood thus obtained to cure hemorrhages or hemorrhoids,[45] which was an affliction the Jews brought onto themselves as punishment for their refusal to save Jesus from Pilate. In addition, Christian blood was supposedly consumed to help the Jews rid themselves of their *foetor judaicus*, the Jewish stink,[46] or the Jews drank it during wedding ceremonies to help Jewish women quickly gain fertility during their marriage years.[47] Jews were also accused of using Christian blood in Host desecrations, where the consecrated Host allegedly bled under Jewish torture. And they were charged with utilizing both menstrual blood and the Host as part of their concoction to poison wells, thereby causing the Black Plague—a charge occurring as early as the First Crusade.

The self-proclaimed "scourge of the Jews," the Franciscan Bernadino da Feltre, wanted the Jews expelled from Catholic society. In the mid-1470s in Italy he predicted that Easter would not pass without Catholics fully understanding Jewish evil. Not surprisingly a two-year-old boy named Simonino (Simon of Trent) disappeared on Holy Thursday in 1475. The boy's death led to a ritual-murder accusation against the local Jews and some visiting German Jews. This defamation led to the torture, death, and expulsion of the Jews of Trent.[48] Da Feltre's agitation seemed to spread beyond Italy's borders, where ritual-murder trials took place within a few years at Regensburg, Ratisbon, Endingen, Ravensburg, and in Spain, where the Inquisition fabricated the never-named "Holy child of La Guardia," possibly as a pretext for the 1492 expulsion of Spanish Jews.[49] These false accusations and antisemitic ideas persisted when few Jews were present.[50] As late as the 1912 edition of the *Catholic Encyclopedia*, Dom Raymund Webster wrote that even though in the case of William of Norwich evidence against Jewish involvement "is totally insufficient. It seems, however, quite possible that in some cases at least the deaths of these [ritual murder] victims were due to rough usage or even deliberate murder on the part of Jews and that some may actually have been slain in *odium fidei*."[51] In other words, in the opinion of the standard Catholic reference book, the Jews did ritually murder Christian children on occasion because they hated Christianity.

Defilement of the Sacred Host

As early as the fourth century, St. John Chrysostom had associated the Jews' "inherent evil," their crucifixion of Jesus, and the sacrament of communion.

> I say to you that it is indeed [Christ] that you see [in the Host]; it is he that you touch; it is he that you eat. . . . If you can regard without outrage the traitor Judas who sold his master and the incredibly ungrateful Jews who crucified their king, take care that you do not also render yourself guilty of profaning [Christ's] body and his blood. These miserable people caused the death of the most sacred body of the Lord, and you, you receive it with a soul totally polluted and soiled after having received so many blessings. For he not only made

himself a man but also exposed himself to the insults and outrages of the Jews and to death upon the cross. But beyond this, he also wanted to join himself and unite himself with us in such a way that we should become one and the same body with him. . . . Jesus Christ . . . nourishes us with his own blood, and in every way incorporates us within him . . . through the mystery of the Eucharist.[52]

As long as the "miracle" of the Mass, that is, transubstantiation, comprised a crucial element of Catholic faith, then the "evil" of the Jews could not be forgotten.[53] Jews who were accused of desecrating the Host were seen as recrucifying Christ. As early as the second half of the eleventh century, perhaps during the time of the First Crusade, rumors of Jewish Host profanation led to the slaughter of Jews across France. This may have been the first instance in which all Jews were blamed for the actions of a few.[54] The anti-Jewish Dominican, Giordano da Rivalto (1260–1311), wrote that the Jews continued to murder Christ by stealing the Host and, in a repetition of the crucifixion, attacking it as if it were Christ's body.[55]

The worst massacre of Jews charged with profanation of the Host occurred at Rottingen, where Jews were accused of pounding a wafer until blood flowed. The killing spread over much of central Germany and Austria between 1298 and 1303, when the vengeful followers of the German nobleman Rindfleisch traveled beyond the local area in a "divinely ordained" attempt to murder all the Jews. Some local burghers and bishops vainly tried to protect their Jewish neighbors, as did the Holy Roman Emperor Albert of Austria (d. 1308). Again, all the Jews were held responsible for the mythical actions of a few local Jews.[56] Perhaps one hundred thousand Jews, including converts to Catholicism, in 146 German communities were massacred during this period.[57] Covering the general area of the First Crusade massacres, additional murders took place in 1336–37 when bands of *Judenschächter* (Jew slaughterers) were stirred to bloody action by alleged Host profanations and anti-Jewish propaganda.[58] In Germany, of the forty-seven examples of bleeding Host stories between 1220 and 1514, twenty-two were followed by massacres of Jews.[59] The Church did little or nothing to stop these massacres. Instead, by allowing priests to preach against the Jews, the Church actually encouraged the murders.

Modern scholarship rejects any factual basis for these accusations of Jewish Host desecration. Yet the charges were so widespread[60] and the accusers were so convinced of the truth of this myth that the eminent German scholar and priest Peter Browe, after concluding that the Jews were not guilty of such charges, still questioned whether "it is impossible that all these accusations were simply based on hatred,"[61] which was an argument employed in 1929 by Julius Streicher, publisher of the popular National-Socialist *Der Stürmer*.[62] This defamation tied into the preexisting belief in the fearsome Jew as an international conspirator.

Black Death

Catholics believed that Jews all across Europe, along with the devil, were involved in a kind of international conspiracy against Christendom. As early as 408 in the Christianized laws of the Roman Empire, Jews themselves had been referred to as a plague.[63] The Twelfth Council of Toledo in 681 associated the Jews with the plague and attempted to eradicate Judaism by decreeing that Jewish parents who circumcised their children were to have their property confiscated and their noses cut off. During the First Crusade, Jews were accused of poisoning wells and were made to pay for this rumor with their lives.[64] In 1246, the Council of the Province of Beziers claimed that Jews practiced black magic and that Jewish physicians and Jews in general were always out to murder all Catholics.[65]

In the mid-fourteenth-century, when one-third to one-half of Europe's population died of the Black Plague, massacres of Jews became chronic. Although other groups were at first blamed, Jews were inexorably focused on as the malicious initiators of plague.[66] They were condemned by their Catholic neighbors and by the so-called flagellants as being in league with the devil to destroy Christendom through the plague. Flagellants believed that Christian sin caused the plague and other calamities; as a result, they whipped themselves to pay God the penance that they imagined God required in order to lift the punishment. But such activity often degenerated into lawlessness that resulted in the slaughter of Jews. The Jews were victimized by "a plague within a plague."[67] During this period, tens of thousands of Jews in more than 350 European communities were tortured and murdered as conspirators in the destruction of Christendom.[68]

Massacres, expropriations, and expulsions of Jews occurred in Spain, France, Switzerland, the Germanies, Austria, Poland, Belgium, and Hungary.[69] Most often, Catholics accused the Jews of poisoning the wells. Although lepers, Moslems, pilgrims, and others were also blamed for the plague, they were regarded as mere instruments of the malicious Jews. At Chillon in September 1348, Jews were put on trial for spreading plague by poisoning wells with a powder ground up from portions of basilisk,[70] the most frightful of imaginary medieval animals.[71]

As during the Crusades, it was the Jews' misfortune to be available victims: they were already well-established as public enemies of Christendom;

they were spread across Christendom, weak, divided, and without legal or significant customary rights; they had no military or political power of their own. The Church and its anti-Jewish theology were primarily responsible for putting the Jews in this vulnerable position, keeping them there, and providing justification for the Catholic assaults.

CHAPTER 6

Papal Policy

The Jewish religion is a plague and deadly diseased weed and must be pulled out by its roots.

Pope John XXII

Degradation and Protection

Papal policy was, most often, Church policy. The popes enunciated the will of God—the ultimate sanction for worldly authority. Mendicant orders, Inquisitors, bishops, and Church councils consistently followed papal initiatives. Medieval popes believed that they had inherited Rome's imperial right to rule the Churches of the former empire, the lands of the Western Roman Empire, and the Jews who inhabited this territory. Papal Jewish policy was embodied in the popes' decrees, pronouncements, encyclicals, bulls, letters, and canon law, and also came to penetrate medieval secular law. St. Augustine's theological construct, the "Witness People,"[1] the fading influence of Roman law, and the arbitrary exercise of "Christian mercy and pity"[2] served as the three bases of papal Jewish policy.

The papacy often operated during times of medieval crisis, such as, famine, war, plague, and schism. Later, during the Protestant Reformation of the sixteenth century, the papacy moved in a defensive, militant, and paranoid manner. The popes nevertheless provided Jews some protection—often as a reaction to Jewish pleas for help. Yet at the same time the popes refined, encouraged, and sometimes imposed a contradictory policy of Jewish degradation. The papacy implicitly and explicitly held that Jews were Christendom's public enemies, capable of any crime, a frightful mixture of Cain and Judas, stateless beings who were slaves to the Church and to the Catholic princes, and sinners who must be punished in this world and the next.

Early Popes

The first evidence of a papal position on Jews comes from Pope Damasus I (d. 384). He shared the hostile attitude of his friend St. Jerome. Damasus stated that "[w]hat is found in the Father and Son is good, but what is not resident in the holy spirit is heretical, because all heretics from the Son of God and evil opinions from the holy spirit may be found in the perfidious disbelief of the Jews and Gentiles."[3]

St. Leo I (440–61) dissuaded Attila the Hun (d. 453) from attacking Rome in 452.[4] In his sermons, Leo argued that the blind, carnal Jew could never appreciate the transformation of the darkly veiled Christological meanings of the Old Testament into the revelatory light of the New. Through the sacrifice of Christ, a new and authentic people of God replacing the Jews has been created, with the cross as their symbol. Even though he believed that God intended that Jesus be crucified, he nevertheless held that the Jews should still be considered malicious murderers of Christ.[5] "On you, on you, false Jews and princes of a sacrilegious people, weighs the burden of this crime [of deicide. It] makes you the more deserving of the hatred of the whole human race."[6] Serving as the basis for Carolingian art some three centuries later, Leo's Sermon 53 stated that "Heaven and Earth have thus passed their judgment of damnation on you, you Jews. . . . And since you cried, 'Let his blood come over us and our children' you have received your just reward."[7]

The reforming pope St. Gregory I (590–604) has been called the founder of the medieval papacy and acclaimed as a doctor of the Church. Like Leo, he sought to make Europe a Catholic society, to convince Catholics that the Church expressed Christ's will, and to establish the papacy's supremacy within the Church.[8] St. Gregory was the first pope to establish a policy for protecting the Jews; his policy was limited, ambiguous, and heavily laden with strong anti-Jewish attitudes, yet it set a pattern that would dominate the Church for the next fifteen hundred years.

St. Gregory's letters were written in the context of widespread persecutions of Jews in Spain, France, and Italy instigated mainly by the clergy and Catholic rulers.[9] His Jewish policy, later incorporated into canon law,[10] was based on St. Augustine's theological dictum of the Witness People and on the Theodosian and Justinian Codes, which gave Jews limited legal protection and considered Judaism a legal but dangerous religion.[11] In June 591, he wrote to the bishops of Arles and Marseilles that, unlike pagans, Jews were not to be forcibly baptized but instead persuaded to convert.[12] After all, coercion would lead the Jew "back to his former superstition."[13] In his letter, *Sicut Iudaeis*, of June 598 to the Bishop of Palermo—a bull repeated by twenty-three popes in the twelfth through the fifteenth centuries—Gregory argued that Jews should not be killed, and although they did not have license to do everything they wanted, they were nevertheless permitted what the Church had already conceded to them.[14] Jews could follow their religious practices but must never be allowed to tempt Catholics away from the true faith toward perfidious Judaism; they must never have authority over Catholics, never in any way try to demonstrate any superiority of Judaism over Christianity, and never blaspheme Christianity. These ideas, already established in Christianized Roman law, would be repeated in several Church councils, including the Third Church Council of Toledo in 589 and the Fourth Lateran Council of 1215.

Many of Gregory's writings, private and public, were dominated by images stigmatizing Judaism and the Jewish people. His letters described Judaism as "superstition," "vomit," "perdition," and "treachery," and the Jews as "enemies of Christ."[15] His essays and homilies described Jews as criminal, cursed, and satanically perverse, as "wild asses," "dragons of poisonous ideas," "their hearts the den of a beast," "wicked," "people of Satan," "of the Antichrist," and "of the Devil." They were faithless and cruel deicides who "had delivered up the Lord and had accused him. [For] they were afraid of losing their country; it was for that reason that they have killed the Savior; yet even though they murdered Christ, they lost their country all the same." He also wrote that "Because the hearts of the Jews are without faith, they are offered to the Devil. . . . The more the Holy Spirit fills the world, the more perverse hatred dominates the souls of the Jews."[16] Gregory believed that Judaism, proud and sterile, had lost its *raison d'être* when Christ arrived. He claimed that Judaism was not an authentic "religion" at all; it was a "stone of darkness," a "shadow of death," a "disaster" that would "pollute [Catholics and] deceive them with sacrilegious seduction."[17]

Aligning himself with those Fathers who labeled all heresy as Jewish, Gregory failed to distinguish between the psychological support Jewish opposition to Christianity might unintentionally have given Christian heretics and the heterodox theological ideas of heretical Christians. He wrote to the citizens of Rome in 602 that Judaizing was the work of the Antichrist who sought to ingratiate himself with the Jews; such Judaizing included some Catholic preachers' advocacy that there should be no work on the Jewish Sabbath.[18] In writing to the Byzantine Emperor Maurice, Gregory accused the heretic, Nestorius (d. 451)—who held that the incarnate Christ was two persons, one divine, one human; whereas the Orthodox position held that Christ was two persons in one—of being a Jew, of believing in "Jewish perfidy."[19] Again, in 599, referring to the "perfidiousness of the Jews," Gregory supported the laws of the Visigothic king in Spain,

Reccared, which threatened destitution and exile for those Jews who refused to convert to Catholicism.[20]

Pope Stephen III (768–72) took a similar position. He complained to the archbishop of Narbonne and the kings of Spain and Septimania that the deicidal Jews of the Frankish Kingdom must not prosper. "The Jewish people, ever rebellious against God and derogatory of our rites . . . own hereditary estates . . . as if they were Christian residents; for they are the Lord's enemies . . . liars . . . miserable dogs. [They must have no such benefit] in vengeance for the crucified Savior." Stephen based his letter to the archbishop on Paul's letter to the Corinthians: "What has the [Catholic] society of light to do with the [Jewish] society of darkness, the consensus of the Temple of God with that of idols?"[21] He ended his letter by arguing that if Jews are not punished for their crucifixion of Jesus but are instead allowed to insult Christianity, then the faithful would question the foundations of Catholic theology, that is, they might doubt that the Jews have been rejected and replaced by the new, true, Christian Israel.[22]

The pronouncements of Popes Hadrian I (772–95) and Nicholas I (858–67) also expressed theological antisemitism but without St. Gregory's denigrating descriptions. These popes held that Catholics were not to associate with Jews, nor should Catholics observe Saturday as the Sabbath. In a letter to Charlemagne, Hadrian used passages from patristic literature in comparing the Jews to heretics.[23]

Following St. Gregory and Stephen, Pope Leo VII wrote to Archbishop Frederick of Mainz in 937 that Jews should not be converted by force. But in the same letter he ordered that if preaching did not convert these Jewish "enemies of God," they should be expelled, for Catholics must not allow "God's enemies" to live among them. Using the same imagery as Paul, he asked "Why should light be joined to darkness [and] the holy be given to dogs and pigs?"[24]

The Height of Papal Authority

By the twelfth century, using ecclesiastical powers such as excommunication and interdict popes dominated the minds and behavior of Europeans who held nearly unchallenged ideological control of society and were coming as close to totalitarianism as any institution before the twentieth century.[25] During the pontificates of Innocent III (1198–1216) and Boniface VIII (1294–1303) the papacy reached the apex of its claims to authority in the secular world as well as within the Church. Innocent believed in a divine right of popes: "beyond man, less than God, but greater than man, he is judge of all, and by no one is he judged [except by God]."[26] The pope was a God-man, taking the place of the risen Christ as the only link to God. Though he was humiliated by Philip IV, Pope Boniface VIII's canonists saw him as *coelestis imperator*—the emperor sent from Heaven who "can do whatever God can do."[27] Other terms of adulation were *vicarius Christi*, the Vicar of Christ who dwells on the supernatural level of being, above and beyond the human; *adominus absolutus*, absolute heir of all of Christ's possessions; *dominus Deus noster papa*, the Lord God himself in human form; *persona Ecclesiae*, the mystical head of the Church that rules over all of Christendom.[28]

The medieval papacy went to great lengths to guarantee that its whole program of institutional and legal reform was carried out. Its treatment of Jews was typical. The papacy developed the ideological construct of "Christendom," which identified the Church and all Christian society with a mystical body of Christ that excluded Jews from recognized rights in this world and from salvation in the next. The first canon of the Fourth Lateran Council, called by Pope Innocent III in 1215, stated: "There is one universal Church of the faithful, outside of which absolutely no one is saved, and in which Jesus Christ is himself at once both priest and sacrifice." Pope Boniface VIII's bull *Unam sanctam* of 1302 reiterated this principle.

Influence on Secular Rulers

Gratian and Huguccio, early canonists, had asserted temporal authority for bishops as part of the Church's God-given powers.[29] This authority did not include the exercise of the power of armed coercion or murder-execution— "the sword of blood." This power was delegated to the political authorities.[30] Boniface VIII's bull reasserted the papacy's position on the Church's authority over the state, drawing on Matthew 16:19 and Luke 22:35–38. Matthew reports Jesus as saying, "I will give unto thee the keys of the kingdom of heaven; and whatsoever thou shalt bind on earth shall be bound in heaven; and whatsoever thou shalt loose on earth shall be loosed in heaven."[31] At the Last Supper, Luke has Jesus mention the necessity for having two swords. Boniface held that the Church held the spiritual sword, whereas Church and state contested for the secular sword. He argued the hierocratic view that all power descended from God through His vicar on earth, the pope.[32] In 1442, the Church Council of Florence explicitly articulated the meaning of the Church's claim to power in regard to the Jews: "no one remaining outside the Catholic Church, not only pagans, but Jews, heretics, or schismatics, can become partakers of eternal life; but they will go to the 'eternal fire prepared for the devil and his angels' (Mt 25:41)."[33]

At the height of power and influence, a thirteenth-century pope was rightly called *motor Caesaris*, the true "king of kings and lord of lords," the maker and breaker who could appoint or depose any earthly authority, even the emperor. Though some rulers were less amenable to papal suasion than others, Church policy conditioned their decisions. When popes required secular authorities to stigmatize Jews and make them suffer for the sake of their Jewishness, the princes usually obeyed.[34] After all, medieval rulers were Catholic princes, most of whom were taught from childhood to dislike or despise the Jews.[35] Although no ruling secular prince was ever excommunicated because he offended the papacy by favoring the Jews,[36] the threat of such sanction was often enough to achieve the popes' goals of degraded preservation of the Jews.

The papacy ensured that any secular ruler who allowed a member of the deicide people authority over a Catholic did so at his own peril. The first letter of Pope St. Gregory VII (1073–85) on the Jews condemned King Alphonso VI of Castile and Leon, who had Jews in his court. "You must not permit Jews in your land to dominate Christians. . . . For what is it to set Christians beneath Jews . . . except to oppress the Church of God and to exalt the Synagogue of Satan; you must realize that your desire to please the enemies of Christ is to condemn Christ himself?"[37]

Innocent III was the most articulate pope in asserting his influence over Catholic princes when they allowed Jews some authority. In 1205, he threatened to excommunicate Alphonso VIII of Castile and Blanche of Champagne for favoring Jews.[38] In 1208, Innocent ordered an interdict (the prohibition from the faithful of all spiritual connections with the Church except for communion) on the lands of the Count of Nevers in part because he granted Jews commercial privileges and helped them collect their legitimate debts. The pope replied to the count's appeal as follows:

> Just as the Lord made Cain a wanderer and criminal fugitive over the earth yet marked him with a sign . . . to prevent anyone finding him from slaying him, so the Jews, against whom the blood of Christ cries out, must be kept alive to wander the earth until in shame they seek the name of Jesus Christ. These blasphemers of Christians must not be helped by Christian princes to oppress servants of the Lord. Instead they should be forced into slavery, which they deserve for having raised their sacrilegious hands . . . and called down His blood on themselves and their children. Would you yourself not be angry against a subject of yours if he proved to be of help to your enemy? How much more, therefore, should you fear God's anger because you show favor to those who dared nail to the Cross the only-begotten Son of God, and who still blaspheme against him![39]

Excommunication of Jews

The papacy had religious authority all across Europe. It also ruled areas where no effective secular authority existed, both within the papal states and elsewhere. This put many Jews under the papacy's direct jurisdiction. In 1 Corinthians 5:12–13, Paul mentioned wicked people outside the law. Medieval canonists applied the phrase to excommuncates, schismatics, new converts, and especially pagans and Jews (infidels).[40]

Huguccio (d. 1212) and Hostiensis (d. 1271) were the first canon lawyers to argue that the Church could not logically deprive Jews of a Catholic sacrament, Hostiensis observing that "Jews cannot be excommunicated. . . . Since they are not of the communion of the Church, they cannot be put outside of its communion." Huguccio explained that the Church could coerce Jews "when[, in the Church's opinion,] they sinned or did wrong." At that point, the Church could fine, mutilate, beat, or hang Jews "by order of a bishop or prince."[41] In 1193, Pope Celestine III called the Jews "wickedly depraved and hard-hearted," "damned and greedy" and ordered those who refused to pay tithes to be cut off from all communication with Catholics.[42] The Fourth Lateran Council (1215) held that if a Jew practiced "immoderate usury" against a Catholic, then "all relations with Catholics shall be denied him."[43] Shortly thereafter, the eminent jurist Raymond de Peñaforte's canonical opinion was that the Church "can inflict temporal penalties . . . and even spiritual penalties indirectly, by removing Catholics from communion with [Jews]."[44]

Popes, at least through the fifteenth century, did, in fact, excommunicate Jews. To force Jews to obey them, the popes isolated individual Jews or Jewish communities from the surrounding Christian community, in a sense "excommunicating" the Jews by threatening to excommunicate any Catholic who had dealings with them. Since Jewish households depended on Catholics for their food and services, this would be a fearsome decree.[45] A contemporary decree of excommunication from the south of France forbade Jews to have any of the following relationships with Catholics: they could not share "fellowship and drinking, standing together and speaking, coming or going, buying or selling, eating in any location, affection or intercourse." The Church also excluded excommunicated Jews from bringing any legal cases.[46] In other words, excommunicated Jews were to be totally separated from "the communion of the faithful in Christ."

This excommunication boycott was called a "judgment of the Jews" (*judicium Judaeorum*), and every pope of the thirteenth century issued such decrees, sometimes even against Catholics. For instance, Cluniac monks who claimed exemption from papal authority were nevertheless subject to the *judicium Judaeorum.*[47] In 1212, after a Jew offended a priest, Innocent III ordered the Bishop of Langres to isolate the Jew "by forbidding all Christians to have any dealings with him and to enforce this by the threat of excommunication against Christians who might not comply." In a declaration to Christians of Cologne and to all the European faithful in April 1213, Innocent III arrogated to himself the power to excommunicate Jews. He wrote, "The Jews shall, through sentence of excommunication, be cut off from all trading as well as other relationship with all faithful Christians." Innocent III and the Fourth Lateran Council confirmed that Jews who refused to pay Church tithes or who charged excessive interest were to be excommunicated, that is, "denied all communication with the Christian faithful."[48]

When Pope Innocent IV (1243–54) ordered the Bishop of Constance to force the Jews to wear the Jew badge, he wrote: "You shall compel them to do so by shutting them off from communication with the faithful."[49] In the same century, zealous bishops in the English towns of Hereford, Worcester, Lincoln, Winchester, Oxford, and Norwich threatened to excommunicate Jews or actually excommunicated them.[50] The Ecumenical Council at Basle (1431–43) affirmed that there could be no fellowship between Catholics and Jews, Catholics could not serve Jews nor hire them as physicians, Jews were to be excluded from holding offices, Jews were confined to ghettos,[51] and Jews had to wear stigmatic emblems. It added new canons preventing Jews from obtaining university degrees and forcing them to attend conversionary sermons. Later in the century, the Spanish Inquisition under Ferdinand and Isabella and Pope Innocent VIII compelled rabbis to cooperate with the Inquisition or suffer excommunication.[52]

Papal Protection

Although popes sometimes wrote letters protecting specific Jews in response to appeals by Jews themselves or temporal princes, in the High Middle Ages, the papacy retreated from the general protection that St. Gregory's policy offered the Jews. (Several cities and princes awarded the Jews civil charters that protected them. But in times of crisis, these charters became almost worthless.) Papal letters failed to protect Jews largely because, reflecting the Church's ambivalence toward Jews, they never guaranteed Jews any fundamental social, legal, or political rights. However tenuous, the Jews' *right* to exist as Jews under Roman Law became a *privilege* under the medieval and modern papacy. The papal policy of protection asserted only that Jews should not be murdered; popes could withdraw any concessions the Church allowed the Jews at any time and for any reason.

Pope Calixtus II reissued St. Gregory's bull of protection, *Sicut Judaeis*, between 1119 and 1124. In 1234, the bull was incorporated into Gregory IX's official Code of Canon Law, the *Decretales*, and its principles therefore became perpetually binding on all Catholics.[53] (The letter itself is no longer extant, but its wording can be determined from later papal documents.) Gregory's letter was vacillating and specious from its inception. Addressed "To all the Christian Faithful," the bull urged them to recognize the limited right of the Jews to live among them as observant Jews in peace according to custom and tradition. Although the Jews stubbornly insisted on their distasteful beliefs, he wrote, out of Catholic kindness and in response to the pleading of the Jews they should be granted limited protection: they should not be coerced into converting to Christianity, Jewish cemeteries should not be desecrated, Jews and their property should not be harmed, and a Jew should not be killed except by decision of judicial authorities. Yet Calixtus himself controverted his limited protection by concluding that the only Jews who "deserve such protection are those who do not plot to subvert the Christian faith."[54] But because Jews believed in the validity of the Talmud, this was *prima facie* evidence that Jews plotted "to subvert the Christian faith."

Like Calixtus II, Innocent III hedged his protection of Jews. He stated in his protective bull, *Constitutio pro Judeis* of 1199, that although "the Jews shall not be destroyed completely, . . . only those who have not presumed to plot against the Christian Faith [will be protected]."[55] The validity of his claim to protect Jews comes into question again in his letter to the archbishops of Sens and Paris in July 1205.

> The Jews are plagued by their own guilt for having crucified the Lord, predicted by their own prophets, who came in the flesh to redeem Israel. . . . But we Christians are kind and so we have tolerated these Jews. Yet they have replied to our generosity by ingratitude and to our friendship with contempt. . . . Lest the faithful incur the wrath of God, they should not allow the Jews to do such detestable and incredible things against the faith without punishment. And so, we have asked our dearest son of Christ, Philip the Illustrious King of France, and we have ordered the noble Duke of Burgundy, and the Countess of Troyes, to restrain these Jewish excesses so that the Jews will not dare raise their necks, bowed under by eternal slavery, against the holy Christian faith.[56]

A few months earlier, Innocent had carefully enumerated to King Philip-Augustus of France other Jewish blasphemies and insults to Christianity that he assumed all Jews were guilty of: moneylending, having Catholic servants, building a new synagogue higher than a nearby church, engaging in overly loud religious rites, insulting Catholics by saying that they "believe in a peasant who had been hanged by the Jewish people," appearing in public on Good Friday and laughing at the Catholic adoration of the Cross, opening their doors to thieves in order to fence stolen goods, and murdering Catholics at every opportunity. Associating the Jews with heretics, he ended his letter by insisting that Philip-Augustus should stop these Jewish blasphemies or remove the Jews from his kingdom. This letter supplied the French king with the additional pretext he needed nearly to destroy the Jewish community in France by expropriations, expulsions, and mass murders.[57]

In 1220, Pope Honorius III remarked on "the *perfidia* of the Jews, [who are] condemned to perpetual slavery because they damned themselves and their children when they cried out for the blood of Christ. They are hardly worthy of papal nurturance . . . nevertheless . . . we forbid anyone from molesting you in person or goods so long as you refrain from blaspheming Christ and his faith."[58] Of course, since Jews were frequently accused of blaspheming Jesus in their daily prayer, the conclusion a Catholic could draw from Honorius' remarks is that Jews can, and perhaps should, be molested.

The nearly one hundred bulls Pope Martin V (d. 1431) wrote in a fourteen-year period comprise a case study in papal treatment of Jews. He alternated protection of the Jews with papal assaults on them, changing his mind as he was lobbied first by Jews and then, and more frequently, by anti-Jewish friars.[59] The Jews used money to gain his help.[60] Catholics employed arguments of faith.

Enforcement of Papal Protection

The popes had the power to excommunicate anyone who violated their decrees of protection for the Jews, and papal letters sometimes included warnings of ecclesiastical sanctions if the pope's wishes were violated. The excommunicants would be totally isolated and barred from aid, assistance, employment, nurturance, and protection. Furthermore, the papacy could ask for cooperation from the "secular arm" to jail the excommunicant or worse (in cases where the Church decided on penalties serious enough to require mutilation or death, it relied on secular authorities to carry out the punishment because the Church formed the second, and spiritually superior, arm of God's power on earth).[61] However, the popes rarely followed up their threats by actually excommunicating Catholic offenders for offenses against Jews, which, in turn, indirectly encouraged Catholic violence.[62]

According to Solomon Grayzel, the papacy never removed any official nor excommunicated any Catholic for forcibly converting, torturing, or murdering

Jews.[63] In 1233 and 1236, Pope Gregory IX—responding to letters from Jews begging the pope to intercede, promising not take usury nor to "insult the Christian faith"—complained to the French bishops that to extort funds from the Jews certain lords "tear [the Jews'] finger-nails and extract their teeth, and inflict upon them other kinds of inhuman torments." Some of the French nobles intended "to exterminate the Jews." But he put no sanctions in his letter of protection and refused even to suggest excommunication.[64] Responding initially to a petition from the Jews of Vienne, Innocent IV wrote a series of letters between May and July 1247 to John de Bernin, the archbishop of Vienne, bishops in Germany and France, and all Christians, rejecting the blood-libel and appealing for piety and kindness toward the Jews.[65] Yet in another letter, the pope reacted to the expropriation, imprisonment, and torture of Jews falsely accused of involvement in ritual murder by simply requiring the archbishop "to warn" the offending bishop of Trois-Châteaux and several aristocrats to release the Jews and restore their property. He specified no punishment for Draconet, lord of Montauban, who had, without evidence of Jewish malfeasance, "cut some of them [Jews] in two, others he burned at the stake, [as to] others he castrated the men and tore out the breasts of the women."[66]

The double standard that runs through papal Jewish policy is evident in comparisons of papal letters that purport to protect Jews with letters that threatened Jews or defended the Catholic faithful. Within one month, Pope Gregory IX severely reprimanded minor Jewish offenses against Christians and threatened to employ secular military forces against the Jews, yet only mildly reproached Crusaders who "try to wipe [the Jews] almost completely off the face of the earth."[67] (Ironically, Gregory was accused by many of having protected Jews only because they bribed him.[68]) In March 1233, Gregory commanded the bishops of Germany "completely to suppress" Jewish attempts to convert Catholics, hold public office, and avoid their stigmatic Jew badges.[69] He added: "[So that the Jews] should not again dare to straighten their neck bent under the yoke of slavery and dispute with Christians about their faith, [the bishops] may call in for this purpose the secular arm." Several popes, including John XXII, Clement VI, and Martin V, granted absolution to Catholics who had persecuted or participated in the murder of Jews.[70]

Anti-Jewish Rhetoric

The protective power of papal letters was also tempered by their intentional and persistant use of abusive language.[71] Popes claimed to protect Jews but continued to assert the Jews' essential lack of value and dignity as human beings as well as their danger to Christians and Christendom. A small sample of papal anti-Jewish rhetoric from the thirteenth and fourteenth centuries alone indicates the extent to which the Jews were denigrated:

"Blind Jewish perversion of Faith,"
"the sons of the crucifiers, against whom to this day the blood cries to the Father's ears,"
"slaves rejected by God, in whose death they wickedly conspired,"
"the *perfidia* of the Jews, condemned as it is to perpetual slavery because of the cry by which they wickedly called down the blood of Christ upon themselves and their children,"
"blasphemers of Christ,"
"it is a crime that . . . the Christian religion should be polluted by being subjected to infidels,"
"Jewish blindness,"
"perverse,"
"the damned faithlessness of the Jews,"
"old and corrupt Jewish blindness, . . . deadly weed,"
"accursed rite,"
"malicious deceit,"
"death-dealing study [and] poisonous diet,"
"dangerous sickness,"
"the darkness of the Jewish *perfidia*,"
"detestable stubbornness."[72]

Papal letters that at once protected the Jews and emphasized their status as religious pariahs served to increase rather than diminish popular awareness of the Church's persistent anti-Jewish doctrine.

Papal Reactions to the Crusades and Other Violence

Pope Alexander II sent similar letters of praise to the archbishop and viscount in Narbonne after the Jews were attacked there in 1063. But these letters, like other papal bulls regarding the Jews, were ambivalent. Alexander observed that the Jews were "*perhaps* destined for salvation." He noted further that the Jews were to "live in servitude." The most damaging part of his letter stated that although the Jews were protected by God's mercy, nevertheless with their homeland and liberty lost, "in everlasting penitence, damned by the guilt of their ancestors for spilling the blood of the Savior, they live dispersed."[73]

Mass murder of Jews during the Crusades and other medieval crises was not officially condoned, but every level of the Church accepted it. During the First Crusade, arguably "a papal enterprise from beginning to end," no papal pronouncements urging protection for the Jews were issued even though thousands of Jews were slaughtered. Pope Urban II remained silent when Crusaders massacred Jews.[74] Papal silence in the face of crimes against the Jews was a pattern that was to be followed for most of the last millennium of European history.

During the early Crusades, the papacy issued no letters of protection for Jews; during the later Crusades, although some letters of protection were written, the popes' anti-Jewish rhetoric inspired the Crusaders to take a full measure of revenge against the Jews. The Crusaders knew that papal language was often extremely hostile to Jews, and they had good reason to believe that the papal policy of protection of Jews was inconsistent and half-hearted. Calixtus II's protective bull[75] opposed forced baptism, but since the bull was issued twenty years after the First Crusade,[76] it could have had no effect on the anti-Jewish activities of the First Crusaders. Only Antipope Clement III had *any* comment on the Crusaders' actions against the Jews when in either 1097 or 1098 he complained to Bishop Rupert of Bamberg that Jews forcibly converted during the Crusade had been allowed to revert to Judaism.[77]

During the Second Crusade (1145–49), the papacy remained mute concerning the Jews, except for Pope Eugenius III's single bull of protection, which was not preserved and was an indication of its lack of importance in the eyes of the Church. At any rate, this letter was not effective in preventing Crusader attacks on Jews.[78] Eugenius also decreed that Crusaders need not repay interest on any debts to Jews.[79] Perhaps as a result of this papal letter, Louis VII of France felt justified in forgiving the Crusaders the obligation to pay back any loans from Jews.[80]

In 1208, Innocent III ordered a Crusade against the heretical Albigensians in the south of France. Just months before the start of this Crusade, in which Jews were murdered along with Albigensians, Innocent wrote to the Count of Nevers that although Jews should not be killed, "the blood of Jesus Christ calls out against them." The Jews ought to be forced into slavery, which they deserve since they had "raised sacrilegious hands" against Jesus and "called down his blood upon themselves and their children." The Jews are "enemies of the Cross."[81] Several of Innocent's letters permitted Crusaders to avoid repaying Jewish loans and threatened to "excommunicate" Jews who did not remit usury to Crusaders.[82] Innocent III did not raise the issue of protection until 1215, when he commanded the bishops of France to forbid Crusaders to hurt the Jews. Again, the full text of this bull has not survived.[83] If it were typical of papal pronouncements on the Jews, no significant penalties were attached. Again, the loss of the document itself—only the rubric remains—may indicate that the Church did not value it very highly.

Popes Alexander III, Clement III, and Celestine III issued bulls of protection for Jews during the Third Crusade (1187–92) and the years just preceding it, at the same time these popes issued several bulls urging Crusade.[84] Alexander's and Celestine's bulls did not survive.[85] They claimed to be "based on Christian piety" and forbade forced baptism, wounding, stoning, beating, or killing of Jews, and desecrating Jewish cemeteries—all of which indicates what the Crusaders were actually doing.[86] These bulls combined with Jewish precautions and princely assertiveness helped somewhat to protect Jews during this Crusade.[87] But none of the papal letters appeared precisely when needed. Only Clement's letter came during the Crusade itself and nearly two months after the worst anti-Jewish violence had occurred, in March 1188.[88] Other contemporary papal letters applied to the Jews such hostile phrases as "the blindness of the Jewish *perfidia*," "the ungodly cult of the Jews," "hard-hearted Jewish depravity," and "damned Jewish greed."[89] Alexander noted the Jews' stiff-necked obstinacy, called Judaism a superstition and Jews the enemies of Christ's cross, and described the reversion of a Jewish convert to Judaism as the returning of "a dog to his own vomit."[90] The loss of two of Alexander's and Celestine's major protective bulls suggests that the papacy neglected them. Shlomo Simonsohn has concluded that the frequent repetition of these bulls meant that they were ineffective or ignored.[91]

The papacy again showed little response to anti-Jewish violence engendered by the so-called Shepherds' Crusade, the riots against the Jewish communities of southern France and Aragón.[92] Already hostile to Judaism, which he regarded as an "error and depravity of Jewish blindness" and "a damnable *perfidia*," "a filthy Jewish superstition,"[93] John XXII, the Avignonese pope, seemed interested in saving Jewish property and Catholic lives but not Jewish lives during this crisis. On June 19, he hesitantly asked the archbishop of Narbonne to compel the shepherds only to desist from killing Catholics and from plundering Jewish goods. The pope also did not specify any punishment for those who violated his wishes. Later that month, John recommended stronger measures against the shepherds to the archbishop of Toulouse but seemed more concerned with the "danger that results from the behavior of riotous mobs" who are acting "prematurely," before King Philip V authorized Crusade. Pope John issued a concurrent letter to the seneschal of Toulouse, suggesting spiritual and secular force be employed against the shepherds; the pope expressed concern that excesses against the Jews and their property could harm the king of France, since he could no longer exact taxes from the Jews should Jewish property be destroyed. On July 9, the pope reminded the Catholic secular authorities in France that Jews should be "defended since they bear witness to [the validity of] the Catholic faith." Even here, however, John did not specify any penalty for noncompliance with his directives. By the end of July, the pope again noted "the blindness of Judaism" and his "detestation of the old Jewish treachery."[94]

In September of 1320, when the shepherds were suppressed, Pope John authorized another assault on the Talmud for blasphemy and error. Noting "the damned initiatives of the perfidious Jews," he ordered that "the plague and deadly diseased weed [of Judaism] must be pulled out by its roots." The notorious Franciscan Inquisitor Bernardo Gui (c. 1261–1331) proclaimed himself "Inquisitor into the perverse heresy and perfidy of the Jews in the realm of France sanctioned by the Apostolic See."[95] Bernardo was authorized to place the Talmud on trial again, since, as Pope John insisted, Catholics must be kept away from the Jewish pestilence. The Talmud must be examined and. if blasphemies were found therein, it must be burned and both judaized Catholics and Jews were to be punished according to canon law. Found guilty of blasphemy, the books of the Talmud were burned in Toulouse and Perpignon. John also took advantage of the Jews' vulnerability at this time and sent special preachers to them in the papal cities of southern France, hoping for mass conversions. When the Jews still refused baptism, their synagogues were destroyed and they were sent into exile. Citing "the elimination of the filthy Jewish superstition and replacing it with the worship of the Lord, the Holy Virgin, Mother of God, and the Saints," the pope himself supplied funds to build churches on the sites of the razed synagogues.[96]

When the Black Death first raged through the papal enclave of Avignon, Pope Clement VI (1342–52) responded to Jewish petitions by issuing a series of bulls of protection in 1348 and 1349. He tried to restrain the Catholic crowd's murderous attacks against the Jews, arguing that the plague was God's punishment of Catholic sin.[97] Repeating Innocent IV's letters of "protection," he threatened to excommunicate any Catholic who killed Jews without trial, forced baptisms, or robbed Jews. But he vitiated his own mandates in a number of ways. He referred to Jews in terms of their stubborn refusal to accept Christ. He addressed them as a "perfidious," "stubbornly hard-hearted" people, who, "unwilling to understand the words of their prophets and their own arcane Scriptures and to come over to Christianity, deserve to be despised."[98] Clement promised to reverse the excommunication of Catholics who violated his protection for Jews if they "make amends with the proper recompense."[99]

His later order to the bishops in October 1349 to suppress the flagellants was probably motivated more because they raised havoc among Catholics than because they murdered Jews, since outrages against the Jews were listed as but one among a number of flagellant offenses.[100] Moreover, although the flagellants had been murdering masses of Jews since at least July 1349, the bull was issued three months later.[101] Measures such as Clement's afforded Jews little real protection; like other Catholic authorities, Clement suppressed the flagellants to protect Catholics.[102] Between Catholic persecutions and plague, less than half of Europe's Jewish population survived past 1350.[103]

The Papacy and Ritual-murder

Moved by theology, pragmatism, and morality, several popes—Innocent IV and Gregory X in the thirteenth century, Clement VI in the fourteenth, Martin V in the fifteenth, Paul III in the sixteenth, and Clement XIII and XIV in the eighteenth[104]—responded to Jewish petitions following Catholic massacres of Jews[105] with declarations that Jews were not involved in murder, blood libel, or the outbreak of the plague. Innocent III himself contributed to the ritual-murder myth when, in January 1205, he wrote to Philip-Augustus, king of France, that "the Jews [who] remain living among Catholics take advantage of every wicked opportunity to kill in secret their Catholic hosts. Thus it has recently been reported that a certain poor scholar has been killed and found dead in their latrine."[106]

Despite several papal disclaimers, such as Pope Innocent IV in 1247 and Pope Benedict XIV in 1758 (who appointed Cardinal Lorenzo Ganganelli—later to become Pope Clement XIV—to examine and report on ritual murder, from which he exonerated the Jews in a document that remained hidden to the outside world for more than a century[107]), papal letters denying the validity of anti-Jewish defamations were ambivalent or ambiguous.[108] Moreover, as mentioned above, the Church beatified several of the alleged ritual-murder victims of the Jews, among them Andreas of Rinn and Simon of Trent, although Pope Sixtus IV unsuccessfully attempted to save the Jews accused of murdering Simon.[109] Andreas was beatified in Benedictine XIV's bull, *Beatus Andreas* in February 1755, which reasserted the "facts" of ritual murder.[110] Simon of Trent was beatified in the late sixteenth century. In 1965, the Sacred Congregation of Rites forbade all veneration. In 1975, on the five-hundredth anniversary of Simon's death, the papacy finally absolved the Jews murdered in Trent from any implication in his murder.[111]

The Papal Assault on the Talmud

Another of the papacy's activities that weakened protection of Jews was its assault on the Talmud, one of the foundations of Judaism. As early as the sixth century, the Christianized Emperor Justinian issued a law that condemned the Mishna. Gregory was scandalized to discover that another Jewish holy book besides the Torah existed. More damaging, several popes believed, like Peter the Venerable, St. Thomas Aquinas, and St. Louis, that the rabbinic Talmud kept contemporary Jews under the sway of the same malicious rabbis who had engineered the death of Jesus.[112]

In 1244, Pope Innocent IV asked Louis IX "to strike down with merited severity all the detestable and heinous excesses" of the Jews, which insult God and injure Christianity and which the king has already begun to prosecute. The Talmud of the hateful and dangerous Jews must be "burned in fire." Later, while he was resident at Lyon in 1247, Innocent IV did briefly reverse himself on the Talmud, because of the pleas of Jews to whom he was then more accessible. But in the next year he allowed his legate, Odo, Bishop of Tusculum, to examine and condemn the Talmud again.[113]

In 1286, Pope Honorius IV wrote to John Peckham, Archbishop of Canterbury, that the "damned Jewish *perfidia*" was being treated too leniently in England. Learning all sorts of vices from the Talmud and associating with converts, the Jews "curse Christians and commit other evils. [Judaism] is a dangerous plague."[114] Four years later, the Jews were expelled from England.

As a result of the papal initiative, the Talmud was tried, convicted, and burned at the stake for containing heresy in France, Spain, Germany, and Italy.

Pressure on the Jews to Convert

The Church believed that the sincere conversion of Jews confirmed the validity of Catholicism and that the baptism of most Jews would pave the way for the Second Coming of Christ. The popes were so intent on achieving baptism for Jews that the popes violated the prevailing theological notion that baptism should be purely voluntary. They did not hestitate to apply extreme moral and psychological pressure on Jews. As early as 418, Pope Zosimus tacitly approved the bishop of Minorca's forced conversion of Jews. The Fourth Council of Toledo in 633 required the separation of Jewish children from their parents. "We order that the sons and daughters of Jews, lest they become further ensnared in the errors of their parents, be separated from living with them, and put in monasteries or with Christian men or God-fearing women, so that they may be taught the religion of Faith."[115] Two centuries later Agobard advocated the removal of Jewish children who were converted through unsanctioned baptism from their parents. The Church Council of Meaux-Paris in 845–6 also ordered that Jewish children "should be separated from their parents and given to Christians."[116]

All medieval canonists agreed that when one Jewish parent converted to Catholicism, all the children would become Catholics. But the canonists objected to forced conversions of Jewish children because, from a legal standpoint, injuring any person, including Jewish parents, was wrong. Forced baptism of Jewish children also presented a theological problem: it would allow no remnant of Jews to remain to be saved at Jesus's Second Coming. [117]

During the First Crusade, Urban II refused to release forcibly baptized Jews from their vows. During the same Crusade, in violation of canon law, Antipope Clement III condemned Emperor Henry IV, who in 1098 had sent out letters of protection for Jews, for permitting forcibly baptized Jews to return to their faith. [118] In the thirteenth century, both Nicholas III and Nicholas IV ruled that Jews who were baptized while fearing for their lives but who later returned to their Judaism were to be considered relapsed heretics and burned at the stake. Because they were "not absolutely or precisely coerced," reversion to Judaism would insult the sacrament of baptism and Christ himself. Because after a year in prison, these Jews persisted in their "Jewish blindness," Nicholas III permitted the Inquisitors to proceed against them as heretics. [119]

With the popes' approval, the Dominicans and Franciscans also intruded into Jewish daily life by censoring the Talmud, forcing Catholic sermons on Jews, and sometimes rousing crowds to attack them. Their goal was to convert the Jews or, should that fail, to end their "threat" to Christian identity by having them expelled. [120] In 1298, Pope Boniface VIII also ordered the Inquisition to persecute as relapsed heretics those Jews who had been baptized as children or as a result of their fear of death, and to treat those who help these Jews as if they were aiding heretics. [121] This principle soon found its way into canon law. [122]

In 1497, Pope Alexander VI did not oppose Portuguese King Manoel's baptizing all Jewish children, four to fourteen, in order to force their parents to convert to Christianity. The baptized children were removed from the family. These were Jews who had been forced from Spain in 1492 and settled in Portugal because of a royal promise that they would be safe to practice the Judaism of their fathers. [123] The plan to force the parents to convert was rarely effective. The more usual result was the kidnapping of Jewish children who were then scattered and raised as Catholics apart from their parents. [124]

Between 1572 and 1585, Popes Paul IV, St. Pius V, and Gregory XIII required Jews residing in the ghettos of the papal states to listen to weekly sermons; those Jews who did not pay attention were flogged. This practice continued under their successor, Sixtus V (1585–90), who, apparently in response to Jewish bribes, removed most restrictions on Jews in the papal states in 1586. [125]

Nevertheless, the papal states maintained an Inquisition well into the nineteenth century. *Conversos* (also, *marranos*, that is, pigs, Spanish Jews who had converted to Catholicism[126]) living in Italy in the mid-sixteenth century who reverted to Judaism were burned as relapsed heretics by Pope Julius III (1550–55). Popes Paul IV (1555–59, formerly Chief Inquisitor Giampietro Cardinal Carafa), and Paul V (1605–21) urged conversion on the Jews with renewed vigor. They saw Jewish existence as a test for the missionary fervor of Catholics. Their harsh measures against the Jews were intended to coerce them into conversion. A 1555 bull of Paul V, *Cum nimis absurdum*, ghettoized those Jews living in Rome and other papal cities, required them to wear badges as a sign of the stigma of their Jewishness, and forced conversionary sermons on them. This bull gained the support of the Spanish founder of the Society of Jesus, St. Ignatius of Loyola (1491–1556), who desperately wanted Jews to convert.[127]

In 1747, Pope Benedict XIV (1740–58) ordered that Jewish children over seven could be baptized against the will of their parents and contrary to the procedures of canon law. In 1751, he punished Jews who changed their minds about becoming Catholics,[128] stirring the kidnapping of Jewish children and their forced baptism.[129] In 1775, as the Jewish "Middle Ages" came to a close, Pius VI ordered Jews who lived in any papal state to listen to conversionary sermons delivered in the synagogues after the Sabbath services, forbade them to associate in any way with Catholics, ride in carriages, leave the ghetto, sell food to Catholics, sing religious songs, or erect tombstones over their dead; the Jews' books were censored and the study of Talmud was prohibited.[130] A visitor to Rome in 1783 observed that "The situation of the Jews in Rome is worse than anywhere else. . . . [W]hen will Christians become more tolerant?"[131]

In 1815, when Pius VII was restored to Rome after his Napoleonic exile, he stripped Jews of whatever gains they had achieved under the French occupation and reinstituted the embarrassing and painful Jewish participation in the Roman Carnivale, conversionary sermons, and the Inquisition. Leo XII reestablished the ghetto, which Napoléon's troops had torn down, and sermons of conversion.[132]

Later in the nineteenth century, Pius IX (1846–78) firmly established the cult of Lorenzino of Marostica whom the Jews had allegedly crucified and drained of blood, thus reaffirming the medieval defamations of ritual murder and blood-libel.[133] He also adamantly insisted that an involuntarily baptized Jewish child, Edgardo Mortara, must not be returned to his parents and must be raised as a Catholic. As a Jewish infant, Edgardo had been surreptitiously baptized and later, as a six-year-old, seized from his parents by the papal Inquisition; he was raised as a Catholic and died as a missionary priest. Pope

Pius IX exclaimed to the Jews of the Roman ghetto, "Could I reject the child who wanted to become a Christian? Besides, if the Mortaras had not had a Christian servant all of this would not have happened." The Jews were then allowed to kiss the papal hand.[134]

The Inquisition

The Inquisition was an indispensable arm of the medieval papacy's Jewish policy. A prince or prelate could request the establishment of an Inquisition, but it was fundamentally a papal institution. In 1184, Pope Lucius III established the "Inquisition of Heretical Depravity" in order to repress heresy. Convicted, heretics would be excommunicated and handed over to the secular authorities for punishment. Fifteen years later, Innocent III declared heresy a treason against God and sent Dominic Guzmàn (founder of the Dominican Order) to preach against the Albigensian heresy in the south of France. This Inquisition, approved by the Fourth Lateran Council, would develop into the Albigensian Crusade, strongly supported by the papacy, and result in the deaths of tens of thousands of faithful Catholics, Alibigensians, and Jews.

Innocent's successor, Honorius III (1216–27), who recognized the Dominican and Franciscan orders, approved the severe penalties for heresy promulgated by Frederick II in the Holy Roman Empire and Louis VIII in France. Gregory IX ruled that the Apostolic See held jurisdiction over Jews if they contravened moral laws or "invented heresies against their own law."[135] In 1231, he handed the papal Inquisition over to the Dominicans, "the watchdogs of Christianity," who would eventually supplant the inquisitional authority of ordinary clergy.[136] Innocent IV (1243–54) allowed the Inquisitors to use torture and to absolve each other for the sins involved in using physical violence since it was employed "to promote the work of faith more truly." Clement IV's bull of July 27, 1267, *Turbato corde*, renewed several times by later popes, gave the Inquisition full authority to examine the Jews and their books for heresy. But this letter should be read in conjunction with another, which Clement sent to James I, King of Aragón, just twelve days before, *Damnabili perfidia Judaeorum*, condemning the Jews' ingratitude and their "damned and treacherous faithlessness." Clement ordered the Dominicans and Franciscans to examine the Talmud for heresy. He called the Jews

> a repudiated, a blind, and a terribly sinful people who had rejected and murdered their true Messiah . . . and who have been forced to wander the earth like the fratricide Cain, guilty of a crime too great even for the Lord to forgive. . . . They had brought him down, they had whipped him, they had sacrilegiously killed him by crucifixion, calling down His blood upon themselves and their

children. Even today, the Jews refuse to accept the fact that they are allowed to live among the faithful without serious mistreatment because of our kindness. But here is this perverse generation [of Jews] . . . who repays Christian kindness with insult, friendliness with contempt, benefit with [betrayal].

Clement believed that Judaism, a "damnable religious practice," was attracting Catholics. This "insult to the most sacred name of Christ [and] subversion of the Faith" had to be stopped.[137] He complained that the Jews had set aside their Mosaic Law and replaced it with the Talmud's abuse and blasphemy against Mary and Jesus. And so he ordered the ecclesiastical and civil authorities of Aragón to force the Jews to surrender their copies of the Talmud to the Dominicans and the Franciscans, who were to examine it for heresies and errors. Among the Inquisitors was Paul Christianus, now a Dominican but formerly a Jew, whose purpose, along with the pope's, was to attack Judaism by destroying the authority of the Talmud.[138]

Although Martin IV limited the power of the Inquisition over the Jews in 1281,[139] the Inquisition was given authority to investigate Jews who were accused of blasphemy against Christians or Christianity, of usury, magic, or sorcery, of proselytizing Catholics, or of helping relapsed Jewish converts to Christianity.[140] In January and February 1290, Nicholas IV, a Franciscan, complained that Jews and Judaized Catholics infected the faithful with heresy. Nicholas instructed the Franciscan Inquisition and other ecclesiastical and civil authorities, to "pull out the deadly plant by its roots, . . . purge the infected provinces, . . . and punish these idolators and heretics, denying them any right of appeal."[141]

The notorious Inquisition in Spain, requested by Spanish monarchs and first established in 1451 by Pope Nicholas V at the request of King John II of Castille and Leon,[142] employed secular force extensively and targeted the converted Jews (*conversos*), against whom Catholics complained because *conversos* refused to baptize their children and instead had them attend synagogues and observe Jewish holy days and thereby demonstrate contempt for the Catholic faith.[143] With the full support of the papacy, by 1478, Pope Sixtus IV sanctioned the royal-ecclesiastical Inquisition by authorizing the Spanish sovereigns to appoint three bishops and other churchmen to proceed against heretics.[144] This Inquisition fined, imprisoned, humiliated, expropriated, tortured, and murdered "heretical" *conversos*, as well as those who sympathized with, protected, or sheltered them by "relaxing" them, or handing them over to the secular authorities for the execution of their punishment. The Spanish Inquisition was established to root out apostasy, real or imagined. Although Sixtus IV attempted to regulate some of the Inquisition's abuses,[145] his language often contained traditional antisemitic rhetoric, like "detestable Jewish perversity," "depraved, obscene and diabolic [Jewish] inventions," and "perfidious Jews."[146] Greater in its cruelty than the northern European witch-hunts, the Spanish Inquisition was one of the most effective and longest-lived institutions of persecution in history. It lasted until the nineteenth century, forcibly converted the greatest Jewish community of medieval Europe, and scattered Spanish Jews who refused baptism into a further Diaspora.[147]

These events revealed how bankrupt the papal policy of protection was. The Spanish Inquisition and monarchy destroyed a Jewish culture and exiled perhaps two hundred thousand Jews from their homeland while the papacy remained silent, and two thousand years of Jewish culture was abruptly terminated.

The Papacy and Jewish Ghettos

The papacy also enforced its Jewish policy by establishing ghettos and imposing legislative restrictions on the Jewish residents. Although, as mentioned above, the Jews themselves often chose to live together for reasons of community and religious practice, by the thirteenth century, the Church began to restrict the locations for Jewish residence. These confined areas would ultimately become the unhealthy and humiliating ghetto, one of the most important elements in the papacy's policy of degradation. Eugenius IV (1431–47) commanded that Spanish Catholics not fraternize with Jews (or Moslems); Jews were to dress distinctively and live in ghettos. They were prohibited from many occupations and activities and were not allowed to appear on the streets during Easter Week.[148] Jews were to be allowed no new synagogues; they could not testify against a Catholic in court; they could not ask Catholics to light their fires, prepare their food, or do anything that would enhance their worship on Sabbath or feast days. The pope entrusted the execution of this bull to Giovanni di Capistrano, a notorious Franciscan Jew-hater. Eugenius also convened the Council of Florence (1438–45), which reaffirmed the 1100-year-old Catholic doctrine that no one—pagan, heretic, schismatic, or Jew—existing outside the Church "can have a share in life eternal, but that they will go into the eternal fire which was prepared for the devils."

Between 1503 and 1555, six relatively tolerant "Renaissance popes"—Julius II, Leo X, Adrian VI, Clement VII, Paul III, and Julius III—opposed Jewish expulsions and the establishment of the Portuguese Inquisition.[149] But Paul IV and St. Pius V adopted Duns Scotus' view that the remnant of Jews saved at the end of time need not to be very large. Paul and Pius expelled most of the Jews from papal territories, leaving only a few Jews living in a few "islands" awash in a Catholic sea.[150] Because Pope Paul felt his duty was to preserve the Catholic nature of the papal states from any profanation by the

Jewish spirit, he established ghettos there in July 1555. Opposite the main gate of the Roman ghetto stood a tall cross bearing this inscription in Hebrew from Isaiah 65:2: "I spread out my hands all the day to a rebellious people."[151] Isaiah continued in this summary manner: "you say do not come near me for I am too holy for you; because you insulted me I will condemn you to the sword; when I called, you did not answer, when I spoke you did not listen, but you did what was evil in my eyes. My servants shall rejoice but you shall be put to shame. You shall leave your name to my chosen for a curse and the Lord God will put you to death." These elements were part and parcel of the Church's traditional assault on the Jews.

Paul IV's anti-Jewish bull *Cum nimis absurdum* stated that it was "utterly absurd and impermissible that the Jews, whom God has condemned to eternal slavery for their guilt [in the crucifixion], should enjoy our Christian love and toleration . . . [that Jews] strive for power . . . that Jews venture to show themselves in the midst of Christians and even in the immediate vicinity of churches without displaying any badge."[152] Paul restricted Roman Jews to a small, unsanitary ghetto near the Tiber and limited their livelihood to dealing in old clothes and second-hand goods. In 1556, he ordered twenty Portuguese *conversos* burned in Ancona on the grounds of heresy, for any contact between *conversos* and Jews was deemed heretical.[153] Several Catholic states emulated the anti-Jewish actions of Pope Paul IV and his successors.

Demanding a public sign of Jewish degradation, Urban VIII (1623–44) refused to let the Jews of Rome put their lips to his foot; instead they were to kiss the place where his foot had rested. In 1684, Innocent XI (1676–89) reaffirmed that Jews in the Roman ghetto be restricted to dealing in used goods and clothing. In the papacy of Benedict XIV, prelates and priests strongly opposed attempts by the Bourbon government of the two Sicilies to allow the Jews to settle in Naples and Sicily.[154] Leo XII (1823–29) revoked all civil rights Napoléon had granted the Jews. The Roman ghetto walls were torn down under Pius IX (1846–78), but it took the destruction of the papal states and the secular unification of Italy by Victor Emmanuel in 1870 to destroy the ghetto completely.[155]

Late Medieval Attitudes

The writings of Pope Paul IV's spokesman Marquardus de Susannis reflect the pope's own anti-Jewish ideas as well as those of the whole era of Reformation and Counter Reformation.[156] Marquardus's book described the status of Jews in canon law as well as in secular civil and criminal law, and included an anti-Jewish polemic.[157] It considered the Jews blind to the truths of Christianity and no longer deserving of the name Israel, which now belonged to the triumphant and true Israel, Christianity. According to Marquardus, Jews were religious enemies of Christ and Christians but were tolerated in Christendom primarily because their punishment as a deicide people reminded Catholics of divine justice. Their fifteen hundred years of worldly suffering, Marquardus maintained, was clear evidence of their horrendous sins against God, who was terribly angry at them and continued to punish them. And so these Witness People should be required to wear stigmatized clothing, their Talmud should be suppressed, and their ability to worship and earn a living carefully controlled. Their very existence was rooted not in any rights, but in Catholic piety and charity, or *caritas*. Once Christian piety itself moved into visual imagery of Christ's Passion and meditation on the pain inflicted during those "sacred" moments on Jesus himself, as Father Gerard Sloyan observed, then "the chief actual sufferers from Jesus' death by crucifixion have been—paradoxically—not Christians but Jesus' fellow Jews."[158]

Citing the elite of anti-Jewish theologians who had preceded him—Tertullian, St. Ambrose, St. Augustine, St. John Chrysostom, St. Isidore, St. Gregory, St. Bernard of Clairvaux, and St. Thomas Aquinas—Marquardus included an angry sermon attacking Jews. Reflecting papal attitudes, he proclaimed that the Jews were the "stinking" enemies of God who must continue to suffer unless and until they convert to Catholicism. Jews were not to be permitted usury, for Catholics should profit from Jews, not Jews from Catholics. In fact, all familiarity between Jews and Catholics had best be avoided; for a Catholic man to have sexual intercourse with a Jewish woman was a capital offense, even if they were married, because the Jews were enemies of the Cross and blasphemers of the name of Christ.[159] Jews should be allowed to remain in Christendom as *servi* (servants of the princes and Church) unless they menaced, corrupted, or conspired against Catholics, in which case they should be expelled.

The popes and their theologians were responsible for both the theological propaganda and pogroms against Jews during the Middle Ages. No matter how devout many popes were, most lacked any sense of authentic justice and charity toward the Jews. Only these few believed that even a limited relationship with Jews was acceptable: Antipope Clement VII, Urban VI, Boniface IX, Innocent VII, Gregory XII, and Antipope Alexander V.[160] As has been shown, although many popes responded to the petitions of individual Jews, the popes taught religious hatred of Jews and, with few exceptions, refused the Jews the help they needed. The papacy's theological position that Jews must be degraded and suffer yet at the same time be protected might have been clear to some of the faithful, but most did not understand such niceties.

The popes could not maintain the balance of contempt and toleration that their theological doctrine of triumphalism required. The papacy's failure to cure Christendom of antisemitism and the papacy's success in justifying and elaborating anti-Jewish attitudes during the Middle Ages were momentous for the future. At the threshold of the modern period of European history, religious antisemitism persisted as the "official position of the hierarchical Church."[161] Instead of protecting Jews, the papacy tacitly encouraged Catholics to degrade and do violence to Jews by not intervening during crises and by refusing to declare antisemitism a heresy.[162] The popes also failed to protest the Catholic princes' expulsions of Jews from Western Europe. In a few instances, popes themselves ordered Jewish expulsions.[163] By the early sixteenth century, Western Christendom was almost totally free of Jews.[164] Those Jews who remained in Europe lived in degradation that differed little from their condition during the Middle Ages.

CHAPTER 7

Germany and Austria-Hungary

What are wolves, lions, panthers, leopards, tigers, and men in comparison with these beasts of prey in human form?

Karl Lueger, Speech before *Reichsrat,* 1890

The Influence of Martin Luther

During the period of the Reformation, it was standard practice at every level of society to blame the Jews for the legion of troubles of the era. At a time when the economic condition of the Jews in Western Europe was in reality miserable, almost everyone—from German peasants to Protestants, from reformers to traditional Roman Catholic theologians—considered the Jews deicides, enemies of the Church, a plague on society, and out to steal Christian wealth and lives. Jews were scapegoated for the harsh fiscal policies of Church and state.[1] As during the High Middle Ages, the apocalyptic belief in the imminent appearance of the Antichrist—who was allegedly to be born of the Jewish people, circumcized in Jerusalem, and whose first followers and intimates were Jews—led to further antagonism.[2] Before church and society could be fundamentally reformed, they had to be totally cleansed of their Jewish spirit. Just as in the patristic period and the thirteenth century, there was an attack on the Talmud on the grounds that it contained blasphemous and seditious materal. Could an assault on Jews be far behind? As Heiko Oberman pointed out, "opposition to Judaism in effect became opposition to Jews."[3] The sixteenth century might have provided a climate for more religious freedom than before, but it was meant to be Christian freedom; there was still no place for the Jews.

The German peasants who revolted in 1523–25 were "imbued with a murderous and active hatred of Jews."[4] John Calvin observed that "[t]he degenerate and unlimited stubbornness [of the Jews] has served to justify their unending accumulation of misery without limit and without measure.

Everyone seems cheered by their punishment; no one feels sorry for them."[5] Perhaps the most surprising antisemite among the Catholic humanists was Erasmus of Rotterdam, the so-called prince of humanists. Even though at one point he criticized theological antisemitism—"if to be an authentic Christian is to hate the Jews, then we all are excellent Christians"—he himself fell prey to it. The entire body of Erasmus's thought is permeated by a virulent antisemitism. There was no place in his *societas christiana* for "the most pernicious plague and bitterest foe of the teachings of Jesus Christ." To Erasmus there was no such thing as a fully converted Jew. Christians must be careful even about allowing Jews into the fellowship of the Church. Faced with the stubborn refusal of Jews to convert, he felt that they stood as a constant menace to "the most basic values [of Christian society]: knowledge, the social order, and religion."[6] The Erfurt Augustinian Magister Johannes von Palt accused the Jews of knowingly and willingly torturing Christ. And Martin Luther's teacher and religious superior, Johannes von Staupitz, charged the Jews with inflicting the "harshest" torments on Christ, "savagely" striking him: "O you evil Jew! Pilate teaches you that your character is harsher than a pig's; the pig at least knows mercy."[7] Luther's arch opponent, the priest Johannes Eck, justified the expulsions of Jews from France and Spain as understandable considering that the Jews were so evil.[8]

Within Germany, the former Augustinian priest Martin Luther was especially influential in regard to the Jews. With his enormous corpus of work, written in a stimulating, polemical fashion, and addressed to every level of society, Luther "was the most popularly read man of his age"—and perhaps the most antisemitic.[9] Luther held that by the mere fact of their existence, Jews were a threat to Christians everywhere; as active opponents of Christ, they did not deserve tolerance. In his later writings, he developed the medieval Catholic anti-Jewish defamations and held that Jews were unconvertible and should be slain. His program on how German leaders should deal with the Jews—attack the rabbis, Talmud, and synagogues; expropriate the Jews and force them into labor; expel or murder them—was followed, whether consciously or not, step by step by Adolf Hitler's Third Reich. Luther obscene attacks on Jews—"We must not consider the mouth of the Jews as worthy of uttering the name of God within our hearing. He who hears this name from a Jew must inform the authorities, or else throw sow dung at him when he sees him and chase him away. And may no one be merciful and kind in this regard"—thematically stem from St. Jerome ("[Just as] you see the Jew praying; . . . nevertheless, their prayer turns into sin"[10]) and sound as if they pour from the poisoned lips of Nazi propagandists.[11] His influence from the start was most pronounced on the leaders of German society.[12] "We are even at fault," Luther wrote, "in not avenging all this innocent blood of our Lord and of the Christians which they shed for 300 years after the destruction of Jerusalem, and the blood of the children they have shed since then (which still shines forth from their eyes and their skin). We are at fault in not slaying them."[13]

Perhaps the starting point of the modern version of the myth of the Eternal Jew, the Wandering Jew, occurred in a 1602 German pamphlet titled *Kurze Beschreibung und Erzehlung von einem Juden mit Namen Ahasuerus* (A Short Account and Narrative of a Jew with the Name Ahasuerus). In it the Jew was forever punished, was denied salvation by Christ himself because of the Jew's refusal to believe in Christianity. Although the real author of the pamphlet is unknown, he mentions that his informant about the Wandering Jew had studied with Luther.[14]

Luther's words, "The Jews are our misfortune," ("Die Juden sind unser ungluck") although repeated in the nineteenth century by Heinrich von Treitschke, were used as a slogan hung on banners at Nazi gatherings. Although a Catholic by birth and choice, Hitler spoke in admiring terms of the great Reformer and his brand of antisemitism. In his conversations with Dietrich Eckart, recorded in *Der Bolschewismus von Moses bis Lenin* (Bolshevism from Moses to Lenin) (Munich 1924), Hitler quoted Luther (and Aquinas) against the Jews. Hitler regretted that Christianity had been broken in two by Protestantism, and he was saddened that Luther had early on written a defense of the Jews, "That Jesus Christ Was Born a Jew." Yet he did observe that Luther—whom he called "one of the greatest Germans," "the mighty opponent of the Jews," "a great man, a giant"—had found himself again in his later anti-Jewish writings. "He saw the Jew as we are only now beginning to see him today. But unfortunately too late, and not where he did the most harm—within Christianity itself. Ah, if he had seen the Jew at work there, seen him in his youth! Then he would not have attacked Catholicism, but the Jew behind it. Instead of totally rejecting the Church, he would have thrown his whole passionate weight against the real culprits."[15]

The Reichskristallnacht pogrom took place November 9–10, 1938, Luther's birthday. Although this date was chosen opportunistically by the Nazis, there was certainly the realization that on November 10, the birthday of Martin Luther—"the greatest antisemite of his time, the warner of his people against the Jew"[16]—was celebrated all across Germany. Luther's birthday also served as the Blood Witness [Blutzeuge] day of the Nazi movement.[17] Walter Buch, supreme Nazi Party magistrate and an SS Gruppenführer on November 9, 1934 admitted Luther's influence on Nazi Germany: "When Luther turned his attention to the Jews, after he completed his translation of the Bible, he left behind 'on the Jews and their Lies' for posterity. . . . Many people confess their amazement that Hitler preaches ideas that they have always held. . . . From the Middle Ages we can look to the same example in Martin Luther. What stirred in the soul and spirit of the German people of that time, finally found expression in his person, in his words and deeds."[18]

There was, likewise, a strong parallel between Luther's ideas and feelings about Jews and Judaism and the essentially anti-Jewish *Weltanschauung* of most Germans.[19] It was the traditional anti-Jewish theology of glory, elaborated by Martin Luther, which "prevented any large-scale mobilization of concern for the Jews."[20] Centuries of theological antisemitism combined with notions of *Obrigkeit* (religiously based obedience to the state), nationalism, Luther's *Judenhass*, opposition to democracy and other such modern movements that Germans associated with the Jews, and racism.[21] Streicher referred to Luther in his own defense on the stand at Nuremberg during the war crimes trials. "Dr. Martin Luther would very probably sit in my place in the defendants' dock today [29 April 1946, at the Nuremberg War Crimes Trials], if this book had been taken into consideration by the Prosecution.[22] In the book, The Jews and Their Lies, Dr. Martin Luther writes the Jews are a serpents brood and one should burn down their synagogues and destroy them." Luther's program for dealing with the Jews was, in fact, followed very closely by the National Socialist government. From segregation and loss of rights, through expropriation to mass murder (at which Luther strongly hinted), the Nazi Holocaust of the Jews proceeded apace with Luther's suggestions. Franklin Sherman, a recent editor and translator of Luther, has observed that "[even though] most of the authorities proved unwilling to carry out his recommendations, whether out of horror at their inhumanity or out of self-interest . . . [i]t is impossible to publish Luther's treatise [On the Jews and Their Lies] today . . . without noting how similar to his proposals were the actions of the National Socialist regime in Germany in the 1930s and 1940s."[23]

Luther's writings are a classic case of the impact of the theology of glory in regard to the Jews by the man who invented the term itself. Luther's language clearly shows how close it came to Nazi ideology. Luther's focus on *Judenmission* was to separate him theoretically from the Nazis of the Holocaust—as Luther scholars have so frequently pointed out.[24] But what is so arresting is that even though Luther was not—chronologically could not have been—a Nazi, his language, his policies, and his conclusions about the Jews were identical to those of the pre-1941 Nazi regime and terribly close to Hitler's Final Solution itself.[25]

Early Modern Germany

As we have seen, medieval drama emphasized the contrast between community of saved insiders and the Jews, who stood apart as evil outsiders.[26]

Emphasis on "Christ's sufferings," on Jesus's humanity, on salvation by means of meditating on suffering and death, and on "the humiliated, tortured, whipped, nailed-down, pierced, dying but life-giving body of Christ . . . present in the Eucharist . . . became the dominant icon of the late medieval church."[27] Following this tradition, the thirteenth-century *Meditations on the Life of Christ*—which are more like meditations on the passionate and painful torture and triumph of Jesus—was written for Franciscan nuns. The seven-hour Oberammergau Passion Play was first performed in 1634 resulting from a vow taken by the inhabitants that if God spared them from the bubonic plague sweeping Bavaria, they would perform a passion play scores of times in the first five months of each ten year period with thousands of residents actively participating in the play. The play is composed of spoken dramatic text, instrumental and choral music, and *tableaux vivants* portraying how Christianity superceded Judaism, Judas selling out Jesus, and the crucifixion itself. Since 1930, the audience has comprised about a half-million members. Hitler himself witnessed the play twice, praising it for demonstrating the "Jewish menace." Up through the 1980s, the script, comparing Christ to Abel and the Jews to Cain, stated that "Christ was despised by His brothers, the Jews. And just as Cain was forced to wander, so the Jews were to be expelled and "dispersed over the whole earth."[28] The play demonstrates, depite its post-Vatican II changes, that it still damned the Jews as "Cains," "Judases," and Christ killers.

In the late eighteenth century, the German nun, Anne Catherine Emmerich (d. 1824) wrote *The Dolorous Passion of Our Lord Jesus Christ*, which reconstructs the Passion of the Christ, emphasizing the collaboration of the evil Jews with the devil and their malicious behavior. Emmerich imagined how the Jews insulted and ridiculed Jesus, pulled out hands full of his hair and beard, spat on him, punched him, and stabbed him.[29] Jeremy Cohen recently summed up the contributions of such devotional literature to the history of Catholic and Christian antisemitism. "Passion centered devotion . . . strove to involve Christians in [Christ's Passion]. The gruesome imagery of Jewish brutality [helped remind Christians that] the descendants of Jesus's murderers, of the same nature and equally guilty as their ancestors, were still to be found in the present age."[30]

Nineteenth-century Attacks on the Talmud

Throughout the nineteenth century, German Catholic theologians repeated the medieval charges against "talmudic anti-Christianity," which were that the Jews subverted Catholic life economically, politically, and morally; these theologians added that Catholic culture would be demolished if Jews were to be emancipated and granted equal rights.[31] In 1882, the First International Anti-Jewish Congress met at Dresden with delegates from all over Germany, Austria, and Hungary. Citing the Church Fathers, Catholic spokesmen contended that, from the beginning, Jews were immoral and subversive betrayers and corrupters of Catholic nations, including Germany.[32]

Between 1867 and 1914, there were a dozen ritual-murder trials in Austria-Hungary, where Jews were "caught in a crossfire of ethnic and social conflicts," Magyars against Slavs, Slavs against Germans, and everyone against the Jews.[33] In 1882, August Rohling, German priest and professor of Catholic theology and Hebrew antiquities at the prestigious Charles University of Prague, testified as an expert witness at the Tísza-Eszlár murder trial. Fifteen members of the Jewish community of this Hungarian town were accused of murdering a Catholic child for her blood—the blood-libel defamation being widely believed in the Hapsburg monarchy. The case drew national and international attention when the local Catholic priest reported it to the press and appealed to the leading Hungarian antisemitic politician, Gyözö Istóczy, to help prevent the case from being suppressed by the Jews.[34] The trial was followed by pogroms in Hungary, where Istóczy's antisemitic party won more than twenty seats in the 1884 parliamentary elections.[35] Although the accused Jews were all acquitted, Rohling attested that "the religion of the Jews requires them to despoil and destroy Christianity in every way possible [and that] the shedding of a Christian virgin's blood is for the Jews an extraordinarily holy event."[36]

The prosecution called Rohling as an expert witness because in 1871 his *Der Talmudjude*, published in Germany, alleged that the Talmud, in contrast to the Holy Bible, was a Jewish collection of immoral and irrational superstitions and that the Talmud required Jews to hate Catholics, to practice ritual murder, and to seek domination of the world. Like Aquinas, he believed that contemporary Jews were not biblical but Talmudic. Despite the court's not-guilty verdict in the Tísza-Eszlár case, Rohling's book continued to have a large readership, because so many Catholics wanted to believe in the "factuality" of the ritual-murder defamation.[37] Once Rohling's themes were picked up by the Jesuit journal *Civiltà Cattolica* in its late nineteenth-century antisemitic campaign, it was as if these Judeophobic ideas were awarded a papal imprimatur.[38] Rohling was ultimately discredited by Jewish rabbi Joseph Bloch and had to resign his professorship, though his book continued to be sold, was translated into several languages (including Arabic), and served as a source for Nazi propaganda. In the end, Rohling was defrocked by the Church, not because of his fabrications and lying attacks on Jews and Judaism, which attracted rather than repelled his superiors, but because of another heretical book of his.[39]

Austrian Antisemitism

Jews had lived in Vienna since the tenth century, but were expelled in the 1420s, in 1475, in the 1670s, and in 1938. Between the tenth and thirteenth centuries, the Church pressed secular authorities for ghettos and stigmatic emblems on Jews. Beginning at the end of the eighteenth century through the nineteenth century when the dual monarchy granted freedom and civil rights, the same period was difficult for the Church (the failure of the concordat, the spilt with the Old Catholic Church, the establishment of "confessional equality" with other Christian confessions, and the further emancipation of Jews). The sharp nineteenth-century increase in Austria's Jewish population (Austria contained one of the largest of Europe's Jewish populations) challenged both Austria's self-identity and aggravated Catholic antisemitism. As Lisa Kienzl wrote, "Catholicism was . . . one of the leading aspects in the development of [Austrian] identity and . . . one reason why Jews, as another religion, had become the outsiders . . . the enemy."[40] As Gustav Mahler noted, "I feel like an alien three times over: as a Bohemian among Austrians, as an Austrian among Germans, and as a Jew everywhere in the world."[41] Despite the high level of native antisemitism, Jews supplied a high proportion of Austria's creative geniuses and helped give Vienna its sparkling reputation.[42]

The leading Austrian antisemitic politician at the end of the nineteenth century was Karl Lueger (d. 1910). Mayor of Vienna, representative to the Austrian Parliament, and head of the Christian-Social Party, Lueger drew many of his ideas on Jews from the works of the Austrian cleric Abraham a Sancta Clara (d. 1709), who was the most important Catholic preacher of his time and a virulent antisemite. Trained by the Jesuits, Sancta Clara felt that the Jews were one of Christendom's prime enemies and classified Jews along with gravediggers and witches as causes of the plague. He accused the Jews of desecrating the Host and murdering Catholic children for the sake of the devil. He ranted that "besides the devil, the Jews are the worst enemy of mankind. . . . Jewish beliefs are such that all Jews should to be hanged and burned."[43] Lueger, like the priest Ignaz Seipel, future chancellor of Austria, was also a disciple of Karl Vogelsang (d. 1890), who was the founder of social Catholicism. Vogelsang was a traditional antisemite who wanted to convert Jews and argued that they were opposed to justice and Catholic community.[44] He advocated a "Catholic antisemitism, which was the only moral, Christian, and potentially successful" antisemitism.[45]

Lueger's Christian-Social Party was familiarly known as the Antisemitic Party. It stemmed from the Christian Union, *Vereinigte Christen*, which was founded in 1887 by two priests and was sanctioned by most clergy, especially the Jesuits. The Christian Union's program demanded restrictions on Jewish immigration and the exclusion of Jews from public office, judgeships and the legal profession, the military, medicine, pawnbrokering, retail trade, and teaching Catholic children.[46] Much of Vienna's Jewish population at the time were poor, unassimilated Jewish immigrants speaking Yiddish with Eastern European dress, mannerisms, and religious customs. And Austria's national identity was characterized by a sharp opposition to foreigners.[47]

Lueger's was a Catholic political party supported by middle-class businessmen, the faithful, and the priesthood, and was endorsed by the papacy. The Hapsburg regime and the Austrian Catholic Church hierarchy initially condemned Lueger's party and his election as Vienna's mayor.[48] But in 1894 and 1895, Pope Leo XIII blessed and commended the Christian-Social Party and its newspaper, the *Reichspost*. To obtain the pope's support, Lueger had assured him that his party consisted of traditional Catholic antisemites. The pope, whose desk was later adorned with Lueger's picture, replied, "The leader of the Christian Social Union may know that he has in his pope a true friend who blesses him and treasures the Christian Social effort." Pope Leo's Secretary of State, Cardinal Rampolla, rejoiced at the party's overwhelming victory in Vienna's municipal elections in the mid-1890s, "You see, we have triumphed."[49] With this kind of endorsement, in 1897, Hapsburg Emperor Franz Joseph accepted Lueger as mayor of Vienna, where he and his Antisemitic Party ruled until Lueger's death in 1910.

Lueger openly admitted the opportunistic element in his antisemitism. In reply to criticism that he accepted too many Jewish dinner invitations, Lueger replied that "I myself decide who is a Jew."[50] But his actions and statements more often reflected traditional Catholic antisemitism, which helps explain his great appeal to all levels of Catholic Vienna's society. Lueger's party republished several antisemitic articles (which Hitler may have read) taken from the Jesuit publication *Civiltà Cattolica*. In an 1890 speech before the Austrian parliament, the Reichsrat, Lueger pictured the Jews as "unbelievably fanatical [in their] hatred and their insatiable love of revenge. . . . What are wolves, lions, panthers, leopards, tigers, and men in comparison with these beasts of prey in human form? . . . We object to Christians being oppressed."[51] He remarked that "only Christian antisemitism is national and effective; it measures up to every standard of culture and humanity and proceeds naturally from the eighteen hundred years of Christian life and teaching."[52] In 1897, Lueger wrote in his party's newspaper that Christian antisemitism "fights Jewish treachery against Christian teaching and culture, against a Christian society and state. . . . [It] sees to it that Christian people remain masters in their own home."[53] In the same year, he supported a bill in the *Reichsrat* designed to end Jewish immigration into the empire. The bill described the

Jews as foreigners and "enemies of Christian culture and of nations of Aryan descent."[54]

German and Austrian antisemitic political parties' decline in voting strength toward the end of the nineteenth century was only temporary.[55] Anti-Jewish arguments and violence against Jews, especially among the youth, became a respectable part of public opinion in part because of widespread anti-Jewish propaganda. German and Austrian political antisemitism would expand further once the twentieth century's disastrous political, economic, and social crises occurred.[56]

The German and Austrian Jews were emancipated but Jewishness was not. Catholicism was almost universally recognized as superior to Judaism.[57] Nor were Catholics "emancipated" from their basic religious antagonisms toward Jews. The culture and thought of Christian Europe still treated Jews with varying degrees of alienation and antipathy.[58] Catholics still distanced themselves from Jews socially, politically, and legally. They still associated Jews with the immoral use of money and with a stubborn attachment to a religion that lacked divine sanction.[59] Average Germans, who bought Streicher's Nazi newspaper, *Der Stürmer* (The Stormtrooper), in post-World War I Germany may have felt that the paper went a bit too far in its anti-Jewish onslaughts, but they felt very comfortable with the basic anti-Jewish values it embodied.[60]

German-Catholic Handbooks and Sermons

The influence of German priests in the nineteenth and early twentieth century on their parishioners was as considerable as was their hatred of Jews. The priests disseminated the Catholic Church's antisemitic position on the Jews to their parishioners, the vast majority of whom accepted the Church's outlook.[61] Following the tenets of triumphalistic Catholicism of men like Pseudo-Barnabas and St. Justin Martyr, St. Augustine and Origin,[62] these priests denied the value of the Jewish Scriptures. Like St. Ambrose[63] and his student St. Augustine,[64] these priests accused Jews of being Cains, "thus Jesus was killed by his blood brothers, the Jews." Like St. Cyril of Alexandria,[65] they denied the sanctity of the Jewish sabbath. Like St. Paul[66] they declared that the Torah was "debased and materialistic in nature" and caused the death of the spirit; like St. John Chrysostom,[67] they regarded the synagogue as "an assembly [of] beasts, in their lust for corporal things"; like St. Jerome,[68] they called Jews poisonous "weeds" and "snakes"; like St. Isidore of Seville,[69] they identified Jews with the Antichrist.[70] Professor Bacharach demonstrates that in the century before the Holocaust, Catholic antisemitism was as strong as ever.[71] The antisemitic language of German priests during this period mirrored the writings of the Church Fathers ("murderers, criminals, sinners, despicable, corrupt, impudent, cunning serpents, poisonous, enemies of God, garbage, enemies") or the thirteenth- and fourteenth-century popes ("blind Jewish perversion, *perfidia*, slaves, blasphemers, infidels, perverse, faithless, deadly weed, malicious, deceitful, poisonous, dangerous").[72]

Moreover, as we enter the twentieth century, Catholic anti-modern and anti-liberal attitudes were added to the woeful list of Catholic antisemitic beliefs.[73] In 1935, the Bavarian clerical journal *Klerusblatt* (Clergy Gazette) accused the Jews of corrupting Germany and described Hitler as "an emissary of God who has come to subdue Judaism."[74] Although on occasion denouncing antisemitism, the influential Jesuit periodical, *Stimmen der Zeit*, claimed that Jews threatened German and Catholic civilization.[75]

If German bishops and other Church leaders had spoken out in defense of the innocent, many more Catholics would have tried to protect Jews and far fewer Jews would have been discriminated against, expropriated, deported, and murdered. In a Germany where the press, free speech, and political parties were suppressed, even with the burden of the Vatican's Concordat in place with strong support from the Vatican, the German bishops could have overcome their disinclinations to help the Jews and could have influenced public opinion.[76] There is little doubt that the German bishops knew precisely what was happening to the Jews, *not* from the Vatican, which knew even more than they, but from SS Captain Kurt Gerstein and other sources.[77] The bishops did send a pastoral letter to the faithful asking them not to deny the right to life of hostages, POWs, and "human beings of alien races and origin."[78] (It is obvious that with the bishops calling Jews members of an "alien race," there was little hope that Catholics would respond favorably.) With a few exceptions such as Konrad Preysing, Johannes Dietz, and Josef Frings the German bishops supported Hitler's nationalism, racism, and plans for the Jews. What were German Catholics, even those who followed the path of *theologia crucis*, to think and do when the Church leaders withheld information about the mass murders from them, when the Church leaders taught them to obey the Nazi regime and not oppose state authority in any way? German Catholics needed to know the specifics about death camps and mass gassings that the Vatican knew about but withheld information.[79]

A leading Roman Catholic prelate during the Third Reich was Munich's Cardinal Michael von Faulhaber. During the anti-Jewish activities of the German government in April 1933, Faulhaber opined that there were more important issues for the Church than protecting Jews. He even declined to defend Jews converted to Catholicism since he felt that baptism gave no one leave to expect earthly advantage from it.[80] His position was enunciated more clearly in his Advent Sermons for 1933, where he pointed out that "Israel had repudiated and rejected the Lord's annointed, had . . . nailed Him to the Cross. Then the veil of the Temple was rent, and with it the covenant between the Lord and His people. The daughters of Sion received the bill of divorce, and from that time forth Assuerus [the Wandering Jew] wanders, forever."[81] Historian of the Catholic Church Michael Phayer, calls this "typical Christian antisemitism."[82] In 1934, in response to international comment that he had somehow "defended" contemporary Jews, Faulhaber reaffirmed that anything positive about Jews in his 1933 Advent Sermons had referred only to Jews who lived before Christ.[83] Some Catholic sources considered Faulhaber's writings courageous because he opposed the Nazi interpretation that there were no "Jewish traces in Christianity," but Faulhaber's writings still regarded contemporary Jews with contempt and therefore he, in effect, was legitimizing the Nazi attack on Jews.[84] As late as November 1936, after nearly four years of Nazi rule, Faulhaber proclaimed that "the Reich Chancellor undoubtedly lives in belief in God. He recognizes Christianity as the builder of Western culture."[85] He told Hitler that "as supreme head of the German Reich, you are, for us, the authority willed by God, the legal superior to whom we owe reverence and obedience."[86] Faulhaber also defended "racial research and race culture" and argued that the Church had always recognized the importance of race, blood, and soil—though he warned against hatred of other races and "hostility to Christianity" and in 1943 tried to convince Cardinal Adolf Bertram (Chairman of the Fulda Conference of Catholic Bishops and therefore the German Church's highest ranking prelate) to protest Jewish deportations.[87] Jesuit Fr. Rupert Mayer, whose position was that one could not be a Catholic and a Nazi at the same time, was disappointed in Cardinal Faulhaber for not speaking out in behalf of the Jews.[88]

A Jesuit critic of Bishop Berning's visit to Hitler, Friedrich Muckermann commented: "We face the shocking truth that the only word that a German bishop until today has publicly said about the barbarities of the concentration camps is a word of glorification of Hitler and of a system that has brought about these barbarities."[89] The Church later squelched Muckermann's criticisms.[90] Bishop Hilfrich of Limburg argued that Christianity had not developed from the Jews but instead had progressed in spite of these "God-killers." Cardinal Bertram agreed with Wurzburg Vicar-General Miltenberger that the Church had always recognized the importance of race, blood, and soil. The same perspective had been expressed by Monsignor Groeber, Archbishop of Freiburg, who himself had become a "promotive member" of the Nazi SS in 1933 and had publicly argued for "the national right to maintain unpolluted its racial origin and to do whatever necessary to guarantee this end."[91]

In wake of the Nazi Kristallnacht pogrom in 1938, Dean Bernhard Lichtenberg, Provost of Hedwig's Cathedral in Berlin, deplored Nazism and specifically condemned the German attack on the Jews, for whom he publicly prayed. "What happens today we have witnessed; outside the synagogue is burning, and that also is a house of God."[92] Other Catholics criticized the Church for its collaboration with the Third Reich—these included a number of Jesuits like Augustin Rösch, Lothar Koenig, and Alfred Delp.[93] In 1943, Alfred Delp, a German Jesuit who would later pay with his life for his involvement in an assassination attempt on Hitler, asked at the annual German Catholic Bishops' Conference: "Has the Church forgotten that it must every now and then say *you must not*? Has the Church lost sight of the Commandments? . . . Has the Church forgotten human beings and their fundamental rights?" The Jesuit order split in its support or opposition to Hitler.[94] In 1937, Berlin Bishop Konrad von Preysing wrote a pastoral letter attacking the Hitler regime, accusing the government of violating German consciences.[95] In 1943, von Preysing threatened to resign over the collaborative behavior of the other German bishops, and he unsuccessfully urged Pope Pius XII "to issue an appeal in favor of the unfortunate [Jews]."[96]

Even in Nazi Germany, assertive action, taken with enough aplomb, could and did make the Gestapo back down. In 1937, the Nazi government did nothing when an angry crowd of Catholics cheered Cardinal Clemens von Galen who arrived on pilgrimage at the cathedral at Aachen and gave a "*pfui!*" to Hitler. Two years later von Galen led the successful fight to stop the Nazi Euthanasia program, and late in the war two thousand "Aryan" women successfully protested the Gestapo's decision to remove their Jewish husbands at Gestapo headquarters.[97] Aside from a few scattered Catholics who objected to discriminatory anti-Jewish laws, expropriations, brutalizations, deportations, and ultimately mass murder, the Catholic Church in Germany and the rest of Europe stood publicly silent and privately bemused in the face of Hitler's Final Solution.[98] Sometimes lay Catholics and even prelates voiced goals similar to those of the Nazis.[99]

Hitler

The first half of the twentieth century posed crisis after crisis for Germany: defeat in World War I; postwar revolutions; ultra-liberal Weimar Republic in a politically conservative, if not reactionary, environment; an unprecedented Inflation and Depression; dictatorship; World War II; genocides; and Holocaust. The German Church found itself fighting the effects of socialism, communism, fascism, modernism, liberalism, Nazism, atheism, feminism, and secularism. Most of these "isms" were associated with the Jews. Although Hitler was certainly not "the embodiment of the Catholic Church," Catholic antisemitism conditioned Hitler's ideas and behavior toward Jews. The nation of Hitler's birth and youth, Austria, was the western nation most influenced by Catholic antisemitism.[100] Austrian Catholics regarded the Jews as "the veritable offspring of the devil."[101] After World War I, Austrian and German Catholics, often led and supported by their priests, established numerous antisemitic paramilitary groups. In the last election of the Hapsburg Empire, more than two-thirds of German Austrians voted for candidates who were extreme antisemites. Austrians joined the Nazi Party and the SS at a rate almost double that of Germans. The *Anschluß* (Annexation of Austria to Germany) of 1938 released such powerful antisemitism that the invading Germans had to restrain the Austrian population from attacking Jews.[102] Less than 10 percent of the German population, Austrians comprised nearly half the concentration camp staffs,[103] and Austrians may have been responsible for half of all war crimes.[104] Austrian Bishop Gföllner's pastoral letter of January 1933 stated that although one could not be a good Catholic while being a Nazi, it was the duty of all Catholics to adopt a "moral form of antisemitism. . . . Our modern society . . . should . . . provide a strong barrier against all the intellectual rubbish and moral slime which, coming largely from Jewry, threatens to flood the world."[105]

Hitler and other Nazi leaders—some having previously served as Church officials and theology students—at least gave the impression that they were devout Catholics.[106] Although most Nazis came from a Protestant background, a disproportionate number of the leaders of the Final Solution were Catholics. Austria gave birth to Adolf Hitler, Adolf Eichmann, Ernst Kaltenbruner, Odilo Globocnik, Rudolf Hoess, and Franz Stangl, most of whom were raised in religious families. Other, non-Austrian, Catholics were Josef Goebbels, Heinrich Himmler (the young Himmler had written, "Come what may, I shall always love God, pray to Him, and adhere to the Catholic Church and defend it, even if I should be expelled from it"; he did not formally leave the Church until 1936[107]), Reinhard Heydrich, and Julius Streicher.

Despite Hitler's assertions that his antisemitism occurred later, like most human beings he learned most of his prejudices as a child. The Austrian Church taught its parishioners, as Austrian Bishop Keppler wrote, that the Jews "are a thorn in the flesh of Christian peoples, suck their blood, enslave . . . , and contaminate [their] culture and morality."[108] In 1896, when Hitler was seven years old, a professor at the seminary for priests in Salzburg, Dr. Schöpf, wrote this analysis of antisemitism in the *Wiener Kalendar*

(Vienna Calendar) in connection with the alleged ritual murder of Andreas of Rinn, which was imagined to have occurred in 1492:

> Hatred and revulsion [of the Jew] are implanted in the heart of the child while he is still small. . . . He is told horror tales of blood-suckers and blood libels. . . . The kindly grandmother takes her grandchild to the Jew's stone [in the church] at Hall [where the Jews had allegedly murdered St. Andreas of Rinn] and points to the cruel features. The child is intimidated and cannot free himself of the fearful image. . . . The face of the Jews is distorted to the point where doubts are raised as to whether Jews are human. [On Good Friday], the day of the crucifixion, the *Perfidi Judaei* prayer is recited. The priest must think that the Church itself, in its very hymns, abhors the Jews as *perfidia gens [treacherous people]*, and thus our pious man, *nolens volens* [willingly or unwillingly], becomes an antisemite.[109]

When Hitler was ten years' old, a publication of Catholic Kindergarten stories described Andreas' death and it terms the Jews "these inhuman people."[110]

In Linz, when Adolf was a boy, Germans publicly demonstrated against Jews. Alois, Hitler's father, and Maria, his mother, were also most likely antisemitic. The only teacher he admired was an antisemitic historian and politician.[111] At the Staatsrealschule in Steyr, Hitler did have further contact with Catholic teachings that most likely dealt with the Jews. He took religion classes, where his grades ranged from adequate to satisfactory.[112] The young Hitler was impressed by the masses and sermons at the local Catholic Church. Besides, for two years he received religious instruction at the choir school of the Benedictine monastery at Lambach, where he served as altar boy and choirboy. At this time he developed the ambition of perhaps becoming a priest himself—an intention approved by his devout mother and even his anticlerical father. As he wrote in *Mein Kampf*, "I had an excellent opportunity to intoxicate myself with the solemn splendor of the brilliant church festivals. As was only natural, the abbot seemed to me, as the village priest had once seemed to my father, the highest and most desirable ideal."[113] If the attitudes toward Jews of the abbot Hitler so admired were characteristic of the time, then they were anti-Jewish. As a teenager, he commented to his friend Kubizek as they passed Linz's small synagogue in the Bethlehemstrasse, "That does not belong here in Linz." Moreover, although Hitler talked about race *ad nauseam*, he nevertheless wrote in his autobiography that of the few Jews who lived in his hometown it was their religion and not their race that distinguished them from the other German Austrians. "I saw no distinguishing feature but the strange religion."[114]

Hitler most likely arrived in Vienna already a Catholic antisemite. In Vienna he was struck by the numerous eastern European Jews with Orthodox dress and manners.[115] Hitler wrote: "Among our people the personification of the devil as the symbol of all evil assumes the living shape of the Jew."[116] This image was Catholic, not just Hitlerian or Nazi. This kind of antisemitism spread wherever Catholicism spread. In Vienna, a fellow vagrant, Reinhold Hansich, remembered that Hitler "would hang around the night shelters, living on bread and soup he got there, and discussing politics" and ranting "about conspiracies and Jewish plots."[117]

In Vienna, Hitler was also able to familiarize himself with the Catholic antisemitism of Karl Lueger—the leading Austrian antisemitic politician at the end of the nineteenth and turn of the twentieth century. As discussed in Chapter 6, Lueger was Mayor of Vienna, representative to the Austrian Parliament, and head of the Christian-Social Party (also known as the Antisemitic Party). Although Hitler objected to the Christian-Social's "half-hearted" antisemitism, he wrote that "[i]f Dr. Karl Lueger had lived in Germany, he would have been ranked among the great minds of our people."[118] It was on the twenty-eighth anniversary of Lueger's death that Hitler ordered the German invasion of Austria.

Hitler claimed that while recuperating behind the lines from a wounded leg, he discovered that Jewish "slackers" dominated the war bureaucracy and that "the Jew robbed the whole nation and pressed it beneath his domination." There is further evidence that during the war Hitler believed that Germany would lose because "invisible enemies of the German people were more of a danger than the enemy's biggest cannon." Germany's sudden defeat, in Hitler's view, could not be put upon the Army nor General Ludendorff and the other military leaders, but it had to be blamed on Bolsheviks, democrats, and especially the scheming Jews[119]—"a gang of depraved and despicable criminals." In November of 1918, a Pasewalk priest relayed to the war-wounded in the nearby German military hospital that the war was lost and on the very next day, an armistice was to be declared not only ending the war but also ending the very structure of imperial Germany. Corporal Hitler later wrote that "I staggered and stumbled back to my ward and buried my aching head between the blankets and pillow."[120] Ian Kershaw concluded that, although Austrian Catholic antisemitism was always part of Hitler's persona, his *Judenhaß* did not flower until after World War I triggered, with Hitler's fantasy about his adopted nation being stabbed in the back (the *Dolchstoßlegende*) by unGerman forces, in particular Jews. Kershaw concluded that Hitler authentically believed all the hatred he spewed against the Jews.[121]

Later, Hitler showed that he was also aware of the history of theological antagonism toward the Jews and he privately expressed his admiration for the anti-Jewish ideas of "all genuine Christians of outstanding calibre." He mentioned St. John Chrysostom, Pope St. Gregory VII (who, along with

Revelations and Pope Pius IX, used the phrase, "synagogue of Satan"), St. Thomas Aquinas,[122] Martin Luther, and others.

In his well-known 1936 meeting with Bishop Berning and Msg. Steinmann, Hitler told Pope Pius XI's German representatives, "I reject that [physical racist] book by Rosenberg. It was written by a Protestant. It is not a party book. . . . as a Catholic I never feel comfortable in the evangelical church or its structures . . . as for the Jews, I am just carrying on with the same policy which the Catholic Church has adopted for fifteen hundred years, when it has regarded the Jews as parasites and pushed them into ghettos, etc., because it knew what the Jews were like. I don't put race above religion, but I do see the danger in the representatives of this race for church and state, and perhaps I am doing Christianity a great service."[123] As Bacharach noted, Hitler had absorbed "the terminology used by Catholic preachers and writers [that] was permeated with images taken from death, from the demonic world, and from the insect kingdom, doomed to extermination."[124] We have no report as to what the prelates replied, if anything. But they later described the talks as "cordial and to the point."[125] Bishop Berning, a member of Goering's State Council, in June 1936, visited a number of concentration camps to remind the prisoners "of the duty of obedience and fidelity towards people and state that was demanded by their religious faith." He also praised the guards for "their work in the camp" and ended his visit with three *Siegheils*. The Church raised him to Archbishop in 1949.[126] Steinmann was the Berlin Vicar-General who greeted Catholic faithfuls with "Heil Hitler."[127]

Hitler's public speeches and private conversations indicate that Catholic antisemitism inspired many of his anti-Jewish ideas, which paralleled and interacted with those of his listeners and much of it was antisemitic interpretations of the Gospels.[128] On April 12, 1922, Hitler stated: "I read through the [Gospel] passage that tells us how the Lord rose at last in His might and seized the scourge to drive out of the Temple the brood of vipers and adders. How terrific was His fight against the Jewish poison. Today, after two thousand years, with deepest emotion I realize more profoundly than ever before the fact that it was for this that He had to shed His blood upon the Cross."[129]

In *Mein Kampf*, Hitler called Judaism a "monstrous" religion and the Jew a "product of . . . religious education."[130] One of Hitler's most quoted lines from this book is: "In defending myself against the Jews I am acting for the Lord."[131] This phrase appeared on calendars and posters displayed all over Germany. From May 17 to May 23 of 1936, it served the SS as their "Motto of the Week."

Hitler's 1936 speech to political leaders of the Nazi party at Nuremberg included "an astonishing montage of Biblical texts," especially from the Gospels of Matthew and John.[132] Hitler seemed to consider himself, perhaps only for public consumption, a Roman Catholic. Hitler participated in regular Communion for the first thirty years of his life.[133] Until the very end in 1945, he continued to allow the state to withdraw a tithe for the Catholic Church from his salary[134] without ever publicly indicating that he was a man without belief in the Catholic faith. Even after he came to power, he often times made gifts to small Church congregations. His public image was always that of "a religious man interested in the church."[135] Hitler wrote that "the religious doctrines and institutions of the leader's people must always remain inviolable."[136]

Hitler was aware of the Christian ritual-murder defamation. Between 1880 and 1945 there were as many instances of this defamation—especially in Eastern and Central Europe, but even in the United States—as during the entire Middle Ages.[137] In a private conversation with Dietrich Eckart, Hitler's closest friend up to the 1923 Munich *Putsch*,[138] Hitler observed that "the Jews had continued to perform ritual murders."[139] Many areas of Germany and Austria revered local saints, such as St. Andreas of Rinn previously mentioned, as "martyrs of the Jews." In the 1920s and 1930s, Julius Streicher's Nazi journal, *Der Stürmer*—the most popular of Nazi publications and Hitler's personal favorite—was filled with references to ritual murder and other religious accusations against Jews and in particular their association with the devil. Streicher considered Catholic myths about Jewish ritual murder to be "historical documents."[140] In 1926, *Der Stürmer* published a story and cartoon on Jewish ritual murder. The cartoon showed three Jewish men drinking blood from a slaughtered blonde Polish woman. *Der Stürmer's* famous ritual-murder issue in May 1, 1934 contained many articles on the subject and a front-page drawing of stereotypical Jews catching the blood from the severed veins of blonde women and children who were hanged upside down.[141] After an international uproar, Hitler banned this issue of *Der Stürmer* on the grounds that Streicher's comparison of the Christian sacrament of communion with Jewish ritual murder was an insult to Christianity.[142]

In 1938, in a conversation with Hans Frank, his Minister of Justice, Hitler noted that "In the Gospel, when Pilate refuses to crucify Jesus, the Jews call out to him: 'His blood be upon us and upon our children's children.' Perhaps I shall have to put this curse into effect."[143] On February 24, 1939, three weeks after his Reichstag speech threatening the Jews with destruction should war start, Hitler stated that "Today the Jewish question is no longer a German problem, but a European one." The German people's needs must be satisfied by Jewish expropriation. In this sense, "we are true Christians!"[144] From the Church's point of view, Hitler's works have never been put on the Index of Forbidden Books, nor has he or any other Catholic who participated in the "Final Solution" ever been officially excommunicated from the Church for war crimes.[145] As late as 2003, a Forsa Institute study indicated that 9 percent of Germans explained the Jews' troubles as due to their murder of Christ.[146]

CHAPTER 8

France

We never do evil so completely and cheerfully as when we do it out of religious conviction.

Blaise Pascal, Pensée *794.*

The Enlightenment[1]

Despite changes in the intellectual milieu of French society during the Enlightenment, almost all the French believed the worst about Jews. As Roland Mousnier in his study of France under its absolute monarchs observed, both the average and the educated people regarded Jews with "religious hatred, jealousy, [and] fear." Jews were still blamed for crucifying Christ, "the greatest of sacrileges, the greatest sin against the Holy Spirit."[2] French Catholics believed that the Jews were also cursed by God and in league with the devil. The Jews awaited their Messiah, a conqueror who would allow them to dominate the world. Some Catholics believed that the Jews' malevolence was so deep-rooted that conversion to Catholicism could do nothing to change them. Jews remained Jews: an unassimilable race.[3] No wonder King Louis XIII reissued the Edict of Expulsion in 1615.

Many religious writers of the period declared the Jews to be worse than heretics and witches, since heretics and witches joined Satan voluntarily and individually, whereas the Jewish people were predestined to be eternal associates of the devil and enemies of Christ. In 1609, King Henry IV commissioned Pierre de l'Ancre, a royal counsellor of the Bordeaux Parliament, as grand inquisitor of witches to clean the Pays de Labourd of witchcraft. As Trevor-Roper described de l'Ancre, this "bigoted Catholic" was a "gleeful executioner" who "gloried in his Jesuit education."[4] He had hundreds of witches, including several priests, burned.

Denouncing the superstitious indecency of Judaism, the widely published de l'Ancre regarded Jews not only as witches[5] but also as cruel and rapacious murderers of Catholics who poisoned the wells and forcibly circumcised and ritually murdered Catholic children.[6] He believed that God had withdrawn grace from the Jews who were condemned to crawl about the daytime world like snakes and roam the nights like wolves.[7] Observing that "filth [is] the attribute common to Jews and pigs" and that Jews "were more perfidious and faithless than demons," he concluded that "the Jews deserve every execration, and as destroyers of all divine and human majesty, they merit the greatest torment. Slow fire, melted lead, boiling oil, pitch, wax, and sulfur mixed together would not make tortures fitting, painful, and cruel enough for the punishment of such great and horrible crimes as these people commonly commit."[8]

Both priests and lay people were taught that Judaism had no salvific value and that Jews were paradigmatically hardhearted and diabolically apostate.[9] Every theological text, every catechism, and every author who wrote about the Jews—including many of the best intentioned—expounded these attitudes.[10] The catechism of Jacques Bossuet (d. 1704), the influential bishop of Meaux, orator, historian, and Louis XIV's "official Churchman,"[11] asked, "Why did God cause all these miracles upon the death of His Son?" Bossuet's answer: "As a testimony against the Jews." Bossuet tells us that God favored the Jews so long as they kept to the true religion. But once they rejected the Christ that was predicted in their own scriptures, their legacy passed to the Catholics. "Judea is nothing to God anymore, nor to religion, nor are the Jews; . . . their ruins [are] scattered over the whole earth." He explained that the Jews were condemned to suffer in Diaspora forever, "carrying with them the mark of [God's] vengeance, a monstrous people . . . now the evil spirit and the detestation of the world."[12] The catechism of Abbé André de Fleury (d. 1743), an important influence on Louis XV, stated: "Did Jesus have enemies? Yes, the carnal Jews. . . . What became of the Jews? They were reduced to servitude and scattered throughout the world."[13]

Blaise Pascal (1632–62) approached the Jewish situation as a traditional Catholic. In his early years he was a physicist and mathematician, and near the end of his short life he underwent a mystical experience and turned his mind to religion and the reformist Jansenist movement. His notes for a defense of Christianity were published posthumously as the *Pensées*, which reflect his profound Catholic faith.

Pascal wrote about the sanctity, dignity, humility, happiness, reasonableness, virtuousness, and amiability of the Catholic soul.[14] He based his faith on Jesus. "Without Jesus Christ man is mired in . . . vice, misery, error, darkness, death, despair. . . . Apart from Jesus Christ, we do not know . . . our life, our death, nor God, nor ourselves."[15]

Although Pascal admired the longevity of Judaism and some Jewish values,[16] he disapproved of most aspects of Jews and Judaism. He listed Judaism as one of the "false religions"[17] and the Jews as "irreconcilable enemies" of Catholics.[18] Typical Jews were "carnal," whereas "spiritual" Jews were really Old Testament Christians.[19] Authentic Judaism did not consist of the traditional elements of Judaism, such as the fatherhood of Abraham, circumcision, sacrifices, ceremonies, Ark, Temple, Jerusalem, law, and covenant with Moses. Only the love of Christ characterized real Jews, as well as real Christians. Pascal repeatedly quoted from the Jewish prophets and Christian Scriptures to support his proposition that God had made a new covenant with the Messiah, Jesus of Nazareth, and annulled the old covenant with the Jews. Jerusalem was rejected and Rome admitted to glory.[20] The Jews sold, betrayed, and crucified "the just one," Jesus Christ.[21] Slaves of sin and rejected by God, Jews have become fruitless, ungrateful, unbelieving, and blind.[22] The Jews still exist under a curse but have been scattered abroad[23] "in perpetual misery," in servitude to Christians, and "in frightful darkness" as proof of, and witness to, Jesus's divine nature and the truth of the Catholic faith.[24]

Voltaire

François Marie Arouet (d. 1778), called Voltaire, was perhaps the most important figure of the French Enlightenment.[25] He grew up surrounded by religious antisemitism in his culture, his family, his education, and the Church of his youth. Although he became ferociously anticlerical, Voltaire remained as faithful to the anti-Jewish Catholic animosities that he inherited from his upbringing as any pious Catholic. His mother's friend and the young Voltaire's godfather and "spiritual father,"[26] François de Castagner (the abbé de Chateauneuf) made the young boy memorize and recite antisemitic poetry, like the *Moïsade*, which attacked theology in general and criticized the political uses of religion. It argued that Moses deceived the Jews and invented the Ten Commandments to dominate them politically.[27] Like Diderot, he was educated by the Jesuits at College Louis le Grand in Paris.[28] who exposed him to the Bible and politics that had an indelible impact on his mind and morals.[29]

Arthur Hertzberg regards Voltaire as the great link between pagan and modern antisemitism, a man who established a new kind of neopagan antisemitism, which was secular and cultural rather than religious.[30] But the matter is not so simple. First, Hertzberg accurately indicates that Voltaire saw Jews as having permanently evil traits. Although this may be considered a form of racism, it is also the old Christian notion that Jews reiterate their inherent evil in every generation. Second, although obviously anticlerical, Voltaire was also a deeply religious man, a theist who believed in God, although not in the Church. "My brothers," Voltaire wrote, "religion is the secret voice of God who speaks to all men."[31] Despite his antagonism to the Church, he asserted the existence of a Supreme Being, a loving God the Father. "I am not a Christian, so that I can love you [God] better. They have made you a tyrant, but in you I have discovered a father."[32] Third, while it is true that Voltaire did not emphasize the deicide accusation against the Jews, he came close to admiring Jesus as Son of God and resented the Jews as rejecting Jesus and stubbornly persisting as Jews who were criminal, usurious, and murderers of Christians.[33]

Voltaire was a deistic rationalist who hated Jewish "superstition," but a more basic idea was his traditional Catholic anti-Jewishness, which runs like a sewer through his writings. He was a man who hated the Church but loved Catholic antisemitism. He distanced himself from the Catholic myth of Jewish host profanation but he admitted that something about this defamation still fascinated him. Ritual murder also attracted him.[34] He told the Jews, "Your priests have always sacrificed human victims with their sacred hands."[35]

In the most systematic exposition of his opinions, the *Philosophical Dictionary* (of its 118 articles, more than 30 attack the Jews), Voltaire seemed obsessed with much of the traditional assault on the Jews. In the article, "Jew," the longest in the book, Voltaire followed the traditional religious attack.[36] He maintained that the Jews' "character was at all times to be cruel; and their fate to be punished. . . . They are still vagabonds upon the earth, and abhorred by men, yet affirming that heaven and earth and all mankind were created for them. . . . In short, we find in them only an ignorant and barbarous people, who have long united the most sordid avarice with the most detestable superstition and the most invincible hatred for every people by whom they are tolerated and enriched."[37]

Voltaire implied that if the Jews were unwilling to abandon their Jewish nature, Christians, presumably not including himself, would burn them again in "holocausts."[38] Frank Manuel has recently argued that Voltaire's "ranting" about the ancient Jews' cruelties probably reflected his own cruel antagonisms toward contemporary Jews.[39] Evocative of St. Augustine's association of the Jews with Cain, in a letter written in February 1776, Voltaire argued that all Jews should be marked on their forehead with a sign, "fit to be hanged."[40]

Other articles of his dictionary demonstrate the value-inversions contained in patristic and medieval anti-Jewish defamations. Voltaire agreed with

St. Jerome that the Jewish Holy Land was "the rubbish heap of nature."[41] In "Antropofages—Cannibals," he asked, "why shouldn't the Jews have been cannibals? It was the only thing that was needed to make the people of God the most abominable on earth."[42] In "Genesis," he converted Jewish monotheism into pagan polytheism and opined that it was these Jewish "gods" who had intercourse with human women. His essay on Ezekiel asserts that the Jews ate their bread "smeared with human excrement."[43]

Although Voltaire appeared to reject the Catholic milieu in which he was raised, he sometimes asserted his Catholic identity. He ended his letter to Isaac de Pinto, a Dutch-born Sephardic financier who wrote to him, with the invocation of a title he had purchased in 1746: "*Voltaire, chrétien, gentilhomme ordinaire de la chambre du Roi Très Chrétien.*" "Voltaire, Christian, gentleman in waiting to the Very Christian King."[44] This great opponent of Christianity invoked his title again in 1776 when he argued against six Jews. In these instances, at least, when sides had to be chosen, Voltaire's "rational" attack on the Jews reduced itself to "we Christians against you Jews." In an appendix to the *Philosophical Dictionary*, Voltaire continued to identify himself with Christianity, haranguing fictitious Jews on its behalf.[45]

Voltaire's novels—*Zadig*, *The Princess of Babylon*, and *Candide*—also contain anti-Jewish stereotypes of dishonest, usurious, and lecherous Jews. Thus Voltaire's work helped ensure that antisemitic stereotypes would persist among the educated members of French society.

The French Revolution and Napoleon

Discussion of Jewish emancipation arose first in Germany but emancipation came about first in France.[46] Before the Revolution a pragmatic day-to-day tolerance did exist for the few Jews who lived in France but not until 1784 did Louis XVI abolish the body tax on Jews, a tax also imposed on cattle. When just before the meeting of the Estates General in 1789 a call went out for *cahiers des doléances* notes of complaint, many concerned the Jews and demanded more restrictions.[47]

Some who proclaimed themselves friends of the Jews nonetheless wanted them to assimilate completely, that is, to end their separatism by ceasing to be Jews.[48] Although a proponent of Jewish emancipation and citizenship, the Jesuit abbé Henri-Baptiste Grégoire wanted the Jews to convert to Catholicism so that they would lose their degenerative physical, moral, and political traits. His liberal attitude toward the possibility of Jewish improvement was rare, since most French people assumed that Jews would always be cursed by the biological defects Grégoire catalogued.[49] But like the neo-Jansenists of his time,

Grégoire believed that it was wrong to persecute the Jews and that the Jews could be persuaded to adopt the true faith by means of Christian preaching, charity, and prayer. To this end, he advocated that the Church and state oppose intolerance.

He found much to admire in the Jews. He praised the kindness and charity that Jews demonstrated toward each other and the "talents and virtues [that] shine forth in them wherever they begin to be treated as men." He sought to "reform their hearts"[50] and he argued that Jews were "born with the same [innate] capacities as ourselves." He not only questioned the right of Christians to carry out retribution against Jews but also argued that Christian revenge had been in part responsible for the Jews' miserable state.[51]

Sometimes, however, Grégoire wrote more like an intolerant priest than a liberal politician. He believed the deicide charge to be true, "the blood of J[esus] C[hrist] has fallen on the Jews as they desired," and he wrote of the Jews' "wretched corruption."[52] He also argued that Jews should be forced out of urban areas and coerced into other professions in order to break the hold of the tyrannical rabbis, to mollify their animosity against Christians, and to make them more honest in their business practices.[53] In 1789, he wrote that the Jews' "abominable meanness produces base actions."[54] When the Ashkenazic Jews of Eastern France refused to assimilate, Grégoire requested that the government force them to accept reform. Admiring only those Jews who adopted French Catholic ways, Grégoire could not appreciate any inherent value in Jewishness.[55] He called Yiddish a "Teutonic-Hebraic rabbinic jargon German Jews use, which only serves to deepen ignorance or to mask trickery."[56] He condemned the Talmud as a "vast reservoir, I almost said a cesspool, where the frenzies of the human mind have accumulated."[57] He called Jews "parasitic plants which eat away at the substance of the tree they attach themselves to."[58]

At the beginning of the Great French Revolution, a combination of anti-ecclesiastical radicals, like the Alsacian deputy Rewbell, and traditional Catholics persuaded the National Assembly deputies to defeat the extension of civil liberties to Jews. Abbé Jean Maury and Bishop Henry de la Fare of Nancy led the anti-Jewish forces. Maury argued that the Jews were religiously alien to France and inherently evil. De la Fare agreed and added that "the people detest them. . . . They claim that the Jews speculate in grain, they take up too much room, they buy the most beautiful houses, and soon they will own the whole city."[59] On December 24, 1789, the day following the debate on Jewish emancipation, the Assembly awarded civil rights to Protestants but not to Jews. In January 1790, the Assembly granted citizenship to the three thousand or so Sephardic Jews living in southwest France and in September 1791 to thirty thousand Ashkenazic Jews of Alsace and Lorraine.[60]

But the French goverment's generosity was limited. Freedom was awarded only to those Jews who explicitly renounced their membership in Jewish communities, and although the French government assumed the debts of the Christian Churches, they refused to do so for the Jewish communities.[61] At this point the Revolution was dechristianized and clerical representatives were not present in the National Assembly. Had they been present, the vote in favor of Jewish emancipation was close enough that they could have defeated it.[62]

The level of antisemitism remained high during the Revolution and Napoleonic Empire. Antisemites charged first the king and then Napoleon with favoring Jews or with being Jewish themselves.[63] Reflecting the same attitudes as peasants and local officials, antisemitic agitators in eastern France railed against a potential Jewish inundation. In Alsace on Good Fridays, villagers burned an image of Judas, chanting, "Sticks! sticks! to burn the everlasting Jew!"[64] Alsatian farmers flailed their grain while calling out loud the names of Jews, "Itzig/Nathel/Gimbel." These peasants believed that Jews buried their dead with soil from the Holy Land so that they would have a supply of stones to throw at Jesus.[65]

In this context of widespread French antisemitism, Napoleon suspended the payments on debts to Jews of eastern France in May 1806, although he took no action against Christian usury, and called an assembly of 112 Jewish notables (the Parisian Sanhedrin) to meet in Paris in July. Napoleon's advisor on Jewish affairs, Count Louis Molé, who advocated the repeal of Jewish emancipation,[66] informed the assembly that complaints about Jewish "evil" had reached the throne; he warned that their fate would be "irrevocably fixed by a Christian Prince." Napoleon presented the assembly with a dozen questions about Jews, Judaism, and Jewish relations with Christians to determine whether Judaism could be harmonized with French law and customs. The Jewish notables, who knew that French Jews had been loyally fighting in France's wars for fifteen years, were especially offended when they were asked: "Do Jews born in France, and treated by the law as French citizens, consider France as their country? Are they bound to defend it?" The assembly replied that French Jews had chosen France as their nation and considered themselves "Frenchmen in France; and they consider as equally sacred and honorouble the bounden duty of defending their country. . . . To such a pitch is this sentiment carried among them, that during the last war, French Jews have been seen fighting desperately against other Jews, the subjects of countries then at war with France."[67]

In February 1807, the emperor convened another Jewish Sanhedrin, which reconfirmed that nothing in Jewish culture contravened Jewish participation in French society as reliable citizens. This gave Napoleon the religious sanction he desired. In March 1808, Napoleon ordered the creation of a system of consistories to oversee Jewish affairs, although, unlike similar decrees for Christians, the state was not to pay the salaries of Jewish clergy. A second decree—known to the Jews as the *décret infâme*—postponed, suspended, or reduced the payment of money owed to the Jews living in the east of France; restricted Jewish trade; and prevented Jewish conscripts from hiring substitutes as Christians could.[68] Judaism itself was not granted equal status with France's Christian religions until, in 1831 under Louis-Philippe,[69] the regime agreed to pay rabbis from state coffers as they had been paying Catholic priests and Protestant ministers since the Revolution. The last discriminatory Jewish oath was not abolished until 1846.

Christians in French-occupied nations, under the influence of Christian antisemitism, rioted against both French-inspired liberties and the Jews. In the Roman Vespers of 1798, Catholic mobs rebelled against republicans and Jews residing in Rome. Carrying a crucifix and a statue of Mary at their head, a crowd in February murdered every Frenchman, republican, and Jew they met. After the French left, Pope Leo XII returned the Jews, who had been liberated by Bonaparte, to the ghetto.[70] In 1819, anti-Jewish riots spread from Germany into France.[71]

Nineteenth-century France

Since the Great French Revolution of the late eighteenth century, nearly every shade of the French socio-political spectrum[72] has displayed the taint of theological antisemitism. At the end of the nineteenth century, the French-Jewish writer Bernard Lazare observed that both Christianity and religious antisemitism were "born on Calvary."[73] Most French Catholics identified the Jews as aliens who, along with Freemasons and Protestants, were plotting with the forces of modernism, capitalism, and democracy to de-Catholicize France.[74] In the the first half of the nineteenth century, Fleury la Serve, author of *Génie de Christianisme*, wrote that "Inasmuch as Lyon is almost entirely Catholic, Judaism is here more disliked, mistrusted, and avoided than anywhere else."[75] Meditating on Venice's Jewish cemetery in 1833, the writer and diplomat François de Chateaubriand (d. 1848) thought about "everyone's contempt and hate for those who sacrificed Christ. A quarantine of the Jewish race has been proclaimed from the height of Calvary and will remain until the end of time."[76] In 1836, writing in the conservative *Revue des Deux Mondes*, Charles Didier described the Jews as morally degenerate, rootless, and parasitical. Following the traditional Christian position as well as the revival of Catholicism in post-Napoleonic France, he compared the Jews to Cain, who was marked "as the first murderer of the world" and condemned to eternal rejection. "In killing the son of the carpenter, the apostle of love and liberty, the Jews have placed humanity and God Himself on the cross."[77]

Liberal Catholics,[78] like the priest Félicité de Lamennais, likewise reaffirmed Catholic triumphalism in regard to the Jews.[79] Though he grew disillusioned with the Church, Lamennais repeated its traditional teachings about the Jews[80]: he believed that Jews were blind to the truth of Christianity and had thereby been replaced by Christians as the true Israel. The Diaspora and persecutions of Jews historically proved this fall from grace.[81] Lamennais called the Jews "coarsely carnal" and a "perverse race" and he called the Jewish leadership the "enemies who plotted [Jesus'] destruction." The Jews, "formerly God's people," had become "the salve of the human kind . . . on whom any amount of suffering and disgrace has been unable to rid them of their pride nor their curse." Lamennais regarded the contemporary Jews as sinful as those who killed his Lord; they were inherently evil and capable of any crime. The Jews murdered Christ and his "blood will forever be on them."[82] He concluded that the Jewish people "made itself into slaves; suffering and disgrace have become its nature. . . . It exists silently on earth always as strangers, its course painful and vagabond. All peoples have seen it pass; all have been horrified by it; it was marked with a most terrible sign of Cain on its forehead, a hand of iron had written, DEICIDE!"[83]

Charles Fourier (1772–1837) was a utopian socialist and radical antisemite whose charges against the Jews ran the gamut from parasitism to usury. His writings include themes of betrayal, intolerance, and deceit drawn from Catholic antisemitism. Claiming to be the "prophetic postcursor" of Jesus,"[84] Fourier imagined France taken over by "the Jew Iscariot." He called the Jews "the enemies of God," and he worried that if France held many more Jews it "would have become one huge synagogue." The Jewish religion, he wrote, "furthers vices [and] gives its adherents a dangerously immoral character."[85]

Most of Fourier's followers were antisemitic.[86] Typical was Alphonse Toussenel (d. 1885), who was another early socialist who based his anti-Jewish ideas on the traditional Christian association of Jews with the immoral uses of money. Toussenel was much more influential than his teacher, in part because his writings were also popular among conservatives. He condemned the victimization of Christian France by the Jews, whom he considered the kings of the world.[87] Toussenel believed that the Jews who controlled France economically were also enemies of Christ and Christianity. Jewish exploitation of French society, he argued, was essentially anti-Christian.[88] Like many French Catholic writers, Toussenel regarded the Christian Testament as morally superior to the Old, which was filled with murder and incest. He criticized both Jews and Protestants for preferring the Jewish Scriptures over the Christian Testament that Catholics revered.[89] "I do not call the people of

God the people that put to death mercilessly all the prophets inspired by the Holy Spirit, that crucified the Redeemer of men and insulted him on the Cross. . . . If the Jewish people had truly been the people of God they would not have put to death the son of God; they would not continue exploiting through parasitism and usury all the workers whom Christ wanted to redeem and who are the militia of God."[90]

The religious nature of this early socialist antisemitism manifested itself in the Catholic theologian and writer, Henri Roger Gougenot des Mousseaux (d. 1876), a follower of both Fourier and Toussenel who also used material from liberals like Jules Michelet and Ernest Renan and conservatives like Louis de Bonald. (In 1806, de Bonald was perhaps the first French writer to accuse Jews specifically of being a state within a state, "état dans l'état."[91]) In his book, Le Juif, Le Judaïsm et la judaïsation des peuples chrétiens [The Jew, Judaism, and the Judaization of the Christian Peoples]—which Norman Cohn called the "the Bible of modern antisemitism" and which was published in German by Alfred Rosenberg in Munich in 1921[92]—Gougenot des Mousseaux used the triumphalistic Christian argument that God had rejected the satanic Jews as his chosen because they killed Christ and revered the Talmud. Gougenot des Mousseaux maintained that the Jews were mortal enemies of Christians. That the Jews received rights equal to Christians in France under the Revolution and Napoléon was scandalous. Gougenot des Mousseaux believed in Jewish ritual murder and held that Jews, "the representatives on earth of the spirit of darkness," conspired along with the freemasons to destroy Christian values and control the world. Inspired, he claimed, by his reading of 2 Thessalonians 2—where Paul describes the coming of "the lawless one" who exalts himself above all others, works with Satan, and whom Jesus will destroy—Gougenot des Mousseaux identified the Jews with the Antichrist. Pope Pius IX blessed his work.[93] The Nazi ideologist Alfred Rosenberg, edited and published the first German edition in 1921.[94]

Catholic Antisemitism Before the Dreyfus Affair
Until the start of World War II, the Catholic Church actively supported every antisemitic movement that arose in France.[95] For most Catholics, lay and clerical, Jews remained Cains, Judases, and deicides. The Talmud was an "anti-catechism" in which the Jews learned, "like serpents, all their vices."[96]

Louis Veuillot (d. 1880), one of the century's most influential French-Catholics, wrote in l'Univers religieux (which he edited) that Jewish children could be baptized without parental consent in order to "snatch a soul from Satan."[97] Supporting the kidnapping of the Jewish Mortara child, Veuillot contemptuously attacked the Jews who opposed him as "the deicide people" who ritually murdered Christians. Jews were a foreign element in Catholic

France that plotted to control all of French society.[98] Veuillot railed against the Jews for having substituted the Talmud—the source of their evil—for their scriptures. "The [Jewish] hate for the Christian, the contempt for the Christian, the skill with which the Jew deceives the Christian, the hope of dominating him, crushing, destroying the Christian, that is the spirit of the Talmud, which is now almost totally the spirit of Judaism."[99] The Church received all of "Christ's light," whereas the Synagogue was "blind and unfaithful." Christianity remained the true Mosaic Judaism perfected by God's promises and the coming of the Messiah. Contemporary Judaism was a "Pharisaic heresy" of true Judaism, "it is Talmudism."[100] Veuillot quoted a Parisian Jew as having said, "We will destroy you [Catholics]."[101]

Between 1882 and 1886, shortly after French primary education became mandatory, free, and secular,[102] French priests published twenty antisemitic books. These books blamed France's ills on "the deicidal people."[103] In the 1890s, before the Dreyfus Affair broke out, Catholic priests and writers argued that Jews should be forbidden to own land in France and should be ghettoized, expelled from France, or hung from the gallows "to expiate the harm they have done us."[104]

The Catholic newspaper *La Croix* and the Catholic-oriented *La Libre parole*, two of the most influential antisemitic papers in France, expressed hostility to Jews years before the Dreyfus Case in 1894. A leader of the Augustinian Fathers of the Assumption, which was a relatively new French congregation whose goal was to fight irreligion through education and the press, and who saw their mission as a war of words and actions against the Jews and the Catholic order that published *la Croix*, argued that the Jews were crucifying the Church now just as they had done to Christ. Both Christ and the Church were "betrayed, sold, jeered at, beaten, covered with spittle, and crucified by the Jews."[105] In 1884, *La Croix* accused the Jews of "fomenting hatred of Christ, . . . overthrowing Christian societies and hounding the Church and the pope without mercy." The Jews were a "deicide people" and "enemies of the Christian name." Dominating the economy of France, the Jews must be feared and fought just as they were during the Middle Ages.[106]

In 1808, Jews comprised 0.16 percent of the French population; in 1897, after the influx of Russian Jews, the Jewish population had climbed to only 0.19 percent. Yet in the two decades before and after the Dreyfus Affair, 3 percent of the French officer corps consisted of Jews. (As late as 1939, Jews comprised only three-fourths of 1 percent of the French population.[107]) Aware of this overrepresentation of Jews in the French officer corps, a May 1892 article in *La Libre parole* argued that the army should remain Jew-free. Denying any religious prejudice and asserting that Jews were usurers, corrupt suppliers, and spies, the author noted that most soldiers felt "an instinctive repulsion against the sons of Israel." The Jew was and had always been incompatible with the army's duties, well-being, and honor. Once they controlled the army, the Jews would "assuredly be the masters of all France." The writer ended by noting that his articles were meant to encourage a "sacred battle" against the Jews.[108] In 1893, when Alfred Dreyfus was appointed as the only Jew on the General Staff, many high-ranking officers, like General Pierre Bonnefond, simply did not "want a Jew on the General Staff."[109]

Literary Antisemitism

For traditionalist Catholic writers like Eugène Scribe, the Wandering Jew (*Juif errant*) was the Antichrist. The Wandering Jew myth grew out of the Catholic Church's traditional anti-Jewish theology and reappeared after Jewish emancipation, nationalism, and racial theories provoked contemporary France to fear Jews.[110] Christians identified the Wandering Jew with the Jewish people who had murdered Jesus, suffered but not been wiped out, and wandered for millennia without a homeland.

Because there was no meaningful vocabulary of goodness concerning Jews that could naturally be affirmed within French culture,[111] hundreds of French artists found it easy to portray the falsely accused French-Jewish Captain Alfred Dreyfus, his supporters, and the Jews in repulsive ways—as devils, locusts, rats, serpents, monsters, vampires, Judases. At the same time, pro-Dreyfus artists could not find a convincing, positive image of Jews. The three greatest cartoonists of the time, Willette, Poiré, and Forain, were all antisemitic. Willette was raised in Dijon, the center of great antisemitic agitation, and his parents gave him religious paintings to stimulate his desire to learn. Poiré was a follower of the neo-fascist Marquis de Morès. Forain was raised in a very strict Catholic family and given a Catholic education. Once retired from cartooning, he spent much of his time painting religious works.

The Dreyfus Affair and Catholic Antisemitism

As the Jewish community in France became increasingly isolated, Catholic antisemitism increased dramatically.[112] By the time of the Dreyfus Affair, the Catholic Church, whose other "enemies"—Freemasons, Protestants, and freethinkers—were generally pro-Jewish, became the principal agent of anti-semitic activities.[113] Although the upper-level hierarchy did not intervene in the Dreyfus Affair, most priests and religious congregations[114] expressed hostility to Dreyfus and the Jews, as did the intellectuals, the army, the police, the students, and the crowd.[115] Many, if not most, French Catholic bourgeois saw the Jews—regardless of their typically French values of family, property, and nation—only as traditional opponents of Christianity.[116]

Religious antisemitism was prominent in education. Despite attempts during the 1890s to secularize education, Catholics expanded their own schools.[117] Almost 40 percent of French school children attended Catholic schools under the control of the Brothers of the Christian schools, who published antisemitic texts and regarded Dreyfus' guilt as much a dogma as the infallibility of the pope. Catholic schools in the southwest used a book recommended by several bishops that called the Jews "an accursed race since they sold Our Lord and failed to perceive His goodness. . . . They are dangerous and insatiable parasites who are to be found wherever there are crimes."[118]

During the 1880s and 1890s, more than one-third of the officers graduating from the French military academy at Saint-Cyr had studied in religious institutions, profoundly influenced by Jesuits and Assumptionists, leading antisemitic Catholic orders of the period.[119] Jean-Baptiste Billot, Minister of War, told the vice-president of the French Senate[120] that "I find myself in a den of Jesuits here. . . . The ministry has been invaded by pupils of the Jesuits."[121] When the same charge was made in the National Assembly by *dreyfusard* (Dreyfus-supporter) Socialist Jean Jaurès, a near riot ensued.[122] Many members of the General Staff were faithful readers of *La Croix* and Drumont's popular *La Libre parole*, a newspaper that claimed a daily circulation of three hundred thousand, which nurtured their antisemitic attitudes about Jews. (In 1886, Drumont published *La France Juive*, an incredibly popular antisemitic book.[123]) Between October and December 1894, the Jewish Captain Alfred Dreyfus was arrested, falsely accused of treason, and convicted in a court-martial procedure filled with irregularities.[124]

Nearly all of France, even the Jewish community, except for Dreyfus' own family, initially believed in his guilt.[125] Although Dreyfus may have had the opportunity to betray France, he did not have a motive. He was a nationalist, a conservative Jewish assimilationist, led an exemplary family and personal life, and had no need of the extra money that could be realized by selling secrets. A native of Alsace, then under Prussian-German occupation, Dreyfus loved France in a way that could be matched by only a few Catholic nationalists.[126]

Dreyfus was accused and convicted primarily because he was a Jew. France needed a scapegoat for her serious social, economic, financial, and political problems, and for most French Catholics, the Jews were the perfect scapegoats; they were France's Cains, Judases, Shylocks, and Wandering Jews.

Dreyfus and his circle understood that his Jewishness convicted him. Like many assimilated Jews, Alfred Dreyfus never felt his Jewishness so keenly as when antisemitism victimized him. Proud of his Jewish name, he was married in a Jewish ceremony to a Jewish woman. When depressed and desperate for comfort in Santé Prison in December 1894, he wrote to the Chief Rabbi of

France, Zadoc Kahn, who had married him and Lucie, to come to comfort him.[127] Shortly after his arrest, as well as after hearing the guilty verdict of the court martial, Dreyfus shouted in anguish: "My only crime is to have been born a Jew."[128] Once in prison, he moaned, "My misfortune is to be a Jew."[129] An early *dreyfusard*, Bernard Lazare, a Jewish nationalist, observed that "[b]ecause he was a Jew he was arrested. Because he was a Jew he was convicted. Because he was a Jew the voices of justice and of truth could not be heard in his favor."[130] Lazare was correct when just a few months after Dreyfus' arrest he wrote that the Jews were no longer physically confined to a ghetto but were surrounded by a hostile climate "of suspicion, of latent hatred, of prejudices all the more powerful because unavowed." The Jews could not escape from this kind of spiritual ghetto because it was created by Catholic France's almost complete rejection of the Jewish spirit.[131] Lazare insisted that "[b]ecause he [Dreyfus] was a Jew the voices of justice and of truth could not be heard in his favor."[132] Dreyfus' brother-in-law Joseph Valabrègue also saw the matter clearly. He asked how "entire families could be dishonored for the single reason that they observe a different religion from the majority of the nation."[133]

Catholics believed that the Jews were involved in all of France's recent disasters and difficulties: the disastrous loss of the war to Prussia in 1870–71, the civil war and the horrors of the Commune, Germany's "rape" of the eastern provinces, where the Dreyfus family still maintained its factories. Christian France was also paralyzed by a generalized fear of Germany, a recognition of the inadequacy of the army, a suspicion of spies, a perception of social change destroying valued traditions, a widespread disgust with financial scandals, with the crash of the conservative Catholic bank, the Union Générale, agricultural and financial disasters, and the loss of conservative Catholic influence and power in educational, social, economic, and political matters. Although the real culprit was the bank's Catholic director, the Union Générale's crash in 1882 was almost universally blamed on the Jews, Jewish financial manipulators, and the Rothschilds in particular. In April 1898, Charles Léandre published in *Le Rire* an iconic cartoon of Rothschild as a vampire with a bat-crown on his head, bat wings, and bat claws for hands encompassing the whole globe.[134]

In the nineteenth and twentieth centuries, Catholic teachings and liturgy "perpetually refreshed" antisemitism.[135] Even an author who emphasizes political considerations noted that "the oldest and most deeply rooted form of antisemitism [was] Christian—and essentially Catholic—antisemitism."[136] Although much of the population no longer considered itself Catholic, theologically based antisemitism continued to exert considerable influence.

Similar to the 1930s in Poland and Germany, the potent mixture of nationalism and antisemitism exploded against the Jews during the Dreyfus Affair.[137] Throughout the Affair, the themes of Judas and Christian revenge on the Jews repeatedly surfaced in relation to Dreyfus' "betrayal" of France and to the Jews' "hateful assassination of Christ."[138] An American traveling in France during this period observed that "Dreyfus is a Jew, and to the people who have never been able to rid themselves of the impression that the Jews of today are responsible for the crime of Calvary that is sufficient to justify his conviction."[139]

On Christmas day of 1894, the anti-Jewish Catholic newspaper *La Croix* reminded its readers that "Jews have been traitors ever since the treason of Judas." A few days later, on the first Jewish Sabbath of 1895, Dreyfus was publicly disgraced in an extraordinary ceremony at the Ecole Militaire in Paris, where he had been a student a few years before. The event took place on January 5, 1895 and was scheduled by military authorities, perhaps intentionally, on the Jewish Sabbath.[140] Among Catholics, Dreyfus' public degradation triggered an extreme antisemitism. At one Catholic school a boy reenacted Dreyfus' public disgrace by pulling the wings off a fly.[141]

An antisemitic conservative, Léon Daudet,[142] later a leading polemicist for Action Française (a movement and a journal, the leading beacon of conservative French nationalism and antisemitism) described Dreyfus' degradation. For him, Dreyfus was "assuredly a foreigner, a stray from the ghetto. A steadiness of obstinate audacity persists, and banishes all compassion. It is his last promenade among humans. . . . This wretch was not French."[143]

Charles Maurras, later the chief of Action Française, made it clear that the anti-dreyfusards believed patriotism to be Catholic and Catholic only. "[P]olitically, a patriotic Frenchman knows no other religious interest than that of Catholicism."[144] At Dreyfus' degradation, officers' wives spat on him and the crowd and the journalists shouted, "Traitor! Death to the Jew!" and "Judas! Filthy Jew!"[145] In July 1897, *La Croix* noted that "Judas Dreyfus has sold France."[146] In 1904, two years before Dreyfus' legal vindication, Drumont's newspaper commented, "Instinctively we raise our eyes to see if an image of the traitor has replaced the Christ banished from our halls of justice. But, amazingly, Christ is still there."[147]

Perhaps the deciding event in Dreyfus' first trial was the dramatic moment when the prosecutor asked Major Hubert Henry (a member of the Counter Intelligence Staff who forged evidence to implicate Dreyfus) to swear on his honor that the treasonous officer was Captain Alfred Dreyfus. Making a sweeping gesture with his arm and pointing to the painting of Christ crucified hanging on the wall behind the military judges, Henry cried out, "I swear

it."[148] (At both of Dreyfus' courts-martial, large crucifixes loomed promi-
nently behind the raised platforms on which the judges sat.) This forceful
oath, made in the context of Judas' betrayal of Christ and the crucifixion, was
a key emotional event in Dreyfus' conviction.[149] It was the myth of eternal
Jewish treason, first enunciated in the Gospels and then elaborated and
recounted by countless Christian writers that convicted Dreyfus.

Zola's article, "I accuse" (*J'accuse*), published on January 16, 1898 in
Clemenceau's newspaper, *L'Aurore*, indicted not only France's political and
military leaders for their involvement in the miscarriage of justice but also
France's Catholic spirit and its identification with the army.[150] In Paris, some
priests instructed the faithful to continue the holy war against the deicidal
people during their sermons at Mass.[151]

When Dreyfus was brought to trial a second time in 1899, riots broke out
in Rennes, where priests led two thousand people into the streets, and the
Dominican priest Didon called on Catholic students to "draw the sword, ter-
rorize, cut off heads and run amok."[152] Despite this and the 1898 riots in
Algeria, the secular government of the Third French Republic still maintained order and protected even its Jewish citizens from violence.

The Catholic press all across Europe and the United States was uniformly,
sometimes violently, anti-Dreyfus.[153] The pro-Dreyfus press reached only 11
percent of Parisians and 17 percent of provincials.[154] The Jesuit *Civiltà
Cattolica*, published in Rome and regarded as the "snarling anti-modernist"
mouthpiece of the papacy, argued for decades before the Dreyfus Affair that
the Jews, influenced by the Kabbala and Talmud, were plotting to disrupt
Christian society and ruin the Catholic religion.[155] In 1890 and 1891, the
journal repeated the antisemitic defamations of the last few centuries: The
Jews caused the evils of the French Revolution and democratic society; Jews
"were at the head of the virulent campaigns against Christianity"; Jews were
enemies and foreigners within every country in which they lived, yet they
dominated and ruled these nations, planning ultimately "to take over control
of the entire world."[156] On February 5, 1898, in the midst of the Dreyfus
Affair, the journal argued that "the Jew has been created by God to serve as a
spy anywhere a betrayal is in the making."[157] Similar to the periodical's later
articles published in the 1930s and 1940s, *Civiltà* saw the solution to the
Jewish problem in "the abolition of [the Jews'] civic equality" and Jewish
reghettoization and expropriation.[158]

The Assumptionist Order's *La Croix* was the authoritative journal of
French Catholicism. Until late in the Dreyfus Affair the Church did little to
limit *La Croix's* attacks on the Jews.[159] In 1898, Drumont explained this state
of affairs as the result of Pope Leo XIII's (d. 1903) refusal to "interfere in a

French domestic question of this kind."[160] Pope Leo also permitted the more closely controlled international Catholic press—the Vatican's own *Osservatore Romano* and the Jesuit's *Civiltà Cattolica*—to print antisemitic articles hostile to Dreyfus and Jews until 1899.

The Catholic press in France was more influential than the intellectual journals (most of the popular press at this time was antisemitic as well[161]); its ideas were intimately tied to the religious antisemitism that dominated French culture. This religious propaganda conditioned the minds of the faithful and helped destroy feelings of compassion and justice toward the Jews. Danielle Delmaire has called it a "catechism of antisemitism."[162] Father Vincent de Paul Bailly founded *La Croix* in 1883. Published in nearly one hundred regional editions, *La Croix* in 1890 named itself "the most anti-Jewish newspaper in France, the one that supports Christ, the sign of horror for all Jews." It stimulated and legitimized French antisemitic opinion and behavior. The writers of *La Croix* regarded the Jews as totally evil; and Dreyfus symbolized the Jews. The editors published lists of Jews in the army, in the press, in education, and in public administration. "Jewry . . . is a horrid cancer. . . . The Jews are vampires . . . whether the order be to rob, corrupt, or betray our country, the Jew always leads the charge" (November 14, 1894). In July 1897, *La Croix* printed a full-page poster: "Judas Dreyfus has sold France. . . . Let us unite to . . . boot the Jews out of France." *La Croix* claimed that only Catholics could be real patriots: "True patriotism is that of the baptized."[163] Father Vincent, writing in *La Croix* in 1898, saw the Dreyfus Affair as a war "against the acknowledged enemies of Christ and the Church," with infidels and heretics (Jews and Protestants) on one side and Catholics on the other.[164]

La Croix du Nord, a popular regional edition of *La Croix*, leavened its Catholic disdain of Jews with economic, political, and racist antisemitism. The Jews were "perfidious," "deicides," "monsters of Golgotha." They perpetuated their deicide by attempting to destroy Christian morality and the Church and kill Catholics. "Brought down for having betrayed their vocation as God's people, inspired by the fallen angel, these malicious people would be the ones to hatch a savagely diabolic betrayal. In order to revenge themselves for their 1900 years of slavery, they recrucify Christ in the form of His Catholic Church . . . and the French nation. . . . They will always murder . . . Christians . . . to obtain the blood needed for their religious rites."[165]

Jews murder Christians, especially the young, because Jews "hate the goy" and need Christian blood in their "religious superstitions," and "'the blood of Christian children' leads to health. [Jews use Christian blood] in circumcision; to parody the sacrament of baptism; in marriage; for the holiday of repentance; . . . at the time of death; . . . at Easter time for use in unleavened bread."[166]

Le Monument Henry

Leading anti-dreyfusard writers—Edouard Drumont, Charles Maurras, Maurice Barrès—as well as army officers, priests, students, and bourgeoisie looked at Jews through eyes jaundiced by Christian theological attitudes. They saw something evil in the "Jewish spirit," something alien to France's Christian values.[167] In many ways the Dreyfus Affair was a battle between Christians and Jews.

After Major Henry's forgeries were discovered and he committed suicide, a provincial edition of *La Croix* claimed that he was murdered at Jewish instigation.[168] During the Christmas season of 1898, Drumont's *La Libre Parole* initiated a contribution campaign to raise money for Berthe Henry, the major's widow, to sue Joseph Reinach for defaming her husband's character.[169] About thirty thousand priests subscribed to this antisemitic newspaper; in 1980, there were only 31,500 priests active in all of France.[170] Twenty-five thousand French men and women contributed to what became known as *Monument Henry*, the Henry Memorial.[171] The contributors' comments, printed in *La Libre Parole*, demonstrated the continuing influence of traditional antisemitism on the French people.[172] Secondary-school and university students, Catholic clergy, and soldiers were all significantly overrepresented among the anti-Dreyfus contributors; agricultural, industrial, and commercial occupations were underrepresented.[173]

Contributors to the fund expressed a variety of discontents: fears of economic and social change and of poverty, resentment of liberal intellectuals and professors, and anger at capitalist exploitation. The contributors strongly supported the Church and the army as the basic institutions of the French nation. They regarded the Jews as paradigmatically evil creatures who were polluting France, corrupting the national spirit and honor through capitalistic enterprise, and destroying the most cherished Christian-French values centering on the family, nation, army, and Church.[174] Many saw the Jews (most of whom were extraordinarily patriotic) as an alien factor that upset traditional Christian France:

"[T]he damned Jews are poisoning France."[175]
"The goodness of God stops where the damn Jew begins."
"The damned Jews and their friends are going to the devil."
"Sacred Heart of Jesus, hasten the promised miracle which must exalt your Church and deliver the Catholic nations from the degrading control of those who have crucified you."

Students at a religious school in the provinces adored the army as the "emblem of the nation" and considered themselves "antisemites in their souls."

"May Christ confuse the projects of his enemies, dirty Jews, freemasons, and the judaized."[176]

A French woman agonized "over the Jewish destruction of our traditions."

"A humble curate . . . with pleasure would sing a requiem mass for the last of the God-damned Jews."[177]

Aldous Huxley observed that "If you call a man a bug, it means you propose to treat him as a bug."[178] By the same token, if you call a people deicides, wild animals, plagues, pests, scorpions, pigs, and so forth, you propose to treat them that way. Jews were dehumanized as "disgusting and annoying beast," "Jewish vermin," "Jewish plague," "Jew microbe," "poisonous spiders," "cancer," "synagogue fleas," and "bugs." "The God-damned Jews are not authentic people."[179] "May the dirty Jews be treated like plague and sent to Palestine." "Better eject the black plague and send the dirty Yids to Panama." "Some partisans of the destruction of the dirty Jewish vermin." "For the destruction of Jewry; the true human phylloxera." A history teacher found "the Inquisition an institution publicly useful" and the St. Bartholemew's Day massacre "a work of national decontamination." "For the radical circumcision of dirty Yids, plague of the universe." "To prevent the pollution by the evil race of dirty Yids."[180]

History has shown that actual mass murder of Jews remained nothing more than a threat in France at the time; nevertheless, some contributors threatened violence and murder with an intensity that suggested genocide. One abbé contributed "for a bedside rug made of the skin of God-damned Jews, so that one can step on them every morning and evening."[181] A man from the heavily Catholic Vendée wanted to take down his rifle and "shoot the dirty Jews who are poisoning France." Another writer asked, "Christ! Help us! Take your whip and chase the damned Jewish merchants from the temple of France." An anti-dreyfusard of Le Mans wanted "to have all the damned Jews' eyes poked out." A military doctor suggested that vivisection be practiced "on the dirty Jews rather than on harmless rabbits." "A patriotic coachman" of Savoy proposed "to destroy the damned Jews completely by hammering them to death." "A group of officers on active duty" urged the purchase of "some nails to crucify the God-damned Jews." A resident of Baccarat wanted "to see all the God-damned Jews, their Yid women and their Yid children put into huge ovens." Another patriot sent money "for the transformation of Yid flesh into chopped meat."[182]

With all this hatred, expressed in the most violent terms, one does wonder why the Holocaust did not take place in the France of the Dreyfus Affair.

Novelists are much better than historians at answering such questions. But some obvious facts bear on this issue. Compared to the 1940's, in the 1890s there was no precedent of World War I, with its horrendous trench warfare and the use of poison gas on the battlefield. There was no 1940s technology (from computer cards[183] to poison gas) and, finally, no Hitler: none of the leading French antisemites combined anti-Jewish ideas with rigorous organization and planning, as well as unprecedented determination.

How could the Vatican's millennial anti-Jewish Crusade not have had an impact on the attitudes expressed in the Monument Henry campaign? Articles in the Catholic press, the *Civiltà cattolica, Osservatore romano, Osservatore cattolico, La Croix, La Croix du Nord*, and the rest drummed into the French Catholic mind that the Jews were ritual murderers in league with the devil, out to destroy Catholic society and control the world. Father Vincent Bailly, director of *La Croix*: "The Jew is the enemy . . . Satan's preferred nation . . . ever since their deicide . . . Synagogue of Satan . . . Church of the devil." Another edition in 1882 pictured Jews butchering Catholic children and draining their blood.[184]

The 1930s and 1940s

For men like Charles Péguy, the Dreyfus Affair seemed to demonstrate that the forces of justice could overcome those of prejudice.[185] In 1906, a civilian appellate court determined that Dreyfus was not guilty, and he was restored to the army, promoted, and awarded a Legion of Honor. The extraordinary Georges Picquart, the Head of Counter Intelligence who put justice, his life, and his honor above his antisemitism and was instrumental in Dreyfus' exoneration became the Minister of War. The Republic was strengthened, Catholic conservatism—which had attempted to use the Dreyfus Affair as a political tool against the Republic—was compromised and antisemitism was temporarily discredited. By 1914, a "holy alliance" (*union sacrée*) involved all of France against the Germans. In 1924, Drumont's newpaper, *La Libre Parole*, went out of business for lack of readers.

But the antisemitism that flowered during the Dreyfus Affair and lay dormant during the early part of the twentieth century would flourish again as a powerful force during the economic, social, and political crises of the 1930s and 1940s. These were the same tensions that threatened the Third Republic from within and without.[186] At home, governments came and went, whether Rightist, Leftist, or Centrist, it made no difference who was in power, things kept getting worse. France and the other great democracies accepted Hitler's political and military initiatives in reestablishing German conscription, remilitarizing the Rhineland, helping the fascists during the

Spanish Civil War, developing Fascist alliances, annexing Austria, absorbing Czechoslovakia, and threatening Poland.

The Vatican and Charles Maurras (fountainhead of French conservative and antisemitic thought and founder of the royalist Action Française; it was believed that he had the French episcopate in his pocket[187]) shared many goals.[188] A few months before the start of World War II, Pope Pius XII pardoned Maurras and lifted the sanctions Pope Pius XI had imposed on Action Française in 1926, after the leaders of the movement signed a letter stating their regret for whatever behavior seemed "disrespectful, injurious, and even unjust toward the person of the Pope and to the Holy See." It was a victory for those Catholics who opposed a liberal, democratic society and hated the Jews.

Once the Third Republic was defeated, in the spring and summer of 1940, France was occupied in the north by the Germans and controlled in the south by Vichy, a conservative Catholic regime headed by the World War I hero, Marshal Philippe Pétain, who spoke of returning to France's traditional Catholic values. The Vichy regime was dominated in turn by Charles Maurras' right-wing ideology and Action Française's disciples. Pétain, who was a willing listener and reader of Maurras' ideas, voted for Maurras' membership in the Académie Française and admired him enormously, inscribing a book he sent to Maurras, "To the most French of the French" (*Au plus Français des Français*).[189] Action Française's hatred of Jews and Jewishness inspired Vichy's antisemitic legislation and linked the movement to the otherwise despised Germans. *Action Française's* affiliated journal, *Je suis partout*, also leaned toward fascism, claiming "solidarity with Germany, whose soldiers constitute the last protective rampart of civilized Europe." It called for a hundred Jews to be shot for every French militiaman killed by the Resistance.[190] Such antisemitic associates of Action Française as Xavier Vallat, Raphaël Alibert, and Darquier de Pellepoix led Vichy's Commissariat-General for Jewish Affairs.[191]

The Split in French Society

For centuries, most French Catholics regarded Jews as nasty, greedy evildoers; others tried to treat Jews with respect. These divisions held among members of the French bureaucracy, the police, the intellectuals, and the Church, as well as among average French men and women.[192] Millions of individual Catholics, including priests and nuns, helped Jews, often at great risk to themselves. The Free French forces, headquartered in London and ultimately led by Charles de Gaulle, were widely supported by liberals and Jews. Many Catholics sought to help Jews by joining the anti-Vichy Témoignage Chrétien movement; some were members of ecumenical groups like Amitié Chrétienne of which the Jesuit Pierre Chaillet was a leader.[193]

Many French officials carried out their orders and arrested Jews without compunction, but others either warned the Jews or let some of them go.[194]

But the more frequent response was collaboration with Vichy or silence in the face of evil.[195] Action Française helped incline the more respectable bourgeois periodicals toward antisemitism, and its members and associates dominated the staffs of France's most antisemitic publications. French-Catholic conservatives, friends of Action Française, not only supported the Vichy government's anti-Jewish policies but also joined Vichy's ultra-authoritarian Milice, a French paramilitary organization similar to the SS. The Milice provided the Germans what they needed: a force of French ideologues ready to collaborate with the Third Reich's policies. In January 1944, Vichy appointed the unscrupulous, violent, and antisemitic Joseph Darnand, head of the Milice, as "Secretary-General for the Maintenance of Order." The Milice replaced the French police and the regular German army—both of whom were growing weary of their assault on Jewish civilians—in arresting Jews, and they performed the task with ever more thoroughness.[196] Other French conservatives joined the French SS. Frenchmen serving with the SS's Charlemagne battalion defended Hitler's bunker against the Russians shouting, "Long Live Christ the King!"[197]

The Action Française movement and its journal of the same name preserved Drumont's antisemitic traditions through the end of World War II.[198] Action Française's leader Charles Maurras was Drumont's heir. Dreyfus and the dreyfusard movement symbolized all that Maurras despised in the Third Republic—its liberalism, its democracy, and its anticlericalism. Marshal Pétain appointed Charles Mercier du Paty de Clam, a descendant of the man who arrested Dreyfus, to head the Commissariat-General for Jewish Affairs in February 1944.[199] After the war, when Maurras was convicted of unlawful dealings with the enemy, he exclaimed, "It's Dreyfus' revenge."[200] *Action Française* continually repeated anti-Jewish canards, and many Catholics sympathized with the newspaper's call in October 1942 and July 1943 that concentration camps be set up in France "like those in Germany."[201]

Vichy's anti-Jewish laws, the *Statut des Juifs* (October 3, 1940 and June 2, 1941), were modeled on the German Nuremberg Laws and, like them, were widely accepted in Catholic circles.[202] The Church was but one of several French institutions that could have done something about these laws but did nothing.[203] Both *statuts* defined a Jew as a person having three or more grandparents who were Jewish. The 1940 law's primary aim was to force Jews out of public service, teaching, financial occupations, public relations, and the communications media. Like Xavier Vallat, Raphaël Alibert, the Vichy Minister of Justice and author of the first statute, supported Action Française (the "French Right's fountainhead of thought") and followed this conservative Catholic movement's anti-Jewish policies.[204]

Xavier Vallat, Vichy's first Commissioner-General for Jewish Affairs, was typical of antisemitic officials. A friend of Mauras, Vallat was a convinced Catholic antisemite who regarded the Jewish people as "an evil race, guilty collectively of deicide, cursed to be forever without a homeland." The Jew "is dangerous not because he is a Semite, but because he is impregnated by the Talmud." France's anti-Jewish legislation was based on "precedents in the historical past of our own nation and in that of Christianity."[205] At his postwar trial, Vallat referred to "the anti-Jewish doctrine of the Church" established by St. Paul and St. Thomas Aquinas.[206]

During the war, Catholic antisemites like Vallat played an increasingly important role in the French contribution to the Holocaust. In January 1944, Vallat replaced another militant Catholic antisemite, Philippe Henriot, as Secretary of State for Information and Propaganda. Henriot was popular among many French Catholics who were not Vichy supporters because of his passionately anti-Jewish radio broadcasts. Vallat followed Henriot's lead, lamenting "this ideological war desired by Israel," which would result in a renewal of Jewish domination of France.[207]

Almost eighty-three thousand Jews from France were killed during the Holocaust, nearly all Jews who had fled from Germany to France. Although most French churchmen had no objections to Vichy's anti-Jewish laws in principle,[208] the Vichy seizure of Jewish civilians disturbed some Catholics as excessive. Neither German soldiers nor Gestapo were involved in the round-ups, only French police and the paramilitary Milice.[209] During the round-ups, thousands of Jewish children were separated from their parents, mistreated, and murdered.[210] The orphaned Jewish children of Izieu were arrested in 1943 and murdered at Auschwitz. Just one child was released by the Gestapo and only because they discovered he was a Christian. Total war was waged only against Jews.[211]

The French Church

The French Church—more than any other French institution identified with Pétain's National Revolution—with "near unanimity" and with the Vatican's blessing supported the Vichy regime's policy of discrimination against Jews, so long as it was carried out with "justice and charity."[212] The Church was the only institution in Vichy France allowed to preserve a high level of autonomy, and it could have influenced the consciences of many Frenchmen and women.[213] In August 1941, Msgr. Béguin, archbishop of Auch, told Pétain that "One must be with you or against you. The Catholics and their clergy,

M. le Maréchal, are with you with all their heart."[214] Cardinal Emmanuel Suhard, archbishop of Paris, was an enthusiastic Pétain supporter. Believing Vichy propaganda, he called Pétain, "the Frenchman without reproach."[215] A secret report commissioned in 1944 by Jacques Maritain and written by the respected Jesuit theologian Henri du Lubac indicted most bishops for accepting Nazi and Vichy outrages. The Church remained silent.[216] After the war, eight bishops were forced to resign for their pro-German activities.[217] Emmanuel Suhard, the cardinal-archbishop of Paris, might have accepted Vichy's anti-Jewish laws because he saw them as one element in France's moral revival.[218]

Cardinal Pierre-Marie Gerlier, archbishop of Lyon, felt ambivalent about Vichy's Jewish policy. He was one of the French bishops who protested the deportations of Jews with a pastoral letter read throughout his archdiocese on September 6, 1942. He also supported Pastor Marc Boegner and Fr. Chaillet in their efforts to save Jewish children.[219] Believing that Pétain would force France back to its Catholic roots,[220] Gerlier nevertheless strongly supported Pétain, whom he welcomed to Lyon with these words: "Pétain, c'est la France et la France c'est Pétain."[221] Like many Catholics of his generation, Gerlier occasionally repeated anti-Jewish stereotypes, and, while opposing racial policies, he tended to be "indulgent towards low-grade [traditional] persecution."[222] Gerlier felt comfortable with Vichy's anti-Jewish statutes, and in October 1941, he told the Commissioner-General for Jewish Affairs, Xavier Vallat, that the anti-Jewish law was "not unjust, [merely lacking in] justice and charity in its enforcement" and that "no one recognizes more than I the evil the Jews have done to France." Gerlier added that "[i]t was the collapse of the Union Générale that ruined my family."[223] In 1944, Gerlier attended a Mass in memory of the propaganda minister and militant Catholic antisemite Philippe Henriot.[224] In 1992, information surfaced that Gerlier was one of several prominent Catholic churchmen shielding France's most notorious war criminal from justice—Paul Touvier headed the pro-Nazi *milice* (political-military militia) in Lyon during the war. Others involved in protecting him were Gerlier's successor, Cardinal Jean Villot, who later became Vatican Secretary of State under Pope Paul VI in 1969.[225]

The Church's general approval of Vichy's anti-Jewish policies was interrupted when deportations of Jews first took place in July 1942.[226] A few days later, the French bishops met and sent a message through Cardinal Suhard to Pétain. It noted that Jews had been recently arrested and treated badly. "In the name of humanity and of Christian principles we protest in behalf of the inalienable rights of the human person. We also appeal to the pity of those responsible for these immense sufferings, especially of mothers and children. We ask you, Marshal, to abide by the requirements of justice and charity."[227]

But the bishops never had the protest published,[228] and only five or six of about eighty French bishops followed up the message to Pétain with individual pastoral letters.[229] Bishop Pierre-Marie Théas of Montauban was a courageous anti-Nazi who spoke out for Jews. On August 30, 1942, he reminded his parishes that all people are brothers created by the same God, "Aryan as well as nonAryan; that all men regardless of race or religion deserve respect from individuals and governments. The present antisemitic measures represent a contempt for human dignity." He asked God to strengthen the persecuted and give the world peace, "based on justice and charity."[230] Arrested by the Germans in June 1944, he was liberated from Compiègne just before he was to be deported to his death.[231]

But the response of Mgr. Delay, bishop of Marseille, a Vichy supporter, was more typical of the French Church's attitudes. In September 1942, he wrote that he recognized the difficult problems that the Jewish question posed for the Vichy government, and he justified the government's right "to take all measures needed to defend itself against those who, especially in the last few years, have done so much evil and whom [the government] has the duty to punish severely. . . . But the rights of the state are limited." Because he did not specify precisely how or when the state's actions should be limited, his words reflected the traditional Augustinian approach of degradation short of murder.[232]

Jules-Gerard Cardinal Saliège, archbishop of Toulouse, felt as ambivalent about the Jews as most Catholic prelates. In the fall of 1941, he called the Vichy government's Jewish policy, "from the point of view of Catholic doctrine, *unassailable*."[233] But shortly after the actual deportations began, a Catholic social worker asked the archbishop to intervene to save the Jews from "awful scenes, attempts at suicide, collapses and crises of madness caused by the violent separation of families."[234] On August 23, 1942, Saliège issued a pastoral letter complaining that "Jews and foreigners are real men and women. Everything is not permitted against them, against these men and women, against these fathers and mothers. They are part of the human species. They are our brothers, like so many others. A Christian may not forget this."[235]

He also aided the rescue of Jewish children.[236] Nevertheless, in late September 1942, Saliège restated his loyalty to the Vichy regime and vigorously protested that the anti-Vichy Resistance movement had "indecently" reproduced his pastoral letter in their publications.[237]

After the few protests against the Franco-German anti-Jewish policies in the summer and early fall of 1942, silence fell on the French Church. In October, while trains were deporting Jews from France to their deaths, France's two most influential bishops, Suhard from the Occupied Zone and Gerlier from the Vichy Zone, met Pétain and Laval to pledge their loyalty to Vichy. Their support may have been gained by the Marshal's support for

Catholic education. The papal nuncio, Archbishop Valerio Valeri, praised the government pro-Catholic actions as proof that the French government intended to "build the new France . . . on spiritual values."[238]

In her work to help the Jews of the Holocaust, the courageous young Catholic Germaine Ribière experienced opposition at every turn from the Catholic hierarchs and priests with whom she came into contact. One priest told her that there were more important things to worry about than the Jews; another, after discovering that she had visited Jews in a French internment camp, refused to give her Communion. "You mean you went to see *those* people?"[239] Two Christian traditions confronted each other, Mlle Ribière's Catholic *caritas* (*theologia crucis*) and the priests' anti-Jewish triumphalism (*theologia gloriae*). The same anti-Jewish dynamics that prompted German policies toward the Jews of the Holocaust were at work in these priests.[240] Centuries of anti-Jewish Catholic teachings diminished the value of the Jews as human beings and put them beyond the realm of humane treatment.

CHAPTER 9

Poland

The two saddest nations on earth.

Antoni Slonimski, "Elegy for the Jewish Villages"

Early History

Although its overall history has been peppered with antisemitic riots and pogroms in response to Catholic anti-Jewish defamation and political unrest,[1] Poland in the late Middle Ages and the Early Modern period served as a refuge for Jews, and Jewish orthodoxy flourished there as perhaps nowhere else. In the late eighteenth century, about 80 percent of the world's Jews lived in Poland.[2] Catholic Poles generally coexisted with the large Jewish population whose status was confirmed by secular law and whose presence well-served the Polish economy.[3]

Because of this economic value, secular Catholic authorities often protected Jews. In 1264, Polish Duke Boleslav V gave Jews a charter, the Statute of Kalisz that, "according to the ordinances of [Pope Innocent IV, who denied the blood-libel defamation], [provided that] no Jews in our domain be accused of using human blood, since according to the precept of their law all Jews refrain from any blood." Any conviction of Jews for this crime would require as many Jewish witnesses as Catholic. The charter also stated that should the Jew be found innocent, then the Catholic accuser would have to undergo the same penalty that the Jew would have suffered.[4] The statute further protected Jews as *servi camerae*, servants of the crown, as occurred many times under other secular Catholic princes of Europe. This meant that Jews would have their life and property guaranteed by the crown, and it freed Jews from local jurisdiction, although it made them vulnerable to any predatory behavior on the part of the crown.

The statute was reconfirmed four times for the whole Polish kingdom and expanded in 1453 by Polish secular princes. As Catholic scholar Ronald

Modras indicates, during this period the Polish Jews "enjoyed the status of freemen . . . the most humanitarian regulation of their status anywhere in late medieval Europe."[5] Established between 1551–81, the Council of the Four Lands also gave Poland's Jews the right to collect their own taxes owed to the crown and to elect their own rabbis and judges to govern their local affairs—"more autonomy than anywhere else in the entire history of [the] Diaspora."[6]

The large influx of Jews into Poland during the Middle Ages, however, led to conflict with the Church.[7] The same Statute of Kalisz that protected Jews, also offers a glimpse into the treatment to which Jews had most likely been subject beforehand in Poland and the rest of Catholic Europe. On the assumption that decrees of protection were not issued without reason, it is safe to assume that Jews were assaulted while they traveled, their inheritances taken from them, not allowed to testify in court, their synagogues, cemeteries, and schools attacked, Jewish merchants taxed at a higher rate than those of Catholics, subject to forced baptisms—all common problems in the rest of Europe. Church councils 1267–85 affirmed that only believing Catholics would be saved in the next life, with Jews sent straight to hell; Jews were to wear stigmatic emblems; Jews should be ghettoized so that Christians would not "fall . . . prey to . . . the[ir] superstitions and evil habits," Jews could not hold offices requiring Christians to be subordinate to them, Christians could not socialize with Jews.[8] The Church Council of Kalisz of 1420 reaffirmed earlier anti-Jewish council decrees. In 1454, anti-Jewish riots in Wroclaw and other Silesian cities were inspired by the papal envoy, the notorious antisemitic Franciscan Giovanni di Capistrano, who accused the Jews of profaning the Catholic religion. As a result, Jews were banished from Lower Silesia. When King Casimir IV ignored the anti-Jewish canons of the Church Council of Kalisz, Cardinal Olesnicki of Krakow denounced the king. The Cardinal also invited Capistrano to Krakow, where he preached against the Jews, forcing the king to temporarily revoke Jewish privileges.[9]

This mix of secular tolerance and ecclesiastical contempt was common to other parts of Europe and lasted until the 1648 Bogdan Chmielnicki Ukrainian uprising against the Polish-Lithuanian Commonwealth.[10] When the Jews took up arms to support the Polish government and charges against the Jews of ritual-murder and host profanation were made, the Ukrainian Cossacks and peasants destroyed hundreds of Jewish communities and tortured and murdered up to a half million Jews.[11] The gratuitous anti-Jewish sadism of the Cossacks and peasants took these pogroms beyond the level of simple riots into the realm of radical religious violence.[12] Many Jewish survivors saw only a dark future for themselves in eastern Europe and made their way back to the west. Shabbetai Hacohen described the destruction of Nemirov, the most important Jewish-Polish city, in this way:

The enemy destroyed the synagogue, our surrogate Temple; they rampaged, they removed all the Torah scrolls, both old and new, and tore them to shreds, and cast them aside to be trampled upon by the feet of man and beast, horses and their riders . . . and they cast Scripture to the ground and trampled on the parchment with their feet.[13]

The Augsburger Johann Peter Spaeth (d. 1701) converted to Judaism and took the name Moses Germanus.[14] He wrote,

In Poland and Germany, . . . circumstantial tales are told and songs sung in the streets, how the Jews have murdered a child, and sent the blood to one another in quills for the use of their women in childbirth. I have discovered this outrageous fraud in time, and abandoned Christianity, which can permit such things, in order to have no share in it, nor be found with those who trample under foot Israel, the first begotten Son of God, and shed his blood like water.[15]

From the late eighteenth century—when Poland was partitioned among Russia, Austria, and Prussia—to the early twentieth century Jewish social, political, and economic conditions deteriorated. Catholic Poles saw themselves as victims "of history and conspiratorial forces (in the first place the Jews)."[16] Although some liberal intelligentsia got on well with their Jewish neighbors, even these Poles felt comfortable only with Jews who repudiated Jewish values and assimilated into Polish culture, language, and society, that is, Polonized themselves. As in other parts of Europe, these liberals regarded Jewishness as a stigma.

Interwar Period

As Poland approached the twentieth century, discrimination and violence against Jewish neighbors[17] alternated with "good-natured" contempt.[18] Polish attitudes were shaped in great part by the Catholic Church, which served as the major "guardian of national values"[19] and which looked to the Holy See in Rome for leadership.[20] Many Poles believed in the age-old Catholic defamations—which were oftentimes propagated by Catholic clergymen—that claimed Jews were ritual-murderers, host-desecrators, Christ-killers, and corrupters of Christian values.[21] Already hostile to Jews as middlemen and moneylenders (positions forced on them because of their legal and customary exclusion from other pursuits, see Chapter 4), Catholic Poles commited pogroms and judicial murders of Jews, who were also forbidden to travel, banned from holding positions of authority over Catholics, and subject to extraordinarily high taxes.[22] A "mix of exclusion and toleration, hostility and benign neglect. . . . Jews and Poles lived side by side, but not together . . . divided by religion, culture, and . . . language."[23]

The first half of the twentieth century posed enormous difficulties for Poland as it did for Germany: the heritage of more than a century of partitions, large ethnic minorities, the dislocations of World War I, another war with Bolshevik Russia, a chaotic introduction to parliamentary democracy, the economic Depression, dictatorship, World War II, genocide, and Holocaust. The Polish Catholic Church, like Germany's, found itself fighting the effects of socialism, communism, fascism, modernism, liberalism, nazism, atheism, feminism, and secularism. Most of these "isms" it associated with the Jews.

After World War I, even though Jews suffered more than any other group, Poles, Russians, and Ukrainians scapegoated them for their national problems.[24] In the Polish pogroms of 1918–19, such as that of Lwow, the Polish Catholic perpetrators acted as if they were celebrating the despoliation, humiliation, and murder of Jews. The Catholic rioters (pogromchiks) behaved as if the Jews owed them their goods and their lives. The rioters felt, as Catholics, that they had the moral right to act this way because they imagined that the Jews were guilty of poisoning Poles, aiding Poland's enemies, fomenting the war, and, perhaps most of all, *not* remaining defenseless, passive, and powerless—which was the Jewish condition that the Church insisted on. Moreover, as did the Germans during the Holocaust, Catholic rioters desecrated Jewish religious identities and sites, burning synagogues, hacking up Torah scrolls, humiliating young Jews, cutting beards off old Jews and then murdering them, "taking righteous revenge for the temporal and spiritual faults they ascribed to their victims. . . . The profanation worked upon Judaism seemingly sought to rob it in anti-Jewish minds of its magical aura and spiritual legitimacy."[25]

When such post-World War I pogroms[26] provoked many Jews to attempt to immigrate to the United States, the U.S. Congressional Joint Committee on Immigration and Naturalization remarked on a bill to allow these Jews into the United States that "If there were in existence a ship that could hold three million human beings, then three million Jews of Poland would board to escape to America." (Even though Ukrainians slaughtered tens of thousands more Jews than Poles did, world opinion blamed Poles, which confirmed in many Polish minds the "reality" of an international Jewish conspiracy.[27]) That Jews were being butchered in Poland was irrelevant to most members of Congress.[28]

In 1918, Pope Benedict XV sent the future Pope Pius XI, Monsignor Achille Ratti, on a special diplomatic mission to size up the chaotic situation in Poland. He was instructed to look into the killings of Jews. Ratti did no such thing. Instead, he reported back, falsely, that Jews were an "extremist [party] bent on disorder," that Jews were "numerous [and] subsist through . . . contraband, fraud, and usury," that "one of the most evil and strongest influences that is felt here, perhaps the strongest and the most evil, is that of the Jews." Ratti left Poland and put the completion of his work into the hands of his trusted and even more antisemitic assistant Monsignor Ermenegildo Pellegrinetti, who added the antisemitic fantasies that "the Jews constitute a major cause of weakness in the Polish state [controlling] the banks, the press, and many important offices . . . and backed by their international organization, they seek the formation of a Judaic Poland," that Jews were a threat to Polish integrity because they believed that "Poles and Jews should live with equal rights," and that Jews represent "a danger . . . from a religious point of view" [which is] fortunately . . . diminished by the national antipathy for them."[29]

During the 1930s, Ratti, now Pope Pius XI, said nothing about Polish antisemitism. When, in July 1938, he made his offhand remark that "spiritually we are semites," it made headlines internationally, yet it was never reported at all in Poland.[30]

Since Poland would become the locus of most of the mass murders of the Holocaust, the Church's influence there and the papacy's attitude toward Polish antisemitism were crucial. Most Poles were zealously devoted to their Church, because it had served as the major unifying institution in Poland for a thousand years. The modern Polish striving for political unification was identified with the crucified Christ, whose resurrection came as surely as Poland's freedom and independence would take place.[31]

Although Polish antisemitism ebbed and flowed during the interwar period, hostility won out.[32] The Jewish spirit was regarded as a direct threat to a vulnerable Polish Catholic self-identity. A Polish Jewish writer, Abraham Brumberg, observed that the conditioning power of the Roman Catholic Church and its allies the nationalist intelligentsia was the main cause of the contemptible popular image of the Jew "as an enemy of Christendom and of the Polish national essence."[33]

The Catholic press and educational establishment were for the most part strongly antisemitic and inevitably had a pernicious influence on most Polish people.[34] Ronald Modras' massive study of Polish-Catholic newspapers and periodicals, Polish-Catholic polemics, and Polish-Catholic pronouncements indicated that the Catholic Church discouraged only the most extreme forms of violence but encouraged discrimination, economic boycotts, and the stigmatizing of Jews as spiritual and political enemies.[35] The Polish press justified widespread national antisemitism claiming it was extensive all across Europe, so why not in Poland, the locus of three million of Europe's Jews, with Warsaw's population being 30 percent Jewish. This "wave of antisemitism" was simply a return to "traditional religious, political, and social concepts" by Catholics who recognized that Jews were the leaders of all the modern movements upsetting Europe.[36] No other nation wanted Jews, why should Poland have to host them? Professor Modras concludes that "theological reasons for antisemitsm were never far below the surface of the political reasons."[37]

After Jozef Pilsudski came to power in May 1926, the Polish government sometimes acted on the Jews' behalf, although it continued to support anti-Jewish discrimination. But after the dictator died in May 1935, things got much worse for the Jews. The political parties, nearly all of which were anti-Jewish, exploited Poland's political and economic instability and called for discrimination, economic boycott, expulsion, and physical violence against Jews (sixty-nine killed and eight hundred wounded in pogroms in 1936[38]). The Polish intellectual, Jan Blonski, has written that if before 1939 Catholic Poles "had behaved only more humanely, genocide would perhaps have been less imaginable . . . more difficult to carry out, and almost certainly would not have met with the indifference and moral turpitude of the society in whose full view it took place."[39]

The post-Pilsudski government officially favored anti-Jewish measures that fit the programs of the Catholic Church.[40] Boguslaw Miedzinski, a leading Pilsudski heir, observed that "of uncommon importance, separating the Jewish question from all other nationality problems" was religion. Of all Poland's inhabitants, only the Jews were not Christian. "It would therefore be impossible to deny the reality of the ethico-religious distinctness of the Jewish masses. [It] wipes out any criteria of a moral nature."[41] The nationalist party (Endecja) ideologue and spokesman, Roman Dmowski, noted that "the whole tradition of [European] society is alien to him, is opposed to everything with which the Jewish soul has become imbued in the course of immutable generations. The Jew treats with aversion the entire past of European nations; he harbors hatred toward their religions."[42] The government enacted several laws that indirectly discriminated against Jews and a law was proposed that would have disenfranchised the Jews as did the Nazi Nuremberg Laws. Though this law was not enacted, its proposal elicited a rousing round of applause on the floor of the Sejm, Poland's national parliament. The worst effect of these legislative measures, these "necessary cruelties," was in dampening the Jews' sense of civil equality and security and in aggravating anti-Jewish boycotts and discrimination.[43] In 1937, two North American missionary ministers, members of the International Missionary Council's Committee on the Christian Approach to the Jews—a leading rescuer of converted Jews from the Third Reich—were shocked that Polish churches were selling antisemitic literature as vile as Streicher's Nazi *Der Stürmer*.[44]

In the Polish universities, students expressed opinions about Jews similar to those of their parents and priests. Though opposed by Jews and Catholic liberals, nationalist students, supported by Polish university administrations, forced Jewish students into segregated "ghetto benches" in the classrooms. The antisemitic students argued that Poland would not be safe until every Jew left Poland. The Catholic Church and press supported the students' discrimination but opposed student rioting against Jews.[45] In the mid-1930s, several major anti-Jewish riots erupted that, combined with boycotts of Jewish merchants, echoed the 1933 boycotts against Jews in Germany.

The primate of Poland during the thirties, August Cardinal Hlond, was considered a moderate, far less nationalistic and antisemitic than many other Polish clergy, and a careful follower of Vatican policy. Yet in 1932 and 1936, while attacking Polish Catholics' enemies—Bolsheviks and free-thinkers—he used the phrase from Revelations, "synagogue of Satan," resonant of Jews, Judaism, and the Jewish spirit. In 1936, he issued an anti-Jewish pastoral letter that Pius XI sanctioned by his silence. Following the traditional precepts of the theologians and the policies of the Church, Hlond opposed public violence but advocated discrimination and boycott of Jews until they converted to Catholicism. Hlond and other Polish Catholic leaders and press believed that a "Jewish problem" existed in Poland, where neither assimilation nor conversion seemed to work—only emigration. Identifying Jews with communists and atheists, prostitution and swindling, as well as supporting the boycott against Jewish merchants, Hlond wrote that Jews corrupted Polish morals.[46]

A Jewish problem exists, and will continue to exist as long as the Jews remain Jews. . . . It is a fact that the Jews fight against the Catholic Church, they are free-thinkers, and constitute the vanguard of atheism, of the Bolshevik movement and of revolutionary activity. It is a fact that Jewish influence upon morals is fatal, and their publishers spread pornographic literature. It is true that the Jews are committing frauds, practicing usury, and dealing in pornography. It is true that in schools, the influence of the Jewish youth upon the Catholic youth is generally evil, from a religious and ethical point of view.

But—let us be just. Not all Jews are like that. . . . I warn against the fundamental, unconditional anti-Jewish principle, imported from abroad [Nazi-style racism]. It is contrary to Catholic ethics. It is permissible to love one's own nation more; it is not permissible to hate anyone. Not even Jews. . . . One ought to fence oneself off against the harmful moral influences of Jewry, to separate oneself against its anti-Christian culture, and especially to boycott the Jewish press and the demoralizing Jewish publications. But it is not permissible to assault Jews, to hit, maim or slander them. . . . When divine mercy enlightens a Jew, and he accepts sincerely his and our Messiah, let us greet him with joy in the Christian midst. Beware of those inciting anti-Jewish violence.[47]

Hlond and other Catholic spokesmen "conformed exactly to the ancient witness theology, launching a torrent of anti-Jewish vituperation but calling for restraint and charity in action, telling the faithful that they should not follow the logic of the antisemitic assertions they have just launched into the air."[48]

When a delegation of rabbis met with Warsaw's Cardinal Kakowski, he condemned violence but he pointed out that Jews were fighting against Catholicism and "inundating" Poland with their pornography, depraving Poland and all of Christendom with their Jewish values. Living among Jews hindered a Catholic's salvation. Catholics must drive out Satan and all of his allies. This is what caused "regrettable excesses." In other words, Polish Catholics attacked Jews only in self-defense. Self-defense was the typical justification of the Catholic press for anti-Jewish violence.

During the interwar period, while softly condemning such violence in Poland—as well as in Germany and Austria—Catholic journalists and clergy created an antisemitic "climate of opinion" involving Polish victimization and Jewish pariahship that enabled the death factories to operate more easily against the Polish Jews during the Holocaust.[49] Based on the traditional theology of glory, the Church served as a bastion of Polish antisemitism.[50] As Hitler saw the Jews behind anti-German conspiracies, many, perhaps most, of the Polish clergy saw the Jews behind modernism, liberalism, communism, and freemasonry; the Polish clergy saw Jews as adherents to these ideologies, along with liberty, equality, and fraternity, which meant that the Jews sought to destroy Catholic Poland and establish a dictatorship of Jews. When any aspect of these ideologies clashed with traditional Polish Catholic culture, Catholic leaders cried, "Judaization"[51]—a fear seventeen-centuries in length that Christians would be influenced by Jews.[52]

Using the Spanish Civil War as the context, Mgr. Stanislaus Trzeciak accused the Jews of being the Catholics' greatest enemy—a position widely held throughout the Catholic world. As Professor Modras notes, many Polish Catholics asked themselves if Jews were such a threat in Spain where no Jews lived, how dangerous would they be to Poland, where three million resided?[53] Jews *seemed* prominent to most Poles even though they comprised only about 10 percent of an ethnically diverse Poland whose total "ethnically foreign" population amounted to 30 percent of the nation's inhabitants. (This prominence may have been caused by the disproportionately distributed Jewish population in urban areas; Jews lived in relatively few places but in relatively large numbers.)[54]

The leaders of the Polish Catholic Church were convinced that they followed the same path as the Holy See in regard to their opposition to modern "Jewish" values.[55] The Holy See, in turn, considered Poland "the bastion of Christianity" that was always loyal to the Vatican.[56] In response to Pius XI's encyclical *Mit Brennender Sorge* (With Burning Concern), the Polish Catholic press—which directly influenced hundreds of thousands of Catholic Polish readers and indirectly influenced, through the priesthood, millions of Poles—did not back down from its antisemitic pronouncements. If anything, the encyclical stirred more antagonism to religious Jews as enemies of Poland in race and in spirit, as threats to Poland's nationhood and Church, as masters of Poland's economy and as destroyers of Poland's morals. Assimilated Jews were doubly dangerous both as disbelieving and perverse Jews who killed Christ, who took Satan as their lord, and who carried with them all the evils of the modern, secular world.[57] For Poland's Catholic leaders, most Catholic clergy, and Polish nationalists, Jewish involvement in the economy meant Jewish influence in Poland's education, arts, and literature, which in turn meant Jewish secularization, which in turn meant the destruction of "Poland's traditional Catholic culture."[58]

A large part of the clergy sanctioned or fomented daily humiliation and hatred of, and sometimes physical violence against, Jews.[59] The Church said nothing about a popular prewar calendar, for example, that showed a devil next to a Talmud, the caption reading, "The books of Judah; Satan himself must have written them with the blood and tears of non-Jews."[60] Father Jozef Kruszynski, a professor at the University of Lublin whose antisemitic books are still in print in Poland, writing in a Jesuit newspaper, considered Jews guilty of an anti-Catholic "Talmud mentality" that prevented assimilation. Those Jews who did assimilate wormed their way into the media, arts, and education and were doubly dangerous to Poland's Catholic culture. A war against the Jews, though the violence was regrettable, was the only way for Polish Catholics to defend themselves against the Jewish enemy that was more of a threat in Poland, where there were more Jews than in any other nation.[61]

Sometimes, Polish antisemitism was framed in racist terms. The Catholic press sought a Poland that was free of Jews and Jewishness, a Poland that was not "foreign [or] semitized."[62] The antisemitic press quoted Poland's greatest poet, Adam Mickiewicz: "A culture and civilization truly worthy of humankind—must be Christian."[63] But they ignored Mickiewicz other comments: "I would not want the Jews to leave Poland. . . . I believe that a union of Poland and Israel would be a source of spiritual and material strength to us.

We would most efficiently prepare Poland's rebirth by removing the causes of its eclipse and reviving the union and brotherhood of all races and religions that regard our motherland as their home."[64]

The Polish bishops believed that Freemasonry, which intended to destroy the Church, was "derived from Judaism, closely linked to Judaism, and serving the interests of International Jewry" and that Poland's Jews supported Freemasonry.[65] The Catholic bishops also believed in the essence of the antisemitic fantasy, *The Protocols of the Elders of Zion*, which was exploited by Catholic and Protestant antisemites all across Europe and the United States to "confirm" Jewish conspiracy with evil. The bishops identified Jews with the evils of the modern world and with those who "do not want Christ to rule over us."[66] Even the canonized Franciscan Polish monk, Maximilian Kolbe, edited several Church newspapers that in the 1920s had associated the Jews with Communism and Freemasonry and in the 1930s supported economic discrimination against Jews "in the name of the interests of the Polish nation and of Western, Christian civilization." This occurred despite the fact that, just like the masses of Catholics, the Jews *en masse* did *not* support the Communists.[67] Like the Roman Catholic Church in general, Kolbe may have been anti-racist and anti-Nazi, but he (and his antisemitic Knights of the Immaculata publishing house and mass-market newspapers) believed in the same anti-Jewish stereotypes that the Nazis of his day promoted about the Jews. Following the anti-modernist trend within the Church, he argued that the Jews specialized in "pornography, divorce, fraud, and corruption [and] the poisoning of young souls."[68] These themes mimicked the anti-Jewish propaganda of the Jesuits of *La Civiltà Cattolica*, the propaganda of the Third Reich,[69] and Catholic antisemitism all over Europe.[70] Not only this, but the Polish-Catholic Church's leadership was much more supportive of antisemitism than secular Polish Catholics, among whom were counted thousands of Righteous Christians like Jan Karski.[71]

Before the Holocaust, a tiny minority of Catholic Poles from almost every walk of life spoke out in defense of the Jews: liberals, professors, students, socialists, communists, journalists, writers, and members of the one Catholic organization in Poland opposing antisemitism, *Odrodzenie* (Renaissance), a social-justice group. The priest Antoni Szymanski, a mentor of the group, a professor of Catholic Ethics, and editor of *Prad* was not a liberal. He believed in the superiority of Catholicism to Judaism but at least he publicly opposed racial antisemitism.[72]

The Holocaust

During the Holocaust, the Germans devastated Poland and its Catholic population suffered "immense losses."[73] Despite the automatic death penalty for

Poles and their families who aided Jews, about fifty thousand Jews survived the Nazi Final Solution in the Polish ethnic area of Poland, meaning that, most likely, tens of thousands of courageous Catholic Poles were involved in their protection.[74] Thousands of Polish names are engraved at the Yad Vashem Holocaust Memorial. At the German death camp Belzec, alone, from March 1942, six hundred thousand Polish Jews were killed. At the same camp, 1,500 Poles were murdered for attempting to help Jews.[75] Despite a lack of direction from the Roman Catholic Church hierarchy, a small minority of Catholic clergy—a few dozen priests and nuns—helped Jews at great risk to themselves, although only Karol Niemiera sought to organize rescues. Poland's Main Commission for the Examination of Nazi Crimes reports that the Nazis killed eleven priests and monks and ten nuns for aiding Jews.[76]

Zofia Kossak was an antisemitic author, prominent lay Catholic, and underground leader who sought to create a Catholic Poland before the war without harming Polish Jews. Kossak and other Catholics organized Zegota (the only Catholic organization in Eastern Europe devoted to saving Jews) to help Jews survive *even though* they considered the Jews alien and dangerous to Poland's Catholic culture.[77] Of the 2,500 Jewish children Zegota saved, 500 were protected in Catholic establishments. Overall, 180 Catholic institutions run by 37 Catholic women's orders contributed to saving Jewish children.[78]

When the Warsaw ghetto uprising took place, Kossak wrote admiringly of the ghetto fighters but complained about Jews who "allowed" themselves to be murdered; her opinion was that the ghetto fighters were negating the Jews' shameful and cursed history, a history of cowardice, stealth, deviousness, and the instigation of many of Europe's wars.[79] A seeming contradiction, Kossak, despite her traditional Catholic antisemitic beliefs, nevertheless in action adhered to the Catholic tradition of *theologia crucis*, a moral position that required its adherents to follow a path in *imitatio christi*, which meant taking up the cross in replication of Christ if need be. Kossak did not like the Jews, but her Christian morality was so strong that she was willing to risk her life to do no harm to them and ended up helping to save some.

Whereas some priests helped Jews despite their own antisemitism,[80] many priests admired the Nazis' Jewish policy, seized Jewish property, discouraged their parishioners from helping, denounced Jews from the pulpit.[81] Indeed, most Poles were indifferent and many actively collaborated in getting rid of the "Jewish pest." This behavior is attested to by almost all Jewish survivors. Moreover, although some Catholics worked actively to save Jews, this was often done not for the sake of humanity but in order to make converts of the desperate Jews.[82]

Usually in the countryside, the most respected person was the village priest. According to Jan Gross, priests "evoked in their sermons an image of Jews as God-killers, particularly at Easter, making the season a perennial occasion for antisemitic violence."[83] Gross also comments that in order to prevent pogroms, bishops and priests "in Poland often had to be appeased with gifts from the Jews."[84] In June and July 1941, some Catholic Poles did more than stand by, indifferent to Jewish suffering. They actively participated in several massacres of Jews, including the most notorious, the Jedwabne slaughter where Polish residents murdered about one thousand neighbors— Jewish men, women, and children.[85] These massacres occurred under the pressure, and with the example, of the German occupation, but they were made more likely given the antisemitism rampant in Poland and in the Polish Catholic Church. A few weeks before the massacres, the local parish priest prevented the populace from attacking Jews; he argued that the Germans were handling the situation. But he made no efforts to stop the July 10 massacre.[86] For a month, the Jews' neighbors tried to starve the Jews out. Before the mass burnings, the Poles forced Jewish men "to enact grotesque rituals before being butchered; women were raped and beheaded; babies were trampled to death." The Poles doused the Jews with kerosene and "played raucous music in order to muffle their screams." As George Steiner writes, "Though encouraged and sometimes initiated by the Nazi occupiers, the actual mass murders were the work of . . . the vast majority of the local Polish communities, who watched the carnival of Jewish agony with derisive indifference or active approval. When Jewish women strove to drown themselves and their babies in order to escape torture and incineration, there were Poles who stood on the banks cheering them on."[87] (The carnival atmosphere and the burning of Jews to death had occurred on a lesser scale in 1918 in the Lvov pogrom and during the German destruction of the Warsaw Ghetto in 1943 on a greater scale.[88])

There were several instances of Poles carrying out anti-Jewish pogroms after June 22, 1941, but the degree of violence and the number of Jews murdered was much lower than the Jedwabne massacres. Usually, Catholic Poles murdered Jews with clubs or knives, drowned them or shot them. But the burning alive of the Jewish victims was unique to Jedwabne and Radziłów.[89] In the *shtetl* (small villages), Orthodox Jews often resided among premodern Polish Catholic peasants who regarded them as pariahs and as a threat to their Catholic identity. According to University of London Professor Joanna Zylinska, "The death of the Jedwabne Jews in a neighbor's barn, to some extent paradigmatic of death in a camp, can perhaps be interpreted as an attempt to 'enclose' alterity, to put an end to it. It was an act of 'devouring the Jews' alive, internalizing them by an inverted reenactment of antisemitic stories claiming that Jews use the blood of Christian children to make their bread."[90]

The Nobel-prize winning Lithuanian-born Polish Catholic poet, Czeslaw Milosz, called antisemitism and nationalism during this time "ills that like cancer were consuming Poland."[91] In his "Campo dei Fiori," filled with poetic tones reminiscent of Bruegel's painting *The Fall of Icarus*, Milosz laments from Warsaw in 1943 that the carousel's carnival tunes and the noise of the laughing crowds in the Catholic area of Warsaw "drowned the salvos from the ghetto wall." The Catholics of Warsaw "haggle, laugh, make love / as they pass by [Jewish] martyrs' pyres."[92] A Jewish survivor tells of the Polish family who saved his life by insisting that he curse the Jews as Christ-killers so that the other children in the neighborhood would not be suspicious of his "authentic Catholic" identity.[93]

The late Jewish historian Emmanuel Ringelblum, who perished in the Warsaw ghetto, has been praised by Polish historians for the accuracy of his observations. He noted that interwar Poland was "the leading antisemitic country in Europe, second to Germany alone"; the Polish police played a "most lamentable role in the extermination of the Jews of Poland" and were "enthusiastic executors of all the German directives regarding the Jews"; that many Poles were happy "that Poland was *judenrein* [free of Jews]."[94]

During the 1940s, Pope Pius XII's silence about the slaughter of Jews matched Pope Pius XI's silence about antisemitism in the 1930s—both of them followed a millennial tradition of papal silence and inconsistency in regard to Jewish suffering. The Bishop of Berlin, Cardinal Konrad von Preysing, mentioned the massacres of Jews carried out in German-occupied territory to Pius XII,[95] but "the Vatican's primary informant" for Poland, Prince-Archbishop Adam Sapieha (who replaced Poland's leading Church official Cardinal Hlond after he fled to France), mentioned not a single word about the Nazi slaughter of Jews in Poland. In October 1942, even though Sapieha was Archbishop of Krakow, he made no mention of the massive and brutal destruction of the Krakow ghetto, the murders and deportation of its Jews taking place in a sense in front of his eyes. Archbishop Sapieha did mention the German depredations against the Polish Church and the Polish Catholic populace, but he felt no "moral injunction regarding the Jews." Furthermore, Poland's primate, Cardinal Hlond, joined Sapieha in not mentioning the extermination of Polish Jews. In Hlond's wartime reminiscences about the years preceding the outbreak of war, Cardinal Hlond refers to "Jewish depravity," and in his musings on Poland's future, he warns that Poland's economy must not fall into the hands of a "nameless . . . Jewish oligarchy." Professor Dariusz Libionka concludes that the Polish Catholic hierarchy kept silent about the Jews because they perceived them "as aliens and threats."[96]

A summer 1941 "Church Report from Poland" smuggled from Poland to London contains an extraordinary statement concerning the Polish Catholic Church's perception of the Jews of the Holocaust: "It is necessary to consider it a peculiar decree of the Lord's providence, that the Germans alongside the multitude of offenses that they have done and continue to do to our country, have made a good start on one score, in that they have shown the possibility of freeing Polish society from the Jewish plague and have pointed out for us the road, which naturally less savagely and brutally but consistently, we must take."[97]

The report goes on to foresee a postwar Poland that included ghettoization of, and discrimination against, Jews with the ultimate goal of making Poland Jew-free.[98] Although the author(s) of this report are unknown, Professor Libionka concluded that these attitudes were "close to those of a large part of the clergy."[99] Only a small minority of clergy called for Catholic-Jewish solidarity against the Germans.[100] Agreeing with the sentiments of the report, Bishop Kruszynski observed that Jews were "microbes." He later added: "I often thought that the Jews would get theirs from the Germans. I didn't know I would live to see this moment."[101]

Professor Modras' concluded that Catholic antisemitism of the period was only one component of a Church that considered itself under attack by liberals, Communists, socialists, and Freemasons, as well as Jews, whom the Church believed were the driving force behind its other foes; the Church concluded that it was in a fierce battle to preserve Catholic culture and Christianity, against such destructive forces of modernity. Given the latest revelations of the Church's behavior in regard to the Jews and judging on the basis of the standards of *theologia crucis*, the Polish liberals, Communists, socialists, and Freemasons, "were much more Christian and Catholic than the leadership of the Roman Catholic Church."[102]

Postwar

After the Holocaust "ended," pogroms killing thousands of Jews occurred, often stirred by ritual-murder accusations, the most notable took place at Krakow and Kielce in 1946. Jewish leaders approached the leading Polish prelates, Sapieha and Hlond among them, for help but received none.[103] (Six months before the Kielce massacres, a hand grenade was thrown into the Kielce Jewish Community Center. When Jewish leaders appealed to local bishop Kaczmarek to admonish the faithful not to commit violence against the Jewish community, he replied that when Jews insult national sensibilities he was not surprised that Kielce Catholics had acted violently.[104]) Ignoring the realities of the Kielce pogrom, Cardinal Hlond—whose first sermon upon returning to Poland from France reminded the faithful that the Jews had betrayed Christ and brought God's punishment upon themselves—held a press conference where he refused to condemn the pogrom or appeal to Polish Catholics to stop killing Jews, arguing that all Jews were Communists or supporters and that Polish antisemitism was caused by the Jews who participated in the Communist government: "[Jews] may have to pay dearly for it. While it is true that Jews are suffering, [Catholic] Poles today [are] suffering incomparably more."[105] The Jewish Committee asked the bishop of Lublin, Stefan Wyszynski, to issue a statement against antisemitism after Kielce. Like Hlond, he refused to condemn the pogrom and blamed it on Polish Catholic dislike of Jews involved in politics and in killing Catholic children, and he said that "Jewish contribution to Polish life is minimal. . . . The Jews should work very hard to achieve their own state."[106] With the exception of one bishop, the Polish clergy rationalized the attack on the Jews.[107] The Catholic press reacted to Kielce by denying that any Polish Catholics could have been involved. In the next half decade, the Catholic press denied that the Church had ever condoned antisemitism and claimed that Poles had only helped Jews.[108]

These criminal acts were lost in a national amnesia, as was the Jedwabne and other such Polish massacres of Jews during the Holocaust. As Polish cultural anthropologist Joanna Tokarska-Bakir noted, "Our memory is the place from which Jews are missing."[109] Joanna Michlic-Coren of the University of London has concluded that the Church reacted to post-Holocaust violence against Jews just as it reacted to interwar violence, by "the shifting of responsibility for anti-Jewish violence onto the Jewish ethnic minority . . . condemning physical violence but . . . blaming Jews themselves for anti-Jewish incidents, thereby reinforcing the myth of the Jew as the Threatening Other."[110]

In the mid-1960s, the Jewish population of Poland was far less than 1 percent, twenty-five thousand out of thirty-two million Catholic Poles, without even a single rabbi. Yet in March 1968, fearing social unrest, Poland's Communist leaders attacked the Jews with all the old charges from the 1930s.

Vatican Council II's ecumenical teachings in *Nostra Aetate* in regard to Jews in 1965 have been neither widely published in Poland nor integrated into Polish Catholic culture. Yet, antisemitic publications were and are still widely sold in Poland, sometimes, as in the 1930s, in churches.[111] Even in the Poland of the 1990s, it was still being taught that the Jews killed Christ and continue to murder Christian children. Antisemitic graffiti could still be seen: "Jews to the gas chamber." [*Zydzi do gazu.*][112]

In contemporary Poland, the Catholic Church hierarchy is not openly preaching antisemitism but many priests are, and the hierarchy is tolerating them even though Jews comprise less than 1 percent of the population.[113] In 1990, the Polish Catholic bishops issued a pastoral letter on Jewish-Catholic relations, acknowledging the complicity of Polish Catholics who stood indifferent or collaborated in the murders of the Jews during the Holocaust. But the bishops did *not* address Polish antisemitic attitudes of earlier decades nor the antisemitic position of the Polish Catholic Church, the hierarchy, the clergy, and the Catholic press. The reason, in part, was that at that time the Vatican had not admitted its own guilt. Antisemitic pronouncements by Polish clergy are standard fare, according to The Stephen Roth Institute for the Study of Contemporary Antisemitism at Tel Aviv University.

In October 1997, Father Henryk Jankowski denounced the expected appointment of Bronislaw Geremek to the post of foreign minister because of Geremek's Jewish heritage. Jankowski stated that there was no place for Jews in the Polish government. The priest has also denounced the Polish government's apology for the 1946 Kielce pogrom. "Apologizing to Jews is an insult to the Polish nation," he said in a July 28, 1996 sermon. Though Jankowski's remarks drew sharp criticism from some Church leaders, his punishment was only a one-year ban from preaching.

Perhaps the most influential source of antisemitic propaganda in Poland today is the popular Torun-based radio station Radio Maryja, which has a Catholic priest as its station director. In January 2000, the station presented a talk show devoted to the theme "What is the Auschwitz Lie?" in which Holocaust denier Dariusz Ratajczyk claimed Jewish prisoners died of overwork and illness.

The *Warsaw Voice* quoted an old woman leaving one of Father Jankowski's masses: "'What the priest says is the real truth; this church is our Poland. We are ruled by Jews, so we have to fight them. And here is our weapon,' she said, pointing to her rosary."

Many Poles, including those well-educated, continue to insist that Jews caused World War II.

On the sixtieth anniversary of the Jedwabne massacres, Polish President Aleksander Kwasniewski stated that Poles should ask "forgiveness" from the Jewish victims.[114] In contrast, in a radio address in March 2001, Polish Primate Cardinal Glemp—who refused to attend the sixtieth anniversary ceremony—declared: "I don't want politicians to tell the Church how it should express its sorrow for crimes committed by some group of its believers. Nor should they propose an ideology to be expressed by the Church." In a radio address, Glemp's apology for "Polish 'sins' was addressed not to the Jews but only to God."[115] He made the following five points:

1. The murders carried out through the burning alive of the Jewish population driven into the barn by Poles are an undeniable fact.
2. It was a crime carried out by a group of believers, but who had morally descended into barbarism.
3. The facts of the murder and the group of killers are known.
4. The only current that systematically persecuted Jews was Nazi totalitarianism.
5. The Church accepts the words of Chief Rabbi Schudrich, that the murder of innocent people in Jedwabne was not a local tragedy but the tragedy of the whole world. It is entered into the tragedy of great crimes of the 20th century alongside those in Katyn, Dachau, Auschwitz, in Rwanda, in the Balkans or among neighbors in Palestine. We mourn for the innocent blood shed among every nation.[116]

In a follow-up interview, Cardinal Glemp seemed to retract his admissions about the role of Poles in the Jedwabne massacres and blamed Polish antisemitism on "traditional unscrupulous Jewish mercantile practices, Jewish sympathy for Communism and the 'bizarre customs' of Judaism."[117] In a Poland that remains 90 percent Catholic, this was the position taken by the Catholic Church in regard to the Polish Catholic slaughter of Jews.

But there were other voices in Poland's Catholic Church that opposed such "contextualization" that denied the immorality of the crime of Jedwabne: Archbishop Zycinski of Lublin, Archbishop Muszynski of Gniezno, Bishop Tadeusz Pieronek, and those of other priests, such as Michal Czajkowski, Lukasz Kamykowski, Stanislaw Musial, and Stanislaw Obirek.[118] It is possible that these voices may someday come to predominate in Poland. Indeed, the latest Institute for Jewish Policy Research reports, "Antisemitism and Xenophobia Today" in 1996, 1998, and 2001 concluded that there have been slowly growing improvements in Catholic-Jewish relations.[119]

Yet when *The Passion of the Christ* opened in Krakow, many in the audience reacted with contempt for Jews. One of the audience "felt afraid of the people of Herod. The Jews, the people who killed him." Comparing the film to medieval passion plays, a priest, editor of an independent Catholic journal that often challenges the Church, worried that the "film unearths an old and terrible view that Jewish people are a source of evil, somehow more culpable for Jesus' death than others." A Polish Jewish film director observed that the film "grotesquely fill[ed] the screen with blood. . . . I saw terrible hatred for the Jews, in the way their faces were depicted and the way they were shot by the camera." The head of the Krakow Polish Committee of Christians and Jews feared that the "film could spark an uprising in antisemitism. . . . The film tells people that Jews are the ones to be blamed for Jesus' death, and that they deserve to suffer as a result."[120]

As late as 2007, Maciej Giertych, an influential member of the nationalistic, Catholic-based League of Polish Families (a partner in Poland's ruling coalition) and Polish member of the European Parliament, published a booklet titled, "Civilization at War in Europe," claiming that Catholic Europe's culture cannot coexist with Torah-based Judaism and that "the biologically different" Jews are (mirroring the arguments of St. Jerome identifying all Jews with Judas) "greedy conspirators," unethical separatists, and "a tragic community" because they refuse to accept Jesus Christ as their Messiah. Giertych's son is Poland's Minister of Education, Deputy Prime Minister, and heads the League—a revival of Endejca, the pre-Holocaust political party that teamed with Catholic students to force a reduction of Jewish students and faculty at universities.[121] Equally important, Giertych claims that his position is based on that of Polish historian and philosopher Feliks Koneczny, a Catholic antisemite who flourished in the 1930s and who blamed the "immoral Jews" for Nazism.[122] Giertych's book was published in connection with a new European Parliament grouping of French, Austrian, Romanian, and Bulgarian parties with a history of antisemitism.[123] The German President of the European Parliament, Hans-Gert Poettering, called the booklet "objectively a serious breach of the fundamental rights, and in particular the dignity of human beings to which our house so strongly adheres."[124]

CHAPTER 10

Modern Papal Policy

The popes regulated the antisemitic campaigns conducted in the Catholic press. . . .
At the same time, through their diplomatic service, they worked quietly to shape the
political use of antisemitism.

David Kertzer, The Popes Against the Jews

The Modern Papacy

Until 1965, the popes continued to follow the fifteen-hundred-year-old tradition of St. Augustine's "Witness People" in regard to the Jews, whom the Church still considered deicides and the world's leading evil-doers who should suffer but not be killed. In 1904, Theodor Herzl made a plea for Vatican support for a Jewish homeland.[1] The papal Secretary of State Cardinal Merry del Val—who, along with Pope Pius X, was sympathetic with many of the goals of Charles Maurras' Action Française, as was most of the French Church[2]—told him that "[a]s long as the Jews deny the divinity of Jesus, we certainly cannot make a declaration in their favor. . . . To us they are the indispensable witnesses to the phenomenon of God's term on earth. . . . In order for us to come out for the Jewish People in the way you desire, they would first have to be converted."[3]

The improbability of Herzl's achieving Vatican support for his goal was already evident when in the 1890s the Churches were the main propagandists of anti-Jewish feeling in Palestine. During the same visit, Pope Pius X told Herzl that Catholics related to Jews by means of "courtesy" and "philanthropy." Pius recognized the Jewish faith as "the foundation of our own," but because if was "superseded by the teachings of Christ, . . . we cannot admit that it still enjoys any validity."[4]

As David Kertzer writes,

In their public pronouncements, the [modern] popes generally avoided any specific mention of the Jews at all, permitting the Vatican to deny that the

Holy See bore any responsibility for the antisemitic movement in Europe. But out of the limelight, and with the assistance of their secretaries of state, the popes regulated the antisemitic campaigns conducted in the Catholic press. . . . At the same time, through their diplomatic service, they worked quietly to shape the political use of antisemitism.[5]

Earlier, the Church had to contend with the crises of the Middle Ages, the Reformation, the anti-clerical age of the Scientific Revolution and Enlightenment, state sovereignty, and nationalism that lasted until the end of the twentieth century. In the nineteenth and twentieth centuries in particular, the papacy had to cope with the development of liberal societies, the loss of papal secular authority except in the Vatican itself, the political upheaval of the Dreyfus Affair, the Russian and other Communist Revolutions, the Depression, and two world wars. Popes found Jews to be a convenient scapegoat to blame for much of what was going wrong in the modern world. They associated Jews, for example, with everything they hated about modern liberal society: freedom of speech and religion, legal equality, and respect for the rights of non-Catholics. Using the Catholic press to revive traditional defamations such as the ritual-murder charge and cozying up to fascist regimes as dams against liberalism, the Holy See fought what it considered "Jewish capitalism" as well as "Jewish bolshevism." The papacy's traditional antisemitism, the most deep-seated of any Western institution's, made the Church the natural ally of fascist regimes and prepared the faithful to be their supporters. In 1894, Father Henri Delassus wrote in a well-known French Catholic weekly that "antisemitism and Catholicism are one and the same thing." In 1911, Pope Pius X appointed him apostolic prothonotary and monsignor and later personally congratulated him on his golden anniversary as a priest.[6]

Jews in the nineteenth-century papal states lived as if it were still the Middle Ages: restricted to ghettos, forced to wear stigmatic Jew-emblems, prohibited from social relations with Catholics, forbidden to own property, to enter the professions or university, and to travel without permission. It was as if Pope Innocent III still ruled on the basis of the canons of the Fourth Lateran Council of 1215, the very first canon of which declared that each and every Jew would roast in hell for all eternity (at least until the Second Judgment): "There is one Universal Church of the faithful, outside of which there is absolutely no salvation." Other canons (67–70) accuse the Jewish "blasphemers of Christ" of "treachery" and "cruel oppression" in charging interest on loans to Catholics; decree that Jews must wear clothing that distinguishes them from Catholics because "through error [male] Christians have relations with the women of Jews . . . , and [male] Jews . . . with

Christian women. Therefore . . . we decree that such Jews . . . of both sexes in every Christian province and at all times shall be marked off in the eyes of the public from other peoples through the character of their dress"; claim that "it is absurd that a blasphemer of Christ [read "Jew"] exercise authority over Christians [in] public offices"; and, finally, order that Jews who had converted to Christianity were to be prevented from going back to Judaism.[7]

The reasons behind the Vatican's Byzantine decisions were best revealed in Catholic publications—newspapers, journals, pamphlets, books—that the Holy See supported or controlled. In 1825, for instance, a long article in Rome's *Ecclesiastical Journal* began a campaign of attacks on Jews that would last more than a century. Inspired by the Cardinal Vicar of Rome Annibale della Genga (who would later become Pope Leo XII), Father Ferdinand Jabilot (Procurator General of the Dominicans) attacked Jews for deicide, lust for money, and conspiracy to destroy Christianity; "they wash their hands in Christian blood, set fire to Churches, trample the consecrated Host, kidnap [Christian] children and drain them of their blood, violate [Christian] virgins." As if taking his text from canon 67 of the Fourth Lateran Council of 1215, Father Jabilot argued that Jews dominate Christians through their moneylending, "deceptions and frauds." Anticipating Dickens' *Oliver Twist*, Jabilot argued that Jews' houses were depots for goods stolen by Jewish "pickpockets, thieves, swindlers, assassins." The Talmud inspired the Jews' "hard, inflexible, tyrannical" behavior in regard to Christians. Catholics must stay alert to fight off this Jewish plot to enslave them. Jabilot's article was subsequently reprinted four times as a pamphlet. According to ex-friar Achille, Cardinal della Genga gave Jabilot "the task to write all the worst he could think of against the Jews. . . . He marshalled all his ingenuity not to discover but to imagine the darkest accusations to hurl against this poor people. Then subsidized by that same [Pope] Leo [XII] had the book printed and distributed it for free even to those who did not want a copy."[8] During this period, Italian Jews constituted less than two-tenths of 1 percent of the Italian population and had not had received civil rights anywhere in Europe.[9]

Popes from the medieval period to the modern period have wanted to be perceived as a moral authority in political life. In the twentieth century, the papacy's prestige and leadership, after a hiatus of centuries, began to reassert itself and the nations of the world were coming to recognize the popes as moral spokesmen for all Christians and for all humankind.[10]

But the reality was that the papacy's primary considerations have been self-interest and realpolitik. During conflicts between Christian nations, as in World Wars I and II, for example, the popes avoided specific political recommendations, not because the papacy had no interest, but because any explicit papal stand in favor of one Christian nation over another would be sure to alienate one of the belligerents. During World War I, Pope Pius X—who died a few weeks after the war's start—and Pope Benedict XV refused to condemn the German invasion of neutral Belgium. But in August 1917, Benedict issued a peace plan that favored the Central Powers apparently to reward Germany for offering to return the city of Rome to the Holy See and to strengthen Germany against a resurgent Orthodox Russia or a "godless" and anticlerical Soviet government. After the war, concerned about drawing up concordats with European states to ensure the Church's political and economic interests, Benedict sent the future Pius XI as apostolic visitor to Poland and the future Pius XII as nuncio to Germany. These two men would become the popes of the Holocaust.[11]

Theology of the Jews During the Holocaust

Like their medieval counterparts, Popes Pius XI and XII adhered to a Jewish policy that mixed realpolitik (political self-interest) with half-hearted protection and degradation of Jews, a program rooted in the basic canons of the Church's anti-Jewish theology.[12] During the Holocaust, 1933–45, the vast majority of Europeans were self-proclaimed Christians, most of them Roman Catholic and still influenced by the Church.[13] Most of France and Italy, 40 percent of Germany, and two-thirds of the populations of the nations occupied by the Third Reich were Catholic. The Catholic Church was an extremely well-organized ecclesiastical institution that had great potential for helping the Jews. A strong stand by the Roman Catholic Church at almost any point between 1933 and 1945 would have affected the way Catholics reacted to the Hitler regime.[14]

Despite proclamations to the contrary, the twentieth-century popes still believed that the Jews were Christ-killers with no fundamental right to reside among Christians.[15] When asked why Pius XII acted the way he did toward the Jews, Dr. Eugen Dollmann, Hitler's SS confidant and interpreter for his visits to Rome tendered a succinct explanation: "After all, it was inherent in traditional Catholic teaching: you know, Christ-killers and all that."[16] Radical Italian Fascist Roberto Farinacci also observed that oppression of the Jews was a logical continuation of papal Jewish policy, since anti-Jewishness was fundamental to Catholic doctrine.[17]

Ritual Murder Defamation

Though some earlier popes denied the existaece of Jewish ritual murder, the twentieth-century papacy still permitted the celebration of four Catholic martyrs allegedly murdered by Jews. As late as 1957, Pius XII acknowledged

San Domenichino de Val of Saragossa, calling him "the holy child, honored by the people of his blood." The Domenichino affair of 1250 was the first ritual-murder libel against Jews in Spain, and it symbolized the rising tide of antisemitism at the time.[18] The papacy also permitted an annual week-long commemoration of the slaughter of the whole Jewish population of Deggendorf in Bavaria after an allegation of Jewish "host desecration" in the fourteenth-century. These observances included the presentation of a play written by a Benedictine monk that called the Jews the children of Judas and of the devil. A local sculpture of the massacre of the Jews contained this inscription: "God grant that our fatherland be forever free from this hellish scum."[19] Finally, Andreas of Rinn and Simon of Trent were two beatified "victims" of Jewish ritual murder from the fifteenth century whose deaths the Church still remembered. Technically, the Church had not formally beatified Andreas and Simon. The Church claimed only that they were killed *in odium fidei*, due to (the Jews') hatred of the (Catholic) faith. Nevertheless, Simon's corpse, containers of his blood, and the torture devices allegedly used by the Jews were displayed in the Trent church until 1965, when the Church finally terminated Simon's veneration.[20]

By permitting the commemorations of these medieval anti-Jewish ritual-murder defamations, the papacy aggravated the disastrous contemporary political situation of the Jews in Europe, and the National-Socialists, among others, used these events in their continuing anti-Jewish propaganda. The popes must have known that such persistent celebrations of medieval myths would feed the worst fears and angers of the faithful and continue to poison the historical atmosphere for both Catholics and Jews.

The influential Jesuit periodical, *La Civiltà Cattolica*, provided the most candid expression of Vatican attitudes. In April 1950, Pius XII congratulated its editors and observed that its constitution was given to it "by the Roman Pontiffs." In 1990, *Civiltà* officials described the journal as "a non-Vatican publication at the service of the Vatican."[21] One of the Jesuits' basic premises was loyalty to the papacy. From the beginning of the Jesuit Order in the sixteenth century, St. Ignatius Loyola dictated that Jesuits must obey with mind and heart, "setting aside all judgment of their own," the infallible Catholic Church, whose authority is embodied in "the Highest Pontiff."[22] This journal often expressed ideas and attitudes that the modern papacy hesitated to acknowledge officially. *Civiltà* was founded in 1850 specifically to defend papal religious and political views as evidenced by the fact that editorials and major articles were reviewed by the Vatican Secretariat of State. Andrew Canepa has described *La Civiltà Cattolica* as "the principal organ of the anti-Jewish movement, lending antisemitism the intellectual prestige of the Society of Jesus and the authority of a publication universally considered

the oracle of orthodox Catholicism."[23] The Vatican-controlled Jesuit periodical *Civiltà Cattolica* publicized Jewish ritual murder. The Jesuits who wrote
these articles in *Civiltà* denied any antisemitic intentions and instead
affirmed that their intent was to prevent Catholics from getting too close to
Jews and to supply Catholics with the means of doctrinal self-defense.
However, between October 8, 1881 and February 24, 1882, a series of nine
antisemitic articles were so hostile to Jews that the author, Fr. Giuseppe
Oreglia, received a cautionary letter from his Jesuit superior. In his reply,
Father Oreglia stated that "I have been writing on Liberals and Masons for
many years, but I have never seen as much interest as now when I write on
the Jews. It's as if I have hit on a sore tooth." He also observed that his aim
had been "to reduce at least a little of the dangerous friendship and esteem
and familiarity [between Catholics and] Jews that is so forbidden by the
Church."[24] He claimed to have "irrefutable proof" that ritual murder and
hatred of Christianity was a requirement of Talmudic law.[25]

Disregarding the doctrine of papal infallibility, Father Oreglia argued that
Pope Innocent IV's thirteenth-century skepticism in regard to Jewish ritual
murder was in error since the pope was ignorant of the fact that the Jews consumed Catholic children's blood while leaving the hearts intact. According to
Oreglia's December 1881 article, papal disclaimers could not efface the fact
that the Jews were capable of any crime or sin. Another article stated that ritual murder was "generally proved [as] a general law binding on the consciences of all Hebrews to make use of the blood of a Christian child
primarily for the sanctification of their souls, and also . . . to bring shame and
disgrace to Christ and to Christianity."

Oreglia further argued that Jews ritualistically mixed blood with wine and
flour to make the Passover ceremony valid and that Jews needed Christian
blood for four other religious ceremonies: circumcisions, weddings, Tish B'av
(the day memorializing the destruction of the Temple), and Purim.
Sometimes, the blood was baked into the traditional Jewish Purim pastry, the
Hamantaschen, as a further insult to the Trinity. Oreglia maintained that during Purim each Jew was allowed to get drunk and actually kill one Christian
instead of symbolically hanging Haman.[26]

Oreglia himself claimed that his series on ritual murder was vigorously
supported by the bishops of Modena and Padova and by members of the
Vatican Secretariat of State.[27] Over the next twenty-five years, antisemites
cited Oreglia's articles and other *Civilta* articles like them. In France, Edouard
Drumont, the leader of the antisemitc movement, also based his charge of
Jewish ritual murder on Oreglia's articles.[28]

During most of the Dreyfus Affair,[29] Leo XIII refused to censure the antisemitic articles carried in the French Catholic newspaper *La Croix*, in

L'Osservatore Romano, in *La Civiltà Cattolica*, and elsewhere in the Catholic press. Reflecting the Vatican's concern that the Church's role in the Dreyfus Affair could result in an anticlerical reaction, only in late August 1899 was the Catholic press ordered to cease its passionate and partisan discussion of the Dreyfus case.[30] *La Civiltà Cattolica's* antisemitic articles disappeared between 1901 and 1914, but in April 1914, *Civiltà* returned to its ritual-murder and blood-libel defamations in a two-part series by a Catholic "expert" on Judaism, Professor Justin Pranaitis, a Polish priest who described a Jewish "dogma of blood." *Civiltà's* Jesuits published Father Pranaitis' articles even though in 1893 he authored a pamphlet[31] charging Jews with ritual murder, which had been discredited as filled with errors and falsifications. In 1911, he had served the antisemitic Russian government as an "expert witness" against the Jew Mendel Beilis at his ritual-murder trial in Kiev when no important Russian Orthodox priest could be found to support the government's case. (A Russian jury found Beilis not guilty.) According to Father Pranaitis, the Talmud allegedly urged Jews to murder Christians, as each death of a Christian, serving as a substitute for the Temple sacrifices, would hasten the arrival of the Jewish Messiah. The Talmudic and Torah prohibitions about consuming blood were circumvented, according to Pranaitis, by boiling the blood.[32]

The Vatican and the Catholic Press

An examination of the papal press reveals the subtleties of papal thinking in regard to the Jews. Beginning with the reign of Pope Leo XIII (1878–1903), several articles in *La Civiltà Cattolica* dealt with the Jews. Many of the unsigned articles—written by the editors Jesuit Father Giuseppe Oreglia de San Stefano, whose brother was a cardinal, and his *protégé*, Father Raffaele Ballerini—scapegoated the Jews to explain the Church's inability to bring the Kingdom of God into history and to help reestablish the Church's faded influence in society by associating the morally corrupt Jews with revolution, capitalism, liberalism, and socialism—in fact, with all the modern ideas, movements, forces, and organizations that so harried the Church.[33]

In later pieces published in the late 1880s and the 1890s, *Civiltà* reminded Catholics that the "eternal Jew" still awaited his Messiah, or the Antichrist, so that together they could dominate the material world and ruin Christianity. In 1896, Father G. G. Franco, a Jesuit specialist in demonology and parapsychology, wrote that in the Jewish-controlled lodges of the Masons, "the obscene worship of objects . . . is always a part of the cult of Satan . . . and of hatred of the Christ of God." Franco accused Jewish organizations in Germany, France, and the United States (the B'nai B'rith), along with the

Masons, of being dedicated to the worship of the devil.[34] As a result, the Jews have been and are enemies of Christianity and of all nations in which they live. Personifying the evils of capitalism, the Jews are cancerous parasites who do not work but live from the labor of others. Another Jesuit wrote that if the Jews had their way, freedom would come to this: "In the Rome of the popes, if the Cross of Christ is carried in procession through the streets of Rome, it is a crime; but if Giordano Bruno's snout and the horns of Satan are carried, then it is a noble homage rendered to civilization."[35]

In articles on January 24 and February 5 of 1898, the same author, following the traditional Augustinian doctrine of the Witness People, noted that God had condemned the Jews to be dispersed and persecuted all over the world and thus the Jews served as witnesses to the truth of Christianity. He suggested that "the race of Iscariot" be awarded the status of strangers, with legal protection but without full rights of citizenship. He saw the solution to the Jewish problem in "the abolition of their civic equality," their reghettoization, expropriation, and "the return of temporal rule to the Holy Throne of the Papacy."[36] *Civiltà's* contemporary models for how to deal with the Jews were the antisemitic legislation of nineteenth-century Russia and the open hostility of Lueger's anti-Jewish Christian-Social Party in Austria.

The Vatican's official newspaper was *L'Osservatore Romano*, which not only published Vatican releases but also often reprinted articles with whose arguments it sympathized. It joined *La Civiltà Cattolica* in expressing anti-Jewish themes during the last decade of the nineteenth century, exuding enthusiasm for Karl Lueger, the antisemitic mayor of Vienna and favorite of Pope Leo XIII.[37] In a chilling premonition, on August 23, 1892 *L'Osservatore Romano* warned the Jews that "they had better beware, for . . . God would inevitably grow intolerant of their behavior and then people's patience would be at an end. Then disturbances and horrible crimes could result, but who will be responsible [if not the Jews themselves]?" During this same period, the apostolic nuncio to France made an equally disturbing threat when he wrote that "the Jewish danger is everywhere, it threatens all of Christianity . . . and all means should be used to crush it. . . . The Catholic Church has reserved special indulgences for those who, when the good cause demands it, spill the blood of Jews and pagans."[38]

In 1898, *L'Osservatore* published a series of articles accusing the Jews of threatening Christian society and attacking the Church.[39] Since a second deicide was impossible, the Jewish rabbis allegedly displaced their hatred against the savior and his partisans, using Christian blood in Jewish rituals and plotting the total destruction of Christian society.[40] The newspaper observed that "[t]he Jew has chosen to lead a life in excessive and immediate abandonment to the innate passion of his race, fundamentally usurious and invasive, . . .

which has justified a thousand times over the natural aversion of Christian people to the deicide people." It concluded that the Jews needed a special legal status in view of "the natural repugnance that everyone feels for this deicide people."[41]

Pius XI

Pope Pius XI, whose papacy lasted from 1922 until 1939, has been idealized as an anti-Nazi opponent of antisemitism. Pius did oppose Hitler's attack on Catholic educational, social, and cultural institutions and condemned racial doctrines violating Catholic theology. But Pius also took Germany's part on international questions before the Concordat with Hitler in 1933, and during most of Hitler's regime he stood silent before the anti-Jewish policies of the Third Reich. Neither he nor his successor, Pius XII, were pro-Nazi but they were also not anti-fascist.

For most of his reign, Pius XI accepted antisemitism without objection.[42] Consistent with his admiration for St. Ambrose, St. Augustine, St. John Chrysostom (whose oratory he taught in the Seminary of Milan), for St. Thomas Aquinas,[43] and for St. Ignatius Loyola, Pius XI held traditional anti-Jewish views. As Peter Godman points out, Pius XI modeled himself on the eleventh-century pope St. Gregory VII, who made an emperor humiliate himself at Canossa.[44] The same St. Gregory VII referred to the Jews as "the synagogue of Satan."[45]

As mentioned above, when the future Pius XI, as Monsignor Achille Ratti, was sent on a papal mission to Poland in 1918, in the midst of pogroms against Jews, he reported back falsely that Jews were an "extremist [party] bent on disorder," that Jews "subsist through . . . contraband, fraud, and usury," and that "perhaps the strongest and the most evil [influence felt here], is that of the Jews."[46] Following traditional papal policy, Pius XI said nothing about Polish antisemitism during the 1930s.

The attitudes of Pius XI, refined in Poland, infused his papacy. In 1923, Pius XI praised Monsignor Ernest Jouin—who had described the *Protocols of the Elders of Zion* in this manner: "From the triple viewpoint of race, of nationality, and of religion, the Jew has become the enemy of humanity"— for "combatting our mortal enemy." Then Pius proceeded to raise Jouin to apostolic prothonotary. In 1925, Jouin praised the Germans who, "better than we, recognized the Jewish peril."[47]

In March 1928, Pius XI quickly confirmed a retrogressive decision of the Congregation of the Holy Office—from 1967 called the Sacred Congregation for the Doctrine of the Faith, the modern incarnation of the Holy, Catholic, and Apostolic Inquisition—to abolish the Catholic society called "Amici Israel" (the Friends of Israel), founded by Dutch theologians as a small place within the Church where Catholics and Jews could meet in peace together, but whose main goal appeared to be to convert Jews.[48] Amici Israel's principles were that Jews were not deicides, ritual-murder was superstition, and the Church would no longer support antisemitic movements. When the Amici Israel asked that "the perfidious Jews" be removed from the Good Friday liturgy, Pius XI called this "grave and offensive to the Church."[49] The Holy Office declared the group heretical on the grounds that the Jews were "no longer a people elected by God" and that the "spirit of reconciliation" between Catholics and Jews was "distasteful to the Holy Fathers and to the sacred liturgy of the Church."[50]

Also in 1928, Pius XI approved an article by Father Enrico Rosa, director of *Civiltà Cattolica*, called "The Jewish Danger and the Friends of Israel." Rosa mirrored the discredited *Protocols of the Elders of Zion* when he described Jews as controlling modern nations politically and economically, as architects of France and Russia—in 1932 Pius XI told Mussolini that the Russian hostility to the Church was caused in part by "Judaism's antipathy for Christianity,"[51] as was the recent Hungarian Revolutions, "with all its massacres, cruelty, and savage horrors."[52]

In 1929, Pius XI chose the antisemitic Archbishop Francesco Duca as nuncio to the Kingdom of Italy.[53] Pius' choice in 1930 to replace Cardinal Pacelli, the future Pope Pius XII, as nuncio to Germany was Cesare Orsenigo, a man who in June 1940 informed the German Foreign Office of "his pleasure at the German victories, that he could not wait for Italy to enter the War [on Germany's side], and . . . that he hoped the Germans would march into Paris by way of Versailles." Even German Cardinal Von Preysing and Austrian Cardinal Innitzer concluded that Orsenigo leaned too much toward the Gestapo.[54] Pius did not replace Orsenigo, chide those German bishops who displayed antisemitism, inform German bishops of the details he knew of the early Holocaust, or urge them to oppose the Final Solution on moral or any other grounds.[55]

In 2003, a letter buried in the Vatican archives was finally released seventy years after it was sent by a converted Jew, Edith Stein (from 1998, Saint Teresa Benedicta of the Cross), whom the Nazis murdered at Auschwitz in August 1942. On April 12, 1933, just ten weeks after Hitler came to power, Stein wrote to Pope Pius XI:

> Holy Father!
>   As a child of the Jewish people who, by the grace of God, for the past eleven years has also been a child of the Catholic Church, I dare to speak to the Father of Christianity about that which oppresses millions of Germans. For weeks we have seen deeds perpetrated in Germany which mock any sense

of justice and humanity, not to mention love of neighbor. For years the leaders of National Socialism have been preaching hatred of the Jews. Now that they have seized the power of government and armed their followers, among them proven criminal elements, this seed of hatred has germinated. . . . Within the last week, . . . five cases of suicide as a consequence of [government] hostilities. I am convinced that this is a general condition which will claim many more victims. . . . [T]he responsibility must fall, after all, on those who brought them to this point and it also falls on *those who keep silent* in the face of such happenings.

Everything that happened and continues to happen on a daily basis originates with a government that calls itself "Christian." For weeks not only Jews but also thousands of faithful Catholics in Germany, and, I believe, all over the world, have been waiting and hoping for *the Church of Christ to raise its voice* to put a stop to this abuse of Christ's name. Is not this idolization of race and governmental power which is being pounded into the public consciousness by the radio open heresy? Isn't the effort to destroy Jewish blood an abuse of the holiest humanity of our Savior, of the most blessed Virgin and the apostles? . . .

We all, who are faithful children of the Church and who see the conditions in Germany with open eyes, *fear the worst for the prestige of the Church, if the silence continues* any longer. We are convinced that this silence will not be able in the long run to purchase peace with the present German government. For the time being, the fight against Catholicism will be conducted quietly and less brutally than against Jewry, but no less systematically. It won't take long before no Catholic will be able to hold office in Germany unless he dedicates himself unconditionally to the new course of action.

At the feet of your Holiness, requesting your apostolic blessing,

(Signed) Dr. Edith Stein, Instructor at the German Institute for Scientific Pedagogy, Münster in Westphalia, Collegium Marianum.[56]

So far as we know, Edith Stein was never granted an audience with the pope, and her letter was buried in the archives without a reply. Secretary of State Pacelli indicated that the pope had read the letter and prayed for God's protection of the Church—he mentioned nothing about the Jews.[57]

Pius XI, along with his Secretary of State Cardinal Pacelli, followed the medieval Church's behavior in regard to the Jews during the Crusades. Perhaps Pius XI and Pius XII were condition by fears stemming from the outrages of the Spanish Civil War and the Church's persecution and anticlericalism in Mexico and elsewhere in Latin America. But the fact is that they kept silent as Jews were attacked throughout most of the 1930s. They said nothing when the Third Reich passed discriminatory legislation against the Jews (the Aryan laws) in April 1933, issued the anti-Jewish Nuremberg Laws in 1935 (themselves modeled on earlier Church regulations in regard to Jews and when Pacelli was informed of them, he kept quiet even though the Holy Office was at that time examining Hitler's racism[58]), seized all Jewish property, and marked German passports and identity cards with the letter "J." They were voiceless during the November 1938 *Reichskristallnacht* pogrom—the worst violence against Jews in the twentieth century up to that time. The German bishops were almost unanimously silent, leaving only one prelate to speak out publicly, Bernhard Lichtenberg.[59] Pope Pius XI was likewise silent, part of a strategy of silence that was followed and explained by his successor. In March 1939, Pius XII noted to the German cardinals that "the world should see that we have done everything to live in peace with Germany." Abandoning a policy of silence would be *"nicht klug,"* that is, not clever.[60] As Peter Godman observes: "a symbol for the strategy of both popes would be an ostrich with its head in the sand."[61]

The British *Chargé d'Affaires*, George Ogilvy-Forbes, has testified that in September 1930 the pope was *dis*pleased that the Bishop of Mainz stated from the pulpit that "a Catholic cannot be a member of the National-Socialist Party" and that he ordered his clergy to refuse the sacraments to Nazis.[62]

In 1933, Pius XI signed a Concordat with Hitler, similar to the agreement he had signed with Mussolini's government. The Vatican was not the first state to recognize the Third Reich, and the pope did regard the treaty as protecting Catholic rights in Germany. However, by this action the Holy See, the self-proclaimed moral caretaker of Christendom's conscience, further legitimized the Third Reich in the international community and set the tone for more positive Catholic attitudes toward the Nazi regime. The Concordat put an end to the German bishops' limited resistance to Nazism and legitimized the already-existing German-Catholic theologians', professors', and university students' support for Hitler's regime.[63] This in turn made it easier for the National-Socialists to totalitarianize German society and undermine the very Catholic authority the pope wanted to preserve. As Robert Gellateley has observed, the Church "did little to discourage Catholics from participating in the public life of the regime."[64]

In March 1933, Pius XI—who had been nuncio in Warsaw during the Russian Revolution—told the French and Polish ambassadors that one motive for the Concordat was to reach an agreement with Hitler that Bolshevism was *the* enemy, that is, Satan.[65] Later, Pius must have approved, or perhaps ordered, Jesuit Superior-General Wladimir Ledochowski's to silence Pierre Charles and Friedrich Muckermann, two Jesuits campaigning against the Rome-Berlin Axis. The Jesuits were told that God was using Hitler and Mussolini to create a new order in Europe.[66]

The Pontiff must have also been aware that the Vatican's legal acceptance of Nazi Germany had significant political ramifications for the Jews. In his Christmas address of 1934, Pius complained that justice could not be based on race law.[67] But not until March 1937 did he finally issue a conciliatory encyclical, *Mit Brennender Sorge*, on the subject. Although it repudiated Nazi-style racism and Nazism's totalitarian trends, *Mit Brennender Sorge*— drafted by German Cardinal Faulhaber and edited by Cardinal Eugenio Pacelli, the Vatican Secretary of State and future Pius XII—did *not* categorically denounce National-Socialism on moral grounds. Pius refused to follow the Holy Office's draft of a condemnation of the Nazis. Pius XI and his Secretary of State Pacelli agreed with Faulhaber that the encyclical should not even mention Nazism and should be a peaceful document dealing only with Catholic dogma, not a "polemic." The German bishops and the Holy See sought an alliance with the Third Reich against Communism and not a "rupture with the Nazis."[68] Instead, the encyclical respectfully reproached the Nazi leaders because they violated their Concordat with the Church in attempting to control Catholic education. Pius XI's letter implied that although he had no use for Nazi racism—the most popular Polish Catholic weekly, published by the Archdiocese of Poznan, argued that the pope opposed racism because it interfered with the Church's missionary activity— he otherwise sought a rapprochement with the Third Reich.[69] Pius refused to use such words as "heretical" and "immoral" in regard to Nazism, words so readily employed in other papal encyclicals. Furthermore, the encyclical made no reference to the Reich's persecution of the Jews or to the Nuremberg Laws that discriminated and disenfranchised the Jews.

Instead, the encyclical contained only two veiled references to the Jewish people, both of which reflected traditional Christian antisemitism. First, Pius XI argued that "the Redeemer's death . . . brought the Old Testament to its fulfillment and completion in the New, by which it is superseded." Second, he subtly alluded to the Jews as deicides when he described "the felony" of deicide and "His crucifiers."[70] Besides, Pius took some of the sting out of his criticism of Nazism when he condemned Communism in his encyclical *Divini Redemptoris* (The Promise of a Redeemer), published a few days after *Brennender Sorge* and allowing no compromise or reconciliation, with the Bolsheviks. A month and a half after the publication of *Mit Brennender Sorge*, Cardinal Pacelli responded to Nazi Germany's complaints: the Holy See "will never interfere in the question of what concrete form of government a certain people chooses to regard as best suited to it's nature and requirements. With respect to Germany also, it has remained true to this principle and intends to do so."[71]

Following these encyclicals, Pius XI's Secretary of State, Cardinal Pacelli—the future Pius XII—told the German Ambassador Diego von Bergen that friendly relations between the Vatican and Germany "would be restored as soon as possible," that he had "the greatest sympathy for the German people," and that he welcomed discussions with German Foreign Minister Joachim von Ribbentrop or Hitler's deputy Hermann Goering.[72]

After the *Anschluss* of 1938, Pius XI criticized Austrian Cardinal Theodor Innitzer's pro-Nazi stand[73] and condemned Mussolini's "Race Manifesto" as an Italian copy of German racism because it forbade marriages between Christians and converted Jews.[74] Pius's objections to racial policies were not based on humanitarian moral grounds but on the sanctity of the Catholic doctrine of conversion, the sacrament of baptism. He said nothing when the Italian government ordered Jewish children out of schools, fired Jewish adults from their jobs, and declared Jews *personae non gratae.* Moreover, at this time papal mouthpiece *Civiltà Cattolica* carried an article supportive of anti-semitism, which reasserted Catholicism's "legitimate defense of Christian people against a foreign nation in the nations where they live and against the sworn enemy of their well-being. [Measures are needed] to render such people harmless."[75]

Pius XI neither said nor did anything to discipline the Polish Catholic Church, which served as the great bastion of Polish antisemitism during the entire interwar period.[76] The Catholic press and educational establishment were for the most part strongly antisemitic and inevitably had a pernicious influence on most Polish people.[77] A large part of the clergy sanctioned or fomented daily humiliation and hatred of, or physical violence against, Jews, who amounted to half the European Jews living outside of Russia.[78]

During the thirties, Pius allowed anti-Jewish articles to be published in the Jesuits' *La Civiltà Cattolica* and other Catholic journals in Germany and Italy.[79] In January 1934, *Civiltà* acknowledged the Nazis' contribution to exposing the evil nature of the Talmud and other Jewish beliefs. Between 1934 and 1938, *Civiltà* stressed that since the Jews constituted a serious and permanent danger to society, Jewish civil rights should be revoked and the Jews reghettoized. Only "segregation and identification"—achieved, of course, "without un-Christian hatred"—would render Jews innocuous. Within a few years, Catholic governments all across Europe, including those of Austria, France, Hungary, Italy, Poland, and Slovakia, revoked Jewish civil rights and terminated all Jewish authority over, and relationships with, Christians. All of these Jesuit advocacies fit with traditional papal policy toward Jews, as did another *Civiltà* article, "Concerning the Question of Zionism," in which the Jesuits pictured Judaism as sinister, and Jews, through money and secularism, as plotting to seize the world with the devil as their master. "Judaism is a deeply malevolent religion, inasmuch as it pertains to a nation which presumes itself elect, and . . . it is the religion of corrupt messianism [which] renders Jewry a tinderbox of disorders and a standing menace to the world."[80]

In response to this article, Roberto Farinacci, the editor of the official fascist journal, *Il Regime Fascista*, sarcastically wrote that he was "impressed" after reading *Civiltà Cattolica*. "Both for Italy and Germany there is still much to learn from the disciples of Jesus, and we must admit that both in its planning and in its execution, Fascism is still far from the excessive severity of the people of *Civiltà Cattolica*."[81] The Italian-fascists' and *Civiltà's* anti-Jewish propaganda campaigns coalesced in 1939 when the journal advocated that Jewish civil rights should be revoked and the Jews reghettoized and expropriated in accordance with Peter the Venerable's advice (also cited by Edouard Drumont in his popular antisemitic tome, *La France Juive*.[82])

Pius XI's lack of positive action throughout much of the 1930s, his failure to condemn traditional Christian antisemitism rising all across Europe, his approval of *Civiltà Cattolica's* anti-Jewishness, the triumphalism expressed in his *Mit Brennender Sorge* encyclical, his silence while German Jews were discriminated against, persecuted, humiliated, their synagogues burned, their holy books trampled, and their lives taken indicated both to the faithful and to the National-Socialists that the pope still believed that the Jews were the traditional enemy.

Two pieces of evidence indicate that near the end of his life, Pius may have begun to rethink his views toward the Jews. First, on September 6, 1938, addressing the directors of the Belgium Catholic Radio Agency, Pius stated:

> Abraham is called our patriarch, our ancestor. Antisemitism is not compatible with the thought and the sublime reality that are expressed in this text. It is an antipathetic movement, a movement in which we Christians can take no part. . . . No, it is not possible for Christians to participate in antisemitism. We recognize the right of anyone to defend himself, to take means to protect himself against all that threatens his legitimate interest, but antisemitism is inadmissible. Spiritually we are Semites.

The reader should note: (1) Pius cannot bring himself to use the word "Jew" in his statement. Just think of the difference in tone had he said, "Spiritually we are Jews." (Throughout World War II, Pius' successor, Pius XII, even in diplomatic documents, usually used the Nazi word for Jew, "non-Aryan."); (2) *Civiltà cattolica*, with Vatican approval, *continued* to run its antisemitic attacks on Jews during this period; (3) Pius XI's statement was completely omitted from all Italian press reports of the audience, from the semi-official

Vatican newspaper *l'Osservatore Romano*, and from the *Acta Apostolicae Sedis*, the official record of the Holy See. For the Vatican, what was not in the written record might as well never have existed at all[83]; and (4) Pius XI's words "We recognize the right of anyone to defend himself . . . against all that threatens his legitimate interest"—that is, Catholics may attack Jews so long as Catholics feel threatened in fantasy or reality—stood as a catch phrase for standard papal policy based on St. Augustine's Witness People prescription, namely, the deicidal Jews were to suffer but not be killed, which was a policy followed by the governments in several Catholic nations as well.

This bipolar attitude sixteen hundred years earlier in a homily by St. Jerome: "My enemies are the Jews; they have conspired in hatred against me, crucified me, heaped evils of all kinds upon me, blasphemed me."[84] Then, after damning the Jews, St. Jerome asks forgiveness for them. This is what the Church did when it approved discrimination and at asking for justice and charity at the same time.[85] In 1898, the Vatican's newspaper *Osservatore Romano* attacked the Jews as vampires who sought Christian blood and conspired to destroy the Church, then advocated a "healthy antisemitism."[86] As Eliezer Berkovitz observed, "charity asked for a people that in the same breath is called fallen and faithless has little effect in history."[87]

A second piece of evidence on Pius XI's late attitude change toward Jews is his plan for a new encyclical "Humani Generis Unitas." Only in Catholic fantasy did Pius' proposed encyclical break new ground. It was the same traditional papal policy we have seen in this chapter. Only 14 percent of the document dealt with antisemitism at all, and its main author was Gustav Gundlach, a German Jesuit who, elsewhere, defended "permissible antisemitism," that is, antisemitism that "combats by moral and legal means a truly harmful influence of the Jewish segment of the population." As Father Flannery writes, "Hardly the person to prepare the section on antisemitism at the crucial moment of history!"[88] The encyclical condemned the Jews as "blinded by vision of material domination and gain [and therefore] spiritually blind," failing to recognize Christ, guilty of Jesus's death, and cursed as perpetual wanderers. Catholics are warned of the "spiritual dangers to which contact with Jews can expose souls. . . . The historic enmity of the Jewish people to Christianity [has led to] a perpetual tension between Christians and Jews." There is no mention of Christian antisemitism. The Church asks governments to deal with Jews "with justice and charity" in any measures they undertook to protect Christians from Jews. Even this was "too shocking" for Vatican conservatives, specifically the Jesuit General, who delayed handing the proposed encyclical over to the pope until he was too close to death to read it.[89]

Pius XII

Early on, Cardinal Pacelli (later Pius XII), then Vatican Secretary of State, recognized the moral implications of Hitler's policies,[90] telling the British Chargé d'Affaires Ivone Kirkpatrick in August, 1933, that he deplored Hitler's recent reign of terror against political opponents and German Jews.[91] Although Pius XII had volunteered to act as an intermediary between the Allies and the ineffectual German opposition to Hitler during the first few months of the war,[92] in his address at the International Eucharistic Congress in Budapest Pacelli referred to Jews "whose lips curse [Christ] and whose hearts reject him even today."[93] Pacelli mouthed these traditional Catholic charges while Hungary and the Third Reich and Italy were in the midst of antisemitic surges. As Germany continued its march of conquest in May 1940, the Vatican signaled its withdrawal from any political resistance.[94]

Pius XII's Christmas message of December 1942 was particularly well received by some in the West and annoyed both German Foreign Minister Ribbentrop and the Reich Security Office.[95] This was Pius's strongest public statement on German mistreatment of civilians, and, compared to the lack of Allied concern for the Jews at this time, he did appear in this one instance to stand out as "a lonely voice crying out of the silence of a continent."[96] But even here, Pius XII did not mention Jews by name—he never did publicly or in his private correspondence—and referred obliquely to "the hundreds of thousands of persons who, without any fault on their part, sometimes only because of nationality or race, have been consigned to death or to a slow decline."[97] Even this material consisted of a mere twenty-seven words in twenty-six pages of text. As Michael Phayer observed, "no one, certainly not the Germans, took it as a protest against their slaughter of the Jews."[98]

Pius XII later argued that he could not have been more specific since the Bolsheviks were also committing atrocities and German behavior had been exaggerated by Allied propaganda,[99] but he omitted the fact that he could have mentioned *both* the German and Russian violations of international law. Privately, Pius told both British Ambassador d'Arcy Osborne and Roosevelt's personal representative Harold Tittman that he believed his statement to be a strong one and that he was referring to "Poles, Jews, and hostages" when he mentioned "the killed and tortured." A few months later he wrote to Berlin bishop Konrad von Preysing, who urged a stronger papal response in words and deeds, that the message was a "short but understood" depiction of "what was being done to non-Aryans in the territories under German authority."[100]

Only a week after the Christmas message, the President of the Polish Republic in exile, evidently unconvinced as to the effectiveness of the pope's message, sent another appeal for the pope to speak out. The British

Ambassador to the Holy See during the war, Francis d'Arcy Osborne, reported a week after this that many diplomats were "anything but enthusiastic" about the statement because it was "inferential and not specific, and comes at the end of a long dissertation on social problems."[101] An American Jesuit close to the pope, Vincent McCormick, told Father Leiber, one of the pope's assistants, that Pius' address was "obscurely expressed."[102] On January 22, Chaim Barlas of the Jewish Agency in Jerusalem in vain asked Cardinal Roncalli to request that Vatican Radio declare loudly and clearly that "rendering help to persecuted Jews is considered by the Church to be a good deed."[103]

Unlike the papal-controlled and clearly antisemitic Jesuit periodical *Civiltà Cattolica*, Vatican radio was *independent* of the pope and his secretary of state.[104] In one instance in October 1942, Jesuit Father Emmanuel Mistiaen spoke on Radio Vatican that: "Let us not forget that Jesus had looked at his lambs with love. . . . He demands that we remember them, that we help them through our courage . . . that we look after those who are rejected and damned by men, . . . let us not forget that we also may be called to testify with our blood. . . . All men are children of the same father. . . . They are no longer Jews, Greeks, gentiles: they are only candidates to the universal redemption brought by Jesus Christ."[105] This broadcast was a call to Catholics to follow *theologia crucis* and help the victims of the Third Reich. A few months later, amidst opposition to his broadcasts by the Catholic hierarchy, Mistiaen was removed from the airways.[106]

In Hungary during the last year of the war, almost a million Jews were deported to their deaths while Pius XII still tiptoed around the Jewish issue. Pressured by Jewish groups, by papal nuncio Angelo Rotta, and by the U.S. War Refugee Board—which advocated a papal radio appeal or the sending of a special papal envoy to Budapest—on June 25, 1944, Pius sent a telegram to Miklas Horthy, Regent of Hungary.

> We are being beseeched in various quarters to do everything in our power in order that, in this noble and chivalrous nation, the sufferings, already so heavy, endured by a large number of unfortunate people, because of their nationality or race, may not be extended and aggravated. As our Father's heart cannot remain insensitive to these pressing supplications by virtue of our ministry of charity which embraces all men, we address Your Highness personally, appealing to your noble sentiments in full confidence that you will do everything in your power that so many unfortunate people may be spared other afflictions and other sorrows.[107]

International pressures, Pius' telegram, along with Allied bombing of Budapest helped achieve the temporary suspension of Jewish deportations, to be resumed shortly afterward. Even though nuncio to Hungary Angelo Rotta informed Pius in 1944 of the suffering and murder of hundreds of thousands of Hungarian Jews, Pius restricted himself to dead-end diplomacy instead of public condemnation.[108]

Perhaps the most significant activity undertaken by Pius was his releasing Catholic priests and nuns from obligations that would have precluded them from helping Jews, many hundreds of whom may have been hidden in the Vatican itself. Moreover, he did not prevent lay Catholics from following their consciences in the matter of saving Jews.[109] As a result, individual Catholics—both clergy and laypeople—did help save hundreds of thousands of Jewish lives with or without violating Church regulations.[110] But these righteous actions took place not because of the pope's leadership or public example (although he made several private, diplomatic efforts to help converts), but rather because of the moral and physical courage of individual Catholics who took the initiative upon themselves. Never did Pius XII state what Maria Langthaler stated after she helped escapees from Mauthausen concentration camp: "I am a Christian, and as a Christian I am obligated to help when someone is in need. The Lord God is for the whole world, not only for the Germans. . . . I asked nothing at all; that made no difference to me. Only because they were human beings."[111] In 1999, the Jesuit priest, Stanislaw Musial, former Secretary of the Commission of the Polish Episcopate for Dialogue with Judaism from 1986 to 1994, and editor of the liberal Catholic weekly *Tygodnik Powszechny*, said: "We [Catholics] were in silence during the Shoah. Maybe Pope Pius XII was a good man, but he did not lead as a shepherd, or help form a consciousness of 'Thou shall not kill.' And for this reason, we should not falsify the historical perspective."[112] Had Pius XII, the Vatican, or the bishops organized any kind of significant institutional response to the Holocaust, had they urged Catholics to help Jews, many more Catholics would have helped and many more Jewish lives would have been saved.[113]

Proficient in history and Church law, a professor and a scholar like his predecessor, Pius XII adhered to Leo XIII's dogma that "it is always urgent, indeed, the chief preoccupation, to think best how to serve the interests of Catholicism."[114] According to Hitler, Pius was the strongest man in Rome, much stronger than Mussolini or the Italian king.[115] Taking Hitlerian hyperbole and ulterior motives into consideration, it is obvious that Pius XII was not a risk taker, no matter the moral imperative. Pius's mottos were opportunism and restraint. Like Pius XI, Pius XII followed a secretive ecclesiastical realpolitik, and he was not the kind of pope who would speak out strongly on moral issues, especially when they concerned the Jews. Pius XII's Jewish policy differed little from that followed by nearly all of the ninety popes who spoke or acted on the Jewish issue. Pius XII was *not* a friend of the Nazis, he was not frozen into silence because he feared for his own life, he did not sponsor Bishop Hudal's ratline that ferried Nazis from Europe to Latin America. The truth is that Pius helped many Jews though not publicly, that after the war Italian Jews expressed their gratitude toward him, that he was sometimes wise. But even the wisest person is not "wise every day."[116] Moreover, based on a policy of self-interest as well as on St. Augustine's precept that Jews should suffer degradation (Sergio Minerbi has commented that the Church was willing to protect Jews only if "it would help them stay alive as sufferers, for they are indispensable to the Church as witnesses of divine punishment"[117]), Pius never made a strong public statement of protection at the right time for the Jewish people. In fact, Pius' policy was less protective than that of many medieval popes, for sometimes, at least, they had admonished both secular and religious princes that Jews must not be tortured *or* killed. To paraphrase Own Chadwick's criticism of Pius: There may be moments when prudence is not the first quality on demand, when what a moral situation needs is an explosion and let prudence be damned.[118]

In the face of enormous political difficulties during the war,[119] many of Pius' decisions were based on the Church's self-interest rather than moral principle. Owen Chadwick lists three items of a "real charge sheet" against Pius XII:

[1] He was not quite the right man in the right place. . . . This was a quiet man, shy, other-worldly, rather remote from ordinary people but charming at need, trained in that world at the end of the nineteenth century when the Vatican walls felt very high, like a sanctuary against a hostile world, good at languages and cultured, but very hesitant in making decisions. His personality . . . heaven-bent, contemplating haloes, static, distant.

[2] He knew [about the slaughter of Jews in Eastern Europe]. He must speak. What he was to say went through draft after draft after draft. . . . There are moments in history when it is better just to speak without thinking.

[3] He kept Mgr Orsenigo as his nuncio in Berlin. . . . The Pope knew how weak with the Nazis he was. . . . Yet the Pope kept Orsenigo in Berlin throughout the war.[120]

There are more charges against Pius than Chadwick lists. Within a few months of his coming to office in 1939, in consultation with the French bishops and based on Action Française's leaders' vague assurance that they would "respect . . . the Catholic religion in the future," Pius decided to lift his predecessor's thirteen-year interdict on the antisemitic and anti-democratic journal, *Action Française*.[121] On June 29, 1943, at the height of the Nazi mass murders, Pius XII published an encyclical, *Mystici Corporis Christi*, which identified the Church with Christ's mystical body. Pius did mention Jews, but following St. Augustine, Pope Innocent III, and the Fourth Lateran Council's first canon, Pius reaffirmed that the members of the uniquely saving Roman Church must be baptized Catholics; while the Nazis murdered the Jews in this life, Pius XII's infallible opinion reminded Catholics that Jews could not be saved in the next.

Pius' attitude to the Jewish predicament is also revealed in his secret correspondence contained in *Actes et Documents du Saint Siège relatifs à la Seconde Guerre Mondiale*. To support the Church's claim that Pius was not informed as to the nature of the Final Solution, several items potentially damaging to Pius' reputation have been omitted:

- SS officer Kurt Gerstein's attempt to communicate his information about the gassings at Treblinka and Belzec to Pius (even though Gerstein's information did reach the Vatican through the auxiliary bishop of Berlin Heinrich Wienken, the Vatican "allowed Gerstein's information . . . to die" without being relayed to France where Jews had not yet been deported)[122];
- information about the Holocaust in Catholic Croatia[123];
- Pius' discussions with American special envoy Myron Taylor and German ambassador Ernst von Weizsäcker;
- the World Jewish Congress memo of March 1942 to the nuncio to Switzerland Filippi Bernardini verifying Jewish extermination;
- a written report of French priest Marie-Benoit submitted to the pope describing the deportation of Jews from France and from the Italian-occupied zone of France[124];
- of Berlin Bishop Preysing's 13 letters to Pius XII in 1943 and 1944, only 2 have been included.[125]
- The Vatican volumes also ignored individual Catholics' attempts to rescue Jews when done on their own initative without Pius' involvement.[126]

Actes et Documents discloses Pius' occasional concern for Jews, mostly for baptized Jews, limited by the parameters of traditional papal policies and the political self-interest of the Church. The documents also demonstrate that the pope and his secretary of state, Cardinal Luigi Maglione, seldom discussed the Jewish issue with officials of the Third Reich. When discussions did take place, they were extremely cautious, and papal concern seemed to the Germans and others half-hearted and unconvincing. Pius seemed to have little objection to a limited and "humane" anti-Jewish policy, and he did nothing to object when Church officials like Archbishop Andrea Cassulo, nuncio to Romania, argued that God was employing the horrors of the Holocaust to gain new converts for the Church.[127] Moreover, in spring 1942 reports to the Vatican from at least nine nations, including Poland and Italy, that eighty thousand Slovak Jews were being deported and murdered in Poland with language like "incredible killings take place every day," nevertheless the Vatican refused to acknowledge the mass murder of European Jews.[128] Catholic historian Michael Phayer asks, "what kind of confirmation" was the Vatican looking for?[129] Not only this, but the Vatican's failure to exchange the atrocity information it collected with the Allies gave them less reason to consider helping the Jews.[130] Moreover, the Vatican kept all the information about the deportations and mass murders of Jews in gas chambers it received and confirmed secret until the end of 1944, not sharing it with the Allies, bishops, resistance organizations in German-occupied nations, or anyone until it was too late for millions of victims—millions. This was an intentional concealing of information and facts of the Holocaust.[131] What shall we make of it? In a diary entry of October 1942, British Ambassador d'Arcy Osborne who, like the pope, noted that "a policy of silence in regard to such offences against the conscience of the world must necessarily involve a renunciation of moral leadership.[132] In December 1942, Osborne noted in his diary that Pius "does not see that his silence is highly damning to the Holy See." And on December 22 he wrote, "The Vatican will be the only State which has not condemned the persecution of the Jews."[133]

Pius claimed several times that information and facts about the Holocaust were kept secret and the condemning of Germany was not done "for fear of making the plight of the victims even worse." This author agrees with Michael Phayer that this "justification cannot be taken seriously."[134] Pius XII said and did nothing when the *Catholic* regime in Croatia was slaughtering Jews and he said nothing *after* Jews were deported to their deaths.[135] In contrast, Croatian archbishop Stepinac, though maintaining ties with the fascist government, protested its murderous antisemitic policies and actions and disciplined collaborating priests.[136] A well-informed Vatican ignored deadly deportations of Jews from Catholic Slovakia, whose population was generally opposed to the deportations and needed clear leadership from the Church (which was lacking) to focus their opposition, while vigorously protesting the use of Jewish women as prostitutes and while the Slovakian bishops issued a pastoral letter reminiscent of *Mit Brennender Sorge* attacking Jews as rejecting their redeemer and preparing "an ignominious death for him on the cross."[137] At the most, the pope comforted himself with minor diplomatic measures.[138] The moral issue of Germany's and other nation's collaboration with Germany's Holocaust was not a priority with Pius XII, whose concerns about the destruction of Church buildings in Rome and diplomatic "priorities put the Jews at mortal risk."[139] The pope apparently "cried like a child" when he was informed about mass murders.[140] He obviously did not want the Jews murdered, but he seemed overcome by his attempt to balance traditional Christian antisemitism with his own feelings of charity, more specifically, St. Augustine's prohibition against killing Jews with the need to have them degraded. Although Pius had to face enormous wartime difficulties,[141] he usually made the worst of the situation. In April 1943, Maglione's assistant, Msgr. (later Cardinal) Domenico Tardini, accurately represented the pope's attitude when he indicated that the Church was protesting the Slovakian government's deportations of Jews more from its universal "duty of charity" rather than "from sympathy with the Jews, [who] will never be particularly friendly to the Holy See and to the Catholic Church."[142]

Several persons close to the pope criticized Pius' decision not to speak out clearly against the Final Solution.

1. Austrian Cardinal Theodor Innitzer (who moved toward opposition to Hitler after asking clergy to vote for *Anschluss*) complained in February 1941 that Jews who had been baptized Catholics were being ignored by the Church they had put their faith in.[143]
2. On June 11, 1940, French Cardinal Eugène Tisserant, the only non-Italian member of the Curia (the papal court, the Vatican's bureaucracy) and called by some Cardinal de Gaulle (the stubborn leader of the Free French Forces) made a devastating criticism if not of Pius himself then of his policies. Realizing that the Catholic conscience, especially that of the young, was being conditioned by fascist ideology and Hitlerism, Tisserant wrote "in righteous anger" to Cardinal Suhard of Paris that for months he had "persistently requested the Holy See to issue an encyclical [Tisserant's reference to an encyclical indicates that he meant his criticism for Pius XII] on the duty of the individual to obey the dictates of conscience, because this is the vital point of Christianity. . . . I fear that history may have reason to reproach the Holy See with having pursued a policy of convenience to itself and very little else."[144]
3. German Cardinal Konrad von Preysing asked Pius on January 17, 1943 "to issue an appeal in favor of the unfortunate [Jews]." But the pope replied in April that the Holy See had acted with material and moral

charity for both non-Aryans and believing Jews, given "the limits of its responsibilities."[145]

4. Besides his previously noted comments, on May 1942, British Ambassador d'Arcy Osborne asked in his dairy, "Is there not a moral issue at stake which does not admit of neutrality?" On June 13, he observed that "moral leadership is not assured by the unapplied recital of the Commandments." In a diary entry of October 1942, Osborne noted that "his Holiness has already publicly denounced moral crimes arising out of the war. But such occasional declarations in general terms do not have the lasting force and validity that, in the timeless atmosphere of the Vatican, they might perhaps be expected to retain."[146] Osborne logged this entry on December 13, 1942, "I am revolted by Hitler's massacre of the Jewish race on the one hand, and, on the other, the Vatican's apparently exclusive preoccupation with the effects of the war on Italy and the possibilities of the bombardment of Rome."[147]

5. In May 1942, the American Chargé d'Affaires, Harold Tittman, reported to the State Department that the pope occupied himself with spiritual matters, charitable acts, and rhetoric while adopting at the same time an ostrich-like policy towards atrocities that were obvious to everyone."[148] In July, Tittman observed that the Vatican's silence was "endangering its moral prestige and undermining faith both in the church and in the Holy Father himself."

6. In September several Vatican diplomats requested that the pope end his public silence on German atrocities. To this complaint, Pius replied, "But I have already done so much!" He argued that his help was more effective in private, that publicity would make things worse, and that his words were censored by the Germans.[149] Pius' frequent response to Jewish and Christian leaders' desperate appeals to help the Jews was typical of the Vatican's usual reply—"the Holy See has done, is doing, and will do all in its power to help."[150]

7. In June 1939, Austrian Jesuit John Oesterreicher complained that Pius XII was grievously erring in praising Hitler "instead of speaking out truthfully."[151]

8. On August 20, 1941, Msgr. Domenico Tardini *unintentionally* criticized Pius when he observed on another issue that "complaints, suggestions, and protests are completely useless if they remain secret."[152]

Christian virtue, bureaucratic sloppiness, and Italian acceptance of bribes were just what the Italian Jews needed for their salvation.[153] The Germans had anticipated that Pius, as bishop of Rome, would lead the way and publicly protest against German deportation of the Jews of Rome. German

Ambassador Ernst von Weizsäcker, a devout Catholic, had written to the German Foreign Ministry that "they say that when comparable incidents occurred in French cities, the bishops there took a firm stand. The pope, as head of the Church and bishop of Rome, cannot be more timorous than they."[154] But, at a time when he knew that arrest was a prelude to the mass murder of Jews, the pope refused to enter any public protest when, in October 1943, the Germans rounded up the Jews of Rome. (Pius did not speak out in December when Mussolini ordered all Jews living in Italy to be interned and expropriated. Pius did relax canonical restrictions to allow about five thousand Jews to be hidden on Church property.) The pope may have feared making matters worse for the Jews, Italians, German Catholics, or himself by a strong intervention. (When, in September 1943, SS Lt. Col. Herbert Kappler, Chief of Security in Rome, tried to extort 50 kilograms of gold from the already condemned Jewish community, Pius did assent to a *loan* if the Jewish attempt to secure the gold fell short, which it did not. In addition to the Jews, many individual Catholics, including a few priests, contributed their own gold.[155]) Ironically, had Pius taken an assertive stance in trying to prevent the round-up of Roman Jews, he apparently would have gotten support from the local German authorities.[156]

On the day of the Roman raid, two German diplomats, Albrecht von Kessel and Gerhard Gumpert, took the initiative and proposed a letter of protest on behalf of the pope to send to the General Stahel, local military commandant of Rome, who would then forward it to Berlin. Pius agreed to this plan. He selected his friend, Bishop Alois Hudal, resident at the German College in Rome, an Austrian antisemite and Nazi sympathizer, to sign a letter prepared by Kessel and Gumpert; the letter was delivered to Stahel just a few hours after the end of the raid.

Who was this man, Alois Hudal, whom Pius XII trusted with the "protest" letter?[157] Hudal had written a book admired by then Cardinal Pacelli, who kept it off the Church's Index of Forbidden Books until 1936.[158] In it, Hudal argued that Nazism, so long as it violated no Catholic dogma, was compatible with Christianity. He offered the National-Socialists a partnership with the Church against Bolshevism, "whose entire middle and lower party apparatus is *Judaized*." Hudal also claimed that the Jewish ghetto of Rome was a "state within a state" in which "the Semitic race" conspired with democracy and cosmopolitanism to control Rome. He observed that the Church had no reason to defend the soulless and materialistic Jews. He justified the anti-Jewish Nuremberg Laws, writing that "they should not be objected to even if these anti-Jewish measures do not comply with what one would expect from a modern state based on the principle of law."[159]

On October 16, Pius ordered Vatican Secretary of State Maglione to discuss the Roman raid with Weizsäcker. When Weizsäcker asked what the pope would do if the German government persisted in its present Jewish policy in Italy, Maglione replied that "The Holy See would not want to be put in the position of having to utter a word of disapproval." A listener to this byzantine conversation would conclude that this was a half-hearted threat, which was never intended to be effectuated. After the German ambassador complimented the Holy See for its "perfect even-handedness," he asked Maglione's approval to keep the meeting secret. Maglione gave his assent, adding that the pope was being "cautious so as not to give the German people the impression that [he] has done or has wished to do even the smallest thing against Germany during this terrible war."[160] In his report to the German Foreign Office on the meeting, Weizsäcker (who was typical of many members of the German Foreign Office who opposed Hitler's policies and thought that "if it were possible to do anything at all for peace, it could be done at or through the Vatican"[161]) confirmed that the pope continued to do everything he could "not to burden relations with the German government and German agencies in Rome."[162] As a result of the "protest" letter and these conversations, Himmler issued no stop order; on the contrary, the arrests of Italian Jews continued on the very next day.[163] Catholic historian Michael Phayer summarized the situation: "Having known in advance what would befall the Roman Jews, the pope said nothing to forestall it. Afterward, he said nothing to condemn it."[164]

Pius' inner circle was dominated by Jesuits: Robert Leiber was his closest advisor; Wilhelm Hendrich, his librarian; Gustav Gundlach drafted many of his public statements on social issues; August Bea, later cardinal, was his confessor; another close associate of Pius', Giovanni Montini, the future Pope Paul VI, had a Jesuit education. Pius himself had been trained by the Jesuits.[165] It was also said that the Jesuit Superior General, Fr. Ledochowski, was more influential with Pius than the Italian cardinals in the Curia.[166] Pius was closer to *Civiltà Cattolica* than other modern popes, and he was responsible for the publication of its ideas and in that sense they were his.[167] During the greatest period of mass murder of Jews, Pius allowed the Jesuits of *Civiltà Cattolica*, whose material was under daily review by the Vatican, to publish anti-Jewish material, including, as previously mentioned, the ritual-murder defamation.[168] In 1941 and 1942, *Civiltà* attacked the Jews for mythic sins, "malice . . . injustice, impiety, infidelity, sacrilege." In December 1941, a month before many of the top German bureaucrats met at Wannsee to finalize details of Jewish deportation and the Final Solution, *Civiltà* reminded its readers that the Jews were the most visible actors in the drama of deicide and that they repeated this crime by means of ritual murder "in every generation."[169] In

March 1942, another article in *Civiltà* cited the Acts of the Apostles as condemning Jewish "perversity [and] furious hatred" against Christ. That Jews condemned Christ to crucifixion—"the crime of the sons of the Synagogue"—was an inexpungeable "stigma."[170] This journalistic antisemitic Crusade occurred just before SS head Heinrich Himmler began his own campaign to stir fears of Jewish ritual murder.[171]

As revealed earlier in this chapter, the Church's negative attitude toward an increased number of Jews in Palestine existed decades before the reign of Pius XII. In the eyes of the Church, Palestine meant the Holy Land, and the thought of an important Jewish presence there stimulated many feelings that had given rise to Catholic triumphalism in the first place. The historic rights of the Church were considered more important than the Jewish lives that could have been saved if Palestine had become a land of refuge for the harried Jews of Europe during the Holocaust. Vatican Secretary of State Maglione believed that "Palestine, under Jewish dominance, would cause new and serious international problems, would displease Catholics all over the world, would provoke the justifiable protest of the Holy See, and would not be appropriate considering the charitable concern that the same Holy See has had and continues to have for the non-Aryans."[172] Maglione's assistant, Msgr. Tardini, also expressed fear about a movement of European Jews into the Holy Land. He appeared unconcerned that this immigration could save Jewish lives when no other haven was available. "The Holy See," he wrote in May 1943, "has never approved of the attempt to make Palestine a Jewish homeland. . . . And the question of the Holy Places? . . . Palestine is by this time more sacred for the Catholics than . . . for the Jews."[173] Even Archbishop Angelo Roncalli, the future saintly Pope John XXIII, then apostolic delegate at Istanbul, felt ambivalent about allowing Jews to immigrate to Palestine. Roncalli was at the time perhaps the Vatican hierarch most aware of the tragedy of the Nazi murder of millions of Jews and one among only a handful of diplomats who actually did something about it. Yet he did not want Catholic charity to lead to the Jewish control of the Holy Land. He was disturbed by the possibility of increased Jewish immigration, writing to Maglione during the war that

> I admit that the idea of seeing the Holy See concern itself with helping Italian Jews escape to Palestine where they could build a Jewish state arouses in my mind a kind of anxiety. . . . It does not seem good to me that a simple act of charity by the Holy See may encourage the possibility of or give the appearance of a collaboration, even indirect, in the establishment of a messianic dream. This may be perhaps only a personal qualm. . . . The reconstruction of a Jewish state can never amount to anything more than a utopian dream.[174]

Pius XII also refused to support Jewish pleas for greater immigration, especially of Jewish children, from occupied Europe into parts of Palestine, the only place on earth where a large portion of the population (Palestinian Jews) would have welcomed them. As Baron Alfredo Porcelli, a Catholic friend of Chaim Weizmann, wrote at the time, "It is only necessary to read *Osservatore Romano*, the *Civiltà Cattolica*, *L'Ora* and similar papal organs, to see the rancorous hatred for the Jews that underlines all their articles. It necessarily must be so because Rome aims at supremacy." These periodicals deplored the possibility that the enemies of Christianity might control the Holy Places; declared that the Jews were in Diaspora because of their sins and that only after converting to Christianity could Jews return to the Holy Land; and argued that the Jewish deicides must never be allowed rights in the Holy Land.[175]

Despite denials of his defenders,[176] Pius was well-informed, without knowing everything, about the Holocaust. However, precisely because Pius did know so much about the monstrous capabilities of the National-Socialists, one could argue that he feared the reprisals that a clear and assertive public condemnation of Nazi crimes could bring. Pius' lack of assertive behavior on behalf of the Jews in occupied Europe may thus have been due to fear for his personal safety or for the safety of millions of Catholics under the Reich's control who would be put at risk had they obeyed ecclesiastical directives to help Jews. But these fears should have been allayed by Pius' knowledge that Hitler had already retreated before Church opposition in other matters. Hitler squelched his anti-Church campaign once the encyclical *Mit Brennender Sorge* was published in 1937. In France, despite the Church's temporary public opposition to the deportations of Jews in 1942, Hitler ordered no massive Nazi attacks on the Church.[177] In November 1940, when the Holy Office condemned the Nazi euthanasia program, Hitler cut back the killings without reprisals against the German Church, which opposed it. In fact, the Nazis almost always considered upper clergy inviolable.[178] Besides, throughout the war, Pius had to be aware of Hitler's concern that severe attacks on the churches would demoralize the German fighting forces, so many of whom were devout Catholics. These points are certainly not meant to deny that the Third Reich also victimized and murdered Catholics, including thousands of priests and nuns.

A scholar who has studied rescue attempts for Jewish children during the Holocaust has written that Pius' silence was "the canonical example of collusion and collaboration."[179] The argument that Pius' silence was due to fear of the Nazis may certainly be challenged on other grounds: When Pius was free of direct fascist and Nazi threats—before the German occupation of Italy, as well as after (Rome was liberated on June 4, 1944, and the war ended almost a year later)—he remained voiceless as Nazi crimes became widespread and well-known. At this juncture, Pius himself apparently became self-conscious, stating to both the Americans and British that he would not forgive himself, nor would history, if he made no effort to save lives.[180] But by 1945, Pius was still silent when most Catholics were out of danger. Pius was still silent when the Reich crumbled. Pius was still silent when Hitler killed himself and Germany surrendered. Pius was still silent when the murder camps were discovered. Pius was still silent when the survivors sought refuge. Pius was still silent when the Vatican (Ratline) worked to save the lives of accused war criminals, Nazis and others, seeking to escape from Allied-occupied Europe, thousands of whom the Vatican supplied with false identity papers and helped ship out of Europe.[181]

Because Vichy's leader General Pétain seemed to genuinely want and need the approval and cooperation of the Church for his policies, a strong protest by the pope against his government's round-ups and deportations might have stopped them or at least slowed them down. But Pius, as well-informed as anyone outside of the leading Nazi figures, never ordered papal nuncio to France Archbishop Valeri to protest the murder of Jewish men, women, and children. Instead, although he was surprised at the brutality of the French police, the pope held, in the words of nuncio Valeri, a "prudent wait-and-see attitude and enlightened restraint."[182] On January 18, 1943, Vichy Ambassador to the Vatican Léon Bérard reported that in a meeting with the Archbishop of Paris, Cardinal Suhard, Pope Pius XII praised Marshal Pétain "and his work in warm and sensitive terms and took a keen interest in the actions of the government which augur well for a renewal of religious policy in France." Pius was undoubtedly enthusiastic about Pétain's reversal of the Third Republic's anticlerical policy, but nothing was said about the Jews.[183]

Pius XII's cooperation could have bolstered the protests of individual prelates against deportations of Jews, but without papal leadership and coordination from Rome, most of Catholic France stood mute before the "Jewish problem."[184] A month later, during the next round-ups of Jews for shipment to Auschwitz in February 1943,[185] Cardinal Suhard wrote to the Marshal not to protest the deportations themselves but to note that "at issue is the way in which actions against the Jews are carried out. . . . We would at least like to see that they not be executed with excessive severity and inhumanity."[186] From this time onward, no Catholic bishop publicly criticized the Vichy regime's Jewish policy.[187] The French Church, as well as the Vatican, achieved an accommodation with Vichy.[188]

Pius complained that, had he condemned the Nazi atrocities, he would have also had to criticize the Anglo-American policy of saturation bombing involving civilian populations, as well as the various Soviet outrages. The pope told Bérard, who reported it back to Vichy, that "if he [Pius] had mentioned the Nazis by name he would have also had to mention the Communists by name."[189] Pius meant this as an exculpatory argument. But an outspoken moral leader would have done just what Pius would not do, namely, condemn crimes against humanity no matter which side committed them.

Whether in Germany, France, Italy, Poland, Slovakia, or Hungary, Catholics depended on their religious authorities to tell them specifically what to do about the Jews. The Church and "God's self-proclaimed vicar on earth," the pope, could have reminded Catholics that Jews were their neighbors, not remote or hated objects. Pius XII never publicly and specifically repudiated the Nazi Final Solution of the Jewish Problem; never reminded Catholics not to involve themselves in mass murder; never condemned mass murder of innocent Jewish civilians; never threatened ecclesiastical sanctions against Catholics who were involved in the Final Solution, from Hitler on down. (In 1940, French premier Edouard Daladier instructed the French Ambassador to the Holy See, Wladimir d'Ormesson, to inform the pope that he "ought to intervene—he ought to pronounce excommunications *ex cathedra*.")[190]

Many of those close to Pius were unclear and upset as to why he failed to express unmistakable moral outrage and was unwilling to teach specific Catholic ethical principles (based on theologia crucis) to the faithful concerning "the unprecedented crime against humanity of Hitler's campaign of extermination of the Jews."[191] When he spoke as pope, Pius' rhetoric was typically periphrastic, his denunciations undefined, his approach restrained, and his leadership hesitant and inhibited. Instead of attacking specific malevolent actions, Pius condemned evil in general. When he made ethical statements, they were without pragmatic moral force. As Catholic historian John Morley observed, "the sad conclusion is that the tragic events in Poland were not able to move the pope [Pius XII] or his secretary of state [Maglione] to face the reality of a situation whose cruelty was unparalleled in human history."[192]

POSTSCRIPT

Catholic Racism

A little Jewish blood is enough to destroy the world.
  Vicente da Costa Mattos, Breve discurso contra a heretica perfidia do judaismo

The Catholic magisterium distinguishes between religious and racial prejudice toward Jews, between so-called anti-Judaism and anti-semitism. Practicing Catholics are generally accustomed to hearing the distinction used in official statements of the Catholic hierarchy. Nevertheless, a case can be made for a form of religious racism as one of the fundamental elements in the Church's antisemitism. Denying the possibility of change or conversion, racism in its most essential definition—whether expressed by nineteenth-century Social Darwinists and nativists or by the Church Fathers and seventeenth-century Jesuits—holds that different groups of human beings are permanently different and unequal physically, intellectually, socially, and morally, and that individual members of a group always manifest the same traits as the rest of the group.[1] Catholic and Jewish writers, philosemites and antisemites, have often used the word "race" as a synonym for "people" or "nation." But this is not the usage here. The standard definition of racism is that (1) different groups of human beings (races) are permanently, genetically different; (2) each individual within a group always manifests the same traits as all other members of their group; and (3) inevitable consequences follow from the differences between groups. Racists assume that in the hierarchy of races, theirs is superior, whereas the others are inferior. Whereas some racists refer to physical differences, others refer to spiritual differences.

Prima facie, it seems incredible that any sort of Catholic thought, even Catholic antisemitism, could contain racism. In particular, the Catholic sacrament of baptism is supposed to wash away all stink of prior unbelief, whereas racism voids baptism, holding that once a Jew, always a Jew. Theologically, baptism is a commanding doctrine instituted by Christ himself, instant and indelible. The baptized Catholic becomes an irrevocable element of Christ's mystical body and a permanent part of the one, true, holy Catholic Church. Baptism is such a momentous sacrament that not only can water of any sort be used but also any lay Christian or non-Christian can perform the ritual. Until recently the Roman Catholic Church accepted that an illiterate Catholic teenager's baptism of a Jewish child without the parents' consent and without corroborative witnesses was still a valid sacrament.[2] Marcel Simon claims that Catholic theological anti-Jewishness and racial anti-semitism are totally different because "from the Church's point of view, at any period, . . . if [a person] was converted, [this person] ceased to be a Jew."[3] But because Catholic writers and Church officials have often conceived of the Jews as intrinsically evil and essentially unconvertible, Catholic theology has all too easily slipped into racism—a racism institutionalized in the Church. On its surface, this sounds incredible. How could an institution like the Roman Catholic Church that treasures the sacraments of baptism and mar-riage be racist in regard to the Jews?

Although baptism and racism seem polar opposites, Christian anti-semitism has bridged the gap. Traditional religious antisemitism existed side-by-side with racist antisemitism for nearly two thousand years. From the early history of the Church onward, many Catholics found an inherent theological *and* physical repulsiveness in Jews.[4] They claimed, despite the obvious and intimate connections between Judaism and Christianity, that the Jews were fundamentally and repugnantly uncatholic and that Jews transmitted indeli-bly and permanently evil characteristics to their offspring. Because Jews were in their eyes permanently evil, many Catholics doubted that baptism would work to improve Jews. How could it?

As we have already seen in Chapter 2 of this book, often basing their belief in regard to the Jews on the Gospel passage that alleges the Jewish crowd in Pilate's courtyard cried, "Let his blood be on our heads and the heads of our children," early Catholics held that, despite the obvious and intimate con-nections between Judaism and Catholicism, every Jew was so fundamentally and repugnantly unchristian that there was not enough baptismal water to wash away the stink of unbelief. Catholic writers consistently considered Jews hardly human, an inherently evil race intimately associated with the devil or, as St. John Chrysostom put it, "the Jews danced with the devil." St. John doubted whether any Jew could be authentically converted to Christianity. The second-century Christian apologist Justin Martyr argued that God had given Moses' Law to the Jews in an attempt to keep in check the evil of the inherently sinful Jews. St. Augustine observed that all Jews shared the stigma of the denial and murder of Christ. The evil of the Jews, "in their parents, led to death." (*Occidistis Christum in parentibus vestris*)[5] St. Jerome claimed that all Jews were "Judases", innately evil creatures who betrayed Jesus Christ for money.[6] St. Isidore of Seville wrote that a Jew could no more become a good person than an Ethiopian could change his skin color or a leopard his spots.[7] In the fourth century, St. John Chrysostom called Jews "*inveterate* murderers, destroyers, [and] men possessed by the devil"[8] with no chance for "atonement, excuse, or defense."[9] The eighth century John of Damascus wrote that God gave the Jews the Sabbath not as a reward for good behavior but because Jews needed time off from their "absolute propensity for material things."[10]

Likewise, in the Middle Ages, St. Augustine's observation was echoed in the Dominican Thomas of Cantimpré, who stated that ever since the Jews of Jesus's time called out to Pilate that "his blood be upon us and on our children," all Jews, even to the present time, had to suffer perpetual slavery. "The curse of the parents falls on the children."[11] St. Thomas Aquinas called Jews an inherently cruel people.[12] It was for this reason that God taught them how to slaughter animals in a kosher, that is, relatively painless, way.[13] A century before, another extraordinarily influential Catholic powerhouse, St. Bernard of Clairvaux, wrote about the papal election of Cardinal Pietro Pierleoni (Anacletus II)—the great-grandson of a converted Jew—that "it is an insult to Christ that the offspring of a Jew has occupied the chair of Peter."[14] Arnulf, later bishop of Lisieux, argued that Anacletus' Jewishness could be seen in his face and that his family "had still not been purified from the yeast of Jewish corruption." Four cardinals calculated that Anacletus had been elected at the very moment that Christ was crucified.[15] At the end of the thirteenth century, when Pope Nicholas III ordered "sermons and other means for the conversion of the Jews" as part of the apostolate of the Franciscans and the Dominicans, "lesser authorities in the hierarchy" refused to admit Jews to conversion.[16] Most likely because they felt the effort was wasted on the Jews.

Every Crusade started out murderously attacking European Jews. Sometimes, the Crusaders gave the Jews the chance to save themselves by converting. "Either the Jews must convert to our belief, or they will be totally exterminated—they and their children down to the last baby at the breast." (*"Entweder müssen die Juden sich zu unserm Glauben behehren oder sie werden vertilgt sammt Kind und Säugling!"*)[17] But other times Crusaders did not give the Jews a chance to convert. Indeed, if the Crusaders had wanted simply to convert Jews, surely Jewish children would have been saved and raised as Christians. This was seldom done.[18] Instead, the Crusaders often seemed intent on destroying all the Jews rather than baptizing them.[19] Crusaders were convinced that Jewishness was an inexpungeably evil characteristic.

After the Middle Ages, these racist beliefs were reflected in Catholic humanists like Erasmus of Rotterdam[20] and articulated in the former Augustinian priest, Martin Luther.[21] In Spain,[22] the state joined the Church in institutionalizing this idea of Jews bearing permanent evil.[23] Léon Poliakov has pointed out that Spanish theologians believed the Jews' rejection and murder of Christ had "biologically" corrupted them down to their latest descendants.[24] Ferrant Martinez, Deputy to the Bishop of Seville and Confessor to Queen Mother Leonora, led a massive anti-Jewish campaign at the end of the fourteenth century. Like St. Ambrose, Martinez called for the razing of synagogues[25] "in which the enemies of God and the Church practice their idolatry." When he became administrator of the diocese of Seville in 1390, in sermons permeated with religious fanaticism and antisemitism Martinez again demanded the destruction of Jews and Judaism. His beliefs and sermons instigated an anti-Jewish movement that spread to Andalusia, Castile, and most of Spain. The violence, encouraged by the royal authorities' half-hearted requests that Martinez desist, began on Ash Wednesday in 1391 and lasted on and off for decades.[26] The common people as well as noble families and priests were involved in the crimes.

The Spanish monarchs Ferdinand and Isabella originally created the Inquisition in Spain to support the Church and to purify Spain of Jewish *conversos*. But soon the Inquisition attacked Jews, heretics, Moslems, free-thinkers, and Protestants as unchristian elements. Ferdinand and Isabella combined nationalistic motives with preexisting religious antisemitism to Christianize, expropriate, murder, or expel the Jews from Spain. In 1483, the crown, along with Pope Sixtus IV, selected the Dominican prior Thomas de Torquemada as Inquisitor General.[27] More than 90 percent of the Inquisition's victims were of Jewish origin.[28] Rather than accept the new Christians into Spanish life and culture, the Inquisition set out to destroy the Jewish presence.[29] At its most extreme, the Inquisition considered anyone who believed in the Talmud and the future arrival of the Messiah, that is, *any* Jew or Judaizer, a complete heretic who deserved to be burned.

Spanish theologians agreed that all Jews were impervious to baptism and salvation. Both Jews and *conversos* maintained Jewish traits of "cunning, sharpness, and a boundless lust for money and power defying all moral scruples."[30] "Noble dogs" could smell out Jews even when they dressed as Christians.[31] In 1604, Father Prudencio de Sandoval wrote that even one Jewish ancestor "defiles and corrupts." Indeed, all the major Catholic orders in Spain adopted clearly antisemitic racist regulations. By the early seventeenth century, for example, the Jesuits ordered that no man could become a priest unless his Christian heritage could be traced back five generations. This "impediment of origin" remained until 1946.[32] In 1623, the Portuguese Vicente da Costa Mattos argued that "a little Jewish blood is enough to destroy the world."[33] Later in the century, Father Francisco de Torrejoncillo warned that Jews desire every kind of evil and with simply one Jewish parent, a Jew was surely "an enemy of Christians, of Christ, and of his Divine Law." Furthermore, Jewish wet nurses should be forbidden to suckle Christian children because "Jewish milk, being of infected persons, can only engender perverse inclinations."[34]

In Germany, the Catholic nun, Anne Catherine Emmerich, meditating on the Passion of Christ, reflecting on her visions, wrote that "I imagine I hear that frightful cry of the Jews, His blood be on us, and upon our children. . . . This curse, which they have entailed upon themselves, appears to me to penetrate even to the very marrow of their bones—even to the unborn infants."[35]

The National-Socialist Nuremberg Decrees of 1935 defined a Jew as having one parent or two grandparents who were Jewish by religious identity. But the papacy sanctioned a narrower definition of racial discrimination when in 1461 Pius II decreed that the administrators of a loan fund must have four generations of purely Christian blood on both mother's and father's sides.[36] In 1495, Pope Alexander VI similarly approved a statute that excluded New Christians (*conversos*) and their descendants down to the fourth generation from Catholic religious orders.[37] Although in the early sixteenth century the warrior pope Julius II reversed the Church's racist momentum, describing such discrimination as "detestable and corrupt and contrary to the wishes of Christ and St. Paul,"[38] in 1525, Pope Clement VII allowed Observant Franciscans to exclude men with Jewish blood from their order.[39] The racial exclusion was later extended to the Dominican Order.[40] Pope Paul III was inconsistent in his policies, sometimes approving racial principles, other times denying them.[41] In 1569, Pope Pius V expelled the Jews from most of the papal states as criminal "dead sheep," hopelessly unconvertible.[42] In 1588 and 1600, Popes Sixtus V and Clement VIII approved a Portuguese law that forbade men from Jewish families from being ordained as priests.[43]

In the sixteenth century, Christian racism developed in the rest of Europe as well. The Catholic priest and humanist Erasmus, for example, maintained that Christians must be careful about allowing Jews into the fellowship of the Church, for a fully converted Jew was inconceivable since a Jew was always pernicious. Erasmus wrote to Pirkheimer and Reuchlin in November 1517 that the Jewish apostate Johannes Pfefferkorn was a typical Jew, whose ancestors attacked Christ, whereas he had betrayed all of Christendom, lying when he claimed to have become a Christian.[44]

The former Augustinian priest Martin Luther sometimes wrote as if Jews were a race that could never authentically convert to Christianity. Indeed, like so many Christian writers before him, Luther, by making the Jews the devil's people, put them beyond conversion. For Luther, trying to convert the Jews was like "trying to cast out the devil."[45] He observed that Jews had not learned a thing from their suffering during fourteen hundred years in exile. "Much less do I propose to convert the Jews, for that is impossible."[46] In a sermon of September 25, 1539, Luther tried to demonstrate through several examples that individual Jews could not permanently convert to Christianity,[47] and in several passages of *The Jews and Their Lies*, Luther wrote that talking to Jews about the law, aside from the Ten Commandments, is like "preaching the gospel to a sow." Luther continued that "From their youth they have imbibed [a] venomous hatred against the Goyim from their parents and their rabbis, and they still continuously drink it. . . . It has penetrated flesh and blood, marrow and bone, and has become part and parcel of their nature and their life." Luther ends on this unhappy note: "Dear Christian, be advised and so not doubt that next to the devil, you have no more bitter, venomous, and vehement foe than a real Jew who earnestly seeks to be a Jew. . . . Their lineage and circumcision infect them all. . . . Even if the Jews were punished in the most gruesome manner so that the streets ran with blood, so that their dead would be counted not in the hundred thousands but in the millions, [it would not be] possible to convert these children of the devil! It is impossible to convert the devil and his own."[48] These "formal writings" agreed with *Luther's Table Talk*, where he wrote: "If I had to baptize a Jew, I would take him to the river Elbe, hang a stone around his neck and push him over with the words 'I baptize thee in the name of Abraham.'"[49]

In 1609, French King Henry IV commissioned Pierre de l'Ancre, a royal counselor of the Parliament of Bordeaux, as grand inquisitor of witches to clean the Pays de Labourd of witchcraft. This "bigoted Catholic" was a "gleeful executioner" who, wrote Hugh Trevor-Roper, "gloried in his Jesuit education."[50] De l'Ancre denounced the Jews as "blasphemers . . . just another kind of witch."[51] He attacked Jews as werewolves, murders of Christians, poisoners of wells, and ritual murderers of Christian children.[52] "By their filth and stink, by their sabbaths and synagogues" Jews disgust God so much that they can never be converted to good Christians.[53]

During the late nineteenth-century Dreyfus Affair in France, *La Croix du Nord* claimed that Jews were fighting a

war to the death that, since the original fall, separated the divine race of the liberator of the human kind from that of the hellish serpent. . . . They are a race, a foreign race, encamped among us; a race without our blood, without our instincts, without our morality, without our ideals; an essentially cosmopolitan race, a race without country; a stubborn usurious race without any moral sense, a race capable of any kind of selling and any kind of buying.[54]

Father Umberto Benigni, who later founded the Sodality of St. Pius V that functioned as an international secret service for Pope Pius X wrote in *Piccolo Monitore* that Jews were "a rabbinical race that still today in 1891 [slit] the throats of little Christians for the Synagogue's Passover." Later, Benigni was honored with a powerful position in the Vatican's Secretariat of State.[55]

Edouard-Adolphe Drumont (d. 1917), called "the Pope of antisemitism," wrote the best-selling French book of the nineteenth century, *La France juive*. Published first in April 1886, dozens of editions appeared in France, Germany, Italy, Poland, Spain, and the United States. In one year the book was reprinted a hundred times.[56] Although he sometimes paraded as a socialist, Drumont was a conservative who sought to preserve such Christian values as family, Church, and nation.[57] Sometimes, denying any religious antisemitism, Drumont expressed himself in thoroughly racist terms—Aryans were good; Jews, who were unbaptizable, were evil.[58] Drumont combined physical and spiritual, secular and Catholic racism.

First, he observed in the first chapter of *La France juive* (Jewish France) that Jews had peculiar physical characteristics, such as "hooked nose, blinking eyes, clenched teeth, protruding ears, . . . overly long torso, flat feet, the soft and melting hands of the hypocrite and the traitor." But he defined race in a non-physical, value-oriented manner, as "a collection of individuals thinking the same, a totality representing a certain number of sentiments, beliefs, aspirations, aptitudes, traditions."[59]

Second, although he neglected to perform Catholic rituals from 1867 to 1878, Drumont saw himself as a conservative Catholic, one who was "infuriated" with what he believed to be the corruption of old Christian values by the Jewish spirit. As his antisemitism developed, he began faithfully performing his religious duties. He attended daily Mass at his parish church in Paris, and in the next year he was married to his mistress in a Catholic ceremony. He always regarded himself as a defender of the faith, and the clerical press praised him as "this respectful son of the Church."[60] The final illustration in the book portrayed Drumont in prayer, reciting a Pater Noster and Ave Maria for France.[61]

Third, Drumont found support for his anti-Jewish activities in every layer of French Catholic society—writers, priests, and lay people. Drumont himself claimed that he had become an antisemite when the Benedictines were expelled from France in 1881.[62] In 1890, Drumont organized the first public antisemitic meeting in the Paris suburb of Neuilly at the suggestion of his wealthy Jesuit friend, Father du Lac.[63] In fact, only one bishop and a few priests criticized Drumont's antisemitism. Auguste Chirac, a self-styled independent socialist writer and a radical atheist, grew closer to the Church as he became friendlier with Drumont.[64] Drumont published his first anti-Jewish works in the *Revue du monde catholique*,[65] where between 1865 and 1867 he was a literary critic, and in *Revue contemporaine*—both of which were Catholic journals. Arsene Guérin of *Revue du monde catholique* praised him for "having served the cause of Christ."[66] In 1885, the archbishop of Paris's quasi-official journal, *Le Monde*, hired him as an editor.[67]

Four, Drumont went out of his way to have the proofs of *La France juive* examined by a priest for any theological error. The busy Drumont traveled to Canterbury in 1884 to submit his long document to Father du Lac. In the same year, he attacked Jews in the journal *Le Livre*, for "destroy[ing] the foundations of Christian society, if not of Christianity." The Vicar-General of Paris and Rector of the Catholic Institute, Monsignor d'Hulst, wrote in praise of the book; most clerical publications, including the most antisemitic and widely read of the Church press, the Assumptionists' *La Croix* with two million readers a week if *La Croix*'s provincial supplements are figured in, enthusiastically reviewed the book. *L'Univers religieux* praised Drumont's "instructive and courageous book" and reprinted the book's conclusion so that all French Catholics should be reminded that as Jesus had risen after being murdered by the Jews, so France should rise again from the domination of the Jews. Drumont himself prayed daily in his parish church for his book's success.[68] Drumont concluded *La France juive* with these words, "I see one face and it is the only face I want to show you: the face of Christ, insulted, covered with disgrace, lacerated by thorns, crucified. Nothing has changed in eighteen hundred years. It is the same lie, the same hatred, the same people."[69]

The chief Jesuit journal *Civiltà Cattolica*, sponsored and controlled by the Vatican, conducted with *papal imprimatur* and *nihil obstat* a racist antisemitic campaign from the Dreyfus Affair in last decades of the nineteenth century at least through 1945. In 1880, under Pope Leo XIII, Jesuit Father Giuseppe Oreglia had written in the journal: "The Jews [are] eternal insolent children, obstinate, dirty, thieves, liars [they compose a] barbarian invasion by an enemy race, hostile to Christianity and to society in general. . . . Oh how wrong and deluded are those who think that Judaism is just a religion like Catholicism, paganism, Protestantism, and not in fact a race, a people, a nation. . . . The Jews are . . . Jews . . . especially because of their race." Even should they convert, he went on to say, Jews remain Jews for all eternity. The next year, Oreglia added that inspired by the devil, Jews cannot become members of another nation or race, "they are born Jews and must remain Jews. . . . Hatred for Christians they imbibed with their mother's milk."[70] In 1897, still during the reign of Pope Leo XIII, in *Civiltà Cattolica*, Jesuit Father Raffaele Ballerini warned the Catholic world that "the Jew remains always in every place immutably a Jew. His nationality is not in the soil where he is born, nor in the language that he speaks, but in his seed."[71]

During this same period, in 1898, a French Catholic daily *La Croix du nord* portrayed Jews as a "race, a foreign race camped among us, a race that has neither our blood nor our ideals, a race that is cosmopolitan by its nature, a race without a country, an intransigent, usurious race lacking moral sense, a race capable of selling and buying anything." In 1906, another French Catholic newspaper wrote that "the Church of Satan is incarnated in the Jewish race."

In 1923, Pope Pius XI praised Monsignor Ernest Jouin for "combatting our mortal [Jewish] enemy." Then the pope raised him to apostolic prothonotary. In 1925, Jouin praised the Germans who, "better than we, recognized the Jewish peril." Jouin had commented on the antisemitic fantasy and defamation, *The Protocols of the Elders of Zion*, "From the triple viewpoint of race, of nationality, and of religion, the Jew has become the enemy of humanity."[72]

The period of the Holocaust, 1933–45, was filled with racial attacks against the Jews by important Church officials and other leaders of Catholic opinion.[73] The Polish press sought a Poland that was "national and Catholic," not Jewish and "foreign. . . . A spiritually semitized Poland would cease to be Poland."[74] In 1934, a nationalist Polish Catholic journal *Pro Christo* observed that even after seven generations, converted Jews still gave off a Jew-stink—a concept related to the medieval association of Jews with the devil, who smelled like feces.[75] In the same year, *Pro Christo*, argued that anti-Jewish racism on the part of Polish Catholics was reasonable because "Jewish blood infects Aryan blood and spirit"; racism "as a means to avoid the harmful influence of Jews" was "useful, proper, understandable, and moral."[76] Another Polish Catholic periodical published for the clergy, *Ateneum Kaplanski*, in 1939 argued that "a Jew racially and ethnically before undergoing baptism, so racially and ethnically he remains a Jew even after undergoing baptism."[77] Father Jozef Pastuszka wrote that the Jews were a foreign body imposed on European Christendom.[78] Views like these did not reflect the totality of the Polish Catholic press, but they were tolerated by those Catholic hierarchs in charge of overseeing the press.[79]

An observer of the Final Solution in Hungary wrote that medieval Catholic antisemitism is "shockingly close" to Nazi racism.[80] In 1935, German Cardinal Bertram declared that the Church had always recognized the importance of race, blood, and soil. Munich's Cardinal Michael Faulhaber and Wurzburg Vicar-General Miltenberger stated similar ideas. Faulhaber defended "racial research and race culture" and argued that the Church had always recognized the importance of race, blood, and soil—though he warned against hatred of other races and "hostility to Christianity."[81] The same perspective had been expressed by Monsignor Groeber, Archbishop of Freiburg, who had joined the Nazi SS in 1933 and argued for "the national right to maintain the nation's racial origin unpolluted and to do whatever is necessary to guarantee this end."[82] In 1938, *Der Stürmer* published a special picture album for children that headlined "The father of the Jews is the devil." This was followed by eleven quotations along the same line from the Church Fathers and Martin Luther.[83] *Der Stürmer*'s Christmas message of 1941 was "To put an end to the proliferation of the curse of God in this Jewish blood, there is only one way: the extermination of this people, whose father is the devil."[84] "Your father is the devil" referring to Jews is found in the Gospel of John, chapter 8.

During the Holocaust itself, Pope Pius XI, in 1938, permitted the chief Jesuit journal, *Civiltà Cattolica*, to portray Judaism as inherently sinister, and Jews, through money and secularism, as out to seize the world. With the devil as their master, Jews first corrupted, then conquered; and so they continued to threaten everyone. "Judaism is a deeply malevolent religion, inasmuch as it pertains to a nation which presumes itself elect, and . . . it is the religion of corrupt messianism [which] renders Jewry a tinderbox of disorders and a standing menace to the world."[85]

Pope Pius XII also controlled *Civiltà Cattolica*, which in 1941 and 1942 attacked the Jews for mythic sins, "malice . . . injustice, impiety, infidelity, sacrilege." In December 1941, a month before the Wannsee Conference in which many of the top bureaucrats of the Nazi regime met to finalize details of the deportation of Jews to torture and death in concentration camps, *Civiltà* reminded its readers that the Jews were the most visible actors in the drama of deicide and that they repeated their involvement in this crime by means of ritual murder "in every generation."[86] (On January 13, 1941, K. E. Robinson, an official of the British Colonial Office, noted that he considered the Jews "entirely alien in every snese of the word."[87]) In March 1942, another article attacked contemporary Jews as carrying an unexpungeable "stigma" because they condemned Christ to crucifixion, "the crime of the sons of the Synagogue."[88]

During the Vichy regime in the 1940s, minister of justice Joseph Barthélemy noted that the government would not assimilate, kill, or expel Jews; "it is merely forbidding [Jews] the functions of directing the French soul or French interests."[89] He believed that all Jews were "impregnated with the Jewish spirit," which could be inherited. Glossing over Vichy's application of the law to Jewish converts, the French Church supported the anti-Jewish statutes, which in 2007 seem to be in effect in several French cities.[90]

The Vatican itself supported this anti-Jewish racist legislation. The Vichy regime inquired about the Vatican's attitude in early September 1941. Vichy Ambassador Léon Bérard reported to Pétain that an authorized Vatican source (possibly Luigi Cardinal Maglione, Vatican Secretary of State, the papal nuncio in France for many years or Maglione's assistants, Msgr. Domenico Tardini, and Msgr. Giovanni Montini, a close associate of Pius XII and the future Pope Paul VI[91]) had objected only to the part of the second anti-Jewish *statut* that ignored the doctrine of baptism.[92]

Many Christian writers both Catholic and Protestant found "a horrible and fascinating physical otherness" in Jews.[93] Several other Christian racists discerned a spiritual otherness between races. German biblical scholar and nationalist Paul De Lagarde, for example, wrote in 1853 that being German was "not a matter of blood, but of a spiritual state of mind" (*Gemüt, nicht Geblüt*).[94] French journalist and writer Edouard-Adolphe Drumont defined race as "a collection of individuals who think the same, a totality representing a certain number of feelings, beliefs, hopes, aptitudes, traditions."[95] German historian Arthur Moeller van den Bruck wrote of "a race of the spirit."[96] The Anglo-German scientist Houston Stewart Chamberlain agreed with St. Paul (Romans 2:28–29) "when he said: 'For he is not a Jew who is one outwardly in the flesh, but [a] person is a Jew who is one inwardly, and real circumcision is a matter of the heart—it is spiritual and not literal."[97] Xavier Vallat, conservative Catholic and Vichy High Commissioner for Jewish Affairs, believed that the Jew was always alien "not because he is a Semite, but because he is impregnated by the Talmud." The Conservative German lawyer and politician Edgar Jung, writing in the 1930s, argued that the alleged racial dichotomy between Aryans and Semites was not the real issue, which was an opposition of Volk against Volk, spirit against spirit. A few days before Adolf Hitler came to power, Johannes Gföllner, bishop of Linz, observed that Aryans and Christians together had to fight the "dangers and damages arising out of the Jewish spirit."[98] German scientists and writers argued that even should all Jews be killed, their spirit would live on and they would have to continue to fight it.[99] In 1939, Hitler noted "I know perfectly well . . . that in the scientific sense there is no such thing as [a biological] race."[100] On February 13, 1945, Hitler differentiated between a race of the mind and one of the body. "We use the term Jewish race as a matter of convenience, for in reality and from the genetic point of view there is no such thing as the Jewish race. There does, however, exist a . . . spiritually homogeneous group [to] which all Jews throughout the world deliberately adhere . . . and it is this group of human beings to which we give the title Jewish race."[101] He further explained that Jews were "an abstract race of the mind [that] has its origins, admittedly, in the Hebrew religion. . . . A race of the mind is something more solid, more durable that just a [biological] race, pure and simple."[102] Individual Jews embodied an inherently evil Jewish spirit.[103] Of course, to eliminate this "spiritual race," Hitler had to destroy the bodies manifesting this spirit.[104]

For any religious institution to change its dogma (established principles, tenets, and doctrines by definition not open for discussion or dispute) is extraordinarily difficult. Even if the effect of the Church's transformation of its relations with Jews has not yet fully reached all the rank and file faithful, its potential for good cannot be overestimated. Credit must be given to those Church hierarchs and others responsible for amelioration of the official Roman Catholic position on the Jews. Hopefully, these actions will, with due diligence, work toward an authentic and lasting improvement of Christian-Jewish and Catholic-Jewish relations. Perhaps, some day soon, all people will realize that they belong to one human family.

Notes

Introduction

1. Lolly O'Brien, quoting Shirley M. Tilghman, the director of the Lewis-Sigler Institute for Integrative Genomics, "Of Genetics, race, and evolution: What the director of Princeton's new institute for genomics has to say," *Princeton Alumni Weekly*, October 25, 2000, http://www.princeton.edu/~paw/web_exclusives/features/features_05.html.

2. In this book, "Catholic Church" and "Roman Catholic Church" refer to the "One, Holy, Catholic and Apostolic Church" mentioned in the Nicean Creed and the "Holy Catholic Church" [*sanctam, ecclesiam, catholicam*] referred to in the Apostles' Creed. Before the East-West Schism of 1054, both Eastern Orthodox and Roman Catholic held that they belonged to the same one, Holy, Catholic, and Apostolic Church. It was with the great schism of the sixteenth century that the Protestant Churches broke away from the mainline Holy Catholic Church, which became identified as the Catholic Church or the Roman Catholic Church (in full communion with the Bishop of Rome), the single strongest, best organized, and most influential of the Christian churches, with 1,098,366,000 members in 2004, which was one-sixth of the world's population.

3. Marcel Simon, *Verus Israel* (Oxford 1986), 231–32; Robert Wistrich, *Antisemitism: The Longest Hatred* (London 1991), xvii–xviii; F. Lovsky, *Antisémitisme et mystère d'Israël* (Paris 1955); James Parkes, *The Conflict of Church and Synagogue: A Study in the Origins of Antisemitism* (New York 1979); Jules Isaac, *Genèse de l'antisémitisme* (Paris 1956); and Jean Juster, *Les Juifs dans l'Empire romain* (Paris 1914), among others, take the position that Christian theology provided a quantum leap into a qualitatively new kind of antisemitism.

4. Menachem Stern, *Greek and Latin Authors on Jews and Judaism* (Jerusalem 1984), 3 vols., has collected and translated all the relevant primary sources.

5. Simon, *Verus Israel*, 397–98.

6. Arthur Hertzberg, *The French Enlightenment and the Jews* (New York 1968), 10, 313; Hannah Arendt, *Eichmann in Jerusalem A Report on the Banality of Evil* (New York 1963), 297.

7. Wistrich, *Antisemitism*, xvii; Wistrich, *Hitler's Apocalypse: Jews and the Nazi Legacy* (New York 1985), 29. Frank Manuel, *Broken Staff* (Cambridge, MA, 1993), 296, also blames "rogue elements in Christianity" and calls Nazism "a Christian heresy."

8. Peter Pulzer, *The Rise of Political Antisemitism in Germany and Austria* (Cambridge, MA, 1964, 1988), xxii.

9. Alfred Fouillée, *Morale des Idées-Forces* (Paris 1908), 353.

10. Eugen Weber, *Action Française: Royalism and Reaction in Twentieth-Century France* (Stanford 1962), 463.

11. Robert Willis, "Christian Theology After Auschwitz," *Journal of Ecumenical Studies* (Fall 1975): 495. See also Parkes, *The Conflict of Church and Synagogue*, 376; John Gager, *The Origins of Antisemitism: Attitudes Toward Judaism in Pagan and Christian Antiquity* (New York 1983), 13; Davies, *Antisemitism and the Christian Mind: The Crisis of Conscience After Auschwitz* (New York 1969), 39.

12. Otto of Freising indicates that Bernard finally silenced Rodolphe by invoking monastic discipline. Chazan, *European Jewry and the First Crusade* (Berkeley, CA, 1987), 177–78.

13. Rabbi Ephraim bar Jacob of Bonn, in A. Neubauer and M. Stern, eds., *Hebräische Berichte*, 187–88. Otto of Freising quoted in Chazan, *European Jewry*, 170.

14. Cohn, *Pursuit of the Millennium*, 69–70.

15. Heinrich Graetz, *History of the Jews* (Philadelphia 1940) 3:351–52; Vamberto Morais, *A Short History of Antisemitism* (New York 1976), 104.

16. The document is translated in Chazan, *Church, State, and Jew in the Middle Ages* (New York 1980), 101–4.

17. Rabbi Ephraim bar Jacob of Bonn, *Hebräische Berichte*, 188. See also Henry Hart Milman, *History of the Jews* (New York 1939), 2:310.

18. Bernard's letter to the Archbishop of Mainz, in Chazan, *Church, State, and Jew in the Middle Ages*, 104–5.

19. Bernard of Clairvaux, "Epistola CCCLXIII (946)," in *Patrologia Latina*, 182:567.

20. "Bernard's Letter to the People of England," in Chazan, *Church, State, and Jew in the Middle Ages*, 101–4.

21. Bernard of Clairvaux, *St. Bernard's Sermons for the Seasons and the Principal Festivals of the Year* (Westminster, MD, 1950), 1:379.

22. *De Consideratione* I, 4, quoted by Torrell, "Les juifs dans l'oeuvre de Pierre le Vénérable," 342n58.

23. Bernard, *Sermones super Cantica Canticorum*, 60.4, in David Berger, "The Attitude of St. Bernard of Clairvaux Toward the Jews," *American Academy for Jewish Research, Proceedings* (New York 1973), 96.

24. Bernard, *St. Bernard's Sermons*, 2:149, in Berger, "The Attitudes of St. Bernard of Clairvaux Toward the Jews," 104.

25. Berger, "The Attitude of St. Bernard of Clairvaux Toward the Jews," 101–2.

26. Samuel and Pearl Oliner, *The Altruistic Personality: Rescuers of Jews in Nazi Europe* (New York 1988), 170.

27. See Chapters 1 and 2.

28. Luther, "Heidelberg Disputation," Article 21, in *Luther's Works* (Philadelphia 1959), 31: 40.

29. James Parkes, "Antisemitism and Theological Arrogance," *Continuum* (Autumn 1966): 413.

30. Pierre Pierrard, *Juifs et Catholiques Français* (Paris 1970), 298.

31. James Parkes, "Attitude to Judaism," *The Journal of Bible and Religion* (October 1961): 300.
32. Bernard Glassman, *Antisemitic stereotypes without Jews: Images of the Jews in England, 1290–1700* (Detroit 1975).
33. Rosemary Ruether, *Faith and Fratricide* (New York 1965), 147.
34. Frederick Schweitzer, "The Tap-Root of Antisemitism: The Demonization of the Jews," *Remembering for the Future* (Oxford 1988), 879–90.
35. In *The Last Three Popes and the Jews* (New York 1967), Pinchas Lapide estimates that more than six million Jews were murdered by Christians in the centuries before the Holocaust.
36. Walter Zwi Bacharach, *Anti-Jewish Prejudices in German-Catholic Sermons* (Lewiston, NY, 1993), 46.
37. May 1961, quoted in Jeremy Cohen, *Christ Killers* (New York 2007), 170.
38. Gordon Allport, *The Nature of Prejudice*, (New York 1988), 446.
39. See Postscript.
40. Not just Protestants but Muslims as well.
41. Based on Gordon Allport's list in his *Nature of Prejudice* (Cambridge, MA, 1954), 14–15.
42. See Robert Michael and Philip Rosen, *Dictionary of Antisemitism* (Lanham, MD, 2006); Cohen, *Christ Killers*, 117.
43. Manfred Gerstenfeld, "Antisemitism: Integral to European Culture," Jerusalem Center for Public Affairs (March 30, 2004).
44. Working Definition of Antisemitism, EUMC. Discussion Papers—Racism, Xenophobia, Antisemitism, March 16, 2005, http://eumc.eu.int/eumc/index. See Robert Michael and Philip Rosen, "Introduction," *Dictionary of Antisemitism* (Lanham, MD, 2006).
45. See Jeremy Cohen, *Christ-Killers* (New York 2007).

Chapter 1

1. Menachem Stern, *Greek and Latin Authors on Jews and Judaism* (Jerusalem 1974, 1980, 1984), 3 vols.
2. Tertullian, *Apology* 21, 1.
3. Robert Wilken, "The Christians as the Romans (and Greeks) Saw Them," in *Jewish and Christian Self-Definition*, ed. E.P. Sanders (Philadelphia 1980), 1:62–64, 104.
4. Wyschogrod, "Heidegger, the Limits of Philosophy," *Shma* (April 2, 1982): 84; Kenneth Woodward, *Making Saints* (New York 1996).
5. Origen, *Contra Celsum*, in *Patrologiae, Cursus Completus, Graeca*, ed. J. P. Migne (Paris 1857–66), 4, 22. (Hereafter abbreviated *PG*.)
6. Jean Juster I, *Les Juifs dans l'Empire romain* (Paris 1914), 45–48nn1–22, for specific citations.
7. John Gager, *The Origins of Antisemitism* (New York 1983), 33, 267.
8. Gregory Baum, *The Jews and the Gospel: A Re-Examination of the Christian Testament* (London 1961); Baum, *Is the Christian Testament Antisemitic?* (New York 1965).

9. Jacob Neusner, "Christian Missionaries—Jewish Scholars," *Midstream* (October 1991): 30.

10. Samuel Sandmel, *A Jewish Understanding* (New York 1956), 10.

11. Samuel Sandmel, *A Jewish Understanding of the Christian Testament*, xii.

12. Rosemary Ruether, "Christology and Jewish-Christian Relations," in *Jews and Christians After the Holocaust*, ed. Abraham Peck (Philadelphia 1982), 27, 34–35; Jules Isaac, *Jesus and Israel* (New York 1971); Fadiey Lovsky, *Antisemitisme et mystere d'Israel* (Paris 1955).

13. Irving Zeitlin, *Jesus and the Judaism of His Time*, Notes and Bibliography (Oxford, UK 1988), 184–201.

14. Robert Alter, "From Myth to Murder," *The New Republic* (May 20, 1991): 40; and James Young, *Writing and Rewriting the Holocaust: Narrative and the Consequences of Interpretation* (Bloomington IN 1988), 4.

15. Jack T. Sanders, "Professor Jack T. Sanders Responds," *Moment* (April 1991): 8.

16. Robert Michael, *Concise History of American Antisemitism* (Lanham, MD 2005); Robert Michael, *Holy Hatred* (New York 2006).

17. Alan Davies, *Antisemitism and the Christian Mind* (New York 1969), 62.

18. The Book of Mormon also contains comparable anti-Jewish material. *The Book of Mormon: An Account Written by the Hand of Mormon Upon Plates* (Salt Lake City 1978). 1 Nephi, 19:13–14; 2 Nephi: 14–16.

19. William Wilson, *The Execution of Jesus* (New York 1970), 143.

20. For Paul's letters and other biblical quotations, *The New Oxford Annotated Bible*, ed. Michael Coogan (New York 1973) will be used.

21. Rom. 9:1–5.

22. There is no consensus on Paul. See Peter Richardson, ed., *Anti-Judaism in Early Christianity* (Waterloo, Canada 1985).

23. Correspondence with the author.

24. Isa. 29:10; Ps. 69:22–23.

25. Rom. 11:28–29.

26. Rom. 9: 8.

27. Gal. 5:16–18.

28. Cor. 3:4–15; Rom. 2, Phil. 3:2; Gal. 3:13.

29. Phil. 3:2–8.

30. Gal. 5:12.

31. *The New Oxford Annotated Bible*, 1433, 1437; Norman Beck, *Mature Christianity* (London 1985), 44, 90.

32. Thess. 2:3.

33. Thess. 2:13–16 and 2 Thess. 2. See Dan. 9:27, 11:31, 12:11; Mt. 24:15; Mk. 13:14; Lk. 21:5–36; and Rev. 13; Wilhelm Bousset, *The Antichrist Legend* (London 1896), 158, 166–70.

34. Robert Wilken, *Judaism and the Early Christian Mind* (New Haven 1971), 174, 226–28.

35. Beck, *Mature Christianity*, 123–24.

36. Acts 12.

37. Acts 7:58–60.
38. Acts 7:51.
39. Douglas Hare, "The Rejection of the Jews," in *Antisemitism and the Foundations of Christianity* (New York 1979), 38; Acts 9:22–25; 20:3, 19; 23:12–14.
40. Acts 2:1–47; 3:13–15.
41. Louis Feldman, "Is the Christian Testament Antisemitic?" *Journal Theological Studies* 50.2 (1999): 32–35, 50–52.
42. Haym Maccoby, "Jesus and Barabbas," *Christian Testament Studies* (October 1969): 55–60.
43. I would like to thank Prof. Eunice Pollack for her input on the Barabbas issue.
44. Sandmel, *A Jewish Understanding*, 127–29.
45. Mk. 3:31–35.
46. Mk. 3:6. Douglas Hare, "The Rejection of the Jews," 29, 32–35.
47. Mark 14.
48. "The Christianization of Pilate was part of an anti-Jewish polemic that emphasized the responsibility of the Jews for "deicide.'" Lellia Cracco Ruggini, "Pagani, Ebrei, e Christiani: Odio Sociologico e Odio Teologico nel Mondo Antico," in *Gli Ebrei nell'Alto Medioevo* (Spoleto 1980), 110.
49. Mt. 27; Mk. 15; Lk. 23; Jn. 18–19.
50. Mk. 15:11–15.
51. Ellis Rivkin, *What Crucified Jesus?* (Nashville 1986); Weddig Fricke, *The Court-Martial of Jesus* (New York 1990).
52. In a letter from Herod Agrippa I to Emperor Caligula, cited by Philo, "Of the Proofs of God's Power," in *The Jewish Question*, ed. Alex Bein (New York 1990), 67.
53. Tacitus, *Annals*, 15, 44; Clark Williamson, *Has God Rejected His People? Anti-Judaism in the Christian Church* (Nashville 1982), 44.
54. Mk. 15:39. A variant reading is "a son of God." *The New Oxford Annotated Bible*, 1237.
55. Mk. 16:15–16.
56. Mt. 21:42–44; 23.
57. Mk. 8:31; Mt. 16:21.
58. Mt. 21:45; 23:2–3.
59. Mt. 23:34–36.
60. Mt. 23:33, 37; 25:41.
61. The best translation, according to Norman Beck, "The Christian Testament and the Teaching of Contempt," at Baruch-Manhattan Colleges Colloquium on the History of Antisemitism, March 1989.
62. Mt. 23:31–35.
63. Mt. 8:5–13; 23:37–39, 24:1–31; Hare, "The Rejection of the Jews," 39.
64. Mt. 27:22, 23, 25. For Matthew's debt to the Jewish Scriptures on the blood guilt issue, see Jeremy Cohen, *Christ Killers* (New York 2007), 31–32.
65. An unnamed scholar, quoted by Sandmel, *A Jewish Understanding*, 164.
66. For example, Mt. 23:37–39.

67. Haym Maccoby, *The Sacred Executioner* (New York 1982), 103; Beck, *Mature Christianity*, 155; Michael Cook, *Mark's Treatment of the Jewish Leaders* (E. J. Brill 1978); Hare, "The Rejection of the Jews," 27–47; E. Buck, "Anti-Judaic Sentiments in the Passion Narrative According to Matthew," in *Anti-Judaism in Early Christianity*, ed. Richardson (Waterloo, Canada, 1985), 1:177.

68. Lk. 17.

69. Lk. 16:27–31.

70. Lk. 17:11–19, 18:9–14; Hare, "The Rejection of the Jews," 35.

71. See *The New Annotated Oxford Bible*, NT76.

72. Hare, "The Rejection of the Jews," 36; Sanders, "Professor Jack T. Sanders Responds," 7.

73. Lk. 4:16–30.

74. Lk. 23: 13, 18, 21.

75. Eldon Jay Epp, "Antisemitism and the Popularity of the Fourth Gospel in Christianity," *Journal of the Central Conference of American Rabbis* (Fall 1975): 35–57; John Townsend, "The Gospel of [St.] John and the Jews," in *Antisemitism and the Foundations of Christianity*, ed. Alan Davies (New York 1979), 72–97.

76. James Charlesworth, "Exploring Opportunities for Rethinking Relations among Jews and Christians," in *Jews and Christians* (New York 1990), 50; R. A. Culpepper, "The Gospel of [St.] John and the Jews," *Review and Expositor* 84 (1987): 273–88; D. Moody Smith, "Judaism and the Gospel of [St.] John," in Charlesworth, *Jews and Christians*, 76–99.

77. Jn. 8: 30–31, 39–40.

78. Jn. 8: 42–47.

79. Jn. 1:38, 49; 7:1, 19, 25; 8:12, 44.

80. Jn. 19: 15–16; Mt. 24:3–31; Mk. 13:3–37; 1 Jn. 2:18, 2:22; 1 Jn. 4:3; 2 Jn. 7.

81. Parkes, *Church and Synagogue*, Appendix 3B–C, 397–99.

82. In Maxwekk Staniforth, trans., *Early Christian Writings* (Harmondsworth England 1968), 147.

83. Marcel Simon, *Verus Israel* (Oxford: 1986), 70.

84. Jules Isaac, *Genèse de l'Antisémitisme* (Paris 1956), 296–305; Isaac, *Jésus et Israel* (Paris 1948); Isaac, *L'enseignement du mépris* (Paris 1962).

85. Juster I, 299–301.

86. St. Augustine, "On the Creed: A Sermon to the Catechumens," *Seventeen Short Treatises* (Oxford 1847), 563.

87. St. Augustine, "Sermo ad Catechumenos: De Symbolo," Tractatus IV, in *PL* (Paris 1841), 40:634.

88. Isaac, *Genèse de l'Antisémitisme*, 167.

89. Pierre Pierrard, *Juifs et Catholiques français* (Paris 1970), 298.

90. Juster I, 307–26; Louis Canet, "La Prière "Pro Judaeis' de la Liturgie Catholique Romaine," *Revue des Etudes Juives* 6 (1911), 212–20.

91. *Didascalia apostolorum*, 5:14:8, 5:14:21. Juster I, 282, 310–11; Heinz Schreckenberg, ed., *Die christlichen Adversus-Judaeos-Texte und ihr literarisches*

und historisches Umfeld, 1.-11. Jh. (Frankfurt 1982), 213–16, Revel-Neher, *The Image of the Jew in Byzantine Art*, 29. See Amalarius, "De Ecclesiasticis Officiis," Libri IV, in *PL*, 105:1027. also Osborne Bennett Hardison, *Christian Rite and Christian Drama in the Middle Ages*, 115.

92. Jules Isaac, *Genèse de l'Antisémitisme* (Paris 1956), 304; Parkes, *Church and Synagogue*, 245.

93. John Osterreicher, "Pro Perfidis Judaeis," *Theological Studies* (1947); Erik Peterson, "Perfidia Judaica," in *Ephemerides liturgicae*, vol. 50 (1936), 296–311; Bernhard Blumenkranz, *Archivium Latinitatis medii Aevi*, vol. 22 (1952).

94. The prayer for the "perfidious Jews" was removed in 1965 as a result of Vatican Council II. Hugo Hoever, ed., *Saint Joseph Daily Missal* (New York 1950–51), 304–9; F. E. Lasance, ed., *The New Missal for Every Day* (New York 1937), 406–7.

95. Roy Deferrari, ed., *A Latin-English Dictionary of St. Thomas Aquinas* (Boston 1986).

96. Shlomo Simonsohn, *The Apostolic See and the Jews: History* (Toronto 1991), 9.

97. St. Ambrose, *Epistola* 74:3 (*PL* 16:1255) in Simonsohn, *History*, 9n29.

98. Amalarius, "De Ecclesiasticis Officiis," Libri IV, in *PL*, 105:1027; *The Old Catholic Missal and Ritual* (New York 1969), 93; Osborne Bennett Hardison, *Christian Rite and Christian Drama in the Middle Ages* (Baltimore 1965).

99. St. Jerome, *The Homilies of Saint Jerome* (Washington D.C. 1964), 255–57, 263–64, 267.

100. Hardison, *Christian Rite and Christian Drama in the Middle Ages*, 130–31.

101. Cross, ed., *The Oxford Dictionary of the Christian Church*, 1175. For a ninth-century version of the Reproaches, Hardison, *Christian Rite and Christian Drama in the Middle Ages*, 131–34; Lasance, ed., *The New Missal for Every Day*, 408–9; Eric Werner, "Melito of Sardis, the First Poet of Deicide," *Hebrew Union College Annual*, vol. 37 (1966), 192–93; K. W. Noakes, "Melito of Sardis and the Jews," *Studia Patristica* vol. 13 (1975), 244–49; John Townsend, "'The Reproaches' in Christian Liturgy," *Face to Face* (Summer/Fall 1976), 8–11.

102. Pierre Pierrard, *Juifs et Catholiques français: De Drumont à Jules Isaac* (Paris 1970), 298.

103. Robert Wilken, *St. John Chrysostom and the Jews* (Berkeley 1983), 92; Robert Markus, *The End of Ancient Christianity* (Cambridge, England 1990), 100–103.

104. Udo Schnelle, and M. Eugene Boring, *The History and Theology of the New Testament Writings* (Minneapolis: 1998), 355.

105. *The Didache*, in *Early Christian Writings* (Harmondsworth England 1968), 231.

106. Juster I, 282–311.

107. Cohen, *Christ Killers*, 65.

108. Juster I, 282–311; C. J. Hefele, *Histoire des conciles d'àpres les docs. originaux* (Paris 1907–8), 1:714

109. My thanks to Professor Frederick Schweitzer for this observation.

110. Parkes, *Church and Synagogue*, 279.

111. Juster I, 320n3.

112. St. Jerome, "Commentariorum in Amos Prophetam," Liber II, Caput V, in *PL*, 25:1054.

113. H. Villetard, "I Giudei nella Liturgia," in *Rassegna Gregoriana per gli study litugici et pel canto sacro* 9 (1910): 430–44.

114. Parkes, *Conflict of Church and Synagogue*, 394–400.

Chapter 2

1. Clemens Thoma, *A Christian Theology of Judaism* (New York 1980), 131.

2. Martin Luther, "Explanations of the 95 Theses," in *Luther's Works*, ed. Harold Grimm and Helmut Lehmann, (1959); Thesis 58, 31:225–27; "Heidelberg Disputation," Article 21, in Grimm and Lehmann, 31:40.

3. Juster, 1:264n11.

4. Eusebius, *Ecclesiastical History*, l.4.6; St. Augustine, *City of God*, 15.l; and *Against Two Epistles of the Pelagians*, 3.4.11.

5. See St. Augustine, "Contra Adversarium Legis et Prophetarum," in *Patrologiae, Cursus Completus, Series Latina*, ed. J. P. Migne (Paris 1844–80), 42:623. (Hereafter referred to as *PL*.)

6. Hyam Maccoby, "Christianity's Break with Judaism," Commentary (August 1984).

7. Irenaeus, *Contra Haereses* 3.21.

8. Léon Poliakov, *The History of Antisemitism* (New York 1975), 3:28.

9. Adversus Judaeos, 1.6.

10. Richard Rubenstein, *After Auschwitz* (Indianapolis 1966), 72–73.

11. Wolfgang Seiferth, *Synagoge und Kirche im Mittelalter* (Munich 1964).

12. Tertullian, *Apology*, 18:2, 5–6.

13. David Rokeah, "The Church Fathers and the Jews," in *Antisemitism Through the Ages*, ed. Almog, 61; and his *Jews, Pagans, and Christians in Conflict* (Jerusalem 1982).

14. James Parkes, *The Conflict of Church and Synagogue* (New York 1979), 160.

15. Gregory of Nyssa, *In Christi Resurrectionem*, in *Patrologiae, Cursus Completus, Graeca*, ed. J. P. Migne, (Paris 1863), 46:685–86.

16. Parkes, *Church and Synagogue*, 105–6, 160–61.

17. Jaroslav Pelikan, *The Emergence of the Catholic Tradition, 100–600* (Chicago 1971), 15.

18. Stephen G. Wilson, "Marcion and the Jews," in *Anti-Judaism in Early Christianity*, ed. Stephen G. Wilson (Wilfrid Laurier University Press, 1986), 2:58.

19. Parkes, *Church and Synagogue*, 300.

20. Wilken, *Judaism and the Early Christian Mind*, x.

21. Robert Wilde, *The Treatment of the Jews in the Greek Christian Writers of the First Three Centuries* (Washington 1949), 149.

22. Efroymson, *Tertullian's Anti-Judaism*, 15.

23. Jaroslav Pelikan, *The Spirit of Eastern Christendom* (Chicago 1974), 201.

24. In *De Spectaculis*, Efroymson, *Tertullian's Anti-Judaism*, 125.
25. See National Geographic Society, et al., *The Gospel of Judas* (Hanover, PA, 2006).
26. St. Jerome, *The Homilies of Saint Jerome* (Washington, D.C., 1964), 1:255, 258–62 (My italics.)
27. St. Jerome, *The Homilies of Saint Jerome*, 263–64, 255–57, 267.
28. Letter 112 to St. Augustine, in Terrance Callan, *Forgetting the Root* (New York 1986), 88.
29. St. Augustine, *Treatise Against the Jews*, in Migne, *PL*, 42:63.
30. St. Augustine, in Migne, *PL*, 36–37:705.
31. Joshua Trachtenberg, *The Devil and the Jews* (New Haven 1943); Werner Keller, *Diaspora* (New York 1966); Yitzhak Baer, *A History of the Jews in Christian Spain* (Philadelphia 1978); Paul Grosser and Edwin Halperin, *Antisemitism* (Secaucus 1976); Heinrich Graetz, *History of the Jews* (Philadelphia 1940), vol. 4.
32. St. Augustine, "Reply to Faustus, the Manichaean," in *Disputation and Dialogue*, ed. Talmage, 31; Migne, *PL*, 36–7:705.
33. St. John Chrysostom, *Saint John Chrysostom: Discourses Against Judaizing Christians*, tran. Paul Harkins (Washington, D.C., 1979), x.
34. Fred Grissom, *Chrysostom and the Jews: Studies in Jewish-Christian Relations in 4th Century Antioch* (Southern Baptist Theological Seminary 1978), Unpublished Dissertation, 166.
35. *Orations Against the Jews*, l.6. (My italics.)
36. Ibid., 5.1(my italics), also 1.4.
37. Ruether, *Faith and Fratricide*, 180.
38. Manes Sperber, *The Achilles Heel* (Garden City 1960), 122.
39. *Orations Against the Jews*, 6.3.
40. Ibid., 4.7.
41. Ibid., 6.3.
42. Ibid., 1.
43. Ibid., 1.1 (My italics.)
44. St. John Chrysostom, *Demonstration to the Jews and Gentiles That Christ Is God*, 4. (My italics.)
45. Juster, 1:231, n. 7.
46. Malcolm Hay, *Thy Brother's Blood* (New York 1975), 27.

Chapter 3

1. James Parkes, *The Conflict of the Church and the Synagogue* (New York 1979), 158.
2. Simon, *Verus Israel*, 100–103.
3. A. H. M. Jones, *The Later Roman Empire* (Oxford 1964), 2:948.
4. Schiffman, "At the Crossroads: Tannaitic Perspectives on the Jewish-Christian Schism," in *Essential Papers on Judaism and Christianity in Conflict*, ed. Jeremy Cohen (New York 1991), 450, 257; Linder, *Jews in the Imperial Roman Legislation*, 274n2; Lellia Cracco Ruggini, "Pagani, Ebrei, e Christiani: Odio

Sociologico e Odio Teologico nel Mondo Antico," in *Gli Ebrei nell'Alto Medioevo* (Spoleto 1980), 109; Schiffman, "At the Crossroads," 450, 257; Linder, *Jews in the Imperial Roman Legislation*, 274n2; an anonymous author, Altercatio Synagogae et Ecclesiae, included in a volume on St. Augustine, in *PL*, 42:1133, in Parkes, *Church and Synagogue*, 239. Also Wolfgang Seiferth, *Synagoge und Kirche im Mittelalter* (Munich 1964), 36.

5. Jacob Marcus, *The Jew in the Medieval World: A Source Book*, 315–1791 (New York 1979), doc. 19.

6. Ibid., doc. 20: iv.

7. Charles Freeman, *The Closing of the Western Mind* (New York 2003).

8. W. H. C. Frend, *The Early Church* (Philadelphia 1982), 150.

9. Jones, *The Later Roman Empire*, 1:91–2.

10. J. N. D. Kelly, *Early Christian Creeds* (New York 1972), 231–42.

11. Solomon Grayzel, "Jews and the Ecumenical Councils," in The 75th Anniversary Volume of the *Jewish Quarterly Review*, ed. Abraham Neuman and Solomon Zeitlin (Philadelphia 1967), 289.

12. Quoted in Simon, *Verus Israel*, 316.

13. Robert Wilken, "Insignissima Religio, Certe Licita? Christianity and Judaism in the Fourth and Fifth Centuries," in *The Impact of the Church Upon Its Culture*, ed. Jerald Brauer (Chicago 1968), 58.

14. Jones, *The Later Roman Empire*, 2:949; *Codex Theodosianus* 16:8:3. Hereafter referred to as *C. T.*

15. *C. T.* 16:8:1. Linder, ed., *The Jews in Roman Imperial Legislation* (Detroit 1987), 131n17.

16. Parkes, *Church and Synagogue*, 255; Wilken, "Insignissima Religio, Certe Licita?" 53.

17. *C. J.* 1:3:44 and Novella 132 in Revel-Neher, *The Image of the Jew in Byzantine Art*, 31.

18. Linder, *Jews in Roman Imperial Legislation*, 108, 118n3; Simonsohn, *History*, 94; also, *C. T.* 2:1:10.

19. Walter Pakter, *De His Qui Foris Sunt: The Teachings of the Medieval Canon and Civil Lawyers Concerning the Jews* (PhD Dissertation, Johns Hopkins University, 1974), 4.

20. *C. T.*, *Novella*, 3.

21. Paulus, *Sententiae*, 5:22:3–4, in Linder, *Jews in Roman Imperial Legislation*, 118. See also Constantine's law of October 335, *C. T.* 16:9:1.

22. *C. T.* 16:8:24, published on March 10, 418.

23. Linder, ed., *The Jews in Roman Imperial Legislation*, 82.

24. *C. T.* 16:8:1.

25. *C. T.* 16:7:3. Issued by Gratian, Valentinian, and Theodosius II.

26. *C. T.* 3:1:5.

27. The third appendix of the Codex Theodosianus, issued in January 438; a law of March 14, 388, *C. T.* 3:7:2.

28. *C. T.* 3:1:5, 15:5:5, 16:5:44, 16:7:3, 16:8:7, 16:8:19, 16:8:22, 16:9:4, and *Codex Justinianus* 1:9:3, 1:7:5; 1:5:7; Novella 3 to the law of Theodosius II of January

31, 438, in Linder, *The Jews in Roman Imperial Legislation*, doc. 54; Clyde Pharr, tr., *The Theodosian Code and Novels and the Sirmondian Constitutions* (Princeton 1952), 489.

29. *C.T.* 16:8:19.
30. Simonsohn, *History*, 133–34.
31. Jaroslav Pelikan, *The Growth of Medieval Theology* (Chicago 1978), 247; Gavin Langmuir, "The Anguish of the Jews: The Enervation of Scholarship," *Continuum* (Autumn 1966): 624.

Chapter 4

1. Salo Baron, "Ghetto and Emancipation: Shall We Revise the Traditional View?" *The Menorah Journal* (June 1928): 515, 526.
2. Hayim Hillel Ben-Sasson, "Effects of Religious Animosity on the Jews," in *A History of the Jewish People*, ed. Hayim Hillel Ben-Sasson (London 1976), 411; Gavin Langmuir, "Anti-Judaism as the Necessary Preparation for Antisemitism," *Viator: Medieval and Renaissance Studies* 2 (1971): 385; John Van Engen, "The Christian Middle Ages as a Historiographical Problem," *American Historical Review* (June 1986): 545–46, 552; Bernhard Blumenkranz, "The Roman Church and the Jews," in *Essential Papers on Judaism and Christianity in Conflict*, ed. Jeremy Cohen (New York 1991), 225–26.
3. For an exhaustive summary of sources of anti-Jewish Christian material, both textual and artistic, up to the Fourth Lateran Council of 1215; Heinz Schreckenberg, *Die christlichen Adversus-Judaeos-Texte un ihr literarisches und historisches Umfeld: 1.-11. Jh.* (Frankfurt 1982); *Die christlichen Adversus-Judaeos-Texte: 11.-13. Jh.* (Frankfurt 1988).
4. Chazan, *European Jewry*, 133–36.
5. Friedrich Heer, *The Medieval World* (New York 1962), chapter 5; Robert Benson and Giles Constable, eds., *Renaissance and Renewal in the Twelfth Century* (Cambridge MA 1962); R. W. Southern, *The Making of the Middle Ages* (London 1953); Berger "The Jewish-Christian Debate," 494; Simonsohn, *History*, 295–96.
6. *Interioris mentis sordibus*. St. Ambrose, "Exposito Evangelii Secundum Lucam. Libris X," in *PL*, 15:1630; St. Thomas Aquinas, *Exposito Continua*, also know as the Golden Chain, *Aurea Catena in quatuor Evangelia, Expositio in Lucam*. "Commentary on the Four Gospels, collected out of the Works of the Fathers. By S. St. Thomas Aquinas," [85793] Catena in Lc., cap. 4 l.7.
7. To the Jews of the Middle Ages, the *Aleinu* was second in importance only to the *Shema*. See Habermann, *Sefer Gezerot*, in *Church, State, and Jews*, Chazan, 302; David Roskies, *Against the Apocalypse* (Cambridge, MA 1984), 51.
8. The prayer was attacked as late as the sixteenth and seventeenth century. Manuel, *Broken Staff*, 86–90.
9. Berger, "The Jewish-Christian Debate," 499.
10. Frank Talmage, "David Kimhi on the Messianic Age," in *Disputation and Dialogue*, ed. Frank Talmage (New York 1975), 74–81.

11. Richardson, *The English Jewry Under Angevin Kings*, 26–27.
12. Sophia Menache, *The Vox Dei* (New York 1990), 26, 37.
13. Lazar, "The Lamb and the Scapegoat," 49, 78n45.
14. Joseph Reiger, "Jews in Medieval Art," in *Essays on Antisemitism*, ed. Koppel Pinson (New York 1946), 101.
15. Bernhard Blumenkranz, *Le juif médiéval au miroir de l'art chrétien* (Paris 1966), 46, illustrations 44–45.
16. Henry Kraus, *The Living Theatre of Medieval Art* (Bloomington, IN 1967), 155.
17. Pulzer, *The Rise of Political Antisemitism*, 298.
18. Isaiah Shachar, *The Judensau* (London 1974), 34, 36–37, 52–61; R. Po-chia Hsia, *The Myth of Ritual Murder* (New Haven 1988), 61–62.
19. Wolfgang Seiferth, *Synagogue and Church in the Middle Ages* (New York 1970), 136.
20. For Christian positional symbolism, Amalarius, "De Ecclesiasticis Officiis," Libri IV, in *PL*, 105:1027; Osborne Bennett Hardison, *Christian Rite and Christian Drama in the Middle Ages* (Baltimore 1965), 50; and Allan Temko, *Notre Dame of Paris* (New York 1962), 301.
21. Kraus, *The Living Theatre of Medieval Art*, 155; see also Edgar de Bruyne, *Etudes d'esthétique médiévale* (Brügge 1946), 88, 110–11.
22. Kraus, *The Living Theatre of Medieval Art*, 149; also Paul Weber, *Geistliches Schauspiel und kirchliche Kunst* (Stuttgart 1894), 68.
23. Seiferth, *Synagogue and Church*, 97.
24. Heinz Schreckenberg, *Die christlichen Adversus-Judaeos-Texte und ihr literarisches und historisches Umbeld, 1.-11 Jh.* (Frankfurt 1982), 111–13.
25. Seiferth, *Synagoge und Kirche*, illustrations 22 and 20.
26. Louis Réau, *Iconographie de l'art chrétien* (Paris 1957), 2:746 and Kraus, *The Living Theatre of Medieval Art*, 149.
27. Zefira Rokeah, "The State, the Church, and the Jews in Medieval England," in Shmuel Almog, ed., *Antisemitism Through the Ages* (Oxford 1988), 104–11.
28. Langmuir, "Thomas of Monmouth," *Speculum* 59, no. 4 (1984), 820–46; Mary D. Anderson, *A Saint at Stake* (London 1964), 199–200.
29. Rokeah, "The State, the Church, and the Jews in Medieval England," 109.
30. Montagu Frank Modder, *The Jew in the Literature of England* (Philadelphia 1939), 11.
31. Neville Coghill, Introduction to Geoffrey Chaucer, *The Canterbury Tales* (New York 1977), 14, 18.
32. Chaucer, *The Canterbury Tales*, 186–93.
33. Florence Ridley, *The Prioress and the Critics* (Berkeley 1965), 1, 35. See also Albert Friedman, "The Prioress' Take and Chaucer's Antisemitism," *Chaucer Review* 9 (1974), 118–29; Richard Rex, "Chaucer and the Jews," *Modern Language Quarterly* 45 (1984), 107–22.
34. Philip de Thaun, *Bestiaire*, in Jacobs, *The Jews of Angevin England*, 13–14.
35. Robert Levine, "Why Praise Jews: Satire and History in the Middle Ages," *Journal of Medieval History* 12 (1986), 291–96. See stories two and three of the First Day, in Boccaccio, *The Decameron* (Harmondsworth, England 1972), 85, 87–88.

36. See Peter Abelard, *Dialogus inter Philosophum, Judaeum, et Christianum*, in *Patrologiae Latina*, 178:1617–18; Peter Abelard, *Ethics* (Oxford 1971), 62–63. See also, Cohen, *Christ Killers*, 176.

37. Cohen, *Christ Killers*, 212, 214; see also Chapter 7 in this book.

38. John Wasson, "The Morality Play: Ancestor of Elizabethan Drama," in *The Drama of the Middle Ages*, ed. Clifford Davidson, et al. (New York 1982), 320; also, Richard Emmerson, *Antichrist in the Middle Ages*, (Seattle 1981).

39. Stephen Spector, "Antisemitism and the English Mystery Plays," in Davidson, et al., eds., *The Drama of the Middle Ages*, 328–31, 340–41, n16; see also Heinz Pflaum, "Les Scènes de Juifs dans la littérature dramatique du moyen-age," *Revue des études juives* 89 (1930), 111–34.

40. Pflaum, "Les Scènes de Juifs," 119.

41. Spector, "Antisemitism and the English Mystery Plays," 329.

42. Manya Lipschuk, "Jews in the French Literature of the Middle Ages," in *The Jewish Element in French Literature*, ed. Charles Lehrmann (Cranbury, NJ 1961), 58–59.

43. Lazar, "The Lamb and the Scapegoat," 54; Heinz Pflaum, "Les Scènes de Juifs dans la littérature dramatique du moyen-age," *Revue des études juives* 89 (1930), 111–34.

44. Little, "The Jews in Christian Europe," in *Essential Papers*, ed. Cohen, 288; Moshe Lazar, "The Lamb and the Scapegoat," 57.

45. Miri Rubin, *Corpus Christi* (Cambridge, England 1991), 287.

46. Spector, "Antisemitism and the English Mystery Plays," 331–35, 338.

47. *Jeu d'Adam*, II. 900–3, quoted by Lazar, "The Lamb and the Scapegoat," 51–52.

48. Karl Young, *The Drama of the Medieval Church* (Oxford 1967), 1:255, 446, 497–99, 530, 532–33, 587; 2:125–26, 131–32, 192. See also Heinrich Loewe, *Die Juden in der Marienlegende* (Berlin 1912); Seiferth, *Synagogue and Church*, chapter 12; Weber, *Geistliches Schauspiel*, chapters 9–12.

49. Quoted by Little, "The Jews in Christian Europe," in Cohen, *Essential Papers*, 289. See also Pflaum, "Les Scènes de Juifs," 133–34.

50. Seiferth, *Synagogue and Church*, 143–44.

51. Fritz G. Cohen, "Jewish Images in Late Medieval German Popular Plays," *Midstream* (August–September 1989), 21–26; Pflaum, "Les Scènes de Juifs dans la littérature dramatique du moyen-age," 130–33; Hans Holdschmidt, *Der Jude auf dem Theater des deutschen Mittelalters* (Emsdetter 1935); Natascha Bremer, ed., *Das Bild der Juden in den Passionsspielen und in der bildenden Kunst des deutschen Mittelalters* (Frankfurt 1986).

52. Richard Axton, "Interpretations of Judas in Middle English Literature," in *Religion and Poetry in the Drama of the Late Middles Ages in England*, ed. Piero Boitani and Anna Torti (Suffolk England), 179, 195, 195 n21.

53. Lehrmann, *The Jewish Element in French Literature*, 52–56.

54. *The Mystery of the Redemption*, in *Representative Medieval and Tudor Plays* (New York 1942), 152–206; See also Pflaum, "Les Scènes de Juifs," 133.

55. Seiferth, *Synagogue and Church*, 145; Heinz Pflaum, "Les Scènes de Juifs dans la littérature dramatique du moyen-age," *Revue des études juives* 89 (1930): 111–34; Lehrmann, *The Jewish Element in French Literature*, 57n3.

56. Walter Pakter, *De His Qui Foris Sunt* (PhD Diss., Johns Hopkins University, 1974), 41.
57. Romans 9 and Galatians 4. See also Romans 11:10, where Paul quotes from Pslam 69:23.
58. St. Augustine, *The City of God* (New York 1948), 18.46, 2:279; also *Adversus Judaeos*, 7:9.
59. Schreckenberg, *Adversus Judaeos Texte*, 245, 279, 3218, 323–24, 336; Justin Martyr, *Dialogue with Trypho*, 123:6–7; Tertullian, *Adversus Iudaeos*, 1:3–4.
60. Simonsohn I, doc. 37.
61. Simonsohn, *History*, 98n12.
62. Jacobs, *Jews of Angevin England*, 62–63.
63. Simonsohn, *History*, 98.
64. St. Thomas Aquinas, *De Regimine principum et de regimine Judaeorum* (Turin 1924), 117; *Opuscula Omnia* (Paris 1927), 1:488. See also his *Summa Theologiae*, 11–11, Q. 10, a. 12, and 111, Q. 68, a. 10. (Also called *Summa Theologica*.)
65. St. Thomas Aquinas, "Letter to the Duchess of Brabant," in *Church, State and Jew*, ed. Robert Chazan (New York 1980), 200; Liebeschütz, "Judaism and Jewry in the Social Doctrine of St. Thomas Aquinas," n27.
66. See Chapter 8.
67. St. Thomas Aquinas, *Opuscula Omnia*, 1:490.
68. Simonsohn I, docs. 79 and 82.
69. Grayzel I, doc. 74.
70. Guido Kisch, "Research in Medieval Legal History of the Jews," in *Medieval Jewish Life*, ed. Robert Chazan, (New York 1976), 140.
71. Robert Chazan, *Medieval Jewry in Northern France* (Baltimore 1973), 40.
72. Yitzhak Baer, *A History of the Jews in Christian Spain* (Philadelphia 1961, 1983), 1:85.
73. Chazan, *Church, State, and Jew in the Middle Ages*, 66–69, 77–79, 122–23.
74. Chazan, *Church, State, and Jew*, 123–26. See also Gavin Langmuir, "*Tanquam servi*," in *Les Juifs dans l'histoire de France*, ed. Myriam Yardini (Leiden 1980), 25–54.
75. Shatzmiller, *Shylock Reconsidered*, 55.
76. Friedrich Heer, *The Medieval World* (New York 1962), chapter 2.
77. Langmuir, "Tanquam Servi," 50.
78. Biale, *Power and Powerlessness*, 64.
79. Langmuir, "Tanquam Servi," 43.
80. Simonsohn I, doc. 82.
81. Gilbert Dahan, "l'article *Iudei* de la *Summa Abel* de Pierre le Chantre," *Revue des études Augustiniennes* 27 (1981), 110–11
82. Langmuir, *Toward a Definition of Antisemitism*, 139; Baron, "Ghetto and Emancipation," 518–19. See also Yosef Yerushalmi, "Response to Rosemary Ruether," in *Auschwitz: Beginning of a New Era?*, ed. Eva Fleischner (New York 1977), 98–101.
83. Simonsohn, *History*, 139.

84. Chazan, *Church, State, and Jew in the Middle Ages*, doc. 5, 58–63.

85. Lester Little, "The Jews in Christian Europe," in *Religious Poverty and the Profit Economy in Medieval Europe* (Ithaca 1978), reprinted in Jeremy Cohen, *Essential Papers*, 277.

86. Yardeni, *Anti-Jewish Mentalities in Early Modern Europe*, chapter 6.

87. Little, "The Jews in Christian Europe," in *Essential Papers*, Jeremy Cohen, 279.

88. J. Charles Roux, *Costume en Provence*, in *Carrière of Carpentras*, Calmann.

89. Pietro Odescalchi, quoted in David Kertzer, *The Popes Against the Jews* (New York 2001), 73.

90. Brian Pullan, *The Jews of Europe and the Inquisition of Venice, 1556–1670* (Totowa, N.J., 1983), 153–54.

91. Simonsohn I, doc. 255.

92. Travers Herford, *The Legacy of Israel* (Oxford 1927), 123.

93. Hannah Arendt, "The Jew as Pariah," *Jewish Social Studies* 6, 99; and *The Jew as Pariah* (New York); and Max Weber, *Wirtschaftsgeschichte*.

94. Simonsohn, *History*, 137.

95. Mansi, XXIII, 22; Hefele-Leclercq V and VI; Grayzel, *The Church and the Jews in the XIIIth Century* (Philadelphia 1933).

96. The identification of Jews and heretics occurred several times in Roman-Christian law. See, e.g., *Constitutio Sirmondiana*, 6 and 14; *Theodosius II, Novella* 3; *Codex Theodosianus* 16:5:44, 16:8:26, 16:8:27; *Codex Justinianus* 1:3:54, 1:5:12, 1:5:21, 1:10:2; *Justinianus, Novellae* 37 and 45. C.J. 1:5:12 specifically defined heretic as "everyone who is not devoted to the Catholic Church and to our Orthodox and holy Faith."

97. Kisch, "The Yellow Badge in History," 101–2, 104, 106–8, 117–20, 124.

98. R. Edelmann, "Ahasuerus, the Wandering Jew: Origin and Background," in *The Wandering Jew*, ed. Galit Hasan-Rokem and Alan Dundes (Bloomington, IN 1986), 7.

99. E. Isaac-Edersheim, "Ahasver: A Mythic Image of the Jew," in *The Wandering Jew*, ed. Hasan-Rokem and Dundes 205.

100. Dwayne Carpenter, *Alfonso X and the Jews: An Edition of and Commentary on Siete Partidas 7.24 "de los judios"* (Berkeley 1986), 5, 69, 104–5.

101. Ibid.

102. *Codex Theodosianus* 16:8:24.

103. Simonsohn I, doc. 246.

104. Baer, *The Jews in Christian Spain*, 1:130.

105. *Siete Partidas*, 7.24.1, 7.24.3.

106. Carpenter, *Alfonso X and the Jews*, 28, 34, 60, 68, 83–84.

107. Baer, *The Jews in Christian Spain*, 1:375.

108. Marcus, *The Jew in the Medieval World*, doc. 19.

109. Walter Pakter, *De His Qui Foris Sunt* (PhD Dissertation, Johns Hopkins University, 1974), 193–94.

110. Guido Kisch, *The Jews in Medieval Germany* (Chicago 1949), 278.

111. Jacob Marcus, *The Jew in the Medieval World* (New York 1979), doc. 10.

112. "Mercatores, id est Iudei et ceteri mercatores," in the *Leges Baiuwar* of 906 (Section 10, Capitulum 9) in *Monumenta Germaniae Historica, Leges* (Hannover 1835–89), 3:481; *Capitularia* of Lothar I of 832 (Capitulum 19) and the *Conventus Carisiac* of 877 (Capitulum 39), in *Monumenta*, 1:363, 1:540.

113. Richardson, *The English Jewry Under Angevin Kings*, 26–27.

114. Parkes, *Church and Synagogue*, Appendix One, 385; A. H. M. Jones, *The Later Roman Empire* (Oxford 1964), 2:865–66.

115. Little, "The Jews in Christian Europe," in *Essential Papers*, Jeremy Cohen, 280–81.

116. Jean Régné, *History of the Jews in Aragón: Regesta and docs., 1213–1327* (Jerusalem 1978), doc. 2694, in *Shylock Reconsidered*, Shatzmiller, 58.

117. R. B. Dobson, *The Jews of Medieval York and the Massacre of 1190* (York 1974), 42.

118. Anonymous reviewer, "The Uses of Usury," *The Economist* (June 8, 1991): 89.

119. A. Murray, *Reason and Society in the Middle Ages* (Oxford 1978), 55; J. Gilchrist, *The Church and Economic Activity in the Middle Ages* (New York 1969), 712.

120. Jacobs, *Jews of Angevin England*, 109; Roth, *History of the Jews in England*, 15; Salo Baron, et al., *Economic History of the Jews* (New York 1975), 212. For a contrary view, see H. G. Richardson, *The English Jewry Under Angevin Kings* (Westport, CT 1983), 90.

121. *Saint John Chrysostom: Homilies on Genesis* (Washington, DC 1986), Homily 4:5 in 2:403.

122. Morris, *The Papal Monarchy*, 355.

123. Joseph Schatzmiller, *Shylock Reconsidered* (Berkeley 1990), chapters 4 and 5.

124. Colin Morris, *The Papal Monarchy: The Western Church from 1050 to 1250* (Oxford 1991), 45; also, Peter Abelard, *Dialogus inter Philosophum, Judaeum, et Christianum*, in *PL*. 178:1617–18.

125. Simonsohn, *History*, 190–91.

126. Jacques Le Goff, *Your Money or Your Life* (New York 1988), 32.

127. Le Goff, *Your Money or Your Life*, 32.

128. *The Liber Augustalis*, (Syracuse 1971), 12–13, in *Shylock Reconsidered*, Shatzmiller, 44.

129. The Church interpreted Deuteronomy 23:19–20, "To a foreigner you may lend at interest," as justifying Jews' lending at interest to Christians, just as canon law allowed Christians to lend at interest to Jews. The Talmud likewise permitted the lending of money at interest to Gentiles. The Fourth Lateran Council ordered that Jews lending money at "heavy and immoderate" interest should be denied any relationships with Christians. Simonsohn, *History*, 191.

130. Simonsohn, *History*, 410.

131. R. Straus, "The Jews in the Economic Evolution of Central Europe," *Jewish Social Studies* 3 (1941): 20; Cecil Roth, *A Short History of the Jewish People* (London 1948), 206–7.

132. Langmuir, *Toward a Definition of Antisemitism*, 368n59.

133. Marcus, *The Jew in the Medieval World*, doc. 5.

134. Shatzmiller, *Shylock Reconsidered*, 47.
135. Cecil Roth, "Portraits and Caricatures of Medieval English Jews," in *Essays and Portraits in Anglo-Jewish History* (Philadelphia 1962), 22–23, figure 5.
136. Richardson, *The English Jewry Under Angevin Kings*, 79–80, 259.
137. As early as 591, Pope St. Gregory I had ordered the subdeacon of Campagna to compell a Jew to return the sacred vessels he had purchased from a priest. Simonsohn, I, doc. 6.
138. Simonsohn I, doc. 79.
139. Chazan, *Medieval Jewry in Northern France*, 86.
140. Parkes, *The Jew in the Medieval Community*, 336–37; Le Goff, *Your Money or Your Life*, 9–10.
141. Martin Bouquet, et al., eds., *Recueil des historiens des Gaules et de la France* (Paris 1737–1904), 15:606.
142. Little, "The Jews in Christian Europe," in *Essential Papers*, 292.
143. The Bull itself has not survived. Simonsohn I, doc. 46.
144. Grayzel I, doc. 1.
145. Grayzel I, docs. 14, 25, 30, 58, 71, and Appendix on Church Councils.
146. Langmuir, *Toward a Definition of Antisemitism*, 140.
147. Guimar, *Annales Nantaises*, 140.
148. Joseph Schatzmiller, *Shylock Reconsidered* (Berkeley 1990), 97.
149. Marianne Calmann, *The Carrière of Carpentras* (Oxford 1984), 142.
150. Jacques Le Goff, *La Naissance du Purgatoire* (Paris 1981).
151. Little, "The Jews in Christian Europe," in *Essential Papers*, 292.
152. Simonsohn, *History*, 202–3, 210.
153. Chazan, *Medieval Jewry*, esp. chs. 3 and 4; Chazan, *Church, State, and Jew*, 185–88; Simonsohn, *History*, 101.
154. Bernardino de Siena, *Sermoni*, Sermon 43, in Simonsohn, *History*, 219–20.
155. Kisch, *The Jews in Medieval Germany*, 318–20; Pullan, *The Jews of Europe*, 147, 148; Calmann, *The Carrière of Carpentras*, 142; Poliakov, *History of Antisemitism*, 2:312, 317; Simonsohn, *History*, 226.
156. Poliakov, *History of Antisemitism*, 2:316–19.
157. Othlon de Saint-Emmeran, *Liber de cursu spirituali* 7, quoted in Little, "The Jews in Christian Europe," in *Essential Papers*, 289.
158. Robert Michael, "American Literary Antisemitism," in *Midstream* (August–September 1991), 27–29.
159. Rigord de St. Denis, *Gesta Philippi Augusti*, in Marcus, *The Jew in the Medieval World*, doc. 5.
160. Chazan, *Medieval Jewry*, 69.
161. Richardson, *The English Jewry Under Angevin Kings*, 167, 191–92, 224–25.
162. Chazan, *Medieval Jewry in Northern France*, 100–102; John of Joinville, *Vie de St. Louis* (Paris 1867), chapter 76, in *Church, State, and the Jew in the Middle Ages*, 283–87.
163. F. L. Cross, ed., *The Oxford Dictionary of the Christian Church* (Oxford 1990), 838; Hans Mayer, *The Crusades*, 261.

164. Baer, *The Jews in Christian Spain*, 1:148–49.
165. William of Chartres, *De Vita et Actibus Regis Francorum Ludovici. . .*, in *Recueil des historiens des Gaules et de la France*, ed. Bouquet, et al., 20:34.
166. Lindner, *The Jews in Roman Imperial Legislation*, 340; docs. 55A, 55B.
167. John of Joinville, *The Life of St. Louis* (New York 1955), 35–36.
168. Chazan, *Medieval Jewry in Northern France*, 185.
169. Ibid., 192.
170. Simonsohn I, doc. 282.
171. Chazan, *Medieval Jewry in Northern France*, 178, chapters 5 and 6.
172. Ibid., 326.
173. Justinian's *Novella*, 146, in Lindner, *The Jews in Roman Imperial Legislation*, doc. 66.
174. Simonsohn I, docs. 162–65.
175. Simonsohn I, docs. 162, 163, 171; Grayzel I, doc. 96 and 104.
176. Grayzel I, 340.
177. Grayzel I, 339–40.
178. Haym Maccoby, *Judaism on Trial* (London 1982), 23–24.
179. Maccoby, *Judaism on Trial*, 19, 25, 27–31, 35; Langmuir, *History, Religion, and Antisemitism*, 296.
180. Grayzel I, 30; Jacob Katz, *Exclusiveness and Tolerance* (New York 1962), 107–8.
181. According to Jeremy Cohen, there were two hearings. The first was a debate between Nicholas Donin and Rabbi Yehiel under royal control. The second an Inquisitorial interrogation. *The Friars and the Jews*, 62–67. Yehiel left France after the disputation and died in Palestine. Other Jews acting for the defense were Judah ben David of Melun, Samuel ben Solomon of Chateau Thierry, Moses of Coucy. The judges were the archbishop of Sens, bishop of Paris, the king's chaplain, the chancellor of the University of Paris, and the bishop of Senlis. Grayzel, *The Church and the Jews*, 30–31.
182. Tractate Avodah Zarah.
183. Lasker, *Jewish Philosophical Polemics Against Christianity in the Middle Ages*, 6.
184. Katz, *Exclusiveness and Tolerance*, 108, 113.
185. Walter Pakter, *De His Qui Foris Sunt* (PhD Diss., Johns Hopkins University, 1974), 34–35; Alexander of Hales, *Summa Theologiae* 3,8,1,1,2, in Simonsohn, *The Holy and the Jews: History*, 27n95.
186. Grayzel, *The Church and the Jews*, 32n60, 278 n3.
187. Werner Keller, *Diaspora* (New York 1969), 225; Simonsohn, *History*, 303–7, 315.
188. Joel Rembaum, "Medieval Christianity Confronts Talmudic Judaism," 376; Joel Rembaum, *The Jews, the Bible, and the Talmud* (Los Angeles, 1982).
189. The Jewish side is fully reported in Rabbi Nachman's *Vikuah Ramban*, in *Jewish Religious Polemic*, ed. Oliver Rankin (New York 1970), 178–210.
190. Yitzhak Baer, "The Disputation of R. Yechiel of Paris and of Nachmanides," in Chazan, *Church, State, and Jew*, 266–67.
191. Jeremy Cohen, *The Friars and the Jews* (Ithaca 1982), 139.
192. Nachman, "The Disputation," 200–201.
193. Rankin, *Jewish Religious Polemic*, 172–73.

194. Grayzel II, doc. 24; Simonsohn I, doc. 226.

195. Simonsohn I, doc. 229; Grayzel II, doc. 25.

196. Joseph ha-Kohen, *Emek Ha-Bacha* (Crakow 1895), 128–30, in Marcus, *The Medieval Jew*, doc. 34.

197. Isidore Loeb, "La Controverse religieuse entre les Chrétiens et les Juifs au moyen age," *Revue de l'histoire des religions* 17 (1888): 311–37.

198. Kisch, *The Jews in Medieval Germany*, 325.

199. W. Vesper, *Der deutsche Psalter*, 72, quoted in Seiferth, *Synagogue and Church*, 76.

200. Parkes, *The Jew in the Medieval Community*, 87, 142–43.

201. Béatrice Philippe, *Etre Juif dans la société française* (Paris 1979), 49.

202. Keller, *Diaspora*, 238–39.

203. Louis Canet, "La prière 'pro judaeis' de la liturgie Catholique romaine," *Revue des Etudes Juives* 61 (1911): 220.

204. David Katz, *Tradition and Crisis*, 22, and *Exclusiveness and Tolerance* (New York 1971), 9–11.

205. Maccoby, *Judaism on Trial*, 32–34.

206. Lasker, *Jewish Philosophical Polemics Against Christianity in the Middle Ages*, 8–9.

207. Lasker, *Jewish Philosophical Polemics Against Christianity in the Middle Ages*, 19.

208. Anna Abulafia, "Invectives Against Christianity in the Hebrew Chronicles of the First Crusade," in *Crusade and Settlement*, ed. Peter Edbury (Cardiff England 1985), 68–70; Berger, "The Jewish-Christian Debate," 492–93.

209. Berger, "The Jewish-Christian Debate," 487–88, 506–7n12.

210. In 1170, Jacob ben Reuben's *Sefer Milhamot Ha Shem*. Daniel Lasker, *Jewish Philosophical Polemics Against Christianity in the Middle Ages* (New York 1977), 1–2, 13.

211. R. Travers Herford, *Christianity in Talmud and Midrash* (New York 1975), 351–53. The second century Christian writer Tertullian mentions similar Jewish ideas. *Liber de spectaculis*, 30, 5–6, in William Horbury, "Tertullian on the Jews in the Light of De spectaculis xxx. 5–6," *Journal of Theological Studies* 23 (1972): 455–59.

212. Matthew 1:1.

213. Lasker, *Jewish Philosophical Polemics*, 5, 175n28; also Tractate Kallah, Sanhedrin 43a, and Joseph Klausner, *Jesus of Nazareth* (New York 1925), 47–54.

214. Sanhedrin 107b. Jacob Lauterbach, "Jesus in the Talmud," *Rabbinic Essays* (New York 1973), 473–570.

215. "Christian Persecutions, c. 1200–1500," in *Atlas of the Jewish World*, de Lange, 36.

216. Katz, *Exclusiveness and Tolerance*, 3; Israel Abrahams, *Jewish Life in the Middle Ages* (New York 1981), 410; also Alex Bein, *The Jewish Question* (New York 1990), 123–24, 130.

217. Biale, *Power and Powerlessness in Jewish History*, chapter 3.

218. Norman Golb, "New Light on the Persection of French Jews at the Time of the First Crusade," in *Medieval Jewish Life*, ed. Robert Chazan (New York 1976); Robert Chazan, *European Jewry and the First Crusade* (Berkeley 1987); Riley-Smith, *The First Crusade and the Idea of Crusading*.

219. Hyam Maccoby, *The Sacred Executioner* (New York 1982); Cecil Roth, *A Short History of the Jewish People* (London 1943); Trachtenberg, *The Devil and the Jews*; Langmuir, *Towards a Definition of Antisemitism*; R. Po-chia Hsia, *The Myth of Ritual Murder* (New Haven 1988); Gavin Langmuir, *History, Religion, and Antisemitism* (Berkeley 1990).

220. Séraphine Guerchberg, "The Controversy over the Alleged Sowers of the Black Death in the Contemporary Treatises on Plague," in *Change in Medieval Society*, ed. Sylvia Thrupp (New York 1964); Philip Ziegler, *The Black Death* (New York 1969).

221. John Edwards, "Mission and Inquisition Among *Conversos* and *Moriscos* in Spain, 1250–1550," in *Persecution and Toleration*, ed. W. J. Sheils (Papers of the Ecclesiastical History Society 1984); Baer, *The Jews in Christian Spain*; Cohen, ed., *Essential Papers*.

222. Robert Michael, *Holy Hatred* (New York 2006).

223. "Germany and the Jews: Two Views," *Conservative Judaism* (Fall 1962/Winter 1963): 43.

224. Based on Shlomo Eidelberg's translation of *The Chronicle of Solomon bar Simson*; see also Solomon bar Simson, in Chazan, *European Jewry*, 252, 256.

Chapter 5

1. Morris, *The Papal Monarchy*, 152

2. Chazan, *European Jewry*, 204.

3. "Entweder müssen die Juden sich zu unserm Glauben behehren oder sie werden vertilgt sammt Kind und Säugling!" An anonymous chronicler of Mainz in Adolf Neubauer and Moritz Stern, eds., *Hebräische Berichte über die Judenverfolgungen während der Kreuzzüge* (Berlin 1892), 176, 169; Robert Chazan, "The Hebrew First-Crusade Chronicles," *Revue des études juives: Historia Judaica* 33 (January–June 1974): 249–50, 253; Bernold, *Chronicle in Monumenta Germaniae Historica, Scriptores* (Hannover 1826–96), 5:465.

4. Golb, "New Light on the Persecution of French Jews at the Time of the First Crusade," 19.

5. In the fourth and fifth centuries many Christian attacks on Jewish communities had also taken place in the Near East.

6. Economic consideratons also played a role.

7. For a similar analysis, Ben-Zion Dinur, ed., *Yisrael ba-Golah* (Tel Aviv 1958–72), cited by Chazan, European Jewry, 198.

8. Cohn, *The Pursuit of the Millennium*, 61.

9. Golb, "New Light on the Persecution of French Jews at the Time of the First Crusade," 318–29.

10. Mayer, *The Crusades*, 8, 23, 30–33, 36; Morris, *The Papal Monarchy*, 150–52; Cohn, *Pursuit of the Millennium*, 61.

11. Mainz Anonymous, in *European Jewry*, Chazan, 226; and Shlomo Eidelberg, ed., *The Jews and the Crusaders* (Madison 1977), 100; Colin Morris, *The Papal Monarchy* (Oxford 1991), 355; Mayer, *The Crusades*, 40.

12. Robert Chazan, "The Hebrew First-Crusade Chronicles," *Revue des études juives: Historia Judaica* 33 (January–June 1974): 248.
13. Riley-Smith, *The First Crusade and the Idea of Crusading*, 52.
14. Riley-Smith, "The First Crusade and the Persecution of the Jews," 57; Chazan, *European Jewry*, 81.
15. Golb, "New Light on the Persection of French Jews at the Time of the First Crusade," 24.
16. Riley-Smith, *The First Crusade and the Idea of Crusading*, 53; Riley-Smith, *The Crusades* (New Haven 1987), 17.
17. Chazan, *European Jewry*, 247.
18. Raymond of Aguilers, "Historia Francorum qui ceperunt Jerusalem," in *Recueil des historiens des Croisades: Historiens occidentaux* (Paris 1844–95), 3:300; Norman Cohn, *Pursuit of the Millennium* (New York 1980), 68.
19. Riley-Smith, *The First Crusade and the Idea of Crusading*, 53–54; Chazan, *European Jewry*, 269, 289–90; Mainz Anonymous and Solomon bar Simson, in *European Jewry*, 227, 245; Solomon bar Simson, in *European Jewry*, 246–47, 251, 253, 269.
20. Mainz Anonymous in *European Jewry*, 227–28; Chazan, "The Hebrew First-Crusade Chronicles," 249; Solomon bar Simson, in, *European Jewry*, 253, 260–61; Mainz Anonymous and Solomon bar Simson, in *European Jewry*, 233, 249; Solomon bar Simson, *European Jewry*, 274; Solomon bar Simson, in Narrative of the Old Persecutions, in Eidelberger, ed., *The Jews and the Crusaders*, 101–2; Chazan, *European Jewry*, 288.
21. Morris, *The Papal Monarchy*, 478, 484.
22. Elisabeth Revel-Neher, *The Image of the Jew in Byzantine Art* (Oxford 1992), 17.
23. Graetz, 3:502–3; Morris, *The Papal Monarchy*, 446.
24. Golb, "New Light on the Persection of French Jews at the Time of the First Crusade," 295.
25. Gui Alexis Lobineay, *Histoire de Bretagne* (Paris 1707), 1:235.
26. J. M. Vidal, "L'Emeute des Pastoureaux en 1320," in *Annales de St. Louis des Français* 3 (1898), 138.
27. Bernard Gui, Vita Joannis XXII, in *Vitae paparum Avinoniensium*, ed. E. Baluze (Paris 1814–1937), 1:161–63; John, Canon of St. Victor, in Baluze, *Vitae Paparum*, 1:128–30; Solomon Ibn Verga, Shebet Yehuda (Hanover 1856), 4–6, in Cohn, *The Pursuit of the Millennium*, 103–4.
28. Yitzhak Baer, *A History of the Jews in Christian Spain* (Philadelphia 1978), 2:15; Chazan, *Church, State and Jew in the Middle Ages*, 181–83.
29. Graetz, *History of the Jews*, 4:57–58.
30. See Chapter 1.
31. Langmuir, *Towards a Definition of Antisemitism*, 127.
32. Trachtenberg, *The Devil and the Jews*, 148.
33. Frederick II's Charter of 1236, King James II of Aragón's Letter of 1294, in Chazan, *Church, State, and Jew*, 114–16, 123–68.
34. Magdalene Schultz, "The Blood Libel: A Motif in the History of Childhood," in *The Blood Libel Legend*, ed., Alan Dundes (Madison 1991), 273–303; Ernest Rappaport, "The Ritual Murder Accusation," in *The Blood Libel Legend*, 326.

35. R. Po-chia Hsia, "Jews as Magicians in Reformation Germany," in *Antisemitism in Times of Crisis*, ed. Gilman and Katz, 119.

36. Julius Streicher, "Special Ritual-Murder Edition," *Der Stuermer* (May 1934); Randall Bytwerk, *Julius Streicher* (New York 1983), 127–30, 199–200.

37. Langmuir, *Toward a Definition of Antisemitism*, chapter 9.

38. He died in 1144; a second case occurred in 1168, Harold of Gloucester.

39. Langmuir, *Toward a Definition of Antisemitism*, 307; The Life and Miracles of St. William of Norwich by Thomas of Monmouth, quoted in Chazan, *Church, State and Jew*, 142–45.

40. Langmuir, *Toward a Definition of Antisemitism*, 307.

41. Richard of Pointoise. Morris, *The Papal Monarchy*, 356.

42. Chazan, *Medieval Jewry in Northern France*, 37; Morris, *The Papal Monarchy*, 356. Also, Chazan, *Church, State, and the Jew*, 114–17; Béatrice Philippe, *Etre Juif dans la société française* (Paris 1979), 18.

43. Gen. 22; Deut. 18:10; Jer. 2:35–35, 19:4–6.

44. Lev. 3:17, 7:26, 17:10–14; Deut. 12:15–16, 23–25.

45. Cecil Roth, "The Feast of Purim," 524.

46. Trachtenberg, *The Devil and the Jews*, 6, 47–50, 116, 149–50, 227–28; Israel Levi, "Le juif de la legende," *Revue des Etudes Juives* 5 (1890): 249–51; Léon Poliakov, *The History of Antisemitism from the Time of Christ to the Court Jews* (New York 1974), 142–43; Little, "The Jews in Christian Europe," in *Essential Papers*, ed. Jeremy Cohen, 288.

47. Trachtenberg, *The Devil and the Jews*, 6, 31, 50–51, 83, 124–55; Hyam Macoby, *The Sacred Executioner*, 152–60.

48. Simonsohn, *History*, 83; Hsia, *The Myth of Ritual Murder*, 43–45.

49. Simonsohn, *History*, 85; Léon Poliakov, *The History of Antisemitism* (New York 1974), 1:148; Lazar, "The Lamb and the Scapegoat," 58, Roth, *A History of the Marranos*, 52; Henry Charles Lea, "Santo Niño de la Guardia," *English Historical Review* 4(1889): 229–50.

50. Jean Stengers, Les Juifs dans les Pays-Bas au Moyen Age (Brussels 1950), 55–56; Bernard Glassman, *Antisemitic Stereotypes Without Jews: Images of the Jews in England, 1290–1700* (Detroit 1975).

51. Dom Raymund Webster, "St. William of Norwich," http://www.newadvent.org/cathen/15635a.htm.

52. John Chrysostom, *Homilies on Matthew*, 82:4–5; also 33:40; Saint Jean Chrysostome, *Commentaire sur l'évangile selon Saint Matthieu in Oeuvres Complètes* (Bar-le-duc 1874), 8:37–8; and Chrysostom Homilies on 1 Corin., 24:4.

53. In legend, the Jews often converted because the miracle caused them to recognize the "validity" of Christianity.

54. Mentioned by Josef ha-Cohen in *Emek ha-bacha, Vallée des Pleurs* (Vale of Tears) (Paris 1881), 28.

55. Cohen, *The Friars and the Jews*, 239.

56. Léon Poliakov, *Histoire de l'Antisémitisme* (Paris 1965), 1:99, 316 n131. See the historical map in Nicholas de Lange, *Atlas of the Jewish World* (New York 1984), 36.

57. Keller, *Diaspora*, 235–36, 230–31; Poliakov, The History of Antisemitism, 1:99–100; Graetz, *History of the Jews*, 4:35–37; Salo Baron, *Social and Religious History of the Jews* (Philadelphia 1952–69), 11:265–66.

58. Edward Flannery, *The Anguish of the Jews* (New York 1985), 108–9; Graetz, *History of the Jews*, 4:97–98; Baron, *Social and Religious History of the Jews* 11:416–17.

59. William Monter, *Ritual, Myth, and Magic in Early Modern Europe* (Brighton 1983), 18; Grosser and Halperin, *Antisemitism*, 126–31.

60. Hsia, "Jews as Magicians in Reformation Germany," 122.

61. Browe, "Die Hostienschändungen der Juden im Mittelalter," in *Römische Quartalschrift für christliche Altertumskunde und für Kirchengeschichte* 34 (1926): 197. See also Peukert, "Ritualmord," in *Handwörterbuch des deutschen Aberglaubens* (Berline 1935–36), 7:727–39.

62. Dennis Showalter, *Little Man, What Now? Der Stürmer in the Weimar Republic* (Hamden 1982), 106.

63. *Codex Theodosianus* 16:5:44. This law also associated the Jews with heretics.

64. Grayzel I, 109.

65. Grayzel I, 333.

66. Séraphine Guerchberg, "The Controversy over the Alleged Sowers of the Black Death in the Contemporary Treatises on Plague," in *Change in Medieval Society*, ed. Sylvia Thrupp (New York 1964), 209.

67. In one instance, the surviving Jews were protected by King Peter IV of Aragón, Chazan, *Church, State, and Jew*, 128–31.

68. Keller, *Diaspora*, 237; also Cohn, *Pursuit of the Millennium*, chapter 7.

69. Grosser and Halperin, *Antisemitism*, 129–31.

70. Philip Ziegler, *The Black Death* (New York 1969), 98, 100–102.

71. Ziegler, *The Black Death*, 103; also Friedrich Closener, Strassburger Deutsche Chronik, in J. Höxter, *Quellenbuch zur jüdischen Geschichte und Literatur* 3 (1927): 28–30.

Chapter 6

1. St. Augustine, "Reply to Faustus, the Manichaean," in *Disputation and Dialogue*, ed. F. E. Talmage (New York 1975), 31; and Commentary on Psalms 58 and 59, in J. P. Migne, ed., *Patrologiae, Cursus Completus, Series Latina*, 36–37:705.

2. Pope St. Gregory IX to the abbot of Cluny, January 23, 1234. Grayzel I, doc. 74.

3. *PL* 13:363–64, in Shlomo Simonsohn, *The Apostolic See and the Jews: History* (Toronto 1991), 9n27.

4. Walter Ullmann, "[St.] Leo I and the Theory of Papal Primacy," *Journal of Theological Studies* 11 (1960): 25–51.

5. St. Leo I, "Sermones XXX, LIX, LX, LXIII, LXVI, LXXI, XCV," in *PL* 54: 234, 340, 343, 357, 365–66, 389, 461.

6. St. Leo I, "Sermo LIX," in *PL* 54:339.

7. Seiferth, *Synagogue and Church in the Middle Ages: Two Symbols in Art and Literature* (New York 1970), 34–35.

8. J. N. D. Kelly, *The Oxford Dictionary of the Popes* (Oxford 1986), 65–69.
9. Simonsohn, *History*, 41–42.
10. Bat-Shiva Albert, "St. Isidore of Seville," 208.
11. *Codex Theodosianus* 16:8:9.
12. Grayzel, "The Papal Bull *Sicut Judeis*," in *Essential Papers*, ed. Jeremy Cohen, 234.
13. Simsonsohn I, doc. 5.
14. Simsonsohn I, doc. 19; Grayzel, "The Papal Bull *Sicut Judeis*," in *Essential Papers*, 231–32.
15. Simonsohn I, docs. 5, 12–13, 24–26.
16. St. Gregory, *PL*, 75:748, 76:26, 62, 428, 430–31, 504–6, 673.
17. St. Gregory, *Monumenta Germaniae Historica, Epistolarum* III, 37, 1:195; IV, 31, 1:267.
18. Simonsohn I, doc. 27.
19. Epistle V:20, quoted in Parkes, *Church and Synagogue*, 300–302.
20. Simonsohn I, doc. 26. Grayzel, "The Papal Bull *Sicut Judeis*," in *Essential Papers*, 234.
21. Corinthians 6: 14–15; *Codex Theodosianus* 16:8:28.
22. Simonsohn I, doc. 29.
23. Bernhard Blumenkranz, ed., *Les auteurs chrétiens latins du moyen age sur les Juifs et le Judaisme* (Paris 1963), doc. 128a–b.
24. Simonsohn I, docs. 29–32, 34.
25. Walter Ullman, *A History of Political Thought* (Baltimore 1970), 105; Guido Kisch, *The Jews in Medieval Germany* (Chicago 1949), 339; Jaroslav Pelikan, *The Growth of Medieval Theology* (Chicago 1978), 268.
26. Pope Innocent III, "Sermones de Diversis, Sermo II, In Consecratione Pontificis Maximi," in *PL*, 217:658.
27. Friedrich Heer, *The Medieval World* (New York 1962), 336.
28. Michael Wilks, *The Problem of Sovereignty in the Later Middle Ages* (Cambridge, England, 1963), 153, 164–71, 275–76, 474.
29. A. K. Ziegler, "Pope Gelasius I and His Teaching on the Relation of Church and State," *Catholic Historical Review* 27 (1942): 412–37.
30. *Gladium sanguinis*, in *De His Qui Foris Sunt*, ed. Pakter, 13–14.
31. Matthew 16:19.
32. Pakter, *De His Qui Foris Sunt*, 330–31.
33. Quoted by Richard McBrien, *Catholicism* (Minneapolis 1981), 2785.
34. Wilks, *The Problem of Sovereignty*, 275–77.
35. Philippe de Mézières, *Le Songe du vieil pèlerin* (1389), ed. G. W. Coopland (Cambridge Eng. 1969), 225.
36. Grayzel II, 34n72.
37. Pope St. Gregory VII, "Epistola II: Ad Alphonsum Regem Castellae," *PL*, 148:604–5; in Blumenkranz, *Les auteurs chrétiens*, doc. 238.
38. Grayzel I, docs. 17 and 18.
39. Simonsohn I, doc. 88.

40. Walter Pakter, *De His Qui Foris Sunt: The Teachings of the Medieval Canon and Civil Lawyers Concerning the Jews* (PhD Dissertation, Johns Hopkins University, 1974), 10–11.

41. Pakter, *De His Qui Foris Sunt*, 12–14, and William Jordan, "Christian Excommunication of the Jews in the Middle Ages," *Jewish History* (Spring 1986): 35.

42. Simonsohn I, doc. 66.

43. Simonsohn, *History*, 191.

44. Raymond of Peñaforte, "Summa de poenitentia et matrimonio," in *Church, State, and Jew in the Middle Ages*, ed. Robert Chazan (New York 1980), doc. 4, 40.

45. *Ravyah*, 452, in *Exclusiveness and Tolerance*, ed. Jacob Katz (New York 1975), 39.

46. Joseph Shatzmiller, "Jews 'Separated from the Communion of the Faithful in Christ' in the Middle Ages," in *Studies in Medieval Jewish History and Literature*, ed. Isadore Twersky (Cambridge, MA, 1979), 307–14.

47. Pakter, *De His Qui Foris Sunt*, 16, 336n45.

48. Simonsohn I, docs. 91, 92.

49. Simonsohn I, docs. 203.

50. Zefira Rokeah, "The State, the Church, and the Jews in Medieval England," in *Antisemitism Through the Ages*, ed. Shmuel Almog (Oxford 1988), 113, 125 n75.

51. Simonsohn I, docs. 357–59.

52. Baer, *The Jews in Christian Spain*, 2:339.

53. Simonsohn I, doc. 44.

54. Solomon Grayzel, "Popes, Jews, and Inquisition," in Grayzel II, 4–5, 26–27.

55. Simonsohn I, doc. 71.

56. Ibid., doc. 82.

57. Ibid., docs. 79, 82, 86–91; also Chazan, *Church, State, and Jew*, 287–89; Simonsohn, *History*, 46.

58. Ibid., doc. 105.

59. Simonsohn, *History*, 32–3, 70.

60. Heinrich Graetz, *History of the Jews* (Philadelphia 1940), 4:220.

61. Shatzmiller, "Jews 'Separated from the Communion of the Faithful in Christ' in the Middle Ages," 308–9; John of Joinville, *Joinville and Villehardouin: Chronicles of the Crusades* (Harmondsworth 1963), 177–78.

62. Grayzel I, 22–82; Malcolm Hay, *Thy Brother's Blood* (New York 1975), 36, 102; Cohen, *The Friars and the Jews*, 243–44; Norman Cohn, *Pursuit of the Millennium* (New York 1970), 63; Walter Ullmann, *Medieval Papalism* (London 1949), 77–81, 141; Charles Lea, *History of the Inquisition in Spain* (New York 1908), 1:82.

63. Grayzel, "The Papal Bull *Sicut Judeis*," in *Essential Papers*, ed. Jeremy Cohen, 249.

64. Grayzel I, doc. 70.

65. Ibid., docs. 113, 114, 116, 118.

66. Ibid., doc. 114.

67. Simonsohn I, doc. 154; Grayzel I, doc. 87.
68. Ibid., 219n2.
69. See also Simonsohn, *History*, 154.
70. Simonsohn I, docs. 333, 347, 348, 369, 653.
71. Simonsohn, *History*, 47.
72. Grayzel I, docs. 13, 14, 18, 41, 49, 53, 59; Grayzel II, docs. 26, 27, 33, 50; Simonsohn I, docs. 379, 434.
73. Simonsohn I, docs. 35–38. also Chazan, *Church, State, and Jew*, doc. 7, 99–100; Simonsohn I, doc. 39; Blumenkranz, "The Roman Church and the Jews," in *Essential Papers*, ed. Jeremy Cohen, 199.
74. Mayer, *The Crusades*, 39.
75. *Sicut Judaeis*, issued between 1119 and 1124. Simonsohn I, doc. 44.
76. Grayzel, "The Papal Bull *Sicut Judeis*," in *Essential Papers*, 235; Simsonsohn, *The Apostolic See and the Jews: History*, 16.
77. Simonsohn I, doc. 42.
78. Grayzel, "The Papal Bull *Sicut Judeis*," in *Essential Papers*, 237.
79. Simonsohn I, doc. 46.
80. Neubauer and Stern, *Hebräische Berichte*, 64; Jean-Pierre Torrell, "Les juifs dans l'oeuvre de Pierre le Vénérable," *Cahiers de civilisation médiévale* 30 (1987): 345.
81. Simonsohn I, doc. 88.
82. Ibid., docs. 89–90, 92.
83. Ibid., doc. 95.
84. Ibid., doc. 49.
85. Ibid., doc. 64.
86. Ibid., docs. 49, 63, 64.
87. Chazan, *European Jewry*, 141–42.
88. Ibid., 140.
89. Issued by Popes Lucius III (in 1184–85) and Celestine III (in 1193). Simonsohn I, docs. 60, 61, 65, 66.
90. Simonsohn, *The Apostolic See and the Jews: History*, 17.
91. Ibid.
92. There had already been a less extensive Shepherds' Crusade c. 1250, when the papacy was also silent.
93. Simonsohn, *History*, 30.
94. Simonsohn I, docs. 302–8.
95. Simonsohn, *History*, 345.
96. Simonsohn I, docs. 302–9, 312–14.
97. Ibid., docs. 372–75. See also Diana Wood, "Infidels and Jews: Clement VI's Attitude Toward Persecution and Toleration," in *Persecution and Toleration*, ed. W. J. Sheils, (Oxford 1984), 121–24.
98. Simonsohn I, docs. 373 and 374 (September 26 and October 1 of 1348).
99. Ibid., doc. 374.
100. Ibid., doc. 375.
101. Mordechai Breuer, "The 'Black Death' and Antisemitism," in *Antisemitism Through the Ages*, ed. Almog, 141–51; Ziegler, *The Black Death*, 103, 106–7.

102. Simonsohn, *History*, 65 n66.

103. Ibid., 64.

104. Ibid., 93.

105. Graetz, *History of the Jews*, 3:596, 611, 4:101–12, 222–25, 545; Dubnow, *History of the Jews in Russia and Poland*, 1:178–79.

106. Simonsohn I, doc. 79.

107. Cecil Roth, ed., *The Ritual Murder Libel and the Jew* (London, 1934), 26, 30–31; also, Elphege Vacandard, "Question du meutre rituel," *Etudes de critique et d'histoire religieuse*, III (Paris, 1912). Cecil Roth described Ganganelli's report as "one of the most remarkable, broad-minded, and humane documents in the history of the Catholic Church." Roth, *The Ritual Murder Libel and the Jew*, 26.

108. Langmuir, *Toward a Definition of Antisemitism*, 307.

109. Simonsohn I, docs. 982, 984–89.

110. Malcolm Hay, *Thy Brother's Blood* (New York 1975), 129.

111. William Monter, *Ritual, Myth, and Magic in Early Modern Europe* (Brighton, England, 1983), 18; R. Po-chia Hsia, *The Myth of Ritual Murder* (New Haven 1988).

112. See Chapter 4 in this book.

113. Ibid., docs. 162, 163, also doc. 171 and Grayzel I, doc. 96 and 104. See also Grayzel I, doc. 119 and 275–79.

114. Simonsohn I, doc. 255.

115. Quoted in Pakter, *De His Qui Foris Sunt*, 290.

116. Ibid., 291.

117. Ibid., 295, 297.

118. Simonsohn I, doc. 42. Similar protection was offered by Frederick I and Frederick II. Pakter, *De His Qui Foris Sunt*, 290; James Parkes, *The Jew in the Medieval Community* (New York 1976), 79–80, 85. For a Jewish report on Henry, see Hebermann, *Sefer Gezerot*, in *Church, State, and the Jew*, doc. 8, 113–14.

119. In 1278, Simonsohn I, doc. 241.

120. Jeremy Cohen, *The Friars and the Jews* (Ithaca 1982), 85; Simonsohn I, docs. 243–45.

121. Ibid., doc. 278.

122. Simonsohn, *History*, 258.

123. Simonsohn II, doc. 1159.

124. Roth, *A History of the Marranos*, 58.

125. Léon Poliakov, *The History of Antisemitism* (New York 1973), 2:317–18; Graetz, *History of the Jews*, 4:657–59.

126. See Chapter 4 in this book on Judensau.

127. James Reites, S. J., "St. Ignatius of Loyola and the Jews," *Studies in the Spirituality of Jesuits* (September 1981): 16.

128. Grosser and Halperin, *Antisemitism*, 193; Chadwick, *The Popes and European Revolution*, 53.

129. Harry Cargas, *A Christian Response to the Holocaust* (Denver 1981), 10.

130. Paul Grosser and Edwin Halperin, *Antisemitism: The Causes and Effects of a Prejudice* (Secaucus 1979), 198; Nicholas de Lange, *Atlas of the Jewish World* (New York 1984), 37; Sam Waaganaar, *The Pope's Jews*, 232–34.

131. Charles Dupaty, *Lettres sur l'Italie*, in *The Pope's Jews*, ed. Waaganaar, 235.
132. Dagobert Runes, *The War Against the Jews* (New York 1968), 44–45; Waagenaar, *The Popes Jews*, 253–54.
133. Kertzer, *Popes Against the Jews*, 127–28.
134. Peter De Rosa, *The Vicars of Christ* (New York 1988), 194–95; A. Berliner, *Geschichte der Juden in Rom* (Frankfurt 1893), 3:205–8, in Poliakov, *The History of Antisemitism*, 2:325–26.
135. Simonsohn, *History*, 344.
136. Ibid., 343–45.
137. Simonsohn I, doc. 230.
138. Grayzel II, doc. 25, and 96.
139. Simonsohn II, doc. 48.
140. Peters, *Inquisition*, 80.
141. Simonsohn I, docs. 263–64.
142. Simonsohn II, docs. 799–802.
143. Philip Schaff, *History of the Christian Church* (Oak Harbor, WA, 1997). For more on Spanish Inquisition and Catholic racism, see the postscript at the end of this book.
144. Ibid.
145. In letters of January–October 1482. Shlomo Simonsohn, *The Apostolic See and the Jews: docs., 1464–1521* (Toronto 1990), docs. 1017–21.
146. Simonsohn, *History*, 36.
147. Cecil Roth, *The Spanish Inquisition*.
148. Simonsohn II, docs. 740–41.
149. Simonsohn, *History*, 46.
150. Ibid., 38.
151. Chadwick, *The Popes and European Revolution*, 19.
152. Waagenaar, *The Pope's Jews*, 169–75.
153. Ibid., 177; Poliakov, *The History of Antisemitism*, 2:317.
154. Chadwick, *The Popes and European Revolution*, 18–19.
155. Poliakov, *The History of Antisemitism*, 2:316, 321, 323–26.
156. *De Iudaeis et Aliis Infidelibus* [Concerning Jews and Other Infidels], published in Venice in 1558.
157. Kenneth Stow, *Catholic Thought and Papal Jewry Policy, 1555–1593* (New York 1977), 64–65, 125–48.
158. Gerard Sloyan, *Why Jesus Died* (Minneapolis, 1995), 2; see also Sloyan, *The Crucifixion of Jesus* (Minneapolis 1995), 2, 5.
159. *De Iudaeis*, I, Introduction; I, 1–13; III, 1.
160. Simonsohn, *History*, 31.
161. Reites, "St. Ignatius of Loyola and the Jews," 15–16, 32.
162. Jeffrey Russell, *Dissent and Reform in the Early Middle Ages* (Berkley 1965), 52.
163. Simonsohn I, docs. 200, 312 and 324, also docs. 313–14, 321–23, 334; Grayzel I, 292–93.
164. Langmuir, *Toward a Definition of Antisemitism*, 99.

Chapter 7

1. Heiko Oberman, *The Roots of Antisemitism in the Age of Renaissance and Reformation* (Philadelphia 1981), 41–42, 78, 95. (Translation of Heiko Oberman, *Wurzeln des Antisemitismus* [Berlin 1981]).

2. Christoph Peter Burger, "Endzeiterwartung im spaten Mittelalter," in *Der Antichrist und Die Funfzehn Zeichen vor dem Jungsten Gericht* (Hamburg 1979), 43, cited by Oberman, *The Roots of Antisemitism*, 129, n. 31; see also Wilhelm Bousset, *The Anti-Christ Legend* (London 1896).

3. Oberman, *The Roots of Antisemitism*, 26, 43, 50.

4. H. H. Ben-Sasson, "Changes in the Legal and Social Status of the Jews," in H. H. Ben-Sasson, ed., *A History of the Jewish People* (London 1976), 647.

5. Quoted by Jacques Courvoisier, "Calvin et les Juifs," in *Judaica, Beitraege zum Verstandnis des Judischen Schicksals in Vergangenheit und Gengenwart* (Zurich 1946), 206, cited by Alan Davies, *Antisemitism and the Christian Mind* (New York 1969), 109.

6. Oberman, *The Roots of Antisemitism*, 38–40.

7. Ibid., 137 n. 123.

8. Johannes Eck, *Ains Judenbüechlins Verlegung* (Ingolstadt 1541), in *Myth of Ritual Murder*, ed. Hsia, 130.

9. Oberman, *The Roots of Antisemitism*, 9.

10. St. Jerome, *The Homilies of Saint Jerome* (Washington, D.C., 1964), l: 255, 258–62 (My italics.)

11. For a full discussion of Martin Luther's antisemitism, see Robert Michael, *Holy Hatred: Christianity, Antisemitism, and the Holocaust* (New York, 2006), chapters 4 and 5.

12. Salo Baron, *A Social and Religious History of the Jews* (New York 1952), vol. 13, 429n26.

13. Luther, "On the Jews and Their Lies," 261–72.

14. R. Edelmann, "Ahasuerus the Wandering Jew: Origin and Background," in *The Wandering Jew: Essays in the Interpretation of a Christian Legend*, ed. Galit Hasan-Rokem and Alan Dundes (Bloomington IN 1986), 6.

15. Friedrich Heer, *God's First Love* (New York 1967) 130, 284–86.

16. Martin Sasse, quoted by Daniel Goldhagen, *Hitler's Willing Executioners*, 178.

17. Robert Michael, "Theological Myth, German Antisemitism, and the Holocaust," *Holocaust and Genocide Studies* 2, no. 1 (1987): 105–22.

18. Richard Steigmann-Gall, *The Holy Reich* (Cambridge 2003), 226.

19. Robert Waite, *The Psychopathic God* (New York 1977), 34.

20. John Conway, "Protestant Missions to the Jews, 1810–1980: Ecclesiastical Imperialism or Theological Aberration?" *Holocaust and Genocide Studies* 1 (1986): 135.

21. Richard Gutteridge, *Open Thy Mouth for the Dumb: The German Evangelical Church and the Jews, 1879–1950* (Oxford 1976), 308–10.

22. *Trial of Major War Criminals Before the International Military Tribunal* (Nuremberg 1947–49), vol. 12: 318.

23. Franklin Sherman, ed., *Luther's Works* (Philadelphia 1971), 47:268n173.
24. See Gordon Rupp, Martin Luther and the Jews, most recently published in *Face to Face* (Spring 1983).
25. See Chapter 6.
26. See Chapter 4.
27. Quoted by Cohen, *Christ Killers*, 125.
28. Ibid., 215, 219.
29. See ibid., 130–32.
30. Ibid., 132–33.
31. Uriel Tal, *Christians and Jews in Germany* (Ithaca 1975), 89–90.
32. Ibid., 94.
33. Wistrich, *Socialism and the Jews*, 187–88.
34. Katz, *From Prejudice to Destruction*, 276.
35. Robert Wistrich, *Socialism and the Jews* (Oxford 1982), 187.
36. George Berkley, *Vienna and Its Jews* (Cambridge MA 1988), 77–80.
37. Poliakov, *The History of Antisemitism*, 3:456; Berkley, *Vienna and Its Jews*, 77–80.
38. Kertzer, *Popes Against the Jews*, 136.
39. Communication from Professor Frederick Schweitzer; Leon Botstein, "Blooming While the Sun Went Down," *New York Times* (Jan. 14, 1990).
40. Lisa Kienzl, "The Relation Between the Growing Antisemitism and the Development of an Austrian National Identity," *Institut for Historie* (Fall 2006): 2.
41. Quoted in ibid., 17.
42. Harry Zohn, "Fin-de-Siècle Vienna," in Reinharz and Schatzberg, *The Jewish Response to German Culture*, 138–39.
43. Victor Farías, *Heidegger and Nazism* (Philadelphia 1989), 26; Trachtenberg, *The Devil and the Jews*, 42, 108; Pulzer, *The Rise of Political Antisemitism*, 211; and R. A. Kann, *A Study in Austrian Intellectual History* (London 1960), 57, 76–79, 104.
44. Mosse, *Toward the Final Solution*, 137–38, 141.
45. Kienzl, "The Relation Between the Growing Antisemitism and the Development of an Austrian National Identity," 33.
46. Ibid., 35.
47. Ibid., 24.
48. Pulzer, *The Rise of Political Antisemitism*, 161, 175, 211.
49. Henry Cohn, "Theodore Herzl's Conversion to Zionism," *Jewish Social Studies* 32 (April 1970): 101–10; Victor Conzemius, "l'Antisemitisme autrichien au XIXième et au XXième siecles," in *De l'antijudaïsme antique à l'antisémitisme contemporain*, ed. V. Nikiprowetzky (Lille 1979), 197; Peter Pulzer, *The Rise of Political Antisemitism*, 176–77, 198; Berkley, *Vienna and Its Jews*, 98.
50. Pulzer, *The Rise of Political Antisemitism*, 200–201.
51. Wistrich, *Socialism and the Jews*, 197.
52. Berkley, *Vienna and Its Jews*, 384; Mosse, *Toward the Final Solution*, 114; Hermann Glaser, *The Cultural Roots of National Socialism* (Austin 1964), 227.
53. Wistrich, *Socialism and the Jews*, 197.

54. Ibid., 198.

55. Richard Levy, *The Downfall of the Antisemitic Political Parties in Imperial Germany* (New Haven 1975); Katz, *From Prejudice to Destruction*; Pulzer, *The Rise of Political Antisemitism*; Shulamit Volkov, "Antisemitism as a Cultural Code," *Leo Baeck Institute Year Book* 23 (1978): 25–46.

56. Pulzer, *The Rise of Political Antisemitism*, 282, 291–92, 298, 305.

57. Jacob Katz, "German Culture and the Jews," *Commentary* (June 1985): 94.

58. Dieter Hartmann, "Antisemitism and the Appeal of Nazism," *Political Psychology* (December 1984): 636.

59. Fritz Stern, "The Burden of Success: Reflections on German Jewry," in *Dreams and Delusions* (New York 1987), 101; Mack Walker, *German Home Towns* (Ithaca, N.Y., 1971), 271.

60. Dennis Showalter, *Little Man, What Now? Der Stürmer in the Weimar Republic* (Hamden 1982), 14.

61. Walter Zwi Bacharach, *Anti-Jewish Prejudices in German-Catholic Sermons* (Lewiston, NY, 1993), 20–21.

62. Barnabas, Justin Martyr, and St. Augustine quoted in Simon, *Verus Israel* (Eng.), 71, 147. Justin Martyr and Origin also argued that the Jews did not have the right to their own Scriptures. Justin, *Apologia* 1:53, and Origen, *Contra Celsum* 7:26.

63. Ruth Mellinkoff, *The Mark of Cain* (Berkeley 1981), 92–93. In later tradition, Cain became associated with the devil. Jeffrey Russell, *The Devil: Perceptions of Evil from Antiquity to Primitive Christianity* (Ithaca 1977), 240, n25.

64. St. Augustine, "Commentary on Psalm 58."

65. Robert Wilken, "Insignissima Religio, Certe Licita? Christianity and Judaism in the Fourth and Fifth Centuries," in *The Impact of the Church Upon Its Culture*, ed. Jerald Brauer (Chicago 1968), 51.

66. Rom. 2:25–29, Galatians 5, Philippians 3:2–8.

67. *Apostolic Constitutions*, 2.61.1; *Homilies Against Judaizing Christians*, 1.3.1, 1.3.5, 1.4.2, 1.5.1, 1.5.2.

68. Jerome, "Epistolae LXXXXIII and CXXI," in *Patrologiae, Cursus Completus, Series Latina*, ed. J. P. Migne, 22:699, 22:1032.

69. B.-S. Albert, "Isidore of Seville: His Attitude Towards Judaism and His Impact on Early Medieval Canon Law," *The Jewish Quarterly Review* (January–April 1990): 209.

70. Bacharach, *Anti-Jewish Prejudices in German-Catholic Sermons*, 25–27, 36, 37, 51, 54–55.

71. Ibid., throughout, especially chapter 7.

72. Grayzel I, Documents 13, 14, 18, 41, 49, 53, 59; Grayzel II, Documents 26, 27, 33, 50; Simonsohn I, docs. 379, 434.

73. Bacharach, *Anti-Jewish Prejudices in German-Catholic Sermons*, chapter 11.

74. Quoted by Guenter Lewy, *The Catholic Church and Nazi Germany* (New York 1967), 379.

75. Michael Phayer, *The Catholic Church and the Holocaust* (Bloomington, IN, 2000), 9.

76. Ibid., 67–68.
77. Ibid., 45–46, 70.
78. Ibid., 75.
79. Following St. Paul in Romans 13:1–7, which orders Christians to follow the orders of secular authorities because they are ordained by God. Phayer, *The Catholic Church and the Holocaust*, 71–73, 77–81. See Chapter 10 in this book.
80. Richard Gutteridge, *Open Thy Mouth for the Dumb* (Oxford 1976), 306n7.
81. Michael Faulhaber, *Judaism, Christianity, and Germany* (London 1934), 13–14.
82. Michael Phayer, *The Catholic Church and the Holocaust* (Bloomington, IN, 2000), 15.
83. Friedrich Heer, *God's First Love* (New York 1967), 322.
84. Bacharach, *Anti-Jewish Prejudices in German-Catholic Sermons*, 41.
85. Yisrael Gutman and Shmuel Krakowski, *Unequal Victims* (New York 1986), 1–26; Artur Sandauer, "On the Situation of a Polish Writer of Jewish Descent," *Pisma Zebrane* (Warsaw 1985), in Abraham Brumberg, "Poland and the Jews," *Tikkun* (July–August 1987), 17.
86. Peter Godman, *Hitler and the Vatican* (New York 2004), 124–25.
87. George Mosse, *Nazi Culture* (New York 1966), 256–61; Phayer, *The Catholic Church and the Holocaust*, 75.
88. Richard Gutteridge, *Open Thy Mouth for the Dumb* (Oxford 1976), 219n17.
89. Lapide, *Three Popes and the Jews*, 239.
90. Heer, *God's First Love*, 330.
91. Heer, *God's First Love*, 311; Pinchas Lapide, *Three Popes and the Jews* (New York 1967), 239; Léon Papeleux, *Les Silences de Pie XII* (Brussels 1980), 77.
92. Gutteridge, *Open Thy Mouth for the Dumb*, 219n17.
93. Phayer, *The Catholic Church and the Holocaust*, 69, 73.
94. Alfred Delp, *Zur Ende Entschlossen* (Frankfurt 1949); Heinrich Portmann, *Der Bischof von Münster* (Münster 1947); Vincent Lapomarda, *The Jesuits and the Third Reich* (New York 1989), chapter 1.
95. Saul Friedlander, *Kurt Gerstein* (New York 1969), 136.
96. Pierre Blet, et al., eds., *Actes et documents du Saint Siège relatifs à la Seconde Guerre Mondiale* (Vatican City 1965–75), 2:318–27.
97. Lapomarda, *The Jesuits and the Third Reich*, 54n55.
98. Gordon Zahn, "The Church Under Hitler," *Commonweal* 80 (July 3, 1964): 448; Sarah Gordon, *Hitler, Germans, and the "Jewish Question"* (Princeton 1984), 261; Donald Dietrich, "Modern German Catholic Antisemitism," *Face to Face* (Winter 1985); Donald Dietrich, "Catholic Resistance in the Third Reich," *Holocaust and Genocide Studies* 3, no. 2 (1988), 176; Kershaw, "The Persecution of the Jews," 326.
99. Hans Muller, *Katholische Kirche und Nationalsozialismus: Deutscher Taschenbuch* (Munich 1965), 70.
100. John Weiss, *Ideology of Death* (Chicago 1996), chapter 11.
101. Arthur May, *The Hapsburg Monarcy* (New York 1951), 179.
102. Weiss, *Ideology of Death*, 330.

103. Ibid., 173, 277.
104. Ibid., 387.
105. Georg Glockemeier, *Zur Viener Judenfrage* (Leipzig 1936), 106.
106. Herbert Ziegler, *Nazi Germany's New Aristocracy* (Princeton 1989), 83; Eva Fleischner, "The Crucial Importance of the Holocaust for Christians," in *When God and Man Failed*, ed. Harry Cargas (New York 1981), 29.
107. Quoted by Peter Padfield, *Himmler* (New York 1991), 3.
108. Stern, *Politics of Cultural Despair*, 149.
109. Quoted in Joseph Bloch, *Israel und die Völker*, (Berlin, Vienna, 1922), 47. See also "Salzburger Regionalgeschichte des Judentums," Universität Salzburg, Zentrum für Jüdische Kulturgeschichte http://www.sbg.ac.at/zjk/sites_en/index _en.htm. The Judenstein story was recorded by the Grimm brothers. http://www .fordham.edu/halsall/source/rinn.html#Judenstein1.
110. *Katholischer Kindergarten oder Legende für Kinde* quoted by Bacharach, *Anti-Jewish Prejudices in German-Catholic Sermons*, Appendix C.
111. Weiss, *Ideology of Death*, 184, 191–92; Paul Johnson, *A History of the Jews* (New York 1987), 472.
112. Konrad Heiden, *Der Fuehrer: Hitler's Rise to Power* (Boston 1944, 1969), 49.
113. Adolf Hitler, *Mein Kampf* (Cambridge, MA 1943), 6.
114. Hitler, *Mein Kampf,* 52.
115. Weiss, *Ideology of Death*, 163.
116. Hitler, *Mein Kampf,* 57, 324. also Alan Bullock, *Hitler: A Study in Tyranny* (New York 1964), 40; and Elias Canetti, *Crowds and Power* (New York 1962), 47.
117. Simon Rees, "A Slow Fuse: Hitler's World War One Experience," (October 2003) http://www.firstworldwar.com/features/aslowfuse.htm.
118. Hitler, *Mein Kamp*, chapter 3.
119. Kevin Baker, "Stabbed in the Back!" *Harper's Magazine* (June 2006). See also Richard Steigmann–Gall, *The Holy Reich: Nazi Conceptions of Christianity, 1919–1945* (Cambridge, 2003), 16, and Boris Barth, *Dolchstosslegenden und politische Desintegration: Das Trauma der deutschen Niederlage im Ersten Weltkrieg, 1914–1933* (Düsseldorf: Droste, 2003), 167 and 340–41.
120. Simon Rees, "A Slow Fuse: Hitler's World War One Experience," (October 2003) http://www.firstworldwar.com/features/aslowfuse.htm.
121. Ian Kershaw. *Hitler, 1889–1936: Hubris* (New York, 1999).
122. Heer, *God's First Love*, 130.
123. Peter De Rosa, *Vicars of Christ: The Dark Side of the Papacy* (New York, 1988), 5; and Lewy, *The Catholic Church and Nazi Germany*, 111.
124. Bacharach, *Anti-Jewish Prejudices in German-Catholic Sermons*, 117.
125. Lapide, *Three Popes and the Jews*, 90.
126. Ibid., 239; Weiss, *Ideology of Death*, 390.
127. Heer, *God's First Love*, 309.
128. Robert Waite, *The Psychopathic God: Adolf Hitler* (New York 1977), 35–36.
129. Adolf Hitler, *My New Order*, ed. Raoul de Roussy de Sales (New York 1973), 26–27.

130. Hitler, *Mein Kampf* (Boston 1943), 307.
131. Ibid., 65.
132. Kershaw, "The Hitler Myth," 107.
133. Walter Langer, *The Mind of Adolf Hitler* (New York 1972), 44.
134. Michael Schwartz, "Are Christians Responsible?" *National Review* (1980): 956–57.
135. Ernst Helmreich, *The German Churches Under Hitler* (Detroit 1979), 138. Helmreich lists the gifts, 489–90n27.
136. Hitler, *Mein Kampf*, 116.
137. E. Roy Eckardt, *Your People, My People* (New York 1974), 22; Cohen, *Christ Killers*, 115.
138. Hitler, *Mein Kampf*, 687.
139. Eckart, *Der Bolshevismus von Moses bis Lenin: Zwiegespräch zwischen Adolf Hitler und mir* (Munich 1924), 20–21.
140. Bytwerk, *Julius Streicher*, 47.
141. Showalter, *Little Man What Now?* 104–6, 213–16.
142. Bytwerk, *Julius Streicher*, 57, 62, 33.
143. George Bailey, Germans (New York 1974), 196.
144. Hitler, *My New Order*, 597.
145. Friedrich Heer, *God's First Love*, 286, 291–93, 307, 311, 324, 477, 484–86; Nobécourt, *"Le Vicaire" et l'Historie*, 342.
146. Kienzl, "The Relation Between the Growing Antisemitism and the Development of an Austrian National Identity," 24.

Chapter 8

1. For earlier French antisemitism, see Chapters 4–6 in this books.
2. Roland Mousnier, *Les Institutions de la France sous la monarchie absolue* (Paris 1974), 323–25.
3. Mousnier, *Les Institutions de la France*, 323–24.
4. H. R. Trevor-Roper, *The European Witch-Craze of the Sixteenth and Seventeenth Centuries* (New York 1967), 139.
5. Isaiah Shachar, *The Judensau* (London 1974), 48.
6. Trevor-Roper, *The European Witch-Craze*, 139, 112–13.
7. Quoted by ibid., 112–13.
8. Pierre de l'Ancre, *L'incrédulité et mescréances du sortilège pleinement convaincues* (Paris, 1622), 8:446–48.
9. Arnold Ages, *The Image of Jews and Judaism in the Prelude of the French Enlightenment* (Sherbrooke, Canada, 1986), 114, 142, 153; Myriam Yardeni, *Anti-Jewish Mentalities in Early Modern Europe* (Lanham Md 1990), 8.
10. François Delpech, "La Révolution et l'Empire," in *Histoire des Juifs en France*, ed. Bernhard Blumenkranz (Toulouse 1972), 268.
11. Frank Manuel, *Broken Shaft*, 165.
12. Jacques Bossuet, "Catéchisme du diocèse de Meaux," in *Oeuvres Complètes* (Bar-le-Duc 1863), 11:443; Bossuet, *Discourse on Universal History*, in *The Jewish*

Element in French Literature, ed. Charles Lehrmann (Cranbury NJ 1961), 100–102; Bossuet, "Sermon on the Goodness and Severity of God," *Oeuvres Oratoires* (Paris 1913), 158.

13. André de Fleury, "Des ennemis du Christ," *Catéchisme historique* (Paris 1766), Lesson 19; Léon Poliakov, *The History of Antisemitism* (New York 1974), 1:180–81, 184; Leon Schwartz, *Diderot and the Jews* (Rutherford, NJ, 1981), 41.

14. Blaise Pascal, *Pensées*, in *Oeuvres Complètes*, ed. Jacques Chevalier (Paris 1954), no. 487; also, Lionel Cohen, "Pascal et le Judaïsme," *Pascal Textes du Tricentenaire* (Paris 1963).

15. Pascal, *Pensées*, nos. 690, 729.

16. Ibid., no. 600.

17. Ibid., no. 485.

18. Ibid., no. 640.

19. Ibid., no. 497.

20. Ibid., no. 498.

21. Ibid., nos. 535e, 505.

22. Ibid., nos. 584, 613.

23. Ibid., no. 406.

24. Ibid., nos. 505, 773, 600.

25. Haydn T. Mason, *Pierre Bayle and Voltaire* (Oxford 1963).

26. Theodore Besterman, *Voltaire* (New York 1969), 28, 31; René Pomeau, *La religion de Voltaire* (Paris 1969), 31.

27. Abbé Duvernet, *La Vie de Voltaire* (Geneva 1786); Lourdet, "Moïsade," in *Oeuvres de J. B. Rousseau*, ed. Jean-Baptiste Rousseau (Paris 1820), 2:405–7.

28. The Jesuits were a leading antisemitic Catholic order up through the twentieth century.

29. Letter of Voltaire, April 1, 1746, quoted by Besterman, *Voltaire*, 43. Like all the other boys, he served as an altar boy while at school. Pomeau, *La religion de Voltaire*, 46.

30. Arthur Hertzberg, *The French Enlightenment and the Jews* (New York 1968), 10, 313.

31. Voltaire, *Sermon des Cinquante*, XXIV, 438.

32. Voltaire, *Epitre à Uranie*, ed. Ira Wade, *M.L.A.* 47 (1932), lines 95–96.

33. Rose, *Revolutionary Antisemitism in Germany*, 10.

34. Mousnier, *Les Institutions de la France sous la monarchie absolue*, 324.

35. Poliakov, *The History of Antisemitism*, 3:93, 88–89; also William Trapwell, *Christ and His "Associates" in Voltairean Polemic* (Saratoga, CA, 1982), 245.

36. David Levy, *Voltaire et son exegese du Pentateuque* (Banbury 1975), in *Studies on Voltaire and the 18th Century*, ed. Theodore Besterman, 130:253.

37. Voltaire, *Philosophical Dictionary*, *The Works of Voltaire*, tr. William Fleming (New York 1927), 3:266, 268, 277–79, 281, 284.

38. Voltaire, *Philosophical Dictionary*, tr. Fleming, 3: 281, 284.

39. Manuel, *Broken Staff*, 197.

40. Ibid., 195.

41. Voltaire, *Philosophical Dictionary*, ed. Peter Gay (New York 1962), 2:340. Gay persistently understates Voltaire's antisemitism.

42. Ibid., 1:88.

43. Ibid., 1:262, 294–95, a misinterpretation of Genesis 6:1–2 and Ezekiel 4:12.

44. Levy, *Voltaire et son exegèse du Pentateuque*, 130:282, 284–85.

45. Poliakov, *The History of Antisemitism*, 3:88, 3:90.

46. Katz, *Out of the Ghetto*, 75.

47. Beatrice Hyslop, *French Nationalism in 1789 According to the General Cahiers* (New York 1934, 1968), 35–36; Léon Jérome, *Les élections et les cahiers du clergé lorrain aux états-généraux de 1789* (Paris 1899), cited in Ruth Necheles, "The Abbé Grégoire and the Jews," *Jewish Social Studies* 33 (1971), 127.

48. What Frank Manuel calls, "the Napoleonic solution" to the Jewish problem. *Broken Staff*, 245.

49. Yosef Yerushalmi, *Assimilation and Racial Antisemitism* (New York 1982), 34–35n45.

50. *Essai sur la régénération physique, moral, et politique des Juifs* (Metz 1789), in *The Jew in the Modern World*, ed. Paul Mendes-Flohr and Jehuda Reinharz (Oxford 1980), chapter 1, doc. 13.

51. Poliakov, *The History of Antisemitism*, 3:154.

52. Ibid., 3:155.

53. Necheles, "The Abbé Grégoire and the Jews," 123–28.

54. *Essai sur la régénération physique, moral, et politique des Juifs* (Metz 1789), in *The Jew in the Modern World*, ed. Mendes-Flohr and Reinharz, chapter 1, doc. 13.

55. Necheles, "The Abbé Grégoire and the Jews," 140.

56. Poliakov, *The History of Antisemitism*, 3:150.

57. Ibid., 3:155.

58. Ibid., 3:153.

59. Ibid., 113.

60. Halphen, *Recueil des Lois*, 229, in Mendes-Flohr and Reinharz, eds., *The Jew in the Modern World*, chapter 3, doc. 5.

61. Robert Seltzer, *Jewish People, Jewish Thought: The Jewish Experience in History* (New York 1980), 802n5.

62. Necheles, "The Abbé Grégoire and the Jews," 134.

63. Poliakov, *History of Antisemitism*, 3, chapter 7.

64. Michael Burns, *Dreyfus: A Family Affair, 1789–1945* (New York 1991), 17.

65. Eugen Weber, "Reflections on the Jews in France," in *The Jews in Modern France*, ed. Frances Malino and Bernard Wasserstein (Hanover NH 1985), 14.

66. Napoleon's uncle, Cardinal Joseph Fesch, was also an antisemite.

67. Mendes-Flohr and Reinharz, eds., *The Jew in the Modern World*, chapter 3, docs. 10, 11, 13.

68. Seltzer, *Jewish People, Jewish Thought*, 525–27.

69. Richard Cohen, "The Dreyfus Affair and the Jews," in *Antisemitism Through the Ages*, ed. Shmuel Almog (Oxford 1988), 298.

70. Owen Chadwick, *The Popes and European Revolution* (Oxford 1981), 464–65, 549.

71. Burns, *Dreyfus*, 21.

72. Jacob Katz, *From Prejudice to Destruction* (Cambridge MA 1980), 294.

73. Bernard Lazare, "Nécessité d'être soi-même," *Zion* (April 30, 1897), in *The Politics of Assimilation: A Study of the French Jewish Community and the Time of the Dreyfus Affair*, ed. Michael Marrus (Oxford 1971), 188.

74. French writers commenting on the Jews "constituted a publicity lobby on behalf of the Catholic Church." Arnold Ages, "Lamennais and the Jews," *The Jewish Quarterly Review* 63 (1973): 159.

75. Fleury la Sarve, "Les Juifs à Lyon," in *Revue du Lyonnais* 7 (1838): 343, quoted in Edmund Silberner, "Charles Fourier on the Jewish Question," *Jewish Social Studies* (October 1946): 258.

76. Chateaubriand, *Mémoires d'outre-tombe*, vol. 3, in *Etre Juif dans la société française*, ed. Béatrice Philippe (Paris 1979), 156.

77. Charles Didier, "Le Maroc," *La Revue des Deux Mondes* (November 1, 1836), in Jay Berkovitz, *The Shaping of Jewish Identity in Nineteenth-Century France* (Detroit 1989), 135.

78. Ages, "Lamennais and the Jews," 159.

79. Other Catholic publicists were ultramontanists who supported the papacy's authority: Joseph de Maistre (d. 1821), Louis de Bonald (d. 1840), Louis Veuillot (d.1880).

80. Ages, "Lamennais and the Jews," 169.

81. Berkovitz, *The Shaping of Jewish Identity*, 135; also Ages, "Lamennais and the Jews," 158–70.

82. Ages, "Lamennais and the Jews," 166–67.

83. Ibid., 168–69.

84. Poliakov, *History of Antisemitism*, 3:367–68.

85. Quoted by Edmund Silberner, "Charles Fourier on the Jewish Question," *Jewish Social Studies* (October 1946): 249–51.

86. Silberner, "The Attitude of the Fourierist School Toward the Jews," *Jewish Social Studies* (October 1947): 360.

87. Toussenel, *Les Juifs, rois de l'époque, histoire de la féodalité financière* (Paris 1888), in *Etre Juif*, ed. Philippe, 161.

88. Berkovitz, *The Shaping of Jewish Identity*, 240; Zosa Szajkowski, "The Jewish Saint-Simonians and Socialist Antisemites in France," *Jewish Social Studies* 9 (1947): 47.

89. Robert Byrnes, *Antisemitism in Modern France* (New Brunswick 1950), 1:120–21.

90. Quoted by Katz, *From Prejudice to Destruction*, 125.

91. Katz, *From Prejudice to Destruction*, 131; Poliakov, *History of Antisemitism*, 3:344; Katz, *Out of the Ghetto*, 100–101.

92. *Le Juif, Le Judaïsm et la judaïsation des peuples chrétiens* (Paris 1869). Norman Cohn, *Warrant for Genocide* (Chico, CA 1981), 41; Peter Viereck, *Metapolitics: The Roots of the Nazi Mind* (New York 1965), 338.

93. Bernard Lazare, *Antisemitism: Its History and Causes*; Jacob Katz, *From Prejudice to Destruction* (Cambridge MA 1980), 142–44; *Jews and Freemasons in Europe*, 153–55; and Cohn, *Warrant for Genocide*, 42–45.

94. Kertzer, *Popes Against the Jews*, 128.

95. Richard Rubenstein and John Roth, *Approaches to Auschwitz* (Atlanta 1987), 69; Berkovitz, *The Shaping of Jewish Identity*, 239–46.

96. Szajkowski, "The Jewish Saint-Simonians and Socialist Antisemites in France," 47.

97. Ibid., 47.

98. Berkovitz, *The Shaping of Jewish Identity*, 240; Philippe, *Etre Juif,* 157.

99. Arnold Ages, "Veuillot and the Talmud," *Jewish Quarterly Review* 64 (1974): 236–37, 241, 245, 247–48.

100. Ibid., 255–56.

101. Ibid., 256n35.

102. From 1850 to this time, the *loi Falloux* had made Catholic instruction compulsory in public schools, and the Church was permitted to substitute its own primary and secondary schooling for state education. Berkovitz, *The Shaping of Jewish Identity*, 239.

103. Pierre Pierrard, *Juifs et Catholiques Français* (Paris 1970), 20, 29.

104. Jean-Denis Brédin, *The Affair: The Case of Alfred Dreyfus* (New York 1986), 31.

105. Stephen Wilson, *Ideology and Experience: Antisemitism in France at the Time of the Dreyfus Affair* (Rutherford, N.J., 1982), 554.

106. May 10, 1884, 1; December 16, 1884, 1.

107. Albert Lindemann, *The Jew Accused* (Cambridge, Eng. 1991), 60; Eugen Weber, "Reflections on the Jews in France," in *The Jews in Modern France*, ed. Frances Malino and Bernard Wasserstein (Hanover NH 1985), 22; Steven Schuker, "Origins of the 'Jewish Problem' in the Later Third Republic," in Malino and Wasserstein, 135, 147.

108. Comte Paul de Pradel de Lamase, "Les juifs dans l'armée," *La Libre Parole* (May 23, 1892), in *Etre Juif,* Philippe, 180–81.

109. Burns, *Dreyfus*, 91. Dreyfus was not the first Jew on the General Staff. Serving in the Intelligence branch in the 1870s was a Col. Abraham Samuel. Eugen Weber, *France: Fin de Siècle* (Cambridge MA 1986), 133.

110. Marie-France Rouart, *Le Mythe du Juif Errant dans l'Europe du XIXe Siécle* (Paris 1988), 96, 99.

111. Norman Kleeblatt, "The Dreyfus Affair: A Visual Record," in *The Dreyfus Affair*, ed. Kleeblatt (Berkeley 1987), 1–24.

112. Adrien Dansette, *Histoire religieuse de la France contemporaine* (Paris 1951), 2:281.

113. Dansette, *Histoire religieuse de la République* (Paris 1965), 147–49.

114. Brédin, *The Affair*, 347.

115. Roderick Kedward, ed., *The Dreyfus Affair* (London 1965), 75.

116. Paula Hyman, "The French Jewish Community from Emancipation to the Dreyfus Affair," in *The Dreyfus Affair*, ed. Kleeblatt, 22.

117. Norman James Clary, *French Antisemitism During the Years of Drumont and Dreyfus, 1886–1906* (Doctoral Dissertation, The Ohio State University 1970), 168.

118. Pierre Sorlin, *La Croix et les Juifs* (Paris 1967), 181–83.
119. Brédin, *The Affair*, 16–17, 35; Byrnes, *Antisemitism in Modern France*, 1:264.
120. The Senator was Protestant Auguste Scheurer-Kestner (d.1899), an early supporter of Dreyfus and a fellow Alsatian.
121. Joseph Reinach, *Histoire de l'Affaire Dreyfus* (Paris 1929), 2:629.
122. Bailly, *La Croix*, February 8, 1898.
123. See Postscript at the end of this book.
124. Burns, *Dreyfus*; Robert Hoffman, *More than a Trial* (New York 1980), 2.
125. Marrus, *The Politics of Assimilation*, 163.
126. Vicki Caron, *Between France and Germany: The Jews of Alsace-Lorraine, 1871–1918* (Stanford 1988), 118; Marrus, *The Politics of Assimilation*, chapter 7; Hoffman, *More than a Trial*, 42.
127. Brédin, *The Affair*, 99n493. For Dreyfus' Jewishness, Burns, *Dreyfus*, 39, 123, 133, 123, 141, 143, 154, 301, 513n34; Letter to Lucie, August 10, 1897, in *Five Years of My Life: The Diary of Alfred Dreyfus*, ed. Alfred Dreyfus (New York 1977), 210; Dreyfus, *Lettres d'un innocent* (Paris 1898), Appendix; Brédin, *The Affair*, 21–22, 99n493.
128. Dreyfus, *Lettres d'un innocent* (Paris 1898), Appendix.
129. Quoted in Burns, *Dreyfus*, 123, 513n34.
130. Bernard Lazare, "The Truth About the Dreyfus Affair," quoted by Barbara Sapinsley, "The Metamorphosis of Bernard-Lazare," *Midstream* (December 1991): 31.
131. "Le nouveau ghetto," *La Justice* (November 17, 1894), in *The Politics of Assimilation*, ed. Marrus, 178.
132. "Une erreur judiciaire: la vérité sur l'Affaire Dreyfus," in *The Politics of Assimilation*, ed. Marrus, 183.
133. Burns, *Dreyfus*, 118, 120, 143, 302.
134. Hoffman, *More than a Trial*, 88–89; Robert Byrnes, *Antisemitism in Modern France* (New Brunswick 1950), 131–35; Jean Bouvier, *Le Krach de l'Union Générale* (Paris 1960), 146; Jeannine Verdès-Leroux, *Scandale financier et antisémitisme catholique: Le Krach de l'Union Générale* (Paris 1969); Annie Kriegel, *Le Krach de l'Union Générale* (Paris 1985).
135. Weber, "Reflections on the Jews in France," 11.
136. Zeev Sternhell, "The Roots of Popular Antisemitism in the Third Republic," in *The Jews in Modern France*, ed. Malino and Wasserstein, 109.
137. Bernard Lazare, "France at the Parting of the Ways," *North American Review* (November 1899), quoted in Egal Feldman, *The Dreyfus Affair and the American Conscience* (Detroit 1981), 101.
138. Weber, "Reflections on the Jews in France," 11.
139. Quoted by Feldman, *The Dreyfus Affair*, 104.
140. Burns, *Dreyfus*, 149; Hoffman, *More than a Trial*, 7.
141. Francois Mauriac, "Preface," *Cinq années de ma Vie* (Paris 1962), 13.
142. Eugen Weber, *Action Française* (Stanford 1962), 45.
143. Hoffman, *More than a Trial*, 40–41.

144. In *Action Française* (15 Feb. 1902), quoted by Weber, *Action Française*, 35.
145. Burns, *Dreyfus*, 153.
146. Sorlin, *La Croix*, 112–14, 28.
147. Quoted in Burns, *Dreyfus*, 307.
148. Burns, *Dreyfus*, 245.
149. Armand Charpentier, *Les Cotes mysterieux de l'Affaire Dreyfus* (Paris 1930), 70; Burns, *Dreyfus*, 137.
150. Francois Mauriac remembers that as a young boy his chamber pot was called Zola. Brédin, *The Affair*, 288.
151. Pierre Pierrard, *Juifs et Catholiques Français* (Paris 1970), 144–46.
152. Hannah Arendt, *The Origins of Totalitarianism* (Cleveland 1958), 102, 111.
153. For U.S. Catholic antisemitism, see Robert Michael, *Concise History of American Antisemitism* (Lanham, MD, 2005).
154. Arendt, *Origins of Totalitarianism*, 116–17; Sternhell, *Antisemitism and the Right in France* (Jerusalem 1988), 24.
155. Richard Webster, *The Cross and the Fasces* (Stanford 1960), 124. Quoted phrase courtesy of Professor Frederick Schweitzer.
156. Pinchas Lapide, *Three Popes and the Jews* (New York 1967), 80.
157. George Bailey, *Germans* (New York 1972), 183.
158. Lapide, *Three Popes and the Jews*, 81.
159. Sorlin, *La Croix*.
160. Quoted by Feldman, *The Dreyfus Affair*, 126.
161. Zeev Sternhell, *La Droite révolutionnaire, 1885–1914* (Paris 1978), 217.
162. Ibid., 235.
163. Sorlin, *La Coix*, 112–14, 28.
164. *La Croix* (8 February 1898)
165. Danielle Delmaire, "L'antisemitisme du journal *la Croix du Nord* pendant l'Affaire Dreyfus, 1898–1899," in *De l'antijudaisme antique à l'antisemitisme contemporain* (Lille 1979), 222–27.
166. Delmaire, "L'antisemitisme du journal *la Croix du Nord*," 222–27.
167. Hyman, "The French Jewish Community," 13–15, 18–19.
168. Byrnes, *Antisemitism in Modern France*, 198.
169. Clary, *French Antisemitism*, 268.
170. Tridentine Latin Mass docs., published originally *Inside the Vatican* (December 1998), http://www.sandiego-tlmc.org/retlatin.htm.
171. Stephen Wilson, "Le Monument Henry: La structure de l'antisemtisme en France, 1898–1899," *Annales* 32 (1977), 279. also Pierre Quillard, *Le Monument Henry* (Paris 1899); Hoffmann, *More Than a Trial*.
172. Pierrard, *Juifs et Catholiques Français*, 104. Most of the well-known contributors, such as the politicians, were "ardent Catholics." Brédin, *The Affair*, 352.
173. Wilson, "Le Monument Henry," 271.
174. Ibid., 277–83.
175. See Marrus, *The Politics of Assimilation*, 169–70; "Paleologos," *Forward* (September 27, 2002), http://www.forward.com/issues/2002/02.09.27/arts4.html.

176. Wilson, "Le Monument Henry," 278–81.
177. IKedward, ed., *The Dreyfus Affair*, 83.
178. Aldous Huxley, *Eyeless in Gaza* (London 1936).
179. Wilson, "Le Monument Henry," 283.
180. Ibid., 278–80, 285.
181. Kedward, ed., *The Dreyfus Affair*, 83.
182. Wilson, "Le Monument Henry," 278–80, 285.
183. The Third Reich used the first automatic sequence-controlled printing calculator (DEHOMAG D-11, Hollerith electric tabulating system.) IBM electric punch-card and printing device capable of processing millions of punch cards, enabling the Nazis to efficiently identify and mass murder Jews, Gypsies, Poles, and others. The machines were custom-designed for the Third Reich, serviced monthly by IBM-trained Nazi personnel, and enhanced the entire commercial, industrial, and war-making capability of Nazi Germany, as well as enabling the Third Reich to mass murder Jews and others with unprecedented efficiency. Robert Michael and Karin Doerr, *Nazi-Deutsch/Nazi-German: An English Lexicon of the Language of the Third Reich* (New York: 2001).
184. Kertzer, *The Popes Against the Jews*, 172, 175, 226–27.
185. Péguy, "Notre jeunesse," in *Cahiers de la Quinzaine* 12 (1910): 54.
186. Robert Michael, *The Radicals and Nazi Germany* (Washington, DC, 1982) and "The Foreign Policies of the Radical Party, 1933–1939," *Third Republic/Troisième République* (Spring 1984): 1–92.
187. Weber, *Action Française*, 35.
188. Ibid., 219–35.
189. Ibid., 411, 446.
190. Ibid., 201, 509–10.
191. Ibid., 443–44, 446.
192. Fleischner, "Can the Few Become the Many?"
193. Eva Fleischner, "Can the Few Become the Many?" in *Remembering for the Future* (Oxford 1988), and Meyer Weinberg, *Because They Were Jews: A History of Antisemitism* (New York 1986), 76.
194. Webster, *Pétain's Crime*, 127.
195. Byrnes, *Antisemitism in Modern France*, 1:264.
196. Michael Marrus and Robert Paxton, *Vichy France and the Jews* (New York 1981), 335.
197. Piers Paul Read, "In Defence of the Jew of Tarsus," *The (London) Times* (March 28, 1992).
198. Ibid., 200.
199. Marrus and Paxton, *Vichy France*, 333–34.
200. Weber, *Action Française*, 41, 463, 475.
201. Weber, *Action Française*, 451, 463.
202. Michael Phayer, *The Catholic Church and the Holocaust* (Bloomington, IN, 2000), 16.
203. Zeev Sternhell, *Antisemitism and the Right in France*, 9, 17. For Algeria, Michel Abitbol, *The Jews of North Africa During the Second World War* (Detroit 1989).

204. Hoffman, *More than a Trial*, 203.
205. Quoted in Pierrard, *Juifs et Catholiques Français*, 301–3.
206. Nobécourt, *"Le Vicaire" et l'Histoire*, 208.
207. Marrus and Paxton, *Vichy France*, 338–39.
208. Thomas Anderson, "Catholic Antisemitism in the Dreyfus Affair," *Continuum* (Autumn 1966): 354–45.
209. Jacobson, "Yellow Star Points to Anti-Nazis' Courage."
210. Ibid., 115–16.
211. Serge Klarsfeld, *The Children of Izieu: A Human Tragedy* (New York 1984), 34, 92–93.
212. Marrus, "French Churches and the Persecution of the Jews in France, 1940–1944," 327; also Pierre Pierrard, *Juifs et Catholiques Français* (Paris 1970), 294; Webster, *Pétain's Crime*, 123.
213. Marrus and Paxton, *Vichy France*, 274.
214. Weber, *Action Française*, 448.
215. Marrus and Paxton, *Vichy France*, 198.
216. Sydney Rubin, "Theologian: Church Backed Nazis," reported by the Associated Press (February 7, 1992).
217. Webster, *Pétain's Crime*, 132–33.
218. Weber, *Action Française*, 463.
219. Webster, *Pétain's Crime*, 124–25. No Belgian bishop protested Jewish deportations. Maxime Steinberg, "Faced with the Final Solution in Occupied Belgium," *Remembering for the Future* (Oxford 1988), supplementary volume, 466; also Steinberg, *La Persécution des Juifs en Belgique (1940–1945)* (Brussels 2004).
220. Marrus and Paxton, *Vichy France*, 198.
221. Webster, *Pétain's Crime*, 124.
222. Michael Marrus, "French Churches and the Persecution of the Jews in France, 1940–1944," in *Judaism and Christianity Under the Impact of National-Socialism, 1919–1945* (Jerusalem 1982), 315.
223. Marrus, *The Politics of Assimilation*, 125; Marrus and Paxton, *Vichy France*, 32. also Valerio Valeri, *Le Relazioni Internazionali della Santa Sede dopo il Secundo Conflitto Mondiale* (Rome 1956), 23–24; Marrus and Paxton, *Vichy France*, 200, 271; O'Carroll, *Pius XII*, 88; Blet, *Actes et documents*, 8:297.
224. Marrus and Paxton, *Vichy France*, 339.
225. Philip Jacobson, "French Clergy Shielded Man Charged with War Crimes," *The London Times* (January 2, 1992).
226. Xavier de Montclos, et al., eds., *Eglises et Chrétiens dans la IIe Guerre Mondiale: La France* (Lyon 1982); Centre de documentation Juive Contemporaine, *La France et la Question Juive, 1940–44: Les Eglises* (Paris 1981); Jacques Duquesne, *Les Catholiques Française sous l'Occupation* (Paris 1986).
227. Philippe, *Etre Juif*, 265–66. also Marrus and Paxton, *Vichy France*, 278.
228. Marrus and Paxton, *Vichy France*, 271.
229. Webster, *Pétain's Crime*, 132–33.
230. Théas' pastoral letter (August 30, 1942), in *Etre Juif*, ed. Philippe, 265–66.

231. Webster, *Pétain's Crime*, 133.
232. Mgr Delay of Marseille (September 6, 1942), in *Etre Juif*, ed. Philippe, 265–66.
233. Pierrard, *Juifs et Catholiques français*, 296.
234. The recollection of Mgr Louis de Courrèges d'Ustou, aux. Bishop of Toulouse, quoted by Webster, *Pétain's Crime*, 122.
235. August 1942. Reproduced in Philippe, *Etre Juif*, 264.
236. Webster, *Pétain's Crime*, 139–40.
237. Marrus and Paxton, *Vichy France*, 277.
238. Marrus and Paxton, *Vichy France*, 278.
239. Diary entries May 1941–February 1943, quoted in Fleischner, "Can the Few Become the Many?"
240. For Allied antisemitism during the Holocaust, see Robert Michael, *Concise History of American Antisemitism* (Lanham, MD, 2005).

Chapter 9

1. Simon Dubnow, *A History of the Jews in Russia and Poland* (Philadelphia 1946), 155–56, 160–71,
2. Ronald E. Modras, *The Catholic Church and Antisemitism: Poland, 1933–1939* (Chur, Switzerland, 1994), Preface.
3. Ten percent of Poles were Jews, about half the European Jews were outside Russia.
4. Robert Chazan, *Church, State, and Jew in the Middle Ages* (New York 1980), doc. 6, 93.
5. Modras, *The Catholic Church and Antisemitism*, 4.
6. Ibid., 4–5.
7. Bernard Weinryb, *The Jews of Poland* (Philadelphia 1973), 23.
8. Dubnow, *History of the Jews in Russia and Poland*, 48–49.
9. Modras, *The Catholic Church and Antisemitism*, 7–11.
10. M. J. Rosman, "A Minority Views the Majority: Jewish Attitudes Towards the Polish Lithuanian Commonwealth and Interaction with Poles," *Polin*, 32.
11. David Biale, *Power and Powerlessness in Jewish History* (New York 1987), 74. 1648 was also the year in which the Thirty Years' War was ended by the Peace of Westphalia, whose religious-toleration clauses were rejected by Pope Innocent X in his bull *Zelus domus dei*.
12. Jewish chroniclers identified these terrible events with those of Blois in 1171. See Yosef Yerushalmi, *Zakhor: Jewish History and Jewish Memory* (Seattle, WA, 1989), 49–50; Bernard Weinryb, *The Jews of Poland* (Philadelphia 1972), 153; Dubnow, *History of the Jews in Russia and Poland*, 100–102, 143–51.
13. Shabbetai ben Meir Hacohen, *The Scroll of Darkness* quoted by David Roskies, *Against the Apocalypse* (Cambridge MA 1984), 50.
14. Hans Joachim Schoeps, "Philosemitism in the Baroque Period," *Jewish Quarterly Review* 47 (1956–57): 139–44. For English philosemitism during this period,

see David Katz, *Philosemitism and the Readmission of the Jews to England, 1603–1655* (Oxford 1982).

15. Jonathan Israel, *European Jewry in the Age of Mercantilism* (Oxford 1989), 224–31; Heinrich Graetz, *History of the Jews* (Philadelphia 1940), 5:177.
16. Brumberg, "Polish Intellectuals and Antisemitism," 74.
17. Abraham Brumberg, "Polish Intellectuals and Antisemitism," *Dissent* (Winter 1991): 74–75.
18. Robert Blobaum, "Introduction," in *Antisemitism and Its Opponents in Modern Poland*, ed. Robert Blobaum (Ithaca, NY 2005), 2.
19. Laurence Weinbaum, "Penitence and Prejudice: The Roman Catholic Church and Jedwabne," *Jewish Political Studies Review* 14 (Fall 2002):3–4.
20. Modras, *The Catholic Church and Antisemitism*, 2.
21. Janusz Tazbir, "Images of the Jew in the Polish Commonwealth," *Polin: A Journal of Polish-Jewish Studies* 4 (1989): 19–20, 24–5. Some powerless Jews responded to antisemitism by stereotyping Gentile Poles as "dangerous, demonic, and devilish"; most Jews felt ambivalent toward Poles. See Wladyslaw Bartoszewski, "Poles and Jews as the 'Other'" and Rosman, "A Minority Views the Majority," Polin, 7, 37.
22. Owen Chadwick, *The Popes and European Revolution* (Oxford 1981), 16–17.
23. Modras, *The Catholic Church and Antisemitism*, 17.
24. Ibid., 25–26.
25. William Hagen, "The Moral Economy of Popular Violence: The Pogrom in Lwow, 1918," in *Antisemitism and Its Opponents in Modern Poland*, ed. Blobaum, 136–40.
26. Between 1915 and 1921 there were massive pogroms all across Eastern Europe. In fiscal year 1920–21, 119,000 Jews immigrated to the United States.
27. Modras, *The Catholic Church and Antisemitism*, 25–26.
28. *Congressional Record*, December 9–10, 1920, 137, 141, 172, 178–79.
29. Kertzer, *Popes Against the Jews*, 247–61.
30. Modras, *The Catholic Church and Antisemitism*, 356.
31. Lucy Dawidowicz, "The Tide of Antisemitism," *The Times Literary Supplement* (July 22, 1977), 901; Brumberg, "Polish Intellectuals and Antisemitism," 74–77.
32. Yisrael Gutman and Shmuel Krakowski, *Unequal Victims: Poles and Jews During World War II* (New York 1986), 1–26.
33. Brumberg, "Polish Intellectuals and Antisemitism," 74.
34. Jerzy Turowicz, "Polish Rights and Jewish Right," *Tygodnik Powszechny* (April 5, 1987), and in "Poland and the Jews," ed. Brumberg, 87.
35. Ronald E. Modras, *The Catholic Church and Antisemitism: Poland, 1933–1939* (Chur, Switzerland, 1994).
36. Adam Romer, in Krakow's Catholic newspaper *Maly Dziennik* quoted by Modras, *The Catholic Church and Antisemitism, 175–6.*
37. Ibid., 187.
38. Edward Wynot, "'A Necessary Cruelty': The Emergence of Official Antisemitism in Poland, 1936–1939," *American Historical Review* 76 (October 1971): 1037.

39. Quoted by Andrzej Bryk, "Poland and the Memory of the Holocaust," *Partisan Review* (Spring 1990): 231–32.

40. Edward Wynot, "'A Necessary Cruelty': The Emergence of Official Antisemitism in Poland, 1936–1939," *American Historical Review* 76 (October 1971): 1043; Wynot, "The Catholic Church and the Polish State, 1935–1939," *Journal of Church and State* 15 (1973): 223–40; Abraham Brumberg, "The Bund and the Polish Socialist Party in the Late 1930s," and Emanuel Melzer, "Antisemitism in the Last Years of the Polish Republic," in *The Jews of Poland Between Two World Wars*, ed. Yisrael Gutman, et al. (Hanover, N.H. 1989), 83, 128–29.

41. Quoted by Wynot, "A Necessary Cruelty," 1049.

42. Quoted by ibid., 1036.

43. Szymon Rudnicki, "Anti-Jewish Legislation in Interwar Poland," in *Antisemitism and Its Opponents in Modern Poland*, ed. Blobaum, 170.

44. Reverends Canon Gould and Conrad Hoffman Weinbaum, "Penitence and Prejudice."

45. Modras, *The Catholic Church and Antisemitism*, 306–12.

46. Ibid., 315–16.

47. [My italics.] Quoted in ibid., 346–47; and in Heller, *On the Edge of Destruction*, 113; see also Gutman and Krakowski, *Unequal Victims*, 19.

48. Personal correspondence with Prof. Frederick Schweitzer.

49. Modras, *The Catholic Church and Antisemitism*, 315–23.

50. Artur Sandauer, "On the Situation of a Polish Writer of Jewish Descent," *Pisma Zebrane* (Warsaw 1985); and in Abraham Brumberg, "Poland and the Jews," *Tikkun* (July–August 1987), 17. See also Celia Heller, *On the Edge of Destruction: Jews of Poland Between the Two World Wars* (New York 1980), 109–14; Gutman and Krakowski, *Unequal Victims*, 19–22.

51. Modras, *The Catholic Church and Antisemitism*, 243.

52. Bernhard Blumenkranz, "Augustin et les juifs: Augustin et le judaïsm," in *Juifs et chrétiens: Patristic et Moyen Age* (London 1977), 226, 230–31, 235–37.

53. Ibid., 100–101, 172–74.

54. Neal Pease, "Review of Ronald E. Modras, *The Catholic Church and Antisemitism: Poland, 1933–1939*," H-Habsburg (May 1996); Jeffrey Kopstein and Jason Wittenberg, "Mass Politics in Interwar Poland," Laboratory in Comparative Ethnic Processes at Columbia University (November 2004), 8.

55. Modras, *The Catholic Church and Antisemitism*, 268.

56. Ibid., 332.

57. Ibid., "Racism," 151–57, 171.

58. Ibid., 242.

59. Brumberg, "Poland and the Jews," 16; Modras, *The Catholic Church and Antisemitism*, 396.

60. Heller, *On the Edge of Destruction*, 112.

61. *Przeglad Powszechny*, in *The Catholic Church and Antisemitism*, ed. Modras, 210–11.

62. Janusz Rawicz, in *Przeglad* Katolicki, in ibid., 246–47; Kertzer, *Popes Against the Jews*, 210–11; Modras, *The Catholic Church and Antisemitism*, 153, 207. See also

Chapter 10 in this book for further examples of Polish-Catholic antisemitic racism.

63. Ibid., 248.
64. Quoted by Abraham G. Duker, "Mickiewicz and the Jewish Problem," *Adam Mickiewicz: Poet of Poland: A Symposium*, ed. Manfred Kridl (New York 1951), Part I.
65. Kazimierz Morowski's position, supported by the Polish bishops. Ibid., 70–71.
66. Ibid., 117, 352.
67. Jews were prominent in party leaderships. Jeffrey Kopstein and Jason Wittenberg, "Mass Politics in Interwar Poland," 16–19.
68. *New York Times* (November 19, 1982); and *Los Angeles Times* (June 19, 1983); and in Meyer Weinberg, *Because They Were Jews* (New York 1986), 159–60.
69. "The Actors in the Trial of Jesus," *Civiltà Cattolica*, (March 1942), 394–97; Pierre Pierrard, *Juifs et Catholiques Francais* (Paris 1970), 129; Charlotte Klein, "Damascus to Kiev: *Civiltà Cattolica* on Ritual Murder," *The Wiener Library Bulletin* (1974): 18, 25; Stewart Stehlin, *Weimar and the Vatican, 1919–1933* (Princeton 1983), 8; Andrew M. Canepa, "Cattolici ed Ebrei nell'Italia Liberale," *Comunità* 32 (April 1978): 61; Andrew M. Canepa, "Cattolici ed Ebrei nell'Italia Liberale," *Comunità* 32 (April 1978): 55, 83, 86, 101; Peter Pulzer, *The Rise of Political Antisemitism in Germany and Austria* (Cambridge, MA 1988), 200; Owen Chadwick, *Britain and the Vatican During the Second World War* (Cambridge, England 1986), 24.
70. Modras, *The Catholic Church and Antisemitism*, see, esp., his section, "*La Civiltà Cattolica*," 334–40.
71. See E. Thomas Wood and Stanislaw Jankowski, *Karski: How One Man Tried to Stop the Holocaust*, Foreword by Elie Wiesel (New York 1994).
72. Modras, *The Catholic Church and Antisemitism*, 387–94.
73. Eva Hoffman, *Shtetl: The History of a Small Town and an Extinguished World* (London, 1998), 5.
74. Modras, *The Catholic Church and Antisemitism*, 404.
75. Martin Gilbert, "The Final Solution," *The Oxford Companion to World War II* (Oxford, 1995).
76. Libionka, "Antisemitism and the Polish Catholic Clergy," in *Antisemitism and Its Opponents in Modern Poland*, ed. Blobaum 253–54.
77. Modras, *The Catholic Church and Antisemitism*, 278, 397.
78. Libionka, "Antisemitism and the Polish Catholic Clergy," in *Antisemitism and Its Opponents in Modern Poland*, ed. Blobaum, 255–56.
79. Ibid., 251.
80. Ibid., 255–56.
81. Ibid., 259.
82. This is demonstrated in Andrzej Szczypiorski's work, *The Beautiful Mrs. Seidenman* (1989).
83. Jan Gross, *Neighbors: The Destruction of the Jewish Community in Jedwabne, Poland* (Princeton, NJ, 2001).
84. Christopher Orlet, "Small Steps: The 60th Anniversary of the Jedwabne Pogrom (July 10, 1941)," *Central Europe Review* vol. 3, no. 14 (April 23, 2001).

85. In December 2001, the Institute of National Memory (IPN) in Poland, following earlier exhumations conducted in Jedwabne in the summer, completed the investigation into the number of Jewish victims murdered on July 10, 1941. See Zylinska, "'They're All Antisemitic There,'" no. 8. (International Interdisciplinary Conference 'Cultural Studies: Between Politics and Ethics' at Bath Spa University College on 6–8.07.2001)

86. Libionka, "Antisemitism and the Polish Catholic Clergy," in *Antisemitism and Its Opponents in Modern Poland*, 254.

87. George Steiner, "Poland's Willing Executioners," *The Observer, Guardian Unlimited* (Sunday April 8, 2001) http://books.guardian.co.uk/critics/reviews/0,,470067,00.html.

88. William Hagen, "The Moral Economy of Popular Violence: The Pogrom in Lwow, 1918," in *Antisemitism and Its Opponents in Modern Poland*, ed. Blobaum, 142; Czeslaw Milosz, "Campo dei Fiori," *The Collected Poems* (New York, 1988).

89. Pawel Machcewicz and Wlodzimierz Knap, "Jedwabne, 10th July, 1941: An interview with Pawel Machcewicz, Director, Office of Public Education, Institute of National Memory by Wlodzimierz Knap." Translated by Wanda Slawinska, July 11, 2001, *Dziennik Polski* (Kraków, Poland) http://info-poland.buffalo.edu/classroom/J/Mach.html.

90. Joanna Zylinska, "'They're All Antisemitic There': Aporias of Responsibility and Forgiveness," *Culture Machine, Generating Research in Culture and Theory* http://culturemachine.tees.ac.uk/Cmach/Backissues/j004/Articles/Zylinska.htm.

91. Alfred Lipson, "Antisemitism Beyond the Vatican," in *Midstream* (June–July 1991), 30.

92. Czeslaw Milosz, "Campo dei Fiori," *The Collected Poems*, (New York, 1988), 193.

93. Bristol Community College (Fall River, MA) psychology professor Leo Arnfeld.

94. Quoted in Mordecai Paldiel, *The Path of the Righteous: Gentile Rescuers of Jews During the Holocaust* (Hoboken, NJ, 1993).

95. Blet, eds., *Actes et documents*, 2:318–27.

96. Dariusz Libionka, "Antisemitism and the Polish Catholic Clergy," in Blobaum, ed., *Antisemitism and Its Opponents in Modern Poland* , 243–47.

97. Quoted in ibid., 248.

98. Quoted in ibid., 249.

99. Ibid., 249.

100. Ibid., 249–50.

101. Quoted in ibid., 262.

102. Modras, *The Catholic Church and Antisemitism*, 407.

103. Ibid., 263.

104. Michal Checinski, *Poland: Communism-Nationalism-Antisemitism* (New York 1982), 21.

105. Yehuda Bauer, *Flight and Rescue* (New York 1970), 206–11; in Natalia Aleksiun, "The Polish Catholic Church and the Jewish Question in Poland, 1944–1948," *Yad Vashem Studies* (2004), vol. 33, 14.

106. Ibid., 14–15.

107. Bishop Kubina of Czestochowa, ibid., 16.

108. Ibid., 17–20.
109. Joanna Tokarska-Bakir, *Gazeta Wyborcza* (January 12, 2001), quoted by Zylinska, "'They're All Antisemitic There.'"
110. Joanna Michlic, "Anti-Jewish Violence in Poland 1918–1939 and 1945–1947," *Polin* 13 (2001): 46.
111. Weinbaum, "Penitence and Prejudice."
112. Polish Correspondent for *The Economist*, "Never Forgetting," *The Economist* (November 9, 1991): 56.
113. Orlet, "Small Steps."
114. "Never Forgetting," 56.
115. Joanna Zylinska, "'They're All Antisemitic There': Aporias of Responsibility and Forgiveness," *Culture Machine, Generating Research in Culture and Theory* http://culturemachine.tees.ac.uk/Cmach/Backissues/j004/Articles/Zylinska.htm.
116. This summary of the main points of Cardinal Glemp's address on Radio Jozef was composed by Father Adam Boniecki and appeared in an article entitled "Prymas o Jedwabnem" (The Primate on Jedwabne), *Tygodnik Powszechny* (March 11, 2001), quoted in Weinbaum, "Penitence and Prejudice."
117. Ibid.
118. Ibid.
119. http://www.axt.org.uk/.
120. Interviews with Margaret Oldieski, Rev. Adam Boniecki, Agnieszka Holland, Stanislaw Krajewski, in "In Poland, New 'Passion' Plays on Old Hatreds," *Boston Globe* (April 10, 2004): D1, D6.
121. Dinah A. Spritzer, "Jews a Detriment to Europe, Polish Politician Says," *The Jerusalem Post* (February 19, 2007).
122. Joanna Beata Michlic, *Poland's Threatening Other: The Image of the Jew from 1880 to the Present*, University of Nebraska Press, 2006, 179.
123. Dinah A. Spritzer, "Jews a Detriment to Europe, Polish Politician says," *The Jerusalem Post* (February 19, 2007).
124. "Giertych reprimanded by EU parliament," Theparliament.Com: European Politics And Policy (March 13, 2007).

Chapter 10

1. Walter Laqueur, *A History of Zionism* (New York 1989), 212.
2. Weber, *Action Française*, 219–35.
3. Theodor Herzl, *The Complete Diaries of Theodor Herzl* (New York 1960), 1591–95.
4. Herzl, *The Complete Diaries of Theodor Herzl*, entry of January 26, 1904.
5. David Kertzer, *The Popes Against the Jews: The Vatican's Role in the Rise of Modern Antisemitism* (New York 2001), 213.
6. Ibid., 226.
7. Many such decrees were issued at other Church synods before and after the Fourth Lateran Council.

8. Quoted in ibid., 77.

9. Ibid., 64–65.

10. De Rosa, *Vicars of Christ*, 141; Valerio Valeri, *Le Relazioni Internazionali della Santa Sede dopo il Secundo Conflitto Mondiale* (Rome 1956), 23–24. This view was supported by Giovanni Montini, later Pope Paul VI, at the Pontificia Accademia Ecclesiastica (Rome 1951), in *Vatican Diplomacy and the Jews During the Holocaust*, ed. John Morley (New York 1980), 11–12.

11. J. N. D. Kelly, "Benedict XV," *The Oxford Dictionary of Popes* (Oxford 1986), 315.

12. Stewart Stehlin, *Weimar and the Vatican, 1919–1933* (Princeton 1983), vii, 8, 448–50; Sergio Minerbi, *The Vatican and Zionism* (New York 1990), 94.

13. Pearl and Samuel Oliner, "Righteous and Unrighteous Gentiles," Baruch-Manhattan Colleges Colloquium on the History of Antisemitism (March 1989); Ian Kershaw, *The Making of the "Hitler Myth,"* (Oxford 1987), 105; and "The Persecution of the Jews and German Popular Opinion in the Third Reich," in *The Persisting Question*, ed. Helen Fein (Berlin 1987), 341.

14. The Danish Jews, e.g., did benefit from the Danish Lutheran Church's stand.

15. Daniel Carpi, "The Catholic Church and Italian Jewry Under the Fascists," in *Yad Vashem Studies* 4 (1960): 54–56; Richard Webster, *The Cross and the Fasces* (Stanford 1960), 124–26; Renzo De Felice, *Storia degli ebrei italiani sotto il fascismo* (Turin 1972), 286–88, 547–49.

16. Gitta Sereny, *Into That Darkness* (New York 1974), 327.

17. "La Chiesa e gli ebrei," *Realtà storiche* (Cremona 1939), 86–87, cited by Meir Michaelis, *Mussolini and the Jews* (Oxford 1978), 240–41.

18. Yitzhak Baer, *A History of the Jews in Christian Spain* (Philadelphia 1961, 1983), 1:149; *Simon Wiesenthal Center Response* (September 1989), 1.

19. Donald Dietrich, *Catholic Citizens in the Third Reich* (New Brunswick, NJ 1988), 73.

20. Colin Holmes, "The Ritual Murder Accusation in Britain," in *The Blood Libel Legend*, ed. Alan Dundes (Madison 1991), 117; Shlomo Simonsohn, *The Apostolic See and the Jews: History* (Toronto 1991), 85n120.

21. "Editors Asked to Print Only Vatican Views," *National Jesuit News* (February 1990): 2; *Civiltà Cattolica*, April 1950, 8.

22. Ignatius Loyola, "Rules for Thinking with the Church" and "Obedience of the Jesuits," *Spiritual Exercises*, in *Documents of the Christian Church*, ed. Henry Bettenson (London 1950).

23. Charlotte Klein, "Damascus to Kiev: *Civiltà Cattolica* on Ritual Murder," *The Wiener Library Bulletin* (1974): 18, 25; Stehlin, *Weimar and the Vatican*, 8; Andrew M. Canepa, "Cattolici ed Ebrei nell'Italia Liberale," *Comunità* 32 (April 1978): 61.

24. Roma, Archivum Romanum Societatis Iesu, *Civiltà Cattolica*, cartella 1, fasc. IX, nn.1 and 2, Oreglia to Boero (March 6 and 8, 1882), in Canepa, "Cattolici," 83, 86.

25. Oreglia, "Della vera origine e natura dell'antisemitismo," *Civiltà Cattolica*, 12a ser., VI (1884), 479. also Fr. F. S. Rondina, "La morale giudica," *Civiltà Cattolica*, 15a ser., V (1893), 153; *Civiltà Cattolica*, March 4, 1881.

26. Jews are allowed to drink but the murder accusation is nonsense.

27. Letter from Giuseppe Oreglia to Giuseppe Boero (March 8, 1882), in Canepa, "Cattolici," 55.

28. Drumont, *La Libre Parole* (July 13 and 15, 1892).

29. See Chapter 8.

30. Canepa, "Cattolici," 103–4; also Pierre Sorlin, *"La Croix" et les Juifs, 1880–1899* (Paris 1967), 224, 267n331.

31. *The Christian in the Jewish Talmud, or the Teachings of the Rabbis About Christians.*

32. "Jewish Trickery and Papal docs.—Apropos of a Recent Trial," *Civiltà Cattolica*, April 11 and 25, 1914. For Pranaitis, Louis Greenberg, *The Jews In Russia* (New Haven 1965), 2:92.

33. De Felice, *Storia degli ebrei italiani sotto il fascismo*, 32–35; Canepa, "Cattolici," 61.

34. "Le logge israelitiche secrete pienamente illustrate," *Civiltà Cattolica*, 16a ser., VI (1896), 160–76.

35. Ballerini, "Della questione giudaica in Europa," *Civiltà Cattolica* 14, no. 8 (1890): 403–4. A Dominican, Giordano Bruno was declared a heretic by the Inquisition and burned in Rome in 1600. In the nineteenth century, he was associated with anticlericalism.

36. Ballerini, "Il caso di Alfredo Dreyfus," in *Civiltà Cattolica*, 17a ser., I (1898): 273–87; "Della questione giudaica in Europa," *Civiltà Cattolica*, 73, 81–83; also "La dispersione de Israello pel mondo moderno," *Civiltà Cattolica* (1897): 1125:267–71.

37. Canepa, "Cattolici," 56; Peter Pulzer, *The Rise of Political Antisemitism in Germany and Austria* (Cambridge, MA 1988), 200.

38. Monsignor Lorenzelli. Maurice Baumont, "L'Affaire Dreyfus dans la diplomatie française," in *Studies in Diplomatic History and Historiography* (London 1961), 27–28.

39. Canepa, "Cattolici," 101.

40. See, for example, "Il Giudaismo nel mondo," *L'Osservatore Romano* (January 20–21, 1898); also "Semitismo e antisemitismo" (July 5–6, 1898).

41. "L'emancipazione degli ebrei," *L'Osservatore Romano*, (January 24–25, 1898).

42. Stehlin, *Weimar and the Vatican.*

43. Pius' encyclical *Studiorum Ducem* of August 4, 1923.

44. Peter Godman, *Hitler and the Vatican* (New York 2004), 18.

45. Pope St. Gregory VII, "Epistola II: Ad Alphonsum Regem Castellae," *PL*, 148:604–5.

46. Kertzer, *Popes Against the Jews*, 247–61.

47. Quoted in Kertzer, *Popes Against the Jews*, 267–68.

48. Philip Hughes, *Pope Pius the Eleventh* (New York 1937), 5–6, 43.

49. Godman, *Hitler and the Vatican*, 26.

50. Kertzer, 269–70.

51. Ibid., 263.

52. Quoted in Kertzer, 272.

53. Galeazzo Ciano, *Ciano's Hidden Diary, 1937–38* (New York 1953), 141.
54. Memorandum by Woermann (June 10, 1940); Pierre Blet, et al., eds., *Actes et documents du Saint Siège relatifs à la Seconde Guerre Mondiale* (Vatican City 1965–75), 9:93–94; 8:534; Guenter Lewy, *The Catholic Church and Nazi Germany* (New York 1967), 289–94.
55. Michael Phayer, *Protestant and Catholic Women in Nazi Germany* (Detroit1990), 243.
56. http://www.ourgardenofcarmel.org/edithLetterToPope.html. Emphasis added. See also Sacred Heart University, Center for Christian-Jewish Understanding, "FEBRUARY 15, 2003: VATICAN ARCHIVES REVEAL 1933 LETTER FROM EDITH STEIN TO POPE PIUS XI," http://www.sacredheart.edu/pages/12100_2003_2_15vatican_archives_1933_letter_edith_stein_to_pope_pius_xi.cfm.
57. Godman, *Hitler and the Vatican*, 35.
58. Ibid., 80–81.
59. Ethel Mary Tinnemann, "German Catholic Bishops' Knowledge of Nazi Extermination of Jews," in *Holocaust Studies Annual, 1990*, ed. Sanford Pinsker and Jack Fischel (New York 1990), 35–36.
60. Godman, *Hitler and the Vatican*, 163.
61. Ibid., 164.
62. Anthony Rhodes, *The Vatican in the Age of the Dictators* (New York 1973), 166–67.
63. William Harrigan, "Nazi Germany and the Holy See, 1933–1936," *The Catholic Historical Review* 47 (1961–62): 166–67; Victor Farías, *Heidegger and Nazism* (Philadelphia 1989), 180.
64. Robert Gellateley, *The Gestapo and German Society* (New York 1990), 99, and chapters 4 and 5.
65. François Charles-Roux and Wladislaw Skrzynski. Hansjacob Stehle, *Eastern Politics of the Vatican, 1917–1979* (Athens Ohio 1981), 151.
66. Friedrich Heer, *God's First Love* (New York 1967), 330; Owen Chadwick, *Britain and the Vatican During the Second World War* (Cambridge, England, 1986), 142–44; Lapomarda, *The Jesuits and the Third Reich*, 226–27.
67. Hughes, *Pope Pius the Eleventh*, 299.
68. Godman, *Hitler and the Vatican*, 142–47. Even so, the Jesuit General Ledochowski considered the document "a bit hard."
69. *Przewodnik Katolicki* 44 (1938): 551, in Ronald Modras, *The Catholic Church and Antisemitism in Poland, 1933–1939* (Chur, Switzerland, 1994), 154.
70. Henri Lichtenberger, *The Third Reich* (New York 1937), 345–63, especially 350.
71. Pacelli note to Diego von Bergen, German ambassador to the Holy See (April 30, 1937), *Documents on German Foreign Policy*, Series D, 1:649, 964–65, in Lewy, *Catholic Church and Nazi Germany*, 158.
72. Bergen to Berlin (July 23, 1937), *Documents on German Foreign Policy*, Series D, 1:990–92, in Saul Friedländer, *Pius XII and the Third Reich* (New York 1966), 6–7.
73. Friedländer, *Pius XII*, 15; George Berkley, *Vienna and Its Jews* (Cambridge, MA 1988), 223, 229, 323.

74. *Civiltà Cattolica* (July 29, 1938), 373; Chadwick, *Britain and the Vatican*, 24.

75. Quoted in Kertzer, 287.

76. Artur Sandauer, "On the Situation of a Polish Writer of Jewish Descent," *Pisma Zebrane* (Warsaw 1985), in "Poland and the Jews," *Tikkun*, ed. Abraham Brumberg (July–August 1987), 17; see also Celia Heller, *On the Edge of Destruction: Jews of Poland Between the Two World Wars* (New York 1980), 109–14; Gutman and Krakowski, *Unequal Victims*, 19–22; see also Chapter 9 in this book.

77. Jerzy Turowicz, "Polish Rights and Jewish Right," *Tygodnik Powszechny* (April 5, 1987), in Brumberg, "Poland and the Jews," 87.

78. Lucy Dawidowicz, "The Tide of Antisemitism," *The Times Literary Supplement* (July 22, 1977): 901; Abraham Brumberg, "Polish Intellectuals and Antisemitism," *Dissent* (Winter 1991): 16, 74–77; Simon Dubnow, *History of the Jews in Russia and Poland* (Philadelphia 1920), 155–56, 160–71; M. J. Rosman, "A Minority Views the Majority: Jewish Attitudes Towards the Polish Lithuanian Commonwealth and Interaction with Poles," in *Polin*, 32; Owen Chadwick, *The Popes and European Revolution* (Oxford 1981), 16–17; Yisrael Gutman and Shmuel Krakowski, *Unequal Victims: Poles and Jews During World War II* (New York 1986), 1–26; Alfred Lipson, "Antisemitism Beyond the Vatican," in *Midstream* (June–July 1991), 30; Andrzej Bryk, "Poland and the Memory of the Holocaust," *Partisan Review* (Spring 1990), 231–32; Heller, *On the Edge of Destruction*, 112–13; Meyer Weinberg, *Because They Were Jews* (New York 1986), 159–60.

79. Ernesto Rosa, "La questione giudaica e 'La Civiltà Cattolica,'" *Civiltà Cattolica* (October 1, 1938): 3–16.

80. Translated by Joshua Starr, "Italy's Antisemites," *Jewish Social Studies* (October 1938): 118.

81. Pinchas Lapide, *Three Popes and the Jews* (New York 1967), 108; Chadwick, *Britain and the Vatican*, 25.

82. (Paris 1885), 1:526.

83. Pius XI, "Discours aux pèlerins belges, September 1938," *Documentation catholique* (September 6, 1938), col. 1460; René Laurentin and Joseph Neuner, *The Declaration on the Relation of the Church to Non-Christian Religions* (Glen Rock 1966), 50–51; Lewy, *The Catholic Church*, 297; Ronald E. Modras, *The Catholic Church and Antisemitism: Poland, 1933–1939* (Chur, Switzerland, 1994), 355.

84. Mentioned in Chapter 2.

85. St. Jerome, *The Homilies of Saint Jerome*, 255–67.

86. Quoted in Kertzer, 212.

87. Berkovitz, "*The Anguish of the Jews*: A Theology of Intolerance," *Continuum* (Autumn 1966), 419.

88. Rev. Edward H. Flannery, "Good Thing Papal Draft Was Never Signed," *Providence Journal*. National Christian Leadership Conference for Israel, http://www.nclci.org/articles/art-flan-papal.htm.

89. Georges Passelecq and Bernard Suchecky, *The Hidden Encyclical of Pius XI* (New York 1997).

90. Lapide, *Three Popes and the Jews*; Robert Graham, *Pius XII's Defense of Jews and Others, 1944–5* (Milwaukee 1982) and *Pius XII; Years of Praise, Years of Blame* (Supplement to the *Catholic League Newsletter* 16, no. 12 (Milwaukee, WI, December 1989); Robert Leiber, "Pio XII e gli Ebrei di Roma, 1943–1944," *Civiltà Cattolica* (March 4, 1961); Michael O'Carroll, *Pius XII: Greatness Dishonored: A doc.ed Study* (Dublin 1980); Anthony Rhodes, *The Vatican in the Age of the Dictators, 1922–1945* (London 1973). But Sam Waagenaar, *The Pope's Jews* (La Salle, IL., 1974), chapter 40; Deborah Dwork, *Children with a Star: Jewish Youth in Nazi Europe* (New Haven 1991), 292n64; Papeleux, *Les Silences de Pie XII*, chapter "Pie XII et l'allemagne."

91. British Foreign Office Records, in Stehlin, *Weimar and the Vatican*, 441n166.

92. Peter Ludlow, "Papst Pius XII, die britische Regierung und die deutsche Opposition im Winter, 1939–40," *Vierteljahreshefte für Zeitgeschichte* 22 (1974): 357, in Chadwick, *Britain and the Vatican*, 98.

93. Phayer, *The Catholic Church and the Holocaust*, 5.

94. Deutsch, *Twilight War*, 120; Friedländer, *Pius XII*, 52–53; also Phayer, *The Catholic Church and the Holocaust*, 4.

95. Chadwick, *Britain and the Vatican*, 218–19.

96. *New York Times* (December 25, 1942), 16; Chadwick, *Britain and the Vatican*.

97. Quoted by Morley, *Vatican Diplomacy*, 300 n188.

98. Michael Phayer, *The Catholic Church and the Holocaust* (Bloomington, IN, 2000), 49.

99. *Foreign Relations of the United States: Diplomatic Papers, 1943* (Washington, D.C. 1963), 2:912.

100. Blet, eds., *Actes et documents*, 2:318–27.

101. Owen Chadwick, "The Pope and the Jews in 1942," in *Persecution and Toleration*, ed. W. J. Sheils (Papers of the Ecclesiastical History Society 1984), 471–72.

102. James Hennesey, "An American Jesuit in Wartime Rome," *Mid-America* 56 (1974): 36.

103. Blet, *Actes et documents*, 9:88.

104. Jacques Adler, "The 'Sin of Omission'? Radio Vatican and the Anti-Nazi Struggle, 1940–1942," *Australian Journal of Politics and History* 50, no. 3, 2004, 397.

105. Quoted by Adler, "The 'Sin of Omission'?" 405.

106. Ibid., 405.

107. Quoted by The Catholic League, "The Action of the Holy See for the Jews of Europe: Hungary." http://www.catholicleague.org/piusxii_and_the_holocaust/hungary.htm.

108. John Morley, "Vatican Diplomacy and the Jews of Hungary During the Holocaust," Second International Holocaust Conference (Berlin 1994).

109. See, e.g., Hallie, *Lest Innocent Blood Be Shed*; Ewa Kurek-Lesik, "The Conditions of Admittance and the Social Background of Jewish Children Saved by Women's Religious Orders in Poland, 1939–1945," *Polin* 3 (1988): 244–75.

110. Waclaw Zajaczkowski, *Martyrs of Charity* (Washington, D.C., 1988); Susan Zucotti, *Italians and the Holocaust* (London 1987), 209; Phayer, *The Catholic Church and the Holocaust*, chapter 7; also Mordecai Paldiel, *The Path of the Righteous* (Jersey City, 1993); David Gushee, *Righteous Gentiles of the Holocaust* (St. Paul, 2003).

111. Quoted by Gordon Horowitz, *In the Shadow of Death* (New York 1990), 136.

112. In an interview with the Jewish Telegraph Agency (March 1999).

113. Phayer, *The Catholic Church and the Holocaust*, 132.

114. De Rosa, *The Vicars of Christ*, 150; Stehlin, *Weimar and the Vatican*, 363, 365; Klaus Scholder, *Die Kirchen und das Dritte Reich* (Berlin 1977), vol. 1, part 2, chapters 2 and 8.

115. Ernst von Weizsäcker, *Memoirs of Ernst von Weizsäcker* (Chicago 1951), 284.

116. "Pius XII: The Legends and the Truth," *The Tablet* (March 28, 1998), 401. http://www.thetablet.co.uk/cgi-bin/register.cgi/tablet-00163.

117. Minerbi, *The Vatican and the Jews*, 99–100.

118. Ibid.

119. John Conway, "The Churches and the Jewish People," in Asher Cohen, et al., eds, *Comprehending the Holocaust* (Frankfurt 1988), 131.

120. Chadwick, "Pius XII: The Legends and the Truth."

121. Weber, *Action Française*, 251; Michael Marrus and Robert Paxton, *Vichy France and the Jews* (New York 1981), 51, 87–88. also Weber, *Action Française*, 219–35, 251–52; O'Carroll, *Pius XII*, 17; Pierre Pierrard, *Juifs et Catholiques Français* (Paris 1970), 301.

122. Chadwick, "The Pope and the Jews in 1942," 457; Michael Phayer, *The Catholic Church and the Holocaust* (Bloomington, IN 2000), 46, 48.

123. For more information on Catholic Croatia and the Jews, see Michael Phayer, *The Catholic Church and the Holocaust* (Bloomington, IN 2000), especially chapter 3.

124. Phayer, *The Catholic Church and the Holocaust*, 96.

125. Michael Phayer, *The Catholic Church and the Holocaust* (Bloomington, IN 2000), 47, 81. Preysing's letters most likely contained further urging of the pope to say and do something about the Nazi mass murders.

126. David Mitchell, *The Jesuits* (New York 1981), 279; Monty Penkower, "Auschwitz, the Papacy, and Poland's 'Jewish Problem,'" *Midstream* (August–September 1990): 15; Stehle, *Eastern Politics of the Vatican*, 206; Deutsch, *Twilight War*, 114. Based on his experiences during the Holocaust, the heroic priest, Rufino Niccacci of Assisi, wrote *While the Pope Kept Silent: Assisi and the Nazi Occupation* (London and Boston, 1978).

127. Blet, *Actes et documents*, 7:374. also Steven Koblik, *The Stones Cry Out: Sweden's Respnse to the Persecution of the Jews, 1933–1945* (New York 1988), 109–10.

128. Michael Phayer, *The Catholic Church and the Holocaust* (Bloomington, IN 2000), 48–49.

129. Ibid.

130. Ibid., 49; Michael, *Concise History of American Antisemitism*, chapters 5 and 6.

131. Phayer, *The Catholic Church and the Holocaust*, 51–52, 54, 77.

132. Blet, *Actes et documents*, 5:676.
133. Chadwick, *Britain and the Vatican*, 207, 216–18; Chadwick, "The Pope and the Jews in 1942," 466–67; Penkower, "Auschwitz, the Papacy, and Poland's 'Jewish Problem,'" 15.
134. Phayer, *The Catholic Church and the Holocaust* (Bloomington, IN 2000), 54.
135. Ibid., 55.
136. Ibid., 86.
137. Morley, 82, 85.
138. Phayer, *The Catholic Church and the Holocaust*, 54–61.
139. Ibid., 65.
140. See, e.g., Francis d'Arcy Osborne, "Letter," *The Times* (May 20, 1963); Blet, *Actes et documents*, 8:669.
141. Conway, "The Churches and the Jewish People," 131.
142. Blet, *Actes et documents*, 9:233.
143. Ibid., 8:90–92, 116–19.
144. Michaelis, *Mussolini and the Jews*, 247n2, 374; the English translation in Friedländer, *Pius XII*, 54–56.
145. Blet, *Actes et documents*, 9:291–92.
146. Ibid., 5:676.
147. Chadwick, *Britain and the Vatican*, 207, 216–18; Chadwick, "The Pope and the Jews in 1942," 466–67; Penkower, "Auschwitz, the Papacy, and Poland's 'Jewish Problem,'" 15.
148. Chadwick, "The Pope and the Jews in 1942," 446.
149. Chadwick, *Britain and the Vatican*, 211–12.
150. Blet, *Actes et documents*, 2:326; 9:179, 229–30, 262, 512.
151. Quoted by Phayer, *The Catholic Church and the Holocaust*, 6.
152. Ibid., 9:doc. 297.
153. Steinberg, *All or Nothing*, 6, 58–59, 66, 70, 170, 229.
154. Weizsäcker to Foreign Office (October 17, 1943), Nuremberg doc. NG-5027; also Michael Tagliacozzo, "La Comunità di Roma sotto l'incubo della svastica," in *Gli ebrei in Italia durante il fascismo* (November 1963): 30.
155. Susan Zucotti, "Pope Pius XII and the Holocaust," in *The Italian Refuge*, ed. Ivo Herzer (Washington, D.C., 1989), 258–60; Blet, *Actes et documents*, 9:111, 610–11; Robert Katz, *Black Sabbath* (Toronto 1969), 79–88.
156. Michaelis, *Mussolini and the Jews*, 254–62.
157. Weizsäcker to Foreign Office (October 17, 1943), Nuremberg doc. NG-5027.
158. Godman, *Hitler and the Vatican*, 128.
159. Stehle, *Eastern Politics of the Vatican*, 170, 413n51; Godman, *Hitler and the Vatican*, 45, 121.
160. Blet, *Actes et documents*, 9:505–6.
161. Weizsäcker, *Memoirs of Ernst von Weizsäcker* (Chicago 1951), 277.
162. Weizsäcker to Foreign Office (October 17, 1943), Nuremberg doc. NG-5027. Weizsäcker tried to minimize papal involvement.
163. Nurember doc. NO-315, in Michaelis, *Mussolini and the Jews*, 369.

164. Phayer, *The Catholic Church and the Holocaust*, 102.
165. Manfred Barthel, *The Jesuits: History and Legend of the Society of Jesus* (New York 1984), 270; Lapomarda, *The Jesuits and the Third Reich*, 235, 243.
166. Chadwick, *Britain and the Vatican*, 187.
167. Letter from Fr. Lapomarda to the author, February 23, 1990.
168. The *National Jesuit News* (February 1990), 2, noted the oversight of the Holy See. There were, of course, other Jesuits who had nothing to do with the antisemitic attitudes expressed in *Civiltà Cattolica*. Lapomarda, *The Jesuits and the Third Reich*, 230n3.
169. "The Great Dilemma," *Civiltà Cattolica*, (December 1941), 5.
170. "The Actors in the Trial of Jesus," *Civiltà Cattolica*, (March 1942), 394–97.
171. See Nuremberg Doc. 1367, Himmler's letter to Kaltenbrunner, dated May 19, 1943.
172. Blet, *Actes et documents*, 9:271–72, 302.
173. Ibid., 9:184.
174. Ibid., 9:469, also 9:185–86.
175. Minerbi, *The Vatican and Zionism*, 133, 136, 139, 143, 158, 161, 171.
176. E.g., Robert A. Graham, *Pius XII's Defense of the Jews and Others* (Milwaukee 1982, 1987).
177. Ulrich von Hehl, *Priester under Hitlers Terror* (Mainz 1984) and Lapomarda, *The Jesuits and the Third Reich*.
178. Chadwick, *Britain and the Vatican*, 200; Arno Mayer, *Why Did the Heavens Not Darken?* (New York 1989), 383.
179. Dwork, *Children with a Star*, 291n64.
180. Michaelis, *Mussolini and the Jews*, 395.
181. Aronson, *Unholy Trinity*; Fein, *Accounting for Genocide*, 105.
182. Blet, *Actes et documents*, 8:615; and John Morley, *Vatican Diplomacy and the Jews During the Holocaust* (New York 1980), 54–70.
183. Marrus and Paxton, *Vichy France*, 278.
184. Pierrard, *Juifs et Catholiques français*, 298.
185. Webster, *Pétain's Crime*, 133.
186. Marrus and Paxton, *Vichy France*, 278.
187. Webster, *Pétain's Crime*, 132.
188. Gerlier and Suhard attended requiem masses and the Archbishops of Marseille and Bordeaux read eulogies for the violently antisemitic Vichy Minister Philippe Henriot, who had been murdered by the Resistance.
189. Chadwick, "The Pope and the Jews in 1942," 471.
190. Chadwick, *Britain and the Vatican*, 122.
191. British Ambassador to the Vatican, D'Arcy Osborne, quoted by Chadwick, 216.
192. Morley, *Vatican Diplomacy and the Jews During the Holocaust*, 146.

Postscript

1. George Mosse, *The Crisis of German Ideology* (New York 1984), chapter 5; Michael Burleigh and Wolfgang Wippermann, *The Racial State* (Cambridge, England 1991), 23.

2. David Kertzer, *The Kidnapping of Edgardo Mortaro* (New York 1998), 33, 310.
3. Marcel Simon, *Verus Israel* (Oxford 1986), 398.
4. Robert Alter, "From Myth to Murder," *The New Republic* (May 20, 1991): 34, 37–38.
5. St. Augustine, *Adversus Judaeos* 7, 10, see also 8, 11. "Occidistis Christum in parentibus vestris."
6. Jerome, The Homilies of Saint Jerome (Washington, D.C., 1964), 1:255, 258–62.
7. *Contra Judaeos*, 1, 18, in Rosemary Ruether, *Faith and Fratricide* (New York 1965), 130.
8. *Orations Against the Jews*, I. 4.
9. *Homilies Against Judaizing Christians*, 6.2.10.
10. "On the Sabbath," 4:23, in Ruether, *Faith and Fratricide*, 148.
11. *Maledictio parentum currat adhuc in filios*," Grayzel I, 10n7.
12. Pope Leo XIII in *Aeterni Patris*, August 4, 1879.
13. *Summa Theologiae*, 1a, 2ae, 102, 6.8.
14. To German Emperor Lothair III in 1134. Mary Stroll, *The Jewish Pope: Ideology and Politics in the Papal Schism of 1130* (Leiden 1987), 166.
15. Stoll, *The Jewish Pope*, 159–62, 177, 181.
16. Edward Synan, *The Popes and the Jews in the Middle Ages* (New York 1965), 120, 134.
17. An anonymous chronicler of Mainz in Adolf Neubauer and Moritz Stern, eds., *Hebräische Berichte über die Judenverfolgungen während der Kreuzzüge* (Berlin 1892), 176, 169; Robert Chazan, "The Hebrew First-Crusade Chronicles," *Revue des études juives: Historia Judaica* 33 (January–June 1974), 249–50, 253; Bernold, *Chronicle in Monumenta Germaniae Historica, Scriptores* (Hannover 1826–96), 5:465.
18. Norman Golb, "New Light on the Persecution of French Jews at the Time of the First Crusade," in *Medieval Jewish Life*, ed. Robert Chazan (New York 1976), 19.
19. Jonathan Riley-Smith, "The First Crusade and the Persecution of the Jews," in *Persecution and Toleration*, ed. W. J. Sheils (Papers of the Ecclesiastical History Society 1984), 51–52.
20. Heinrich Graetz, *History of the Jews* (Philadelphia 1940), 4:435, 443–44; Shlomo Simonsohn, *The Apostolic See and the Jews: History* (Toronto 1991), 333n101; Heiko Oberman, *The Roots of Antisemitism in the Age of Renaissance and Reformation* (Philadelphia 1981), 30–31, 53; Léon Poliakov, *The History of Antisemitism* (New York 1974),1:215.
21. For Martin Luther, see Robert Michael, *Holy Hatred: Christianity, Antisemitism, and the Holocaust* (New York, 2006), ch. 4. See also Yosef Yerushalmi, *Assimilation and Racial Antisemitism* (New York 1982); Léon Poliakov, *The Aryan Myth* (New York 1974); Albert Sicroff, *Les controverses des statuts de "pureté de sang" en Espagne du XVe au XVIIe siècle* (Paris 1960); Michael Glatzer, "Pablo de Santa Maria on the Events of 1391," in *Antisemitism Through the Ages*, ed. Shmuel Almog (Oxford 1988), 127–37; Cecil Roth, *A History of the Marranos* (New York 1974), 21, 29–30.

22. Yosef Yerushalmi, *Assimilation and Racial Antisemitism* (New York 1982).

23. Simonsohn, *History*, 366; Manuel, *The Broken Staff*, 23.

24. Léon Poliakov, *The Aryan Myth* (New York 1974), 12–13; Albert Sicroff, *Les controverses des statuts de "pureté de sang" en Espange du XVe au XVIIe siècle* (Paris 1960), and Michael Glatzer, "Pablo de Santa Maria on the Events of 1391," in *Antisemitism Through the Ages*, ed. Shmuel Almog (Oxford 1988), 127–37.

25. Every medieval persecution of Jews resulted in attacks on synagogues. Simonsohn, *History*, 124.

26. Roth, *A History of the Marranos*, 14–17.

27. Shlomo Simonsohn, *The Apostolic See and the Jews: Documents, 1464–1521* (Toronto 1990), Documents 1000 and 1040.

28. *Converso* reversion to Judaism was considered heretical. Roth, *A History of the Marranos*, 21, 29–30.

29. *Historia de los Reyes Católicos*, book I, ch. 44, 600, and in Baer, *The Jews in Christian Spain*, 2:327–28.

30. Reites, "St. Ignatius of Loyola and the Jews," 30, 9.

31. Raymond Carr, "'Corruption or Expulsion,' Review of Elie Kedourie, ed., *Spain and the Jews* (London 1992), *The Spectator* (May 22, 1992), 30.

32. James Reites, S. J., "St. Ignatius of Loyola and the Jews," *Studies in the Spirituality of Jesuits* (September 1981): 15, 16, 32.

33. Jerome Friedman, "Jewish Conversion, the Spanish Pure Blood Laws and Reformation," *Sixteenth Century Journal* (1987) 18.1, 16–17.

34. Frank Manuel, *Broken Shaft* (Cambridge, MA 1992), 223–24, and Yerushalmi, *Assimilation and Racial Antisemitism*, 16.

35. Anne Catherine Emmerich, *The Dolorous Passion of Our Lord Jesus Christ*, ch. 28. http://www.jesus-passion.com/THE_PASSION3.htm#CHAPTER%20XXVIII.

36. Shlomo Simonsohn, *The Apostolic See and the Jews: Documents, 1464–1521* (Toronto 1990), Doc. 879.

37. Ibid., doc. 1157. A minority of the order opposed such a rule.

38. Ibid., docs. 1167 and 1206.

39. Ibid., doc. 1334. A minority of the order opposed such a rule.

40. Ibid., doc. 1158, and Shlomo Simonsohn, *The Apostolic See and the Jews: History* (Toronto 1991), 385.

41. Simonsohn, *History*, 387–91.

42. Kenneth Stow, *Catholic Thought and Papal Jewry Policy, 1555–1593* (New York 1977), 58, and "Hatred of the Jews or Love of the Church," in *Antisemitism Through the Ages*, ed. Shmuel Almog (Oxford 1988), 86.

43. Owen Chadwick, *The Popes and European Revolution* (Oxford 1981), 133.

44. Quoted by Sander Gilman, "Martin Luther and the Self-Hating Jews," in *The Martin Luther Quincentennial*, ed. Gerhard Dünnhaupt (Detroit 1985), 84–88.

45. Martin Luther, "That Jesus Christ Was Born a Jew," in *Luther's Works*, ed. Walther Brandt (Philadelphia 1967), 45:213; repeated in "Vom Schem Hamphoras."

46. Martin Luther, "The Jews and Their Lies," in *Luther's Works*, tr. Franklin Sherman (Philadelphia 1971), 137–38.
47. Reinhold Lewin, *Luthers Stellung zu den Juden: Ein Betrag zur Geschichte der Juden während des Reformationszeitalters* (Berlin 1911), 77.
48. Martin Luther, "The Jews and Their Lies," in *Luther's Works*, tr. Franklin Sherman (Philadelphia 1971), 170, 216, 267, 217, 268–69, 285, 269, 286, 253.
49. Martin Luther, *The Table Talk*, ed. William Hazlitt (London 1883), 165.
50. H. R. Trevor-Roper, *The European Witch-Craze of the 16th and 17th Centuries* (New York 1967), 139.
51. Isaiah Shachar, *The Judensau* (London 1974), 48.
52. Trevor-Roper, *The European Witch-Craze*, 112–13.
53. Ibid.
54. Ibid.
55. Kertzer, *The Popes Against the Jews*, 172, 175, 226–27.
56. Frederick Busi, *The Pope of Antisemitism: The Career and Legacy of Edouard-Adolphe Drumont* (Lanham, MD 1986), 73; Michael Marrus, "Popular Antisemitism," in "The Dreyfus Affair," ed. Kleeblatt, 52; Byrnes, *Antisemitism in Modern France*, 1:153; Katz, *Jews and Freemasons in Europe*, 161.
57. Clary, *French Antisemitism*, 314.
58. Busi, *The Pope of Antisemitism*, 61–62, 179.
59. Drumont, *La France Juive*, 2:572.
60. Busi, *Pope of Antisemitism*, 42–46, 53.
61. Byrnes, *Antisemitism in Modern France*, 1:152.
62. Busi, *Pope of Antisemitism*, 42–46, 53.
63. Clary, *French Antisemitism*, 128.
64. Byrnes, *Antisemitism in Modern France*, 1:146, 166, 172, 180–81.
65. Busi, *Pope of Antisemitism*, 11–14.
66. Ibid., 76.
67. Ibid.
68. Byrnes, *Antisemitism in Modern France*, 147–48, 150, 154, 1818, 196.
69. Quoted in ibid., 92–93.
70. Quoted in Kertzer, *Popes Against the Jews*, 136–38.
71. Quoted in ibid., 146.
72. Quoted in ibid., 267–68.
73. George Mosse, *Nazi Culture* (New York 1966), 256–61; Friedrich Heer, *God's First Love*, 311; Pinchas Lapide, *Three Popes and the Jews* (New York 1967), 239; Leon Papeleux, *Les Silences de Pie XII* (Brussels 1980), 77. For the Protestants, see Richard Gutteridge, *Open Thy Mouth for the Dumb* (Oxford 1976). For the Catholics, see Michael Phayer, *The Catholic Church and the Holocaust* (Bloomington, IN, 2000).
74. Janusz Rawicz in *Przeglad* Katolicki, in ibid., 246–47.
75. Kertzer, *Popes Against the Jews*, 210–11; Modras, *The Catholic Church and Antisemitism*, 153.
76. Modras, *The Catholic Church and Antisemitism*, 151–52.

77. Dariusz Libionka, "Antisemitism and the Polish Catholic Clergy," in *Antisemitism and Its Opponents in Modern Poland*, ed. Robert Blobaum (Ithaca, NY 2005), 240.

78. Quoted in ibid., 153.

79. Modras, *The Catholic Church and Antisemitism*, 207.

80. Tamas Nyiri, "In Lieu of a Preface," in *Befejezetlen mult: Keresztenyek es zsidok sorsok* [Unfinished Past: Christians and Jews, Destinies], ed. Sandor Szenes (Budapest 1986), see Asher Cohen, "Review," *Holocaust and Genocide Studies* 3, no. 1 (1988): 104–6.

81. Robert Wistrich, "The Vatican and the Shoah," *Modern Judaism* 21, no. 2, (May 2001): 83–107; Donald Dietrich, "Catholic Resistance in the Third Reich," *Holocaust and Genocide Studies* (1988) 3(2):171–86.

82. Ibid.

83. Lapide, *Three Popes and the Jews*, 90.

84. See, e.g., *Nuremberg Document* PS 2699, *Der Stürmer* of Christmas 1941. See also Robert Kempner, *Eichmann und Komplizen* (Zurich 1961), 132.

85. "Concerning the Question of Zionism," tr. Joshua Starr, "Italy's Antisemites," *Jewish Social Studies* (October 1938): 118.

86. "The Great Dilemma," *Civiltà Cattolica*, (December 1941): 5.

87. Quoted inBernard Wasserstein, *Britain and the Jews of Europe* (London 1979), 47.

88. "The Actors in the Trial of Jesus," *Civiltà Cattolica*, (March 1942), 394–97.

89. Ibid., 99.

90. Reported in early March 2007 in *Nice-Matin, London Times, Le Figaro*. "Nice: Réglements anti-juifs," (March 1, 2007) http://libreinfoswebzine.over-blog .org/archive-03–01–2007.html. See also Marrus and Paxton, *Vichy France*, 198–99.

91. Pierre Blet, et al., eds., *Actes et documents du Saint Siège relatifs à la Seconde Guerre Mondiale* (Vatican City 1965–75), 8:295–97, 333–34; Marrus and Paxton, *Vichy France*, 202.

92. Jacques Nobécourt, *"Le Vicaire" et l'Histoire*, (Paris 1964), 207–8. See Chapter 11 in this book on the origin and use of this concept of just and charitable anti-semitism.

93. Robert Alter, "From Myth to Murder," *The New Republic* (May 20, 1991): 34, 37–38. Walter Sokel has called this kind of anti-Jewishness, "ontological anti-semitism." See his "Dualistic Thinking and the Rise of Ontological Antisemitism in 19th-Century Germany," Sander Gilman and Steven Katz, eds., *Antisemitism in Times of Crisis* (New York 1991), 154–72.

94. Paul de Lagarde, *Die gegenwärtigen Aufgaben der deutschen Politik in Deutsche Schriften* (Munich 1924), 30.

95. Drumont, *La France Juive* (Paris 1885), 2:572.

96. Fritz Stern, *The Politics of Cultural Despair* (Berkeley 1974), 201.

97. Steven Aschheim, "The Myth of 'Judaization' in Germany,'" 230.

98. Pulzer, *The Rise of Political Antisemitism*, 312.

99. Weiss, *Ideology of Death*, 396–97.

100. Hermann Rauschning, *Hitler Speaks* (London 1939), 229.
101. Martin Bormann, *Le Testament politique de Hitler: Notes Recueillies par Martin Bormann* (Paris 1959); Martin Bormann, *The Testament of Adolf Hitler: The Hitler-Bormann Documents, February–April 1945* (London 1960).
102. Hitler, *The Testament of Adolf Hitler*, 55–56.
103. Eckart, *Der Bolshewismus*, 46, in Aschheim, "The Myth of 'Judaization' in Germany,'" in Jehuda Reinharz and Walter Schatzberg, eds., *The Jewish Response to German Culture* (Hanover NH 1985), 240; also Langmuir, *Toward a Definition of Antisemitism*, 348.
104. Hermann Rauschning, *Hitler Speaks* (London 1939), 229; Gavin Langmuir, *Toward a Definition of Antisemitism* (Berkeley 1990), 348.

Index